Gerald Griffin

Tales of the Munster Festivals

The Aylmers of Bally-Aylmer

Gerald Griffin

Tales of the Munster Festivals
The Aylmers of Bally-Aylmer

ISBN/EAN: 9783337249403

Printed in Europe, USA, Canada, Australia, Japan

Cover: Foto ©ninafisch / pixelio.de

More available books at **www.hansebooks.com**

TALES OF THE MUNSTER FESTIVALS.

THE AYLMERS OF BALLY-AYLMER.

THE HAND AND WORD.

THE BARBER OF BANTRY, ETC.

BY

GERALD GRIFFIN,

Author of "The Collegians," "Tales of the Munster Festivals," "The
Rivals," & "Tracy's Ambition," "Tales of the Jury Room," "The
Duke of Monmouth," "Tales of the Five Senses," & "Night
at Sea," "The Invasion," "The Poetical Works," &
"Tragedy of Gisippus," "Life of Gerald Griffin."

New York:
P. J. KENEDY,
EXCELSIOR PUBLISHING HOUSE,
5 Barclay Street,
1896.

"HOLLAND-TIDE".

Straw for youer gentilesse! quod our hoste—
What, Frankeleine! Parde, Sire, well thou woot
That eche of you mote tellen at the lest
A Tale or two, or broken his behest.

CHAUCER

"HOLLAND-TIDE", "All-Hollands", "Hollands-Eve", or November-Eve, was once a merrier time in Ireland than it is at present, though even still its customary enjoyments are by no means neglected. Fortunately for "all the Saints", in whose honour the feast is celebrated, it occurs at a season of the year when the pressure of want is less sensibly felt than at most others, and, among a people who are, generally speaking, so easily satisfied as to the external comforts of life, that a comparative alleviation of suffering is hailed with as hearty a welcome as if it were a positive acquisition of happiness. The peasant sees, at this period at least, the assurance of present abundance around him. He beholds a vast extent of land all cultivated, and burdened with the treasured produce of the soil—gardens of stubble covered with *shocks* of wheat, oats, and barley, which look just as if they were intended to make bread for him and his neighbours; fields of potatoes, some in which the numerous earthen mounds, or *pits*,* have been

There is a curious inversion of signification in the words *pit*, *ditch*, and *dyke*, in the sister isle. A potato *pit* is an *elevated* mound of earth, containing potatoes. A *ditch* is a dyke, and a dyke means a ditch.

already raised; others, in which the nipping frost that is
borne on the November blast has embrowned the stalks
and withered the leaves upon their stem. The stroke of
the flail and the clack of the water-mill are in his ear
—the meadow land is green and fresh with its aftergrass
—and the *haggart*, or hay yard, is stacked into a labyrinth
with hay and corn. He is satisfied with the appearance
of things about him—he thinks he has no business
asking himself whether any of these good things are destined for his use, or for that of a foreign mechanic—he
never stops to anticipate in fancy, while he puts the spade
for the first time into his own little half acre, and discloses
the fair produce of his labour, how many calls from
tithe-proctor, assessed tax-gatherer, landlord, priest, etc.,
may yet diminish his little store: he sees the potatoes;
they are his and his pig's by right, and he and his pig are
merry fellows while they last, and while they can procure
a turfen fire, or the smoke of a fire, to warm the little
cabin about them.

Or, if this last comfort is denied him, he can take his
stick, and his "God save all here", along with him, and
make the best of his way into the spacious kitchen of the
neighbouring "strong farmer", "middle-man", "small gentleman", or "half-sir", when the festival evening above-
mentioned has arrived. Here he can take his place among
the revellers, and pay for his warm seat in the chimney
corner by a joke, a laugh, a tale, a gibe, a magic sleight, a form
of conjuration proper to the time—in short, by adding his
subscription of merriment to the general fun of the meeting.

Just such a quiet, contented, droll fellow, formed one
of a most frolic November-Eve party at the house of
a respectable farmer in the west of Munster, upon whose
hospitality chance threw the collector of these stories
on the 31st of last October. The earthen floor had
been swept as clean as a new pin; the two elderly
rulers of the mansion were placed side by side in two vene-

rable, high backed, carved wooden chairs, near a blazing
turf fire; their daughter, a bright-haired Munster lass
(and Munster is as remarkable for fair faces, in Ireland,
as Lancashire in the neighbouring country), all alive with
spirit and jocund health (that dearest dower of beauty), was
placed opposite, contending with and far overmatching the
wits of two rustic beaus, the one the assistant of the village
apothecary, the other (the more favoured of the two), a
wild, noisy, rude, red-faced savage, son to the agent at
the "great house", as the mother gave me to understand
in a whisper. The schoolmaster, the seneschal, half a
dozen neighbours, and a few shy-looking, rosy-cheeked
girls, looking forward with most unchristian anxiety and
credulity to the cabalistic ceremonies of the evening, and
anxiously longing for the retirement of the scrupulous old
couple, whose presence alone prevented their being immediately put in train, in defiance of Father Maney and
his penances, filled up the remainder of the scene immediately around the fire—while Paddy, the *gorsoon*, and
the two maid-servants, sat whispering together in respectful
distance, seated in shade upon the settle-bed, at the upper
end of the apartment.

Previous to the commencement of the evening sports
the jolly-looking fellow in the corner before mentioned,
throwing himself back on his *sugan* chair, stretching out
his unstockinged, polished, and marbly legs, variegated by
the cherishing influence of many a warm fireside, snapped
his fingers, and made glad the heart of his ancient host,
by leading out the famous old chorus:—

L

'I love ten pence, jolly, jolly ten pence,
I love ten pence better than my life;
   I spent a penny of it,
   I lent a penny of it,
I took eight pence home to my wife.

II.

I love eight pence, jolly, jolly eight pence
I love eight pence better than my life;
  I spent a penny of it,
  I lent a penny of it,
I took six pence home to my wife.

III.

I love six pence", etc., etc.

and so forth, to

"I love two pence, jolly, jolly two pence;
I love two pence better than my life;
  I spent a penny of it,
  I lent a penny of it,
I took NOTHING home to my wife!"

The chorus having died away in a most musical dis-
cord, a clear space was made in the midst, and a fat
faced little urchin, clambering up on the back of one
of the high chairs, lowered from the roof a sort of
apparatus made of two laths crossed, and suspended
from one of the bacon hooks above by a whip-cord,
fastened from the centre. A large bag of apples was
now brought forward from the corner of the room, and
two of the sleekest and largest affixed to the extremities
of one of the cross-sticks, while the other was furnished
with two short bits of candles, lighted. When the balance
was fairly adjusted, and the whole machine lowered to the
level of the mouths of the guests, it was sent twirling round
with a touch of the finger; the fun being now, to see who
would fix his or her teeth in the immense apple while in
rapid motion, and avoid taking, instead, the unwelcome
inch of lighted candle, which appeared to be whisking round
in pursuit.

"E'then, bad mannners to you, Norry Foley", said the
merry fellow with the legs before mentioned, addressing
himself to a modest, blue-eyed, simpering maiden, who advanced in her turn to the "snap-apple", with a sly coquet

tish management of lip and eye, "only mark what a weeny
dawny little mouth she makes at it, because the gintlemin
is looking at her now, all o' one I hadn't seen her myself
many's the time make no more than the one offer at a white-
eye that would make two of that apple".

And, as if to demonstrate the facility of the undertaking,
he advanced in his turn with an easy, careless, swaggering
confidence in his own prowess, and a certain ominous working of his immense jaws, which struck awe into the hearts
of the junior spectators. The orifice which was displayed
when he expanded them, banished the faintest glimmering
of hope; and when they closed, with a hollow sound, upon
the devoted fruit, a general groan announced that the sports
and chances of "snap-apple" for that evening were at an end.

Next followed the floating apple, of still greater dimensions than the former, placed in a tub of clear water, and
destined to become the property of him who should, fairly
between his teeth, and without help from hands or the side
of the vessel, lift it out of the fluid. This created most up-
roarious mirth for some time, until the man with the legs,
in his own quiet, silent way, stalked among the disputants
like the genius of fate, and picking it off the surface as if
it had been a walnut, retired to his corner, followed by the
wondering and envious glances of the gaping juniors.

While these things were transacted above, another group
about the fire were occupied more interestingly, though not
so merrily, in melting the lead through the handle of a key
placed over a *porringer* of water, and conjecturing from the
fantastical shapes which the metal assumed, their own future destiny; in burning the beans* (in which process,
much to the dissatisfaction of the young hostess and her
noisy sweetheart, the village apothecary's lad was observed
to burn quietly by her side, while the former bounced away

* Such is the demand for those articles "coming on" November
Eve, that rural speculators sow bean gardens for the purpose of profit-
ing by the occasion.

with a " pop!" like a shot), and other innocent and permitted arts of the Ephesian letter.   These little minor tricks,
however, were but child's play to the great girls, who were
on thorns until the field should be left clear to themselves
—when they might put in practice the darker and more
daring ceremonies proper to the time—the drying of the
shift sleeve on the three-legged stool, and watching in the
silence of the midnight for the shadowy resemblance of the
future spouse, who was to turn it before the fire ; the sowing of hemp or rape seed ; the adjuration with a sage-leaf,
and all the gloomy and forbidden mysteries of the night,
into which we shall not at present penetrate ; these ceremonies not being peculiar or strictly national, and having
already found admirable historians in the authors of " Hal-
loween ", and of " The Boyne Water ".

After the company had wearied their spirits and memories in search of new matter of amusement, and exhausted
all the accustomed festivities of the evening, the loudness
of their merriment began to die away, and a drowsiness
crept upon their laughter and conversation.   As the noisier
revellers grew comparatively silent, the voices of two or
three old gossips who sat inside the hearth in the chimney-
corner, imbibing the grateful warmth, and seeming to breathe
as freely and contentedly amid the volumes of smoke which
enveloped them as if it had been pure aroma—their knees
gathered up to their chins, and the tails of their cotton or
stuff gowns drawn up over their heads, suffering the glazed
blue or green petticoat to dazzle the eyes of the admiring
spectators—the voices, as we have said, of these old crones
became more audible as the noisy mirth around them began
to decrease, and at length attracted the attention of the
other guests.

" What is it ye're doing there ?" exclaimed the old master of the house, looking towards the corner with an expression of face in which much real curiosity and some assumed ridicule were blended.

" Oyeh thin nothing in the world", replied a smoke-dried, crow-footed, white-haired, yet sharp-eyed hag, whose three last teeth were employed in masticating a piece of " that vile roguish tobacco". " Nothing;—only we to be talking among ourselves of ould times—and things—the quare doings that used to be there long ago—

'Onst on a time
When pigs drank wine,
And turkeys smoked tobaccy':—

whin THEMSELVES used to be seen by the ould and the young, by day and night, roving the fields and places, and not to be scaming about as they do now (maning 'em no disparagement), in a whisk of a dusty road on a windy day,—whin goold was as plenty as bog-dust, and there used to be joyants there as long as the round towers ; when it was the fashion for the girls to come coorting the boys, instead of the boys going after the girls, and things that way, entirely".

" Poh, what nonsense !" exclaimed the hero of the snap-apple, " there's not a word ever to be had out o' the ould woman, passing a chronicle of a fable about the fairies, and priests, and joyants, and things that we never seen, nor that nobody ever come back to tell us about—what kind they wor—or what truth was in 'em. Let somebody sit upright and tell us something that we'll know is it a lie that he's telling, or not".

" Something about wakes and weddings, and them things", said (a note above her breath) the modest, small mouthed Norry Foley.

" Or smugglers, or coiners, or fighting at fairs, or Moll Doyle, or rebellion, or murthering of one sort or another", roared he of the legs.

" Easy now—easy the whole o' ye!—easy again !" said the host, waving his hand round the circle to enjoin si-lence,—there may be a way found to please ye all ! " (this was said with an air of good-natured condescension, as if

1*

the speaker, in his benevolence, were about to tolerate
rather than enjoy the silly amusement which the youngsters
meditated).   " Gather round the fire, do ye, and let every
body tell his story after his own way; and let the rest
hearken, whether they like it or not, until 'tis over, and then
tell their own, if they think 'tis better ".

A clattering of chairs and stools, and a general bustle,
announced the ready concurrence of the company in this
polite arrangement.   In a short time all were hushed into
a most flattering silence, and the following tales passed
round the circle, lulling some to sleep, keeping others
awake, each finding its particular number of indulgent,
gratified, and attentive auditors, though no single one, perhaps, succeeded in pleasing all.

Whether such may be the lot of the narratives among
a more extensive and less considerate audience, remains to
be seen.   Avowing the source from which his materials
were taken, the collector thinks himself entitled to tell the
stories after his own liking, only requesting the critical
reader to keep the pretensions of the book in mind whenever its defects shall arouse the tiger, judgment, within
his breast.   It is not that we absolutely fear the beast,
but we would have him reserve his royal ferocity for a
worthier prey, which a little forbearance in this instance
may induce us, ere long, to lay before him.

THE

AYLMERS OF BALLY-AYLMER.

With pleasure and amaze I stand transported!
What do I see?   Dead and alive at once!

Cato.

"THE mountains!   The Kerry hills!   Alone by yourself,
and at this time o'night!   Now, hear to me, will you, sir,
for it's a lonesome way you're taking, and them mountains
is the place for all manner of evil doings from the living
and from the dead.   Take this little bottle of holy water,
and shake a little of it upon your forehead when you step
upon the heath.   Walk on bold and straight before you,
and if the dead night come upon you, which I hope no
such thing will happen till you reach Tralee any way, you
won't whistle: don't, for it is that calls 'em all about one
if they do be there; you know who I mean, sir.   If you
chance to see or hear anything bad, you have only to hold
these beads up over your head, and stoop under it, and,
whatever it is, it must pass over the beads without doing
you any harm.   Moreover—"

"Easy, easy, Mrs. Giltinaan, if you please.   There is
something of much more consequence to me than those fine
instructions of yours.   Don't mind telling me what I shall
do in case I lose my way, until you have let me know first
how I am to find it".

"Oh, then, why shouldn't I, and welcome, Mr. Aylmer?

listen to me and I'll tell you, only be careful and don't slight *themselves* for all ".

The above formed part of a conversation which took place between the hostess of an humble inn on the west border of the county of Limerick, and a young gentleman whose sharp accent and smart dress bespoke a recent acquaintance with Dublin life at least. As he was a very handsome young fellow, and likely to fall into adventures, perhaps I may be excused for giving some account of him, and in order to do this the more fully and satisfactorily, I shall begin by telling who his father was.

Robert Aylmer, Esq., of Bally-Aylmer, was a private gentleman of real Milesian extraction, residing near the west coast of Ireland. Like most of the gentry around him at that time, he did not scruple to add to his stock of worldly wealth, a portion of that which by legal right should have gone into his Majesty's exchequer. In a word, he meddled in the *running* trade on the coast, a circumstance not calculated at the period in question to attach any thing like opprobrium to the character of a gentleman and a real Milesian. Although he added considerably to his patrimony by this traffic, the expenses of the establishment at Bally-Aylmer were so creditable to the hospitality of its master, that he felt himself sinking rather than rising in the world, and was, indeed, on the eve of ruin, or more properly of an ejectment, when a desperate resource presented itself in the form of a smuggling enterprise, so daring in its nature that none but a Milesian would have even dreamt of putting it in execution. He formed this project, as he had done many others, in conjunction with an old friend and neighbour, Mr. Cahill Fitzmaurice, or as he was called by the smugglers, from his hardiness and cruelty, Cahil-cruvdharug (Cahil of the red hand), a name, however, which, like many other nicknames, was but little appropriate, for Mr. Fitzmaurice was known to mingle much humanity with his enterprise. Those two friends undertook the affair together, succeeded with an ease which they hardly anticipated, and realized a sum of money more than sufficient to have tempted them into danger still more imminent. Gratifying as was his success so far however, this enterprise was of fatal consequence to Mr. Aylmer. Having embarked with his friend on board a Galway hooker (a kind of vessel used for carrying fish or turf along the coast and up the Shannon), for the mouth of the river, they happened to engage in a dispute on some trivial occasion or other which, nevertheless, was made up between them with little difficulty. On the same night however, a very dark one, as the little vessel was *putting about* in a hard gale, a stamping of feet and struggling was heard on the forecastle, and immediately afterwards a heavy plash on the lee bow. Running forward to ascertain the cause, the boatmen found that Mr. Aylmer had fallen overboard, and Fitzmaurice was observed standing near the lee gunwale, and holding by the fluke of the anchor, apparently under the influence of strong agitation. He was seized instantly and questioned as to the occurrence, which he described to be perfectly accidental. A jury of his countrymen subsequently confirmed the allegation, and the innocence of the man was considered to be put beyond all doubt by the circumstance of his adopting the only child of the deceased, William Aylmer, educating him at his own expense, and clearing off all the debts to a very large amount with which his father's patrimony had been incumbered. The youth had been educated with the infant daughter of his father's friend until the age of ten, when he was sent to the metropolis; and he was now returning to the house of his benefactor, after an absence of nine years, during which time he had made himself perfect in all the accomplishments which a college, and subsequently a polite education, could afford.

Having performed the greater part of his journey in a kind of itinerant penitentiary called a jingle, an illegitimate

sort of vehicle, somewhat between a common cart and a
damaged spring-carriage, possessing all the rickety in-
security of the one, with all the clumsiness of the other,
young Aylmer determined to trust to a pair of well qualified legs for the remainder of the route, and was now in
the act of striking off the high road into the Kerry mountains which lay between him and Bally-Aylmer, near which
Mr. Fitzmaurice resided, with the intention of completing
his journey before night.

The "Kingdom of Kerry" is, as Horace Walpole said
of a county in England which happens to be very fashionable at present, a great damper of curiosity.   Among the
mountainous districts in which it abounds, are vast tracts
of barren, heathy, and boggy soil, which are totally destitute of human inhabitants.   The champaign which now presented itself to the gaze of the traveller, was one of the
dreariest that may be easily imagined : heath beyond heath,
and bog after bog, as far as his sight could reach in prospect, canopied over by a low dingy and variable sky, and
rendered still more dispiriting by the passing gusts of wind
which occasionally shrieked over the desolate expanse with
so wildering a cadence as almost to excuse the superstition of
the natives, that the fairies of the mountain ride in the
blast; these formed the prominent characteristics of the scene
which lay before him.

Now and then as he advanced on his route a travelling
tinker touched his hat to him, and a fish-jolter, from the
western coast, nodded a courteous "Dieu ith", as he passed,
in his complete suit of sky-blue frieze, whistling to his
mule ; while, with downcast, meditative look, the patient,
passionless animal plodded on, stooping under the weight
of two large *cleaves* of fish, intended for the next market.
Often, too, the eye of the young collegian found matter
more interesting in the laughing, round, red cheeks, snow-
white teeth, and roguish blue eyes of the country girls,
who hurried past him with a drop curtsy, and a half modest,

half cunning glance, shot from under the eye-lash with an expression which seemed to say, "there be coquets out of Dublin". All traces of cultivation had not yet disappeared— the hardy potato, in all its varieties of cup, white-eye, English red, kidney, London lady, black bull, rattle, early American apple, white potato, etc., etc., etc., diversified the ungrateful plain with several plots or gardens of variegated bloom, and filled the air with sweetness. The young gentleman's pair of velocipedes, however, were so vigorous in the execution of the trust confided to them, as to quickly place him beyond the influence of these outskirts of cultivation, and, after an hour's walking, he found himself far beyond the sight or sign of human habitation, a good hazel stick in his hand, and a Murphy's Lucian in his coatpocket. He had received and noted down in his memory with great exactness the various landmarks by which his course was to be directed, and he felt too unbounded a confidence in his own powers of discrimination, to doubt his being able to recognise them when they should occur. But those who have been similarly circumstanced will easily acknowledge the probability of a miscalculation in this respect. It is even as in the great world—however minute or provident may be the code of instructions with which the young adventurer is furnished at his outset, he quickly finds the number of novel contingencies which thrust themselves upon him, too extensive for any second-hand experience to secure him against all necessity for exercising his own natural judgment.

It was not, however, until he had been journeying for some hours, that Aylmer began to think at all of the possibility of mistaking his route. His mind was occupied with meditations of a far more agreeable nature,—the expectation of speedily revisiting scenes so dear to him, from the recollection of the merry hours he had passed among them, and from their association in his mind with the few friends of his childhood. His benefactor he had seldom seen, for Mr. Fitzmaurice was a silent, solitary, musing man, who loved little company of any kind, after the loss of his friend, and who was not anxious to conceal that a certain natural weakness of temper rendered the sight of the little orphan at no time pleasing to him. Miss Fitzmaurice, however, entertained a very different feeling on this subject: and the childish affection which had swiftly developed itself on both sides, was quite strong enough to supply the want of natural or instinctive fondness. The time that had elapsed since Aylmer's separation from her, had not abated any of the regard which he always cherished towards his fair friend, and he contemplated their approaching meeting with a glee which originated a great deal in real kindness, and not a little in that curiosity which is so frequently mistaken for affection by those who feel it. He had shaped out, with his mind's eye, a thousand full-length portraits of the now womanly Kate Fitzmaurice, from the dusky evening air, and had completed one very much to his satisfaction, when a sudden salutation in a strange voice startled him from his reverie. He looked round him, and perceived now, for the first time, that the night was rapidly closing in. The appearance of the heavens had changed since he had last observed them. Clusters of broken vapour were now hurrying past in swift succession, and there was a bleakness in the air which seemed to portend an approaching change of weather. Turning to ascertain from whom, or whence, the voice proceeded, he beheld a man seated on the heath, his back supported against an in-sloping crag, a gray frieze coat thrown loosely about his person, a pair of brogues well studded with *pavers* (large-headed nails used for the strong shoes of the peasantry in Ireland), and an auburn-coloured felt hat, pressed down upon his brows. There was, nevertheless, something of finery in his address, which seemed inconsistent with this coarseness of appearance.

"A question from a stranger is hardly sinful in such a
place as this ", he proceeded, after Alymer had acknowledged
his courtesy, "particularly as a man has his own choice
about answering it. Do you mean to journey much farther to-night, sir?"

"I hope to reach Bally-Aylmer before the night has
become much darker ".

The stranger shifted his position, and was silent for a
few minutes. "Bally-Aylmer!" he exclaimed at last; "you
are the young master, then?"

"My name is Aylmer ".

"Bally-Aylmer! Um. It is seven long miles from
you now, if you took the nearest way that is, and that is
not possible for any one to do that knows so little of the
mountain-roads or tracks as you do. I was going in the
same direction myself, but seeing the night about to fall
dark, I preferred taking my chance for shelter under this
crag, where I shall lie dry at least, to my chance of a
drenching, and perhaps something worse, among the bogs
and crags that lie about half a mile beyond us. If you
will proceed, you are like enough to have a hard night.
Do you not hear the *Cashen** roar?"

"I do; but the fear of a little rain must not deter me.
I have been out on worse nights ".

"There are other dangers, sir, no less worthy to be
avoided than the chances of pit and bog ".

"Oh, I remember that too—my head is filled with tales
of the Kerry mountains, and their marauders, and bana-
thees, and phukas; but for the one, I am provided with
this amulet", brandishing his beads, "and here is a charm
for the other ", elevating his stout black-thorn in a gay
humour.

---

* The *Cashen* is a stream which empties itself into the Shannon,
at no great distance from Ballylongford, in Kerry. At the approach
of rainy weather, the sound of its waters can be heard distinctly at a
distance of many leagues.

The stranger was again silent for a short time, during
which he seemed to canvass the whole person of the young
collegian with a curious eye, at the same time that, whether
accidentally or otherwise, his own features were almost
entirely concealed by his position. At length, taking from
his pocket a sealed letter, he handed it towards Aylmer,
and said: "I had orders to leave this at Bally-Aylmer,
for some one of the family there. If you will pardon the
liberty of my offering it, you will do me a great service,
and save me a long journey out of my way".

Aylmer readily took the letter, and in placing it in his
pocket-book, caught, for the first time, a view of the stranger's countenance. It was that of an aged man, with
nothing very uncommon in its character; though a flashing, yet wavering and doubtful recollection, seemed to rush
on Aylmer's mind the instant he looked upon it. He felt
satisfied that he had never seen the countenance before,
and yet its expression startled him with a feeling of sudden recognition, for which he afterwards could in no manner account. He had not an opportunity of pursuing his
scrutiny farther, for at that instant the muttering of a
distant thunder-peal, preceded by the falling of a few
large drops of rain, induced the old man to return to his
shelter beneath the rock. Wishing him a courteous farewell, the youth proceeded on his way, puzzled a little at
he knew not what.

"If I were a Pythagorean", said he within himself,
"this adventure might help to strengthen my faith; for,
unless it be a glimpse into another state of existence, I
am at a loss what I shall make of it".

After casting a rather uncomfortable glance at the heavens, which were now darkening above him so rapidly as
to leave him little hope of clearing the mountains so speedily as he intended, he pushed on at a vigorous rate. The
storm which had been threatening, however, in a very
short time burst forth in all its violence. The sky became

one dense mass of black, illuminated only at intervals by the
blue and sheeted lightning, that served to reveal to him the
perils amongst which he was entangled, without assisting to
guide him out of them. He could perceive that the beaten
path which he now followed, lay through a wide morass or
bog, and so indistinctly was it marked out, that he found
himself obliged to proceed with the utmost caution, although
the rain had already begun to descend in torrents upon him.

He was mincing his steps in this manner, and beginning
to feel a greater respect than he had hitherto done for the
recommendation of the old man, when he was startled by
feeling some living creature brush swiftly by his legs, so
as almost to touch them, and presently after, in a pause
of the storm, a loud ringing whistle, followed by a shouting and hallooing at a distance, greeted his ear. A low
grumbling bark, very near him, seemed to give answer
to the sounds; and Aylmer heard the animal which had
been snuffing inquisitively about him just before, bound
and scamper off in the direction from whence the voice proceeded. In the hope of obtaining some assistance, the
adventurer put his lungs to their best use, and endeavoured
to outroar the warring of the elements themselves; but
the effort proved to be a total failure, for he was not
heard, or at least not attended to. He hurried on, nevertheless, with a feeling of greater security, on the path which the
dog had taken, and in a short time was rewarded for his
perseverance by feeling the firm mountain heath beneath
his feet. He now looked round him in the hope of finding
himself in the neighbourhood of some human habitation,
and for once was not deceived. Not more than a hundred yards to his right, in a sudden declivity of the
mound, he perceived a cabin, with half the wicker-door
thrown open, and revealing, in the strong light of a
well-furnished hearth, an abode which seemed to promise
much comfort and accommodation. He made no more
ado, but straightway presented himself at the entrance.

"Boloa irath!"* he exclaimed, as he bent forward over the half-door, willing to conciliate the good-will of the inmates by affecting a familiarity with their habits and language.

"And you likewise", was the answer returned by the "all" whom he had blessed ; a plain-looking aged woman, who sat enjoying the delights of ease and a dhudheen (short pipe) in the chimney-corner. Aylmer drew back the bolt of the wicker and entered. The old woman continued smoking her pipe without expressing either displeasure at his intrusion, or anxiety to do the honours of her house; almost without raising her eyes from the heap of red and blazing turf on which they were musingly bent. Finding whom he had to deal with, and not disposed to lose much time in ceremony, her unbidden guest drew a sugan-chair close to the fire, and while he briefly explained the circumstances which had compelled him to be a trespasser on her hospitality, he made himself perfectly at home with respect to his shoes, stockings, and coat, which he suspended before the blaze, while he received with much satisfaction its full influence upon his person. After he had in some degree elevated his own temperature to the level of the atmosphere in which he was now placed, another inconvenience began to press upon his recollection, which he yet saw no means of removing. He turned his eye in various directions, but could discern nothing that could be useful to a man in want of a supper. At length he ventured to break his mind to his hostess on the subject. She at once directed his attention to a cupboard at the end of the room, to which he repaired with highly excited anticipations. All his anxieties were set at rest by the apparition of a good supply of cold roast mutton, with some oaten bread, and potatoes in great abundance. Laying joyous hands upon his prize, he bore it with much gratification to the deal table which stood in the centre of the apartment, and presently fell to work upon it: his

* Bless all here.

hostess, during the whole time, preserving her attitude and look of indifference or listlessness, of which her guest was now too agreeably occupied to take any cognizance.

While he was yet seated at table, the sound of several voices outside the door diverted his attention, for the first time, from his fare. The occasional broken and hurried sentences of command or remonstrance which were bandied from one to the other of the unseen speakers, were alternated by the low and stifled bleatings of a sheep, which speedily terminated in a quick and gurgling expression of pain, that sufficiently demonstrated the means which had been adopted to secure silence.

"Smaha buhill!" exclaimed one, "faix, she's a joyant of a baste. Take her round to the barn, Will; and do you an Lewy make haste in to your supper. Here Vauria!"

"Vauria is here av you want her", shrilled out the old woman, who had, at the first sound of the voices, made an extraordinary exertion to place a *skillet* of potatoes over the fire before the speakers should enter, and had now resumed her pipe and indolence.

This had scarcely passed, when a stout, able-bodied man, his face smeared with bog-dust, having the appearance of a grazier (and a very ill-looking one), flung himself into the house. His astonishment at beholding a stranger quietly seated at his table, and demolishing his cheer, was so vividly expressed as scarcely for the moment to place his hospitality in a very favourable point of view. It was only after an uninterrupted gaze of a few seconds, that he suffered a half unconscious "Dieu ith" to pass his lips. "Dieu ith agus a Vauria!"* was the reply of Aylmer.

"'Tisn't driven in by the weather you were?" continued the cottager (meaning directly the contrary). Aylmer nodded an assent, as he continued eating. "A smart evening, indeed", was the next observation. "*Sha guthine!*"† replied the collegian, still continuing to use his

---

* God and Mary be with you.   † Yes, indeed.

vernacular tongue, and in every possible way endeavouring
to mystify his real condition.

The querist was about to address the old woman, when,
darting a sudden glance at his guest, he quickly asked
him "if he understood English?" a question which
the infrequency of the accomplishment in those districts
rendered feasible enough. Instantly catching at the
probable motive in which it originated, Aylmer replied at
once in the negative. The cottager and the old woman
soon after entered into conversation in their own broken
and mangled effort at the idiom.

"An who tould him fare the mutton was?" inquired
the owner of the house, after the woman had satisfied
him as to all previous particulars. "In troth it's asy
seen what a thrasheu he meant to give it, when he stript
to the work that way". Here Aylmer was near betraying
himself by the smile which began to struggle on his lips.

"Lewy did a purty piece o' work this evening (night)",
continued the host: " Cahill-cruv-dharug's herdsman will
be missen a ha'porth o' tar in the mornen. One of the
prettiest creatures on the long walk, and fat, ready to
melt in our arms. Take it from me, Vauria, Cahill Fitzmaurice won't be a bit glad to be eased of her, to-morrow
morning".

"Let him score it over against the blood of Robert
Aylmer, then, and he'll be the gainer still, may be",
muttered the old woman.

"Pho! Pho! Easy. What nonsense you talk. Was'nt
he cleared o' that be a judge an jury, in the face o' the
whole country?—Pho!"

"I was aboord the boat that awful night, an I heard
words spoken that ought'nt to pass a Christian's lips,
except he was a Turk. But what's the use of being
talking? There's as much time to come after as ever
went before us, an they say blood will speak if it bursts
the grave for it".

Often as he had heard these circumstances repeated, and enthusiastic as early conviction had made him in the confidence of their utter groundlessness, it was not very easy for Aylmer to support his assumption of perfect listlessness and indifference, while the above conversation was passing. Notwithstanding the feeling of indignation which the rambling imputations of the hag excited in his mind, he could not prevent their sinking deep into his spirits, and taking a hold there which he in vain endeavoured to shake off. The conviction, too, of the immediate and imminent peril in which he was placed — for it was no longer a matter of doubt to him that he had fallen upon a gang of the far-famed Kerry sheep-stealers — contributed not a little to the uneasiness of his situation. He began strenuously to long for an opportunity of withdrawing himself from the chance of further illustrations of their mountain hospitality.

Shortly after, the cottager started up from his seat by the fire, and said rapidly: "There's the white horse on the pzatics; I'll go and and see what is it keeps the boys, and do you get up one o' your old ancient fables, and keep this man by the fire till we come back. We'll talk o' what's to be done abroad".

No sooner had the speaker disappeared than Aylmer began to meditate the most probable means of taking himself out of the cottage and its neighbourhood, without awakening suspicion. He got up from the table—walked towards the fire—resumed all his dress, with the exception of his hat, which still hung in the chimney corner, reeking against the heat: and after all this was done with as great an appearance of carelessness and indifference as he could command, he took his seat by the fire, stirred it up briskly, and made an effort to engage his hostess in conversation; in which, however, to his great satisfaction, he totally failed. The old woman seemed to be one whom time had beaten down into a state of almost negative

existence, and whose only positive enjoyment seemed to
consist in the absence of all exertion. Far from com-
plying with the cottager's desire that she should endeavour
to entertain her guest, she seemed, from the moment of his
departure, to be almost unconscious of the presence of a
second person; and went on exhausting her store of tobacco, and musing over the fire with the comfortable air
of a slave who has been relieved from the presence of the
task-master.

The violence of the tempest had now considerably
abated, although the night still continued dark, and the
wind hissed along the broken thatched roof in fitful and
uneasy gusts. After making some observation on the
change, Aylmer walked towards the little window, as if to
look out upon the night, and in so doing stumbled upon a
new confirmation of his suspicions. Casting his eye,
accidentally, towards the hurdle loft, which was constructed over the ceiling of an inner apartment, he
observed several piles of sheepskins thrust under the
sloping eaves, and heaped towards the centre, the spoils
of many an enterprise similar to that of which he had just
before witnessed the termination.

As the time rolled on, the anxiety of the youth increased, and he determined at length on making some
exertion for his freedom, before the male tenants of the
cottage should return. Leaving his hat where it hung,
in order the more effectually to baffle the suspicions
which his absence might occasion, he made some trifling
remark to the old woman, and passed into the air. After
he had crept a few paces from the house, and felt himself
placed without the immediate circle of the influence of its
possessors, he made a joyous bound on his path, and ran
along for a considerable distance, without a moment's
pause, in the direction from which he had turned aside
during the tempest. The rain had ceased and the wind
abated, but the sky was yet loaded with vapour, and the

wanderer had little more than random conjecture to depend upon in pursuing his route over the mountain heath. Early as it yet was in the night, and totally ignorant as he was of the distance he might have to conquer before he should arrive at the termination of the wilds, he could not avoid feeling an occasional depression of spirits when he reflected on the possibility of his being pursued; in which case the familiarity of his enemies with the passes of the mountain and its bogs, must leave him at a perilous disadvantage. He dashed forward on his way, however, without stopping to calculate disheartening probabilities, and journeyed for nearly an hour without meeting any impediment to arrest his progress, or any piece of good fortune that might assist it.

On a sudden, the disparting of an immense mass of cloud, which had for a long time been condensed on the horizon behind him, betrayed the night-walker to the glances of a few kind stars, and very shortly after the veil was withdrawn from the fair, round, fat face of the winter moon herself, and a welcome flood of light was poured about his path. He now discovered himself to be still surrounded, as far as his sight could reach, with the uneven wilderness of heath, over which he had so long been toiling, and no indication lay, within the wide circuit which his eye was enabled to comprehend, of human neighbourhood. There was no sign of cultivation, no bound of partition, nothing but heath and bog to be discovered, and this circumstance contributed materially to depress the cheerfulness of spirit which the sudden accession of light had awakened within him. This uncomfortable state of mind, however, in some time began to give place to a feeling of more immediate and positive alarm. Whether it was that his imagination, highly excited as it had been by the events of the evening, became over quick at transforming all indistinct sights and sounds into occasions of terror, or that such occasions did in reality

2

exist, Aylmer could not divest himself of a strong consciousness that the chase was up behind.   Now and then,
in the intervals of the distant moaning of the Cashen, his
ear was startled by the fancied or actual echoes of the
baying of a hound upon his track, a sound, however, which
was yet so fine and so equivocal,

>   ——"that nothing lived
>   'Twixt it and silence".

He paused for a moment, and bent his ear to the earth
in order to assure himself.   In a little time he became
convinced of its reality.   The portrait of the cottage
hound which had startled him at first sight by the indications of fatal sagacity which he could collect from its
appearance, "so flewed, so sanded", its head

>   "—— hung
>   With ears that swept away the morning dew,
>   Cross-kneed, and dewlapp'd like Thessalian bulls";

its sullen, blood-shot eye, and lumpish mouth, all rushed
together upon his recollection, and utterly discomfited the
slight feeling of security to which he had just before
begun to deliver himself up.   He grasped his black thorn
club with a firmer gripe, and at once made up his mind
to the most desperate contingencies that could arrive.   If
a much more extensive tract of land lay between him and
the houses of honest men, it was evident he had not the
slightest chance of eluding his pursuers, provided as they
were with so fearful and so infallible a clue to his position.
His only reliance was on a pair of vigorous limbs, which
he forthwith applied to the best purpose possible, and
which he might have calculated on with very great ra-
tionality, had his hunters been altogether human.   As it
was, in spite of all his exertions, he found that they were
gaining rapidly upon him.   He darted forward with renewed speed, and as he panted and stumbled on his course,

in one of those glances of reflection, which even in the
act of the most violent bodily exertion, will sometimes
flash upon the reason, he made a wordless resolution
within his heart, that he never would hunt or course a
hare as long as he lived.

Still he dashed forward headlong on his path, and still
that horrid, sullen, twanging cry became louder and louder
upon his track, until it sounded in his ear, as the trumpet's
charge might be supposed to do in that of a soldier destined to a forlorn hope. The shouting of the animal's
masters, too, cheering their guide upon the game, became
audible in the distance. With a failing spirit, Aylmer
glanced on all sides as he bounded along, but could discern
no means of even possible protection. No stream, no
tract of water by which he might baffle the terrible instinct
of his four-footed enemy, not one of the many contrivances by which he had heard and read this had been
successfully accomplished, here presented themselves. His
brain, his sight, his senses became confused; a fear like
that which oppresses the dreamer in a fit of night-mare,
lodged itself upon his heart; his will became powerless,
and the motion which still hurried him along his path,
might almost be termed involuntary. He thought of
nothing, he saw nothing, he heard nothing, but the fast
approaching terrors in his rear, the heavy, confident baying
of the hound, and the fierce hallooing of his pursuers.
Fortune seemed in every way to conspire against the devoted youth, for in rushing down a slight declivity of the
heath, a small tuft of the weed came in contact with his
foot, and flung him with considerable violence on the
ground. He sprung to his feet again, but fell at the first
effort to proceed; his foot was maimed past all use. One
thrill of utter despair shot through his frame, and the next
moment a perfect indifference came over him. The shouts
of the hunters were now almost close upon him, but, and
he hardly trusted his sense when it first informed him of

it, there was another sound mingled with theirs. He started to his feet, and stood erect in spite of his hurt; he heard the sound distinctly—it was the dash of waters on his left. Clasping his hands together, and offering, in one flashing thought, as fervent a thanksgiving as ever passed sinner's lips, he staggered toward the spot. Coming suddenly over the brow of the hill, he beheld immediately before him a small river, broken in its course by several ledges of rock, and flinging itself in masses of white foam into a kind of basin, whose surface the full winter's moon had lighted up with its gladdening influence, so as to shine "like a welcoming" in the student's eyes. The banks of the stream were fringed with drooping sallows, and a dark angle close to where he stood seemed to offer the closest and securest mode of concealment that he could desire. Without a moment's thought or wavering, he slipped down the bank, and seizing one of the twigs, plunged himself, all recking with perspiration as he was, into the cold, freezing, November flood.

He had not been in this situation long enough to feel the inconvenience of the transition, when his anxieties were renewed by the approach of his pursuers. Creeping under the screen of the hanging sallows, and still clinging to the twig which he had grasped, he remained up to his chin in the water, imitating the action of some species of waterfowl, when conscious that they are under the eye of the fowler. From this concealment, completely enveloped, as he was, in a piece of impenetrable shade, he could see his bandy-legged, shag-eared foe, bound fiercely to the bank immediately above him. The animal stopped short, snorted, looked across the stream, and whisked his head, with an action of impatience and disappointment. He ran up and down the bank, his nostrils expanded and bent to the earth, and snuffed long and argumentatively about the very spot where Aylmer had descended. In a

few seconds after he heard the voices of the mountaineers
at the top of the hill.

"Blessed Saviour o' the airth!—O Lewy! the sthrame!
—We're lost for ever!—Come back here, Sayzer!—The
unnait'rcl, informing Dane! To come among us and make
a fool of a shoulder of as good mutton as was ever dhrov
the wrong way off a sheep-walk; and, I'll be your bail for
it, he'll have the army with us to buckist* in the morning,
av we stay for them (which we won't)—sorrow skreed o'
the mait he left upon the bones, as much as would make
a supper for old Vanria herself".

Aylmer was too uncomfortably situated at the moment,
to enjoy these jests on his prowess at the sheep-stealer's
board, and waited with much uneasiness until the speaker
and his companions might be concluded out of all power
of observation. Day had begun to dawn before he ventured to re-ascend the bank; and never was the benevolent
eye of the morning startled by a more pitiable spectacle
of solitary human misery, than he presented at that
moment. His fingers, stiff and crimpled up with the cold,
refused to close around the shrubs which he attempted to
grasp, his joints were all stark and painful, and his hair
and clothes distilling a hundred streams, as if he were, like a
male Niobe, about to be resolved into a portion of the element
to which he had just been indebted for his existence.
Great as was the general inconvenience which he felt, however, he had the satisfaction to find that the cold im-
mersion had arrested the progress of whatever inflamma-
tory symptoms his sprain in the foot had occasioned, and
he was now enabled to turn the limb to which it apper-
tained to some account. He walked, like a piece of half-
animated stone-work, along the banks of the stream, for
nearly half a mile, and had the pleasure to observe, in
spite of the clouds which the agitations and exertions of

* Breakfast.

the night had still left upon his brain, that he was close to
one of the most frequented public roads of the country.
He had no difficulty in discovering his exact position, and
was not a little comforted at finding that he was no more
than a mile from the residence of his friend and guardian,
Mr. Fitzmaurice. Not willing, however, to present himself before his old friends in the deplorable yet ludicrous
plight to which his mountain adventure had reduced him,
he directed his course toward his own family residence,
which lay at no great distance from him, and which, though
it had only occasionally been occupied by him, was, he
knew, tenanted by the aged widow of his dead father's
herdsman, and her son, Sandy Culhane. At the hands of
those old "follyers" of his family, Aylmer knew he might
calculate on receiving all the accommodation which his
present condition rendered necessary. His long absence
from the country, uninterrupted, as it had been, by even a
visit to his friends at the customary seasons for such indulgence, secured him against all probability of being
recognized on the way to the "great house", and he met
with no interruption in his walk thither, which was easily
accomplished before the sun had well shook himself after
his night's sleep.

Bally-Aylmer was one of those architectural testimonies
to the folly of our fathers, which are scattered rather
abundantly over the face of the green isle. Although the
term has slipped from beneath our pen, there was little
worthy of the name of architecture, about either the principal building or its official appendages. The site of the
house appeared to have been selected in those days when
it was the wont (contrary to modern practice on similar
occasions) to choose the lowest, as the most graceful, as
well as convenient and salubrious position, and when that
position was ascertained by rolling a large round stone
down an eminence, and sinking the foundation wherever it
happened to repose. Aylmer, fatigued as he was, found

a sufficient excitement in the first view of his native place,
to divert his attention in some degree from his sufferings.
Accustomed, as he had been during his absence, to the
splendours of metropolitan architecture, he could not avoid
feeling a momentary sense of humiliation, when he perceived the utter poverty and tastelessness of an establishment which in his childhood he had been used to look
upon as the perfection of elegance, and with which even
his distant recollection had not presumed to quarrel, until
he now brought his classical feeling and experienced
judgment full upon it, in all its hideous and awkward
reality. The entrance consisted of two lean, gawky-
looking piers, built of plain rough stone, and standing
bolt-upright, like young steeples, on each side of a low,
shattered, paltry wooden gate, which had long discon-
tinued the use of its hinges, and was propped up to its
office by the assistance of a few large stones, rolled against
the lower bars, the removal of which, for the admission of
cars (carts) and horses, usually occupied as much time
each day as a carpenter might have lost in screwing on
a fresh pair of hinges. On the summit of one of those
piers, a noseless Banthee, or Banathee, done in limestone, the work of some rustic Westmacott, might be
observed in the act of combing her long and flowing hair,
an action very generally attributed to this warning spirit.
Upon the other, nothing was visible to the naked eye.
That fashionable appendage to modern improvement, a
factitious lake, was not wanted here, though the specimen
presented was rather on the small scale. It consisted of
a sheet of some liquid or other, about twenty feet by
twelve in extent (lying close inside the entrance), and
greeted more senses than one of the incomer, with an intensity which it required no great fastidiousness to de-
precate. The house itself, a square-roofed, lumpish-
looking edifice, sadly out of repair, and de itute of even
a solitary twig or fir to conceal its threadbare masonry;

its line of red binding-tiles broken and blown away;
its chimneys damaged and menacing; and its slated roof
hospitably inviting, in divers-apertures, the visitations of
the winds and rain—all, together, presented as bleak and
comfortless a spectacle as ever greeted even a provincial
eye. Without detaining the adventurous youth any
longer in his uncomfortable deshabille, we shall hasten to
relieve the pain of our sympathising reader, by informing
him that Aylmer was not disappointed in his calculations
on the services of old Ally Culhane, by whose assistance
he was presently rid of his cumbersome habiliments, and
introduced to the consolation of a well aired, well blan-
keted state bed, where he speedily lost all memory of his
night's ramble, in a good, sound, healthy, dreamless sleep.

The only immediately habitable rooms in the venerable
mansion, were that in which its heritor atpresent slumbered,
and the kitchen in which the aged Ally and her son had
domiciliated since the house had been in a great measure
abandoned to them by its original possessors. The others
had been partly stript of their furniture and locked up, or
appropriated to the Irish use of store-rooms and granaries
for the produce of the adjacent acres, which were turned
to the best possible account for the benefit of his ward
by Mr. Fitzmaurice, who seemed never happy, or even
contented, unless when he was occupied in some way or
other about the Aylmer property. Though he was a
native of a country where more apologies are found for the
shedding of human blood than would, if universally admitted, greatly further the interests of society, and although much of his life had passed amid scenes where
homicide was familiar as the day-light, Cahill Fitzmaurice
had, either from a natural quickness of feeling, or from
the influence of that half-animal, half-chivalrous sense of
moral honour which is so often made to supply the place
of system, of principle, or of true religion in the minds of
a neglected people, retained a tetchiness of spirit about

what he was pleased to call his reputation, which, would
come with an ill grace enough from the lips of a smuggler
of the present day. Notwithstanding his "honourable
acquittal" too, by the county grand jury, of the horrible
offence imputed to him, and the assurance of those his
judges, that "he left his dungeon with as unstained a
character as if he never had been called to it"—for
speeches of this kind were among the specimens of cant
in vogue then, as well as now,—Fitzmaurice felt convinced, and the conviction sunk deep into his soul, that
suspicion was a shade of guilt, and that there was, in fact,
no such thing as an "honourable acquittal" from a public
accusation. The consequence of this feeling was, a total
and marked alteration in the character of the man. His
frankness—his hospitality—his broad-faced, laughing good-
humour,—all his social qualities were blasted, as if by a
lightning shock. He was no longer to be seen at the fair
or session; his steward being entrusted with an unlimited
discretion, as to the fate of the flocks and droves which
were transmitted to all places of public traffic. His farm
was, in a great degree, neglected by him; and the only
active business in wich he still continued to take anything
like an active interest, was, as before alluded to, the
improvement of his young ward's inheritance, in which he
was vigorous and successful; having contrived, during the
long period of the youth's minority, to amass for his
future benefit a sum of money which might enable him, at
the proper season, to take possession of his patrimony in
a manner calculated to assure him of an influential station
in his native country. His house and his board were still
open to the traveller, and the welcome was not diminished
either in its warmth or sincerity; but it came no longer from
his own lips,—he never appeared among his guests, and
was seldom visible even to an early acquaintance. His pride,
in fact his Irish pride, had been stabbed to the heart; he
felt that it was in the power of any man who grudged him

2*

the fragment of reputation he still retained, to snatch it
.rom him by a word, a look, a gesture. With this conviction full upon his own mind, he had, in the two or three
efforts which he made immediately after his liberation to
regain his old place among his old friends, entered into
their society with an almost morbid tremulousness of
feeling—a quickness to anticipate the intention of slight,
which is alike the characteristic of the fiery and chivalrous,
and of the weak and sensitive nature, and which, in
various degrees, has been set down as the leading peculiarity of the veritable Milesian by all painters of national
character, from the days of Captain Macmorris down to
those of the knight of Blunderbuss Hall. The embarrassment which this feeling imparted to his manner,
naturally communicated itself to those whom he addressed,
and the unfortunate Fitzmaurice, not possessed of sufficient
philosophy to trace the effect to its real origin in his own
demeanour, attributed it at once to the unquieted suspicions
which his overwrought susceptibility had led him to anticipate, and gave up the attempt at once in a paroxysm
of despair. Thus it was that, with as kind, as generous,
and as benevolent a heart as ever beat, Fitzmaurice found
himself, in the vigour of his manhood and in the full
possession of all those qualities which had for a long series
of years rendered him the delight of his companions, struck
down, by one home-blow, into a branded and degraded
wretch, whom chance had protected from death, but not
from ignominy. The gloom which was thus cast over his
heart, speedily found its way to his brow; and, in a few
years, he would have been a skilful physiognomist who
could have traced, in the sallow, wasted cheek, the indented temples, the contracted, darkening brows, the thin,
colourless lips, and sullen, dark, disappointed eye of the
man, a memory of the broad, red, careless, moon-cheeked
face of the noisy Cahill Fitzmaurice, the Pylades of Robert
Aylmer. No consciousness of innocence could comfort or

support him under the pressure of so grievous, so overwhelming an accusation as that which had been cast upon
him. He had been charged in open court with the murder
of his oldest and kindest friend ; he had even been bowed
down to the ignominy of giving a formal denial to such a
charge. There are imputations the very necessity of dis-
proving which is as blasting to a man's character, as the recording guilty to others ; and Fitzmaurice thought, or felt,
that this was one of them. One merit, however, he at least
possessed amid all the blameful sullenness and darkness of
spirit to which he delivered himself up—he never was
heard to indulge in those "whys" and "wherefores" on
the justice of his fate, in which (very unhappily) so many
sufferers, self-tormentors, and uneasy speculators in matters
of Providence, are apt to look for consolation. Fitzmaurice took the more rational and amiable part of quiet
endurance ; and those who were familiar with his temper
and habits (as he had once been), remarked, some with
wonder, some with pleasure and commendation, that the
doom which seemed to oppress his heart, even to breaking,
never had the power to wring from his lips a single
murmur of complaint against Heaven.

Notwithstanding this sentiment of resignation, or
whatever it might be, it is still doubtful whether the heart
of the man could have borne up long, if it were left to its
own solitary broodings over the events of the past, and
the bleak, dreary nothingness of the prospect which the
future presented to the eye of his sorrow. One consolation, however, had been spared him—one true friend
—unchanged, unchangeable—one wound up in all his interests and feelings, as intimately as even in the help-
lessness of unfriended degradation he could have desired
—one whose duty as well as inclination it was to cling to
him under any circumstances that stopped short of moral
guilt, and who would have died, even at that point,
before the link that bound them together had been sun-

dered. It was his only child and daughter, Katharine, of
whom mention has been made before now in our story.
True, it was not until many years had elapsed after her
father found cause to sigh for a real friend, that Kate had
reached an age sufficiently matured to enable her to comprehend, much less to sympathise in, his distresses; but
her devoted and passionate attachment to her parent
seemed to be born with her, and the slow but sensible
development of a vigorous reason which manifested itself
in the progressive force and eloquence of her consolations
in his hours of depression, came over the spirit of the
broken man with the influence of a gradual summer sunrise. There is so much of vanity mixed up with even the
most amiable sentiments of our nature, that we never
fail to direct all the energies of our affection with
most satisfaction and assiduity, where we perceive them
to be most successful. There is too an unconscious
self-gratification in the exercise of any influence over the
thoughts and feelings of a suffering fellow-being, which
endears him to us at least quite as sensibly as his unhapp
fortunes do; and ill-natured as the conjecture may appear,
perhaps we should not widely err in attributing to a
partial operation of this unintended, undetected self-
seeking some portion of the deep devotedness of love, with
which the merry-hearted Kate abandoned herself in the
full glow of youth, and with the fullest capabilities for the
enjoyment of more congenial society, to the silence, the
solitude, and the gloom of her father's dark oaken parlour
Without once daring to gratify a mean curiosity by as
certaining, or striving to ascertain, the occasion of the
heaviness that oppressed him, she applied all the powers
of her mind and heart to lighten and relieve it. Such
curiosity, indeed, she never was at any time assailed with,
for, however changed her parent might appear to others
who remembered him in the gaiety of his manhood, he had
always been the same in her eyes, always the discomfite

downcast, silent, and fitful, yet kind and affectionate old
man. Her education had taken place altogether under
her paternal roof, and Fitzmaurice had the happiness to
find that he had not injured his daughter by neglecting the
hints respecting a few years' boarding in Killarney convent,
which some religious friends had scattered in his ear.

On the evening, and about (perhaps) the very period
when Aylmer was conversing with the stranger in the
Kerry mountains, the father and daughter were seated in
the large, old-fashioned parlour, the window of which commanded, at a vast distance, a view of the hills or yet
more gentle elevations of the soil which run along the line
of coast, revealing at intervals certain glimpses of the blue
waters of Dingle Bay, which were all massed at present in
one glow of hazy splendour by the influence of the departing sun. Now and then a white sail, glancing like a
speck of light on the waters, appeared and flitted across
those scanty gaps in the horizon, all moving inland, and
relieving by their motion and the associations which they
waked up, a good deal of the still and monotonous repose
of the interjacent prospect. The old man, who had been
more than usually gloomy during the evening, and who had
not spoken during several hours, now sat, his arm-chair
drawn towards the window and fronting the distant bay,
on which his eyes were fixed with an expression varied
only in its intensity, but at all times stamped with the
hue of a consistent and enduring melancholy. Kate,
with the fineness of tact which long habit as well as
native delicacy had given her, perceived that something
had occurred during the course of the day, most of which he
had spent at Bally-Aylmer, to agitate him, and she fel·
that it was one of those moments at which all interference
with, or intrusion upon, his feelings, would jar against his
very nature. She pursued her work therefore in silence
venturing only in an occasional impulse of anxiety to stea
a glance from under her curved eye-lashes at his darkening

dispirited conntenance. Had Kate been gifted with any
portion of physiognomical penetration, she might have
read, in that apparently still and evenly dejected range of
features, the influence of thoughts which should have excited her love, her pity, her sorrow, and her dismay, by
turns. She might have beheld a long train of mournfully
joyous associations, touched from their sleep by the influence of the sweet scene on which his eye was fixed, and
awakening, in their turn, recollections still more remote, all
blended and mixed up with the absorbing event in which
all his misery had originated, and each bringing a new
stimulant to the disease which that event, and its con
sequence, had occasioned in his mind.

While each thus followed up their own fancies " in
social silence ", the attention of Katharine was diverted by
a light tapping at the parlour-door, which, opening presently after, admitted the tip of a polished, pretty nose, a
blue eye, and a section of a broad, bold forehead. The
blue eye was directed on the young mistress of the mansion
and the finger of a hand, yet reeking with soap suds, and
of a wrinkled whiteness, was forthwith protruded to
beckon her from the apartment. Kate obeyed the action
in silence.

" What's the matter now, Norry ? " said the young lady

"It's from Bally-Aylmer, miss", was the reply. "Sandy
Culhane to be to the posht-office to day, and to hav·
letters for yourself and himself".

Without waiting to hear more, her lively mistress
bounded and skipped past the girl to the kitchen, where
stood the welcome messenger, who had, it would seem,
refused to deliver up his precious freight, until he should
have received his *albricias*, either in smiles or commen-
dations, from the lips of the " young missis herself, the
darlen ".

These letters were what Katharine judged them to be,
the avant couriers of Aylmer's return, written about a

month before, and now almost overtaken by him, an event less usual in Irish post-offices at the present day than it was then, when there was no Sir Edward Lees to keep the machinery in working condition. More than half the delight which she felt, however, instantly referred itself to her parent, and her affectionate heart bounded at the thought, that she had at last found something with which she might venture to break in upon the gloom that had taken possession of his mind during the whole afternoon.

" I have news for you, sir ", said she as she reëntered the apartment on tiptoe, her pretty lip pinched up to murder a smile that was still struggling for its life, her half-shut, gray, waggish eyes bent merrily on his, and her whole face beaming with a child-like, irrepressible delight.

" Go, go, you little fool, mind your work ".

" I know who will be the loser then ", retorted Kate, as with an affectation of hoydenish freedom, she leaned over the back of his chair, and flourished the letter before his eyes.

" Who, monkey ? "

"Do you know that hand ? " replied Kate, slipping one soft white arm round her father's neck, and with the other holding the letter steadily before him, while she watched his countenance, as one would that of a child to whom one has just given a new gilt-covered picture-book. While Fitzmaurice put on his spectacles and glanced over the contents of the letter, she felt a quick and hurried pulsation beneath her hand, which at once induced her to withdraw it from his neck. Her intuitive delicacy of feeling made her shrink with scorn from the acquiring an insight into the soul of another by the use of any of those " points of cunnynge ", of which my Lord Verulam, Bacon, gives us so elaborate and philosophical a detail.

" The third ! " said Fitzmaurice, when he had concluded; "then I should not be surprised if we had him here this evening ".

" This evening ! O my ! " exclaimed Kate, as she

glanced first at her dress,' and then, involuntarily, at the ancient pier-glass, with its gorgeous volumes of gilded foliage, on the other side of the room.

" O *my!* O *you!* What you? Poh! what nonsense!" exclaimed Fitzmaurice, as he observed the direction which her eyes had taken. " This young man's arrival, Kate, seems to give you a great deal of pleasure ".

Kate blushed, between a feeling of consciousness and of surprise, and without making any reply, she looked in her father's face with an expression of astonishment, confusion, and curiosity.

" To me", he continued replying to her gesture, " I confess this intelligence brings no unmingled sensation. I believe I have done enough to show that I love young Aylmer well—I like him too, for his own gentle qualities, as much as for his name's sake; but I cannot forget, neither, that to that very name I owe the loss of all I prized in life—all my old friends—my good fame, my poor wife, your sweet mother, Kate, who was lying on a sick-bed when I was dragged from her side, to——— and who mingled her death-groan with your first cry of sorrow, my girl, as she placed you in my arms. But these are unfair and selfish modes of feeling ", he continued, as he saw a tear glisten in the eye of his daughter; " I must learn to conquer them. Only I would be alone for the rest of the evening". And kissing his daughter affectionately, the old man passed to his sleeping apartment.

    *   *   *   *   *   *

During all this while Aylmer has been enjoying a comfortable sleep, and it is high time we should wake him up again for the amusement of our readers, or, to speak more modestly, for the furtherance of our story. The noon of a bright frosty day had just passed when he awoke. So heavy and unbroken had been his rest, that he could scarcely believe his eyes, when he saw the sunbeams strike on a point of noon which he remembered from his child-

hood. Aylmer had not yet passed that happy season of
life when novelty is enjoyment, and change of place and
circumstance seems almost to imply change of being. As
he opened his eyes on the old-fashioned curtains of his old-
fashioned state bed, under whose lofty tester he had often
reposed in childhood, and recognized the faces of many familiar friends on those hangings—the same pike-nosed
grayhound, in the yet unaccomplished act of springing
over the same barred gate, the same hunter, sticking in the
same slough, and the same clumsy squire, kissing the same
funny-looking, blowzy-checked milk-maid—it seemed to
him as if the whole intervening space had been but the
circle of one long night, and all its crowd of events and
changes nothing more than the shadows of a vivid dream.
When he flung back the curtains, however, and tossed his
manly bulk out of bed, the sight of a tolerably rounded calf
gave him, like the beard of Rip Van Winkle, assurance of
their reality.

His toilet, and the preparations for it made by his old
friend Ally, also reminded him of his change from Irish
city to Irish country life. The luxury of soap was what
she appeared to be totally unprovided with, from her
having substituted in its place a handful of dry oatmeal,
and a small, clean piggin-full of new milk, a quid-pro-quo
by no means satisfactory to a young man whose darkening
chin advised him of the necessity of raising a lather. He
now perceived, what in the gray doubtful light of the
morning dawn had escaped his observation, the extreme-ry
dilapidated state of the apartment in which he stood. The
single window was eked out, half glass, half paper; and
the shutters swung crazily on their hinges. The plastering
of the ceiling, as well as of the walls, had fallen away
in various places; and, on one side of the room where
a partition divided it from the kitchen, this circumstance
disclosed a secret of true Munster economy, creditable
alike to the ancient and the present tenants of the

mansion. The partition appeared to be composed of hard *slane*-turf,* which in its smooth coat of mortar and white-wash, had escaped the eyes of inquisitive housewives for a succession of *lustra*, until this unfortunate demolition of the outworks had taken place. On the first occasion for an immediate supply of firing, which subsequently oc-curred, Sandy sent his right leg through the partition, and furnished his hearth from the breach, to which he often afterwards recurred, although a bog lay within twenty perches of the house, declaring that "the ould wall burned like coal". The breach was at present stopped with a dismantled door of an inner room. "No matter!" thought Aylmer, as he plunged his puckered-up, grinning face into the basin of biting cold water, "these things shall be mended when I take the management of the place into my own hands".

As he proceeded in the act of purification, he perceived that his own clothes had been removed from the apartment, as he concluded, for the purpose of being dried; and a suit perfectly strange to him, both from its fashion and its material, was laid across the lofty back of a huge oaken chair in their stead. It consisted of a blue jacket and trowsers bagging toward the ankle in sailor fashion, both closely studded with gilt buttons, strung in rows wherever buttons were admissible, and altogether having a great deal more the air of venerable age, both in their *cut* and texture, than fell in very lovingly with the modern taste of the young student. He put them on, however, in default of better, and was not a little surprised to find himself as exactly fitted as if they had been cut *for* himself, and "upon scientific principles". As he concluded his toilet, he recognized, through the breach, the voice of his old companion, Sandy, crooning over an old fox-hunting ditty, as he sat in the chimney corner, addressing, between

---

* So called to distinguish it from *hand* turf; the one being cut from the soil with an instrument called a *slane*, the other shaped with the hand out of a soft boggy stuff, which is afterwards dried.

occasional bars of the melody, sundry conjectures to his
mother on the probable issue of Aylmer's return:

> " Good morrow, Fox ".— " Good morrow, sir",
> " Pray what is that you're ating ? "
> " A fine fat goose I stole from you :
> Pray, will you come and taste it ? "
>   " Niel flash e piue
>   Niel niesh e giub,
> Indeed I will not taste it ;
> But I promise you, you'll screly rue
> That fine fat goose you're ating ! "

"Eh, mother! O holy saints, protect an' save us! look
there!" cried Sandy, starting from his place, and crossing,
with a face expanded in wonder and awe, to his mother,
as Aylmer suddenly entered the kitchen, and confronted
him.   The old woman, turning her hung-beef countenance
over her shoulder, seemed to catch the alarm from her son,
and flung her withered arms round his neck for protection, while her smoky eyes continued bent on the
astonished youth.

"Hooee! Alilu-war-yeh! Sandy, dear! O, murther!
'Tis it that's there!"

" 'Tis himself, all out!" roared Sandy.

" The liven imidge!" said Ally.

" Jest as if it stept out o' the pictur frame, down!   A
sperrit, no less!"

"An the hair! an the eyes! an the whole tote! It
bates cock-fighten!"

" My good people", said Aylmer, as soon as he had
sufficiently recovered his surprise to cut short the torrent
of their ejaculations, "this may be very amusing to you
and very flattering to me, for aught I know; but would
you be kind enough to explain what it is in my person
that sets you roaring, and kicking, and plunging up in a
corner that way?—eh?"

" Thu! thu—thu—thu! 'Tis master Will, then, him-

self after all!" said Ally, clacking her tongue against the
roof of her mouth, as is usual among the peasant Irish,
when they wish to express surprise, compassion, or perplexity.   After a little time, he was enabled to gather the
occasion of their sudden alarm.   The clothes which he
wore, and which, after a great deal of rummaging among
old chests, presses, and worm-eaten wardrobes, were discovered by Ally in an inner apartment, belonged in times
past to his father, and helped to strengthen the natural
likeness of the son into an almost deceptive similitude.

  " Indeed, it's a burning shame for me to mintion it
Master Will, darling", said Ally, as she laid before him
his breakfast of fresh eggs, butter, jelly, smooth-coated
potatoes, and virgin-white milk; "but I could'nt get a
taste o' tay, high nor low.   But av we have you here to-
morrow, there'll be a *keeler* o' the *beestings**— a trate you
hadn't in the 'cademy, I'll be your bail.   Indeed, Sandy
and meself are trusting now a long while to the milk
o' one stripper; as Mr. Fitzmaurice says we musn't lay
wet finger on the little Kerry cows that fill the firkins for
your ixpences behind up.   Troth, as I tell Sandy, I think
it's in the cow's horns it do be going from us", etc., etc., etc.

  While this chat, and a great deal more equally edi-
fying and imaginative, was gliding forth from between the
old herdswoman's lips, the person addressed was very sa-
gaciously employed on the viands which she had set before
him, and so vigorously did he exert himself, that long
before Ally thought of discontinuing her harangue of
mingled welcomes, and praises, and moanings, and complaints, he cut it short by declaring his intention of
setting off immediately for his guardian's house, where, as
he rightly calculated, it was probable his baggage had
arrived before now.

  * The first milk of a cow immediately after her *accouchement* is
called *beestings* in Ireland; and, dressed in a peculiar way, is considered a delicacy there.—Tastes vary.

It was too cold a morning to think a great deal of love,
and yet, as Aylmer took his way over the crisp and frosty
meadows that lay between him and the residence of the
Fitzmaurices, he could not avoid renewing his conjectures
as to the probable effect of time on the frame and mind of
his fair play-fellow, and repeatedly putting the silent
question to his heart, whether he should now seriously fall
in love, or no. Capitulation, on such occasions, is a very
usual consequence of parley; but as this happens to be one
of those situations of the heart (so useful to a story-teller),
in which the reader is kind enough to find novelty and entertainment even in repetition, just as one thinks the
dinner-bell, at forty years of age, sounds quite as sweetly
as it did at ten, there can be no great harm in following
the steps of the deliberator through all the gradations of
his defeat. His spirit warmed within him, in spite of the
season, as he saw the smoke curling off in the light blue
masses (it is turf smoke we speak of, gentle London
reader) from the chimneys of Kilavariga house (those
classical names are destructive to all sentiment), every
stone, and brick, and tile, and crink, and cranny of which
were as familiar to his memory as the shape of his nose
or the colour of his hair. There was the great avenue
gate, on which Kate and himself, when relieved from the
stern constraint of their guardian's eye, were wont to indulge in a fine romping bout of swinging, and riding, and
shouting, and screaming, and laughing; and which, if the
truth must be told, was the scene of many a serious battle-
royal between the pair, so far as that fray could be called
a battle, in which all the offence lay on the feminine side.
Stepping over the stile on one side of the closed entrance,
a greater number of remembrancers of the olden time
started up before him--the haggard (Irish-English for hay-
yard), behind the stacks of which they had played many a
merry game of *hoop*, and hide and seek; the little pond,
on which they had launched their green flag boats, and

cheered them as they skimmed over the surface, with as keen, and, certainly, quite as philosophical an interest, as the speculators of the T. Y. C. matches on the banks of Father Thames. Leaving all these sweet stimulants of memory behind him, however, Aylmer approached the dwelling of the still sweeter being to whom they were indebted for more than half their interest. As he crossed the lawn, his eyes fixed on the window of the parlour, which (not the gentle instinct of affection, though we would fain assert it, but) his memory told him was her appointed place of work, of study, and of elegant amusement, he saw the light muslin blind withdrawn for an instant, and a fair face, with hair clustering about it, in papers, like ripening grapes, just showed itself, and " vanished, like a shooting star ". The blind was re-adjusted, and Aylmer beheld nothing further of the inmates of Kilavariga, until he had applied himself to the brazen knocker of the hall-door. It was opened almost instantly by (not the dear hand which his throbbing heart had led him to anticipate, but) the more robust and substantial one of Norry, the " getter up of small linen " to the establishment. Those who saw Norry on her return to the kitchen, averred that there were, in the heightened colour of her cheek and the sparkle of her eye, tokens of a welcome on her part, and a greeting on Aylmer's, a little more Irish than the lady of the house might have been pleased to witness—but this is none of our business. Aylmer hurried on, with a pulse throbbing in the tumultuousness of expectation, into the parlour, but he found no one there, although the disposition of the furniture showed him that it had been very recently abandoned by its mistress. The slight feeling of disappointment which this seeming coldness and tardiness gave occasion to was quickly removed, however, by the appearance of two or three curl-papers, dropped near the pier-glass. Aylmer smiled most roguishly and impudently, as he stooped to pick one up; but he was properly punished for his conceit and impertinence. It was torn from one of his own best composed and most poetical epistles.

Humbled and irritated a little, he began, in the absence of his friend, to collect from the objects around him all the indications of the present state of her mind and habits which these could supply. The dark-grained, well-polished oaken floor was strewed (around the work-table) with fragments of dress, a species of feminine carelessness, which, however severely reprehended by mothers and governesses, has always been regarded both by Aylmer and myself with much tenderness, as imparting a very civilized air to a mansion, when disposed with a sufficiently careful negligence. Nothing is more ornamental to a lonely house, in a wild country, than those scattered symptoms of gentle womanhood. A volume of Ferrar's History of Limerick, lying with a thread-paper between the leaves, enabled Aylmer to form a diagnostic of a little female patriotism, while an unmuffled harp, with a music stand and book near the window, rather modestly thrown into the shade, gave indications of higher accomplishments than he had even been led to hope for. All these delightful conclusions were, however, soon cut short by the sound of a light foot upon the staircase without. His heart leaped into his eyes, as he bent them on the door—the handle stirred—it was opened.

"Kate! Kate!"

"Oh, William!"

I know that there are many respectable persons, whose theory as well as practice it is, to make all the impulses of passion and feeling, as well as all the varieties of action and attitude, obnoxious to the rules of etiquette—who can be joyous within limit, or most elegantly disconsolate, as the occasion may require—and to such I can have no apology to offer for the conduct of my heroine at this conjuncture. She received the friend and playmate of her childhood with an ecstacy truly barbarous—there is

no denying the fact—she almost rushed into his arms—
she hardly checked the kiss which he was presumptuous
enough to snatch from her, and very faintly on its repetition; her delight was outrageously unsophisticated and
natural—it was, in fact, an Irish meeting "all over".

When the "Kates", and "Williams", and "my goodness!" and "dear mees!" and bursts of laughter, and all
the other delicious nothings in which this untamed affection
is privileged to indulge itself on such occasions, had been
nearly expended, Aylmer contemplated the face and figure
of his young friend with greater attention, and we shall
now describe what he saw as accurately as possible.

He was not disappointed in any way by either the
countenance or the person of his mistress (for as such, at
the first glance, he had set her down); and, yet though the
latter *was* beautiful, the former fell decidedly short of that
standard.   There was no exquisite combination of colour
in the checks—no lilies and roses—no rubies—no diamonds, and yet the face itself was perfectly captivating.
Her lips were thin, but eternally charged with an expression of arch gravity or undisguised pleasure, which the
restless heart supplied in such continual succession as totally to exclude all thought of considering their pretensions
to mere material beauty.   Her eye was gray and shrewd,
in its moments of comparative inaction, but full of fire, of
passion, of mirth, of thought, of feeling, or of *fun*, according as those varying emotions were stirred up within
her bosom.   The whole countenance fell into a character of
intensity and animation, which gave the fairest promise in
the world of the evenness that might be expected from
the mind and temper.   It was the veritable window to the
heart, for which the philosophic braggart affected to sigh,
and was only to be loved for the revealment of the spirit
which was in it.   "She is not handsome, decidedly", said
the student to himself, after the elegant fashion of his
compeers in T. C. D.; "she is none of your brick-and-

mortar beauties—but I like her the better— there's *vous*
about her. 'Tis a well built forehead, too".

The gentleman was no better satisfied with what he
beheld in the person of the lady, than the lady was with
that of the gentleman. She saw in the figure of her
grown-up friend, a well-looking, clever young fellow,
rather under the stature of masculine beauty, and with, to
a prophetic eye, a promise of rotundity (*not* corpulency)
in his person. His face was a good oval, indicative of
strong intellect, but perhaps quite as much, or rather more
so, of strong passion, his forehead round and resolute, his
eyebrows so Melpomenish, that they would have given a
moped and anxious air to his *masque*, if they were not
corrected by the vigour and bustle of the eye beneath
them : *that* was an article of the greatest advantage to the
character of the whole face. There was no affectation
about it, and yet it was full of meaning, and had a frankness that was royal. His hair, rather black, and doubtful
whether it should curl or no, was thrown back on all sides
in a kind of floating way, an arrangement that savoured
too much of technicality, when it is considered that he was
a haunter of Parnassus, and had moreover once upon a
time been an accomplice in the perpetration of the
" Historical Tragedy " of the " Battle of Aughrim ", in a
cock-loft near Smock Alley, " for charitable purposes ",
on which occasion he represented the heroic St. Ruth,
who, as is pathetically narrated in the drama,

> " Adown a winding valley met his fall,
> And died a victim to—a cannon ball ! "

Aylmer was about to question his fair friend on the
subject of her father, when the door again opened, and
the old man entered. He advanced hurriedly to welcome
his protégé, and scarcely looked at him, until he had
grasped his hand, while his own, as Aylmer felt,
trembled in the effort. He was about to speak when his

3

eyes fell full on Aylmer's person ; he glanced quickly and
rather wildly over his dress and features ; and the words
of welcome stuck in his throat.   He dropped the young
man's hand, and shrunk back with a look of mingled
wildness and distrust.

" Oh, father ", exclaimed Kate, her eyes filling up,
" won't you speak to William ? "

" What is it Kate ?—Come near me, give me your arm,
child ".

" Oh, Mr. Fitzmaurice, is this my welcome home ? "

" Father, dear father ! "

" Let the candles be lighted in my room, the sky is
darkening.   God bless us !   What ails you, Kate ?—I am
well, I am very well.   Stand back, Aylmer ! "

" I am not welcome then ! "

" Stand back, I say ! no——yes——welcome ?——
Kate, keep near me, my darling.   You wrong me, young
man, indeed you do ! "

" How, sir ?—O tell me ! "

" May the great and merciful Lord of the universe
forgive us all !   Surely we are none of us without our
weakness !   William, do I deserve this of *you ?*   The night
has fallen already :—Kate, come with me, and get candles
in my room.   Don't drag me down so, girl ! I have weight
enough upon me : this way ", and gathering the terrified
and weeping girl closer to him, he hurried through the
door, leaving Aylmer overwhelmed with wonder, indignation, and dismay.

It was some time before he heard anything further of
his host.   The night had, as he remarked, fallen with
much suddenness, and the indications of an approaching
snow-storm began to make themselves evident in the
thickening, grayish masses of cloud that drifted close over-
head, so as speedily to spread themselves over the face of
the heavens.   As Aylmer looked from the parlour window,
the dreariness of the change produced a chilling effect on

his excited spirits for the moment, and served to check the resolution which he had formed of instantly quitting the house and returning to Bally-Aylmer. He sat at the window, expecting the return of some of the family, and resolved if possible to obtain some elucidation of the extraordinary scene that had taken place.

He mused in this position for a considerable time, with no other sights or sounds to divert his mind from the anxiety that was gradually deepening around it, but the heavy whirring of the wind as it swept over the whitening plain, the pattering of the snow and hail against the window panes, the cackling of poultry as they ran with expanded tails and disordered plumage right before the wind, to the shelter of the nearest turf-rick, the short dissatisfied grunt of the hog as he stumped it sturdily beneath the window towards the piggery, like a four-footed Caliban driven in a sulk from his feast of "pignuts", and in the intervals of the driving gusts, the solitary cry of a house-sparrow, at finding himself compelled to quit the exposed farm-yard before his little craw was half stored with its thimbleful of the scattered grain, and retire supperless to roost for the night. All those appliances, however, in Aylmer's present state of mind produced only the effect of throwing an additional gloom over his spirits, and filling his heart with wavering and flashing doubts, conjectures, and uncertainties, with which, until the present moment, he had never been disturbed, and which even now resisted all his exertions to turn "them to shapes", and give them an assumed existence.

After he had waited a considerable time in fruitless expectation, his patience again became exhausted, and a feeling of deep and bitter indignation took possession of his mind. The disappointment which his young and ardent heart had met with in the very first burst of its affection, was calculated to sting more keenly on consideration. He had come to his home and his only friends after a nine years' absence, with a breast all glowing with love and ecstacy, and this was his welcome! A cold and almost repulsive greeting, a few short sentences of unprovoked reproach, left wholly unexplained by the utterer, and here he remained, apparently quite forgotten by the family, in a dreary apartment, without a sign of preparation or of kindness. It is in such moments as this that the orphan is most oppressed with the full and bitter sense of his situation, and though Aylmer was the least disposed youth in the world to pule or whine, he could not help exclaiming to his own wounded heart, that it was not so parents were wont to receive their long absent children.

The wormwood of this reflection had scarcely diffused itself over his mind, when the door opened gently, and Katharine entered. Her eyes were red and moist, and her movements still retained much of the agitation into which she had been betrayed by the preceding scene. Her look of distress was sufficient to subdue all the resentful emotions which had sprung up in the mind of the student, and the tenderness with which he took her hand and offered his consolations, would seem almost to imply a consciousness of blame, attributable to his own conduct. Kate, however, did not appear to view the matter in this light: she was the bearer of her father's apologies, and joined to his her own entreaties, that he would endeavour to forget what had passed, and remain the night at Kilavariga. The old man was still, she said, ill to an alarming degree; in fact he had spoken so wildly on many occasions of late, that she sometimes feared —— and a shivering of her whole frame, and a momentary glance of horror, completed the sentence which her lips refused to utter.

The probability of this startling suspicion darted on Aylmer's mind with all the force of truth, and he was instantly struck with a feeling of remorse at the selfishness of his resentment. He affected, however, to make very

light of the conjecture, and succeeded in restoring his
young friend to some degree of composure before they
separated for the evening.

Aylmer used somewhat more care than usual in making
his toilet the next morning, without, perhaps, being himself conscious of any motive for unusual decoration. And
by a curious coincidence enough, a similar degree of care
and taste had been called into use in the female de-
partment of the family, with, doubtless, a similar innocency
of intention. Miss Fitzmaurice was patriotic even in her
gowns, skirts, and bodies (are not our names correct,
ladies?); and she did not depart from her national principle even on this occasion. Her dress consisted of a
grave-coloured Dublin tabinet, bound tight around the
waist (it was the fashion then and there) with a broad
riband, a plain muslin *collar* (is this right too?), as white
as this fair paper which we are blotting with her description, lying close and flat upon the *gorge* at either side:
and that was all the finery about her.

When the young collegian descended, he found Fitzmaurice and his daughter already occupying their places
by a blazing turf fire in the breakfast parlour; the one
domestically occupied in cutting up a large *brick* of home-
made pan-bread into slices for toast, the other plunged
deep into the columns of the last *Dublin Evening Post.*
Both received him cheerfully, and no allusion whatsoever
was made to the occurrence of the preceding evening.
Whatever lingering of mental weakness the old man might
yet labour under, it was soon banished by the frank and
buoyant spirits of the young student, who appeared to
have, and, in fact, at the time *had*, banished from his mind
all thought or recollection of his ungentle reception.

During the progress of their morning meal Aylmer detailed circumstantially his adventure among the sheep-
stealers the second evening before, and Fitzmaurice called
to mind, what he had already heard with indifference, a

complaint of his herdsman, made on the previous morning, respecting the loss of a fat wether, from the long walk. The consequence of the communication was a resolution, on the part of the young man, to lodge informations at once before Mr. Geoffrey Hasset, an estated gentleman and a magistrate, who resided within a few miles of Bally-Aylmer. The old man acquiesced in the proposal as soon as it was made, not that he entertained any longing for justice on his own despoilers, but feeling a satisfaction at the idea that he might thus be rid of the eternal charges of apathy and indolence which were very freely dealt forth by his aged steward, without the necessity of any active personal exertion. Miss Fitzmaurice, too, encouraged the enterprise, as she would have done any other which was likely to occasion some little variety and bustle of circumstance in the monotonous thrum-thrum of Kilavariga life.

Forth accordingly fared our hero; and a few hours' riding brought him within view of the little village, at a gentlemanlike distance from which the clumsy bulk of Hasset-Ville stood, like a *cock-throw*, on the summit of a round, squat hillock near the sea-side, with a few lean-looking elms and alder trees at the rear, which served only to make " barrenness visible ".

An unusual commotion had been occasioned in the village by the unexpected return of the lord of the soil, the above named Mr. Hasset, who had just given his tenantry the first specimen of the benefits of absenteeism since the Union. The loyalty of the parish was fully manifested by the efforts made on the part of its inhabitants to receive their monarch with suitable enthusiasm. As his carriage turned the angle of a rock, some miles distant from his seat, the sound of all manner of villainous instruments rattling away to an inspiring national phlanxty, announced the approach of the villagers, and in a few minutes he was encountered by their advanced guard, a

mounted deputation, headed by a lame carpenter, who
filled his seat on the bony ridge of a wall-eyed, unfed
gelding's back, with the dignity of an orderly on a field-
day, and with the resignation of a martyr. The music
being hushed for the moment into a delicious silence, and
the open carriage drawn up, the schoolmaster of the village
inflicted a harangue on the occupant, which was borne
with gracious patience, and suitably acknowledged; after
which, with tremendous yells, the crowd bounded on the
carriage, emancipated the four-footed cattle, cashiered the
postillions, and fastening two ropes on either side, hurried
the lumbering vehicle along the rough and stony road
with a velocity which caused an expression of real alarm
to take place of the smiling condescension which had before
diffused itself over the gracious countenance of the proprietor. As they whirled him along, amid terrific shouts
and bursts of wild laughter, toward the demesne gate,
the walls and the way-side were lined with gaping and
noisy crowds, principally composed of the younger urchins,
whose scantiness of stature obliged them to make shift in
this manner. One of these had clambered up a gate-pier,
and sitting cross-legged on the back of a stone monkey,
secured his seat by passing his arm round the neck of the
dilapidated pug, while with the other he twirled his little
hareskin cap above his head, and added his share of noisy
triumph to the general voice.

Preparations having been made for the day's amusements some time previously, there was no pause, no lack
of enjoyment after the first burst of welcome had been
exhausted. The demesne was opened freely to all who
chose to mingle in the glee of the time. Tables were
spread before the wooden rustic seats which were scattered through the grounds, and in the interval of the
festive preparation, those who chose to witness or partake
in the sports were summoned to a smooth plot before the
drawing-room window, which was fixed on as the scene of

contention for those who chose to put in their claims for
the several prizes, which the liberality of the proprietor
supplied for the occasion. The great personage was, himself, at the moment, enjoying the scene from the open
casement.

Aylmer had formed one of this last mentioned group for
a considerable time, and joined heartily in the bursts of
laughter which broke from the delighted rustics, at the
various spectacles of fun which were presented to them;
the racing of old women on their *grugs* for a cotton
hankitcher, the grinning through a horse-collar, and
many other sports which it would require the pen of the
author of the Æneid to celebrate with poetical justice.
Suddenly a voice close at his elbow startled him; he turned
quickly round, and gazed on the speaker, who, unconscious
that he was observed, repeated an exclamation of delight
and applause, while the tones of the voice thrilled through
the nerves of the student with a momentary influence of
terror: a glance at the countenance was sufficient to
satisfy him,—he laid his hand softly over the fellow's
shoulder, and fixing a strong gripe on the breast of his
blue frieze coat, dragged him back from the ring.

The scene was instantly changed. The man struggled
to free himself from Aylmer's hold, but the latter clenched
his hand the faster; and there was a consciousness about
the stranger's efforts which enfeebled his strength, and beat
him down almost to a level in point of bodily power with
his captor. Astonished at the sudden confusion, Mr.
Hasset disappeared from the open window, and presently
hurried forth upon the lawn, followed by the seneschal of
the parish, and a posse of domestics.

"Murder! murder! is there nobody for the O'Deas?"
exclaimed the prisoner.

"Man alive! let go your hoult!" shouted a young
countryman, shaking a smoke-dried blackthorn at Aylmer's
head.

"**Will** no one help me to secure a thief and robber? Ha!—Mr. Hasset!"

"Lewy—Oh! Lewy—darling, must it be this way with us?"

"Let go your hold!"

"Help! help! for justice——"

Before another instant Aylmer lay senseless on the earth; and in the same space a well directed blow from behind had done the same rough office for Lewy.

"*Shasthone!* Sandy Culhane, stick by the master!"

"Aisy, av you plaze!" cried Sandy, after he had fixed a similar gripe on the sheep-stealer's throat to that which his young master had been so unceremoniously compelled to relinquish: "Wasn't it in high time I come?—Mr. Hasset, here's your prisoner".

"What has he done?"

"'Pon my life that's more than I can tell—only it's something, no doubt, and the master to seize him: stand a one side, some o' ye, and let us rise him a little – there—pooh! it's nothen. What is it the villian's done to you, Master Will, darling? Mr. Hasset wants to know——"

"Better ask questions within—keep both these men in custody—and remove the young gentleman into the house; he does not appear conscious yet".

"He isn't himself rightly, sure enough; for the eye do be shutting and opening upon me as if it was blind—mark. Indeed I'm but a poor hand at a *kippen* in a fight, and to say that born rogue is able to walk already", as he observed the younger prisoner led off without much assistance, together with his companion, toward the house.

The orders of the magistrate were put in execution, and Aylmer, still half stupefied from the effects of his hurt, though not seriously injured, was assisted to the house by two of the domestics.

It was long before Aylmer had sufficiently recovered himself to identify the mountain marauder, and to explain

3*

to the wondering administrator of petty justice the cause
and manner of the extraordinary scene which had passed
before him.

"And it was by Mr. Fitzmaurice's good will that you
came to lodge informations this way again' me, was it?"
said the sheep-stealer, when Aylmer had concluded.

"He certainly will not be sorry to hear that a thief has
been brought to justice".

"Justice, inagh? O it's justice Cahill is looking after,
is it? Why, then, the Vergin speed him,—and tell him
from me that he'll come by more of it than he's bargaining
for, may be".

"What do you mean, ruffian?"

"Is it asking me what I mane you are? Aisy. Tell
Cahill-cruv-darug, that Lewy Histin, Vauria Histin's first
cousin, that is rearing her this way, said it 'll be a sore day
for him the day that Lewy enters Tralee gaol, barring he
doesn't enter it at all, on his informations".

"You may be very well satisfied that insolence like
this will do you no good with my friend".

"May be not, then. Only you asked me fot I meant,
you see, and I told you plain out. Tell Cahill I said, fot
hurt was it to draw the blood of a little wether, in com-
parishun of an old friend's?—And see if Cahill will ask
you what I mane, do".

As Aylmer was turning away with an expression of
disgust, the prisoner seemed suddenly to call something to
mind, and plunging his rough hand into the pocket of his
frieze, drew from it a dingy piece of paper, folded and
wafered like a letter, which, after sundry efforts to rub it
white again with the sleeve of his coat, a process which
by no means improved its appearance, he handed to the
gentleman. Notwithstanding its piteous condition, Aylmer
was able to recognize the letter which he had received
from the unknown stranger in the mountains, and the ro-

cognition became immediately manifest on his countenance.
It did not escape the observation of the prisoner.

" Aye—it's the very same, indeed. You left it in the
old Caroline as it was drying before the fire, and you see
how honest and safe I *kep* it, although 'tis unknown
to me whether there baint a halter for meself within in it ".

The magistrate, who had been, during the above conversation, buried alive in a digest, now broke in upon it,
to declare his conviction of the sufficiency of the evidence to
warrant a committal. This was made out accordingly, and
Aylmer, declining a handsome invitation to stay the evening,
returned the often neglected letter to his pocket, without
even looking at its superscription, and prepared to depart.

" You'll not forget to take my words to Mr. Fitzmaurice,
sir ? " said the sheep-stealer.

" I shall tell him what you have said, as you seem to
desire it, although I think it would be better for yourself
that I should be silent on the subject ".

" Not at all, indeed !—O, no. Do you mark my words
for it, Cahill will say ' yes ' to my bidding; and a wise
man he'll be when he says that. If he won't say it, come
to me again, and I'll tell you a story that it concerns your
father's child to hear ".

The few sentences which had been dropt in the
mountain-hut by the prisoner and his female companion,
now recurred to Aylmer's mind; and as he proceeded
along, on his way homeward (accompanied by Sandy
Culhane), the uncertain and uneasy feeling of mingled
anger, fear, and curiosity, excited as it had since been by
the scene of the evening before, pressed itself upon him
with an almost irresistible force. Fully convinced as he
was that the threats and insinuations of the man originated in mere malice, he could not yet restrain the ardent,
and, to himself, unaccountable longing which he felt to
search the matter to the very heart, and pluck the plain
truth from its hiding-place. Although he had not yet

thought long enough upon the subject to encourage even
a shadow of momentary suspicion, the misty and uncertain
doubts which he had flung from him with indignation on
their first occurrence, now crowded back upon his mind,
and tortured his imagination with vague and cloudy apprehensions of some approaching horror, while his excited
fancy wasted itself in idle efforts to discover what that
horror could be.

As he approached the house, the appearance of a muff
and bonnet at a little distance directed his meditations
into another channel. He dismounted, gave his horse to
Sandy, who looked a volume of wit and prophecy, as he
saw his young master vault over the stile, and run along
the walk towards his mistress. He leaned with his arm
across the saddle for a few moments, and continued with
mouth expanded, and smiling, gazing in the direction of
the youthful couple, whom he had already paired together
by anticipation in " the incommunicable tie". Aylmer ran
for some time before he overtook Miss Fitzmaurice; she
had the coquetry to quicken her pace as he approached,
and at last feigned a fair flight, which gave opportunity to
a world of laughing, romping, and adjusting of pelerine
and tresses, when she was overtaken. Then there was a
pretty battle about accepting his arm; she drew her little
white hand from the muff, and with a sweet shrinking of
the frame, as she felt the cold air, plunged it again into its
warm nestling-place, from which, however, she was finally
induced to withdraw it, and submit to her fate with the
air of a martyr. None of these manœuvres, delicate and
fine-drawn as the sentiment was in which they originated,
were lost on Sandy.

" Isn't it 'cute she is, then, for all?" he muttered in
soliloquy, as the lovers, arm in arm, glided off and disappeared in a turning of the walk. " E'then, do, look
away ", he continued, addressing the horse, whose eyes
happened to be turned in the same direction, and pat-

ting the animal on the face, "indeed it's no use for you to
be throwing the eye after them. 'Tis to Bally-Aylmer
she'll be going before long, mistress of yourself, and
meself, and all belongen to us, my hand and word to you,
ma copuleen beg". And flinging himself lazily over the
back of the animal, he turned off in the direction of the
avenue, quickening his pace a little as the lengthening
shadows, cast by the hedge-rows across the plain, gave
intimation of the approaching nightfall, for Sandy had no
wish to be overtaken by darkness on his way, in a country
so haunted as his was with smugglers, peep-o'-day boys,
fairies, ghosts, headless equipages, and revenue officers.
This excessive precaution may not appear to coincide with
the account given of Sandy's prowess in the forenoon; but
the fact was, that as there are many men who endeavour
to conceal a conscious timidity beneath the affectation of
nonchalance and braggadocio, so Sandy, on the contrary,
was gifted with a much hardier temperament than he
himself believed, or was willing to allow. His general
anxiety to avoid danger was not merely assumed, but it
was never suffered to be evident except in circumstances
where no real peril existed. He was naturally nervous,
and fond of quiet; but when once convinced that promptitude and exertion were absolutely necessary to his
personal safety, or to that of any other individual in whom
he was interested, he seemed by a sudden impulse to start
into a totally different being, and many instances were
recorded of his heroic prowess, while under the influence
of these chronic affections of valour, which would not
have been unworthy the most daring spirit in the neighbourhood. Sandy, however, was by no means vain-glorious,
and dreading above all things a reputation for valour, on
account of the many troubles he feared it might induce, he
invariably disclaimed in his cooler moments all merit for
that which he had performed, as he believed under the
impulse of some supernatural agency.

As he turned into the avenue, he was suddenly accosted by a man who, from his position in a corner of the way, appeared to have been awaiting him for some time—he stept quickly out upon the road, and laid his hand on the horse's bridle.

" Culhane, stop! I have some questions to ask ".

" Blessed saints! but you startled the heart within me, sir! Isn't it a droll way, that, for you to make out upon a body, as if it was *itself* that was there ".

" No nonsense now, Sandy, we have too much business on our hands. Have you seen old Evans? "

" I did your honour's bidding. But he says, the only way for him, says he, is to deliver himself, round and sound, before the judge at the next assizes, and tell the whole story out o' the face. It's the greatest nonsins in life for him to be afeerd, for though the warrant is still out against him, all the evidence is scattered and lost, and moreover the affair is forgotten a long time now: so that he had best make one bould stroke for his own again ".

The stranger seemed lost in meditation for some time, then suddenly accosted Sandy:

" And the affair here at Killavariga, how does it go on, Sandy? "

" Why thin, smooth enough. I seen himself and herself funnen together a while ago, like two that would be coorten, and not far from the end of it, neither. Av they don't have a hauling home before next Sherrove, call me an honest man ".

" Never, by this book! "* exclaimed the stranger, with vehemence, slapping his hand upon the pommel of the saddle: " I'll prevent that, at all events ".

" And what do you say to Mr. Evans's advice? "

" We'll talk of that another time. You will take care

---

* It does not necessarily follow, when an Irishman swears "by this book ", that the object which he indicates shall be a book, or have any relation to it. The oath is a very usual one.

to be in the way to-morrow, and let our friend Ally have a bed for me to-night, and keep the fire awake until I return, whatever hour that may be ".

" But I have something more to tell you", Sandy called out, in an under-tone, as he saw the stranger prepare ro depart.

" Reserve it for this evening, or to-morrow ".

" 'Tis regarden the Histins ".

" Hang them all up, high ! I want to hear little more of them now ".

The reiterated " But, sir", of Sandy, was lost upon the retreating colloquist, who, as it then appeared, had taken his departure in good time to escape observation, if, as his manner indicated, he were in reality anxious to avoid it. As Sandy turned his horse's head to proceed towards the house, he encountered the plump, little, rosy-cheeked maiden whom we have before mentioned as one of the household of the Fitzmaurices. An Irishman, of whatever rank or grade he may be, thinks it always a serious part of his duty, whenever he meets a woman alone, to begin with a compliment, be it good or bad.

" It's common out rubben snow-balls to your cheeks you do be, this way, that makes em so rosy, I'll be bound", with a smile which he intended should be an arch one.

" Never mind Norry's cheeks, whether they do be rosy or no ", replied the fair one, with a smile that dimpled them into the similitude of buds half-blown, and which, at the same time, confessed that the flattery had not been thrown away (when has it ever been ?)—" only come, as fast as hops, to the master, and don't unsaddle the horse, for he's going to send you of a message ".

" A'then, what's the murder now, Norry, eroo ?"

" All on the 'count of young Master Aylmer, thin. He to come in and to give tidings to the master about how he took the Histins, tne sheep-stalers, and to make out a narraytion o' what Lewy Histin, the born rogue, said concar-

ning the master—and the master to be taken ill, just as
he was, there isn't only a day there sence, when he seen
Mr. Aylmer in the sailor's clothes. The master is like an
innocent, mad intirely above in his bed-room, and the
young missiz with him, fare he's callen for you, all so fast,
there's half an hour there sence."

" It's a droll bizness, Norry, isn't it ?" said Sandy, as
he dismounted, and placing the bridle rein on the hasp
of the kitchen door followed his fair conductress into the
house.

In the meantime Aylmer was left in the parlour, to
ruminate on this repetition of the wonders of the previous
evening.   He could scarcely persuade himself that all
this could be fortuitous, and the deep and festering suspicion had already begun to lodge itself upon his heart,
and to darken on his brow, and in his eye, when it was
again met, and disabled by a piece of frankness on the
part of his guardian. He had, after the first access of
agitation had gone by, freely admitted the occasion in
which it originated. Those very Histins were the only
persons present, when the fatal dispute took place between him and Robert Aylmer, and his young friend
surely could not be surprised, that so powerful a remembrancer of that dreadful night, that night which had been
to him the cause of so much grief, shame, and suffering
(not the least of which might be accounted the loss of an
old and dearly loved associate,) should exercise a more
than ordinary influence upon his spirits. Aylmer could
not but be affected by the justice of this representation,
as well as by the agony of mind in which it was delivered
by the sufferer ; and he had separated from him and his
daughter, after a thousand assurances of perfect confidence
and affection, and various efforts at condolence, which, however, the old man seemed to receive, as was most natural,
with sufficient impatience.

Still, however, there was a restlessness and a working

at his heart, a craving and hungry curiosity, which told
him there was much yet to be learned, and resisted all the
efforts to persuade himself that he was satisfied.   While
he leaned on a table near the window, which looked into
the yard, he heard the clattering of a horse's feet over the
pavement, and presently after the voice of Sandy, addressing some words of grumbling indignation to some person
near him, and alternating his complaints, as was his
manner when under any excitation, with snatches of an
old piece of chimney-corner croonery.

" A fine time o' night it is, indeed, to be senden one a
lonesome road off to Hasset Ville, all a' one the day isn't
long enough.   Stand aizy, you ugly baste (to the horse).
And the O'Deas, the Histins's faction, vowen vengeance
again me early and late, for given Lewy to the law".

" To Hasset Ville!" said Aylmer, starting from his seat,
and looking out into the yard, where Sandy stood tightening the girths of his horse, and grumbling and singing
alternately.

> " ' There was an old 'oman toss'd up in a blanket
> Seventy times as high as the moon :
> Fare she was ——'

" Aye, and the rivinue min out, too, not knowen is it
for a smuggler they'll take me.

> ' Fare she was goen I couldn't emagine
> But in her hand ——'

" To shoot me, may be, unknownst, murder !

> ' But in her hand she carried a broom'.

" Isn't it what they done to Tim Dalton, near the cross
in the bog, and I have to pass that cross, too, and in the
dark, fare they say Tim do be goen about with his head
under his arm doen penance, in regard of cutting corn of a
retrenched holliday ; murder !

> " ' Ould 'oman, ould 'oman, ould 'oman, sis I,
> Erra, fare are you goen up so high ?
> To sweep the cobwebs off o' the sky,
> And av—— ' "

He was cut short in the melody by Aylmer, who threw up the window, and beckoned him close underneath.

" Who is sending you to Hasset Ville, Sandy ?"

" Himself, thin."

" With what message ?"

" With a letter, see, in regard o' the Histins ; and I abn't to show my face, av I don't deliver it to-night—a poor case."

The recollection of the prisoner's words instantly flashed on Aylmer. There was a message for their liberation ! There was a ground for the man's threat ! Aylmer paused a moment, like one who has received a stunning blow, then, addressing Sandy :

" Would you wish to have a brace of pistol bullets in your brain before morning ?"

" O fie ! murder ! Master William darlen, fot do you mane ?"

" That you must not, as you value your life, go to Hasset Ville to-night. Take the horse off to Bally-Aylmer, and have him ready for me to-morrow morning. In the mean time, keep the letter safe until you are called upon to deliver it up."

" And what'll I say to Mr. Fitzmaurice, sir, when he'll ax me concarnin his orders to-morrow ?"

" Keep out of his sight altogether, and I will take all the blame upon my own shoulders ?"

" Murder ! murder ! but it's a droll story," muttered Sandy, secretly rejoiced in his heart at the countermand.

" I'll do your honour's bidden, any way, without any questions. Allilu, murder alive !" and off he rode in very good humour, leaving his young master in a state of mind by no means similar.

On inquiring from a servant, Aylmer learned that the old man still continued ill, and that he had even requested his daughter to retire to her apartment, and leave him alone for the night. The young student's wish, in the first heat of his agitation at the discovery he had made, was to instantly fathom the motives of the old man by a personal interview, but a moment's consideration suggested to him the propriety and advantage of a little caution. He resolved to use every exertion in his power to obtain something like a corroboration, if not confirmation of his doubts. He took the light from the hands of the servant, and proceeded with a loaded and anxious heart toward his sleeping room.

Before we proceed to detail the occurrences of the night, it may be necessary to say something in the way of an apology to the enlightened reader, for what must at first sight appear to be a childish and threadbare essay on his credulity, more particularly as some little efforts have been hitherto made to give the narrative a hue of verisimilitude. We beg to disclaim any unworthy purpose, and only, like faithful chroniclers, record every event, be it wonderful or otherwise, even when we are ourselves unable to find a cause for it " in our philosophy". It will be much the better way, if the reader will suffer his judgment to travel quietly along with the narrative, suspending it where it is offended by improbability, and awaiting the occurrence of fresh incidents to atone for and explain the past.

The side of the bed in which Aylmer slept, was placed towards a large window, at about two yards distance, and the room itself was large and half wrapt in gloom, on which the light which he held in his hand had but a very partial influence. Perceiving that the moonlight fell with an unusual brightness (the natural consequence of the snow showers which had covered the ground and the roofs of the houses within the last few days) upon his bed and im-

mediately around it, Aylmer threw down the heavy dark
curtains on that side, and after having endeavoured to
compose his mind to prayer, proceeded to undress. In the
progress of this ceremony, he happened to put his hand
into the pocket in which he had deposited the mountain
stranger's letter. He resolved, at length, now that he
was perfectly at leisure, to examine it. The superscription, though half erased by the rain and ill usage, was
still sufficiently legible to satisfy him that it was directed
to himself, and with a passing emotion of surprise at the
stupidity of the man, who took so little trouble to make
himself certain into whose hands he was committing the
paper, he broke the wafer, and read the following words :

" Mr. Robert aylmar.   sir, there Is A Scame goen on
bee Tune Cahil-cruv-d rug an His daatur For you to
marry Her, and make Her missis uv bally ayl Mur.   william deer dont Take the hand Thats redd wit your fathers
Blood.   If you Wont bee sed be me yool heer moar in
Time frum
                    an Ould follyer o The famalee".

With something less of persevering industry than might
have enabled him to make tolerable progress in the far-
famed Babylonian slab, Aylmer contrived to extract the
above from the strange mass of hieroglyphics which the
letter presented to him.   Had he opened the paper but
one day sooner, he would have flung it from him with
contempt, and thought no more of its contents ; but the
occurrences of the last twenty-four hours had left his mind
in such a state of excitation, that he would have caught
with eagerness at a much more slender clue to an explanation.   The suspicion was not, at all events, peculiar to
his own breast, and it seemed to be more than a suspicion
with some.   He determined, as he had at length obtained
a guide, that he would thrid this labyrinth to its centre.

and after muttering this resolve between his teeth, he extinguished the light, and threw himself on the bed.

Still it was long before he could sleep. After exhausting all the customary modes of inducing slumber, without producing the desired effect, trying in vain the right side, and the left side, and the right again—pummelling the innocent pillow, and railing in heart at the equally innocent chambermaid, he fairly abandoned himself to his waking meditations, and gave up the attempt to conquer his restlessness altogether. This show of non-resistance, however, he soon found was the very surest mode of achieving triumph in such a case. Sleep, like good fortune. is not always to be taken by a *coup de main*—she will more frequently shed her blessings on the brain that is neglectful of her, than on that which is busy in devising means to accomplish her favour. He lay gazing on the curtain, which the moonlight rendered almost transparent, suffering thought after thought to glide quietly through his brain, each waxing fainter than the other, until at length the power of discrimination became inert, and consciousness itself began to fade away into that soft and gentle delirium which precedes the access of perfect mental repose, and forms one of the most luxurious and exquisite enjoyments which the weary spirit can receive from absence of active exertion. His eyelids were just drooping, and the visual faculty itself was just dormant, when he was suddenly startled by observing the shadow of a human figure thrown upon the bed-curtain that hung between him and the window. It flitted across, and was lost, almost before he had sufficiently roused himself to be certain that it was not a creation of his fancy. After drawing the curtains aside, and demanding: " Who was there ?" without receiving any reply, he dropped them again, and in the moment of their fall, as they rattled on their brass rings, his ear caught, or fancied it caught, a sound like the turning of a door-handle. He listened

again, but "heard nothing only the silence". Satisfied
that his auricular as well as his optical senses had been
playing the antic with him, he flung himself back on the
bed, and was speedily lost in the world of dreams.

In a short time his visions assumed a turbulent and
anxious, though rather whimsical air. They were crowded
with all the horrors of the three last days. He dreamt
first that the letter before mentioned was written in Greek,
and that Doctor ——, one of his college superiors, was
rating him for not being able to read it off at sight; that
it suddenly changed into Gælic, and the Doctor into Mr.
Fitzmaurice, who seized him by the throat, and plunged
him into a bog-hole, where he attempted to stifle him,
while, in endeavouring to remonstrate, he could do nothing
himself but bark and bay like a hound, until at length a
burst of laughter from his tormentor made him look up,
when he saw that it was his own dead father who stood
above him. He was impressed with this conversation
from no other evidence than the arbitrary feeling of a
dream, for he neither remembered his father's countenance,
nor was there in that of the vision the least resemblance
to any one that he had ever seen. The terror which the
sight occasioned him went on deepening in rapid gradations
until an oppression seized him which proceeded almost to
a point of suffocation. It was, in fact, a fit of nightmare
which had been induced, and he speedily fell into that
state of mental consciousness, and mental as well as bodily
impotence, which constitutes one of the most terrific
stages of the disease. His brow and limbs became bathed
with perspiration in the vain efforts which he made to
relieve himself. His eyes opened, and he distinctly saw
the material objects which surrounded him; yet the
visions of his sleep not only in part continued, but began
to assume a frantic sort of reality, from the manner in
which they became combined with these objects. His
waking eyes began to take the part of his yet unregulated

and delirious fancy, and he beheld, or at least strongly imagined he beheld, the figure of an old man standing by
his bedside, holding back the curtain with one hand, while
the other hung in perfectly motionless repose by his side.
His form was so placed, that the dreamer could see little
more than the strongly-marked outline of the shape and
face, which the intercepted moon-light had pencilled out
with the most perfect distinctness, and mellowed by a
silver line of light, which corrected its harshness, while it
revealed its character and expression in all their vigour.
By degrees Aylmer's glance became settled and fixed itself
full upon the figure. The lips, which were before parted
with an expression of kindness, began to move at length,
and another of the young man's senses was called in to
bear testimony to the reality of the appearance.

"I am come to warn you, William Aylmer, of a danger
in which you are placed. Listen to me, for it is your
father that speaks to you".

The young man attempted to stretch out his hands, and
speak, but the effort failed, and the words died in indistinct
murmurs upon his lips.

"Listen, but do not speak", continued the figure, "for
the night is flying fast, and the clouds are already gray in
the east. You have heard of your father's death—the
hand that plunged him living into the waters, was that of
Cahill Fitzmaurice. Beware of him, for he called himself
my friend for five-and-twenty years, and yet was not
ashamed to take me unawares in an hour of weakness and
of sin. He sought my life while I staggered in drunkenness upon the deck that I had died with unatoned blood".

Aylmer's countenance expressed the horror mingled
with curiosity which this last intimation had excited
within him. His informant perceived the meaning of the
gesture, and proceeded :—

"In that affair Cahill had no part. I had taken out the
vessel unaccompanied by him, and in the enterprise that

followed, the blood of a king's servant was shed. We thought more of the peril, then, than of the crime. I have since learned to think more of the crime than of the peril. Mine was not the hand, thank Heaven, that dealt the blow, nor mine the tongue that directed it; but in me, nevertheless, the guilt originated, and the hand of Fitzmaurice only anticipated the vengeance of the law. But these things are past. I have come now to warn you of another matter. Avoid the company of your guardian's daughter! Let all things rest as they are at least for two months, in the space of which time you shall see me again. Till then touch not her hand nor listen to her voice, as you value your parent's peace. To Fitzmaurice I would have you say——"

The slapping of a door in another apartment suddenly cut short the intended commission, and as the figure

"started like a guilty thing
Upon a fearful summons—"

Aylmer had a momentary view of the face, as the moon shone full upon it. There was an appearance of age, a paleness in the complexion probably heightened by the peculiar light, and long flaxen locks depending around either temple. The expression of the countenance, during the instant, was that of anxiety and intense attention. On a repetition of the sound, the strange midnight visitor dropt the curtain which he had been holding, and with a low and gentle farewell blessing, uttered with the softest and kindest tone in the world, such as the lip of a parent alone can breathe, and the heart of a child alone can appreciate, the appearance fled.

Aylmer, in the effort which he made to detain the vision, both by voice and action, found that his nightmare had completely left him, and that, in fact, he had been lying wide awake for a considerable time, though consciousness had stolen by such imperceptible gradations

upon him, that he could not tell at what period of the
scene that passed he had been waking, and when he slept.
It did not, however, escape the metaphisical eye of the
young collegian, that the bed curtain had become wrinkled in the grasp of the spectre, precisely in the same manner as it would have done if the limb had been composed
of material flesh and blood. He sprung from his bed,
and rushed in the direction by which the appearance had
departed. There was no person in the room, but a little
search satisfied him that there existed no necessity either
for a sliding panel, or the other resource, an impassible
state of being, to aid his visitor's flight, for the room door
stood a-jar. It certainly was a very vulgar exit for a ghost,
but the probability that it had been used was more than
feasible.

The morning broke before Aylmer was enabled to subdue, in any degree, the feverish excitement which this
occurrence had induced. The dawn was cold and comfortless, and the cold drifts of snow, amid which it was
ushered in, prolonged the greyish mistiness of its twilight a considerable space beyond its customary duration.
Without waiting to form any resolution as to the immediate line which it would be necessary for him to pursue,
further than might be suggested by the feverish impulse
of the moment, and with his heart and mind and frame
all glowing and trembling with the energy of the terrific
discovery which he had chanced upon, he found himself
hurrying almost instinctively along the passage which led
to the sleeping room of Fitzmaurice, in a distant corner of
the building. The chamber of the murderer!—his father's
murderer! He scarcely knew—he never once thought of
asking himself what his design was in thus breaking in upon the morning slumbers of the old man; but he had an
indistinct, unsifted motive within his breast, which prompted him to take the criminal (if the spirit had not lied), by
surprise, and startle the truth from its resting-place within

4

his soul. A sensation too, perhaps, similar to that which is uttered by the ill-fated Danish prince, in a situation of equal perplexity, might have mingled itself with this unde fined purpose :—

> " ——The spirit that I have seen
> May be a devil ; and the devil hath power
> To assume a pleasing shape ; yea—and, perhaps,
> Out of my weakness and my melancholy
> (As he is very potent with such spirits),
> Abuses me, to damn me : I'll have grounds
> More relative than this—"

"The sudden "Who's there?" that struck his ear as he stirred the door-handle, showed him that the old man had not been surprised in slumber by the awaking day. Without making any answer, he burst in tremulous agitation into the apartment, when the excess of feeling which swelled his bosom and rushed into his throat, compelled him to stop for a moment, and almost gasp for breath. He flung himself at last into an arm-chair by the bed-side, where he lay back for a few moments, oppressed almost to suffocation with the host of fearful and conflicting sensations that had been stirred up within him. The horror of his guardian's crime—the memory of all his kindness—pity for his present sufferings, and the natural instinct that prompted him to the course of justice, all contended for mastery within his soul, and made havoc of the region in their strife. It was the first time that the spear had been struck into the dwelling-place of his stormy passions, and they bounded from their hold with all the ungovernable fury which the novelty and fierceness of the excitement was calculated to produce. The old man had flung back the bed-curtain, and sitting erect, gazed with an expression of amazement, of terror, and cruel anxiety, upon the strange emotion in his young friend. Fear, and (an uncharitable observer might say an instinctive consciousness of its cause, prevented his questioning the

latter, on whom his wild, flickering gaze continued to
direct itself while he waited with panting heart, gasping
lips, and checks and brow made cadaverous with the dread
of the coming horror, for the first speech of the youth.

At length their glances met, and the effect was elec-
trical. Rising slowly to his feet, and uplifting his clenched
hand above his head, while that and every other member
of his frame shook with convulsive energy, and his voice
became thick and hoarse, and his eyes grew red and
watery with passion, he said:—

"Cahill Fitzmaurice, confess to your God and to me,
for the time is come at length. You are the murderer of
my father!"

A low muttering groan, and then a gurgling in the
throat of the accused, were the only answer which the
accuser received. The curtain fell from the hand of the
former, and he lay back motionless on the bed. Fully
prepared, as he had been, for the conviction of guilt,
which the seeming criminal's conscience thus afforded, its
effect on Aylmer was not the less powerful when it flashed
upon him in all its certainty. He felt a sickness at the
heart, a sudden shooting at the eyes, and a reeling in his
brain, which nearly made him stagger from his balance.
Pressing both hands close upon his brow, as if to crush
the burning thoughts that were rioting within, he hurried
out of the chamber, just as Miss Fitzmaurice, in a night-
dress and slippers and with a countenance full of alarm,
entered it by another door.

When he reached his own apartment, he gave full vent
to the whirlwind of emotions which he had been endeavouring to restrain during the last half-hour, and flung
himself upon the bed in a convulsion of feeling. It was
one of those great and extraordinary occasions which, oc-
curring when the character is matured by time and
experience, serve only to strengthen or call forth its
peculiarities, and wear their channels deeper in the heart;

but which, when they come into contact with a youthful, undecided, and susceptible mind, can shake it to its very foundation, and mark its course for good or ill through life. The young man, who had lain down to rest the evening before, a raw, unformed, unfledged spirit, now rose from the bed, a fiery, austere, and resolute being, with a shadow of sternness and gloom struck into his heart, which clung to it during all his after-life.

After the first shock of his agitation was at an end, and he had, not without a passing emotion of shame at his own weakness, reduced his over-wrought spirits into some degree of calmness, he determined instantly to repair to Bally-Aylmer, and there deliberate on the course which it would be necessary for him to adopt.

He flung his *loody* about him, and regardless of the snow which drifted in large flakes into his face, he proceeded towards his family residence.

In the mean time, Katharine had hurried to the bedside of her parent. She had been awakened from her light sleep in the apartment next his (which she always occupied) by the first sound of Aylmer's entering; and unknowing the cause of the intrusion, while she felt indignant that any disturbance should be made in his chamber at that early hour, she hurried on some careless additions to her night-dress, and entered the room at the very moment the door closed on Aylmer's receding figure. Her anxieties being, in the first place, aroused for the immediate condition of the old man, she walked rapidly to the bed, and removing the hangings, discovered, in the gray morning light, a spectacle that made her heart recoil with horror. He lay, half supported by the head of the bed, his jaw hanging, and his eyes watery and motionless, fixed in a stare of stolid terror upon the ground, his forehead covered with a death-like moisture, and his cheeks and lips tinged with the cold, bluish colour which is cast over the features in the extreme agony, and is recognized

as the liveried hue of the grave. Uttering a half-
suppressed scream of anguish, the affrighted girl wound
one arm around the head of her parent, and supported it
upon her bosom, while she pressed the other in an agony
of suspense upon his heart. The organ of life had suspended its function for a short time, and was now, throb
after throb, slowly-resuming its office.

The chamber-door soon after opened, and Norry hurried
to the assistance of her mistress. While the latter endeavoured to recal sensation by the usual physical appli-
cations and resources, sprinkling the face with cold water,
chafing the temples, and placing the body in a horizontal
position, the unsophisticated attendant took the more
effectual course of forcing open the stiff clenched fingers of
the right hand, and making the sign of the cross with her
thumb upon the palm. This feat accomplished, she stood
thumping her bosom, and awaiting its effect in perfect
faith, at the bed's foot.

"Don't mind any more o' the water, Miss Cauthleen;
the little criss-crass I made in his hand will soon lift him
out o' the fit: it's the gentlemen, God speed 'em (here
she crossed herself, and curtsied with much devotion),
that were wantin to hoise him away with them this mornen".

"Hush! hush! girl! fall back out of the light—he is
recovering, God be thanked and praised!"

"Guilty—aye—guilty!" muttered the still unconscious
object of their solicitude.

"God save us! Do you hear him, miss?"

"His senses are wandering yet".

"Where—where is he? Kate, my girl, you shall bear
witness to this—call him! call him back!"

"Whom, my dear father ?—William?"

"Mister Aylmer is gone off, miss", said Norry.

"Gone! I am lost! Ungrateful boy! If I wronged
the father, did I not serve the son? Haste! call him
back! he has my life in his hands".

"Quit the room, Norry!" exclaimed Katharine, stamping her foot against the boards with an expression of anger which was foreign to her nature. The servant obeyed, after a world of wondering gestures, crossings, and muttered ejaculations.

The violence of the action served, in some degree, to recal Fitzmaurice to a perfect consciousness of his situation. "What! Kate, my gentle Kate, grown passionate?" he said, in wonder and tenderness, as he took her warm hand in his, and gazed still with some expression of listlessness into her eyes: "These veins have young and boiling blood within them, my little girl. You must learn to temper and subdue it in time, or it will lay the seeds of a bitter old age, and a fearful death for you".

"I will, sir—you are better, are you not, father?" said the daughter, regarding the speech as a part of the lingering delirium which had seized him, and affecting to coincide with it, in the light and cursory manner which one uses to satisfy the sufferer on all such occasions; and *than* which nothing can be more irritating, if the person towards whom it happens to be adopted should at all suspect its motive.

"You treat me like a child", said Fitzmaurice, with sharpness; "no matter. It may be the time is not far distant, when it will be the act of a fool to mutter a word of reason in my ears", he continued, passing his hand over his brow, and turning his eyes wildly from her glance. "Yes. Many that have ate and drank at my board, would only eat and drink the freer, when the master of the house was in Swift's Hospital. And the mistress of Kilavariga would smile as merrily too. She would be her own mistress then. Go, go! You are like the rest. Go from me, girl, go from me".

Shocked and wounded as she was by these expressions, the horrible indications by which they were accompanied were more than sufficient to stifle all the selfish feelings of wronged and undervalued affection, which would at any other time have burned like a fever stroke within the breast of the devoted girl. Persisting, notwithstanding his pettish repulses, in clinging around her father's neck, she sobbed and wept upon his shoulder, until she felt an assurance of relenting in the renewed pressure of the hand, which he still retained.

"I did not, indeed, think of what I was saying, sir", she exclaimed, in her most repentant tones, perceiving at once that the surest way of redeeming her error, was by adopting the directly opposite course. "But, why will not my father confide in me? I am no longer a child, in whom one should fear to repose a trust, nor am I incapable of feeling and participating in the grief, the secret grief, whatever it is, that is weighing down your heart. Do you not feel I love you, father? Have you not been my only friend from my very childhood? Has not all that I prize and reverence most, my knowledge of right and wrong, my perception of virtue, my religion, been all taught me by you, and you only? and how could I, if I were of the worst nature in the world, do otherwise than dearly love and honour you?"

Surprised, and not a little pleased with the energy and fervour with which the gentle girl made her appeal, the old man paused a moment, while he surveyed her with a moistened and affectionate eye. The very last phrase which she used, however, appeared to jar against his thought, and interrupt the kindly feeling that had begun to diffuse itself over his breast. His brow contracted, and he mused for a moment.

"Aye, Kate", said he, "but will you continue to hold this sentiment? Suppose the time should come when none but you could or would do other than revile and hate me, do you think you would continue to honour your old, and perhaps erring, but fond, fond parent?"

"It was the commandment of the Eternal God Him-

self", exclaimed the maiden, in a burst of staid enthusiasm, "delivered amid the lightnings and thunders of
the Holy Mountain, 'Honour thy Father and Mother!'
and there was no reservation found upon the tablet of
stone. Man may persecute, sickness may change, grief
may depress, poverty may chill, or guilt may blacken the
heart of a parent, but the bonds of the child are never
loosened".

"'Then, should the world call me a guilty wretch, and
prove me little less, I may still have a daughter ?"

" When that day comes, father, I will say my eyes and
ears are false, and trust my heart alone, that will speak
for you against them ".

The old man reclined against the head of the bed for a
few moments, while his eyes closed and his lips moved in
silence. Then, without altering his position, he waved his
hand gently, and said in a soft and broken tone :

" Leave me, Kate, for a few minutes to myself. I will
look for you in the parlour. Clear all signs of anxiety
from your countenance, and prepare yourself for a mournful
confidence ".

Katharine obeyed in silence, and her father, after per-
forming the duties of the toilet, began to deliberate within
his own mind the events of the morning, and their most
probable consequences.

It was a passing comfort to him to know, that he had
at last found one to whom he might show himself such as
he really was, without meeting that quick repulsive horror
and distrust, which he feared worse than conscience ; and
yet it was a bitter humiliation to be reduced to the
necessity of lowering himself in the eyes of his own child,
and directing those feelings of terror and detestation at
vice which his own instructions had generated in her mind,
against himself in person. For one moment, an involuntary wish escaped him, that he had reared his
daughter with a somewhat less acute susceptibility of the

hideousness of crime, and a more qualified admiration of
its opposite, than now formed the groundwork of her
character. It was but a glance of thought, however, in
which neither his reason nor his feeling had any par-
ticipation, and was forgotten even before it was condemned. He concluded by determining to make the
confidence which he meditated, and after praying, for the
first time in many a year, with a somewhat lightened
spirit, he descended to the parlour, where Katharine was
awaiting him.

The young lady in the mean time had been occupied
with doubts and conjectures of an equally agitating,
though a less gloomy character. Notwithstanding the
warmth of feeling, into which she had been hurried by the
enthusiasm of her affection during the preceding scene,
she was very far from anticipating, even in thought, the
possibility that her filial love could be put to so extreme
a test as her words declared it capable of surviving, and
she looked for nothing more in truth than her father had
himself led her to expect—"a mournful confidence".
Even the wild and haggard air which was about his
features and actions as he entered the room, were in-
sufficient to lead her to suspect that his promised secret
could comprise any thing of a darker or more fearful hue.

He motioned his daughter to keep her seat, and after
glancing along the passage by which he approached,
closed the door and slipped the little bolt into its p'ace.
Then, after pacing up and down the room several times,
as if debating with himself the easiest mode of opening a
conversation so replete with humiliation to one party, and
horror to the other, as that which he was about to enter
upon, he stopped opposite his daughter's chair, and fixing
his eye, all lighted up as it was with a thousand fearful
emotions, on her mild and tenderly anxious glance, he said:
"You know not, perhaps, or have not considered the full
extent of the consequence which you draw upon your e'f
4*

by urging me to this confidence. You have not had time to think on the subject, how deeply and closely it will involve your peace of mind, nay, perhaps your health of soul—how intimately and perfectly your fate must become intertwined with that of him, into whose secret heart you are now about to penetrate unbidden".

"There must be safety, father", said the girl, a little startled and confounded by the strangeness of his manner, "there must be peace, wherever you lead me".

"Do nothing on presumption", was his reply. "I wish you to pause, and ponder well, before you have my secret, for when it is once told, I shall hold you bound to me, and to my service, more firmly than ever, though perhaps not equally to my love".

The last words were uttered in so mournful a tone that the current of Katharine's feelings, which had been a little disturbed and qualified by the mysticism of the previous speech, again rushed into their old channel. Her eyes filled up as she grasped her parent's hand in hers, and wetting it with tears of filial love and reverence, she said, in hurried, and yet irresolute accents :

"O father, I do not know what you mean, or what I am to fear; but speak—speak, in God's name; whatever it is that troubles you ought not to be spared to me. If it be a sorrowful tale, I may make its memory sit lighter on your heart, and two, at least, can bear the burden better than one. If it be guilt that—guilt" (she shuddered and was silent one instant, as she detected a word on her lips, which her will had not directed them to utter) —"forgive me, sir, that cannot be, I know—No, father, no", in increasing agony, as she read not the indignant denial she looked so eagerly for in his cold and marbly eye —"you have taught me to love virtue, to adore God, to fear His anger, to deserve His mercy. Father! speak! speak to me—"

"Peace, girl!" said the old man sadly, yet sternly;

"attribute not to the inactive instrument the music which
was made by the divine breath that filled and the hand
that governed it.   He who holds a light to another, is most
like to fall himself. Sit still, and hear me". And replacing
the trembling girl in the chair, which in her agitation she
had left, he stood close at her side, and after a pause,
began:
    "You have heard of the circumstances which attended
the death of William's father?"
    "Yes, yes, sir!" replied Kate, in a low and hurried tone,
with a horrible failure and sinking at her heart.
    "When he died, there was but one friend at his side".
As he proceeded, the sallow and ashy countenance of the
old man became deepened in hue by the rushing of the
scanty currents of life into channels which they had long
ceased to visit, and his eye became gradually fiercer and
fiercer, as the fear and horror that oppressed his daughter
became more manifest in her look and attitude.   "Sit
erect, girl, and hear me steadily.   You have forced me
to say what, except in madness, I thought mortal ears
should never hear me utter, and you must abide the consequence.   Sit still, then, and do not flinch or waver, while
I speak to you, as you value your father's reason".
    "I will, sir.   I am not terrified", whispered the bewil-
dered girl, while a strange mixture of anxiety and listlessness became blended in the gaze which she now bent on
the old man.
    "The two friends", he continued, after a pause of
fearful recollection, "were sitting together by the little
brick hob in the hooker's cabin, and talking gaily enough
about the work they had both been about.   Friends
leagued in crime are but light lovers, though their bonds
are the stronger by the addition of fear and community of
guilt, than those which simple liking ties.   Few words
were necessary to bring the frown and the taunt where
the laugh and the jest were seen and heard a little while

before.   A sharp speech provoked a blow, and the friend-
ship of a long life was dissolved as suddenly as life itself,
when the deathstroke touches it.   The man who received
the indignity remained silent and gloomy during the
remainder of the evening.   Although he did not refuse his
hand when the aggressor sued for reconciliation, the
disgrace was festering at his heart.   Soon after, a dark
and foggy night came on.   Both these men ascended on
deck to speak at greater freedom, and draw a somewhat
purer air than that of the close and smoky cabin where
they had been lying just before.   At a moment when the
vessel heeled more deeply than usual before the blast,
while the steersman was busy at the helm, and his mate
with the foresheet—and while the two stood alone and
unseen (though not unheard) upon the forecastle—one
roaring, laughing, and unsteady with drunkenness and
with triumph; the other equally intoxicated, but after a
darker and more sullen fashion, and from a different cause,
the aggressor staggered a little, reeled, and overhung the
lee-gunwale.   The opportunity flashed like lightning upon
the heart of his enemy; he darted on him, and in the
fierce effort almost precipitated his own fate and mingled
it with that of his victim.   The fluke of an anchor,
however, caught in a part of his frieze great coat, and he
hung suspended between both worlds, while the dying
shrieks of his victim, the gurgling of the death struggle,
the angry dash of the waters, and the whirring of the wild
gale, sounded in his ears like the din of the last judgment.
He was saved, however.   The vessel swept on, and the
voice of the dying man was speedily lost in the distance.
A lie protected his destroyer ".

The old man here paused and sunk back in his chair,
exhausted by the fierceness and horror of his recollected
sensations; while his daughter sat stooping forward, her
eyes fixed in motionless horror upon his, and every
feature bent up, and set hard in an expression of de-

vouring attention; her limbs and frame stiffening with the anguish of the dreadful suspense in which the old man's pause had left her,

> " ——as if each other sense
> Were bound in that of hearing, and each word
> Struck through it with an agony ".

At length he resumed in a faint and hoarse tone, without daring to lift his eyes toward his auditor: "The man who died on that night was Robert Aylmer; and his murderer was——".

Uttering a low, yet piercing scream of agony, the wretched girl cast herself at the feet of her guilty father, in an attitude of deprecation and entreaty.

" No, no, you will not say it, sir. Oh! do not, in the name of the Heaven you have taught me to venerate, plunge us both into such a gulf of horror. What! my father! my kind, good father, in whose bosom I have been fondled—whose lips I have kissed—whose hand has blest me morning and evening for fifteen years—my dear, dear father, do a deed so full of horror and crime—a murderer, a secret murderer!—Ha!" with a cry of exultation, as a momentary flush of burning pride and shame, the impulse of an uncalculating instinct, passed over the brow of the old man at the branding epithet,—"I see it there—I knew it could not be; you are not he of whom you spoke, father? Forgive, forgive me, sir, for so cruel, so insulting an anticipation of your words".

"It is too late for recanting them now", said Fitz-maurice quietly, but with a dreadful ghastliness in his eye: "the blood of my oldest friend is on my hands; I have told my sin, and my soul is lighter".

"Good Heaven! blessed mother of God!" muttered Katharine, as she rose from her knees, and passed one hand in a trembling and hurried manner over her forehead and about her loosened hair, while her eye became

fixed in stupid terror on the earth.   A silence of terr.ble
reflection to both ensued.   Fitzmaurice perceived, at a
glance, that he had for ever lost the esteem of his child.
That was bitter.   Katharine beheld, in one short hour, the
peace, the happiness of her whole existence withered and
parched up; her duty made burdensome as crime; her
heart's warmest and best affections made grievous to her
soul, its faith disproved, its idol broken down, and the
shrine of its worship polluted and made desolate.   This
was more bitter still.

After a pause of some minutes, Fitzmaurice approached
her and held out his hand.   She shuddered, and shrunk
back upon herself with an involuntary action and a half-
stifled exclamation of repugnance.   He attempted to
smile, but his lip grew pale, and his brows were knit in
anguish at the change.

"I thought this, Kate", he said, sadly; "but I do not
blame you for it.   And yet it is a sad promise to me of
what I am to expect from a malignant and suspicious
world, when my own daughter, whom I have reared and
cared for now sixteen years, shrinks from my touch as if
it were that of a viper".

Perceiving that this appeal was ineffectual, and that the
stroke had been too hardly dealt on his daughter's heart,
Fitzmaurice continued, rising: "And now, Kate, though I
put your affection to a strong test before I spoke to you on
this, you shall not find me ungenerous enough to profit by
the hasty enthusiasm of the moment.   I have lost your
love.   I grieve for it, but I do not blame you.   Yet,
without your love I will never allow your service nor com-
panionship.   Go you out at that door—I will take this;
and let that be our final parting.   Go, my loved, my injured child; forget your miserable father,—think of him as
of one departed, but not in crime—for that would make his
memory bitter to you,—but as one who erred, and found
the grace that Heaven treasures for the penitent.   Another

land must be my refuge from the retribution which
my guilt demands, and must afford me time to labour for that divine grace. Farewell, Kate; go and
be gay, and happy, and innocent as ever, and leave
your old parent to his guilt, his sorrow, and his solitude".

This speech had the effect on his hearer which the
speaker wished and intended. The sluices of her soft and
feminine passions had been all dammed and choked up,
almost to suffocation, by the grand and overwhelming
horror that had been thrown about her, and only wanted
a single pressure on the master-spring, one whisper in the
ear of the heart, to set them flowing again, in all the
impetuosity of interrupted feeling. She flung herself into
her father's arms, and twined her own around his neck,
while she leaned her head against his bosom in a
hysterical passion of grief.

"No, no, father!" she exclaimed, as soon as she could
give words to her affliction, "part we shall not, at least.
Whatever you may have been to others, you have been
always kind, and tender, and good to me, and my hand
must not be the first to cast the stone at my only friend.
The changes of the world can affect us but little, for we
have always lived more to ourselves than to it; and a life
of loneliness will be nothing more than a prolonging of
past quiet. Yes, father, my resolution is taken. If you
must leave home for ever, you take all my home with you;
and, for my own heart's ease, I must follow it". It can
hardly be said (for thoughts will often come unbidden,
and make obstinate battle with the will), that we charge
the gentle and affectionate Kate with any selfishness of
feeling, in acknowledging that, while she spoke the last
sentence, a new thought, a new fear, and a new pang,
darted into her heart, and seemed for the moment to have
almost cleft it asunder. William Aylmer! She gasped
for breath, while her aged parent folded her to his

breast, and moistened her neck with the first tears he
had shed for many days.

We will close the scene on this afflicted pair, and cast
our eyes for a short while in another direction.

It will be recollected that Sandy Culhane had received
directions from William Aylmer to hold in readiness for
him on this morning the horse on which he was about to
bear the intercepted letter to Hasset Ville. The winter
dawn had scarcely whitened in the east, when he was at
his post in the old stable, preparing the animal for the
appointment. He was busied after his usual fashion,
rubbing down the pleased and sleek-coated beast with a
" wisp " of straw, while he puffed away the clouds of dust
that enveloped his person and hummed out an occasional
bar of his favourite *madhereen rhu*,* interrupted by
" hirrups! stand over croo! hiss—ss—ss—ss—the little
'omaneen you were—aizy!" when a " God bless all
here ", from the darkening doorway, suspended his
labours; he looked up and beheld an old man in a gray
frieze dress leaning against the jamb, and throwing his
head on one side, to screen it from the snow that drifted
across. It was the herdsman of Kilavariga.

" Yeh, then, isn't it airly you're goen roven this mornen,
Mick? What's the murder now? "

" Whist! whist! Sandy. I have something to say to
you.— Will she kick? "

" O, sorrow a taste! Aizy, you born jade, and let the
nayburs come in ", as he observed the animal throw back
its ears, and use a menacing gesture towards the intruder.
The latter shook down an armful of the sweet hay in a
corner of the stable, and seating himself on it in a fair-and-
easy Irish way, commenced business at once.

" Have you air a thief in your house, Sandy, that wears
brogues and pavers?"

Sandy stared as he replied : " A thief, Mick, eroo? Bad

* Little red fox.

'tess to the thief at all in our house, wit or without the pavers ".

The herdsman paused, and seemed to take thought for a moment; then glancing at Sandy's well greased dogskin shoes, he beckoned him to follow to a little distance, where a long track of footsteps intersected the plain, white surface of the snow-covered lawn. "Would you look here, Sandy?" said he. "The master's turf-rick, the slane turf, was broken last night, and I traced those steps over the little haggard wall, and through the paddock, and by the forge, and here, all the ways to Bally-Aylmer. 'Tis hard to tell the marks o' these steps now, for it was snowen since they wor made, but here's one of 'em close be the wall, put the print o' your crubeen a-nigh that, av you plase ".

Sandy indignantly stamped his foot in the snow, and the investigator, after viewing both impressions, shook his head, as if disappointed.

" They are quite different. There's pavers here wit heads as big as tin-pinnies, and yours hasn't only toe-tacks in 'em, like the gintlemin ".

"Why then, you lahu-muthawn* o' the airth!" exclaimed the insulted Sandy, now that the cause of the herdsman's action was so unmincingly announced, "is it maning that it was meself was at your ould turf-reek you wor?"

" Aisy, aisy, now, Sandy!" said the other, moving on before him towards the stable, with one arm resting on his back, under his long coat skirts, and motioning him back with the other. "There's no offince. I seen the print of a handsome, clever foot in the snow, and where was I to look for it, av it wasn't with Sandy Culhane? But sure I ought to know better, for you shamed it out intirely whin you put your own a-near it. Sure av I wasn't blind, I ought to know, that it isn't sech a *plob* of a fut

* Half-natural.

as that abroad, that could bother Norry Kilmartin's
dreams".

With a heroic effort at forbearance, Sandy mastered his
indignation, and complacently glancing down at a hideously
formed foot, followed the herdsman into the stable, where
he recommenced his labours on the ecclesiastical sides of
the well-conditioned quadruped, while the former resumed
his seat and meditative air on his heap of fresh hay.

" It's droll still who the brogues belonged to ", he continued, after a pause, " but all is one; for if I was to
bring him in bound hand an fut to the master, he'd be the
first to let him off himself.   What do you think did he do
the other day, only relase the Barret's pzaties from the
cant, and bid him say nothen about the trifle o' the rent
that was due, but to set to work agen, fresh on a clear gale ?"

" Wisha, the Barrets are poor craturs ! " was all Sandy's
reply.

" More's the pity to be losing to 'em, since it does 'em
so little good".

" Did you ever hear the ould fable of Jack Finnane and
the white-eyes ? " said Sandy.

" To be sure I didn't ; for what should I ?"

" Sit aisy then, and I'll tell you it.   This Mr. John
Finnane, you see, was a kind of a half-sir, a middleman,
that used to be great long ago, letting out land in acres,
and half-acres, and quarter-acres to the poor people, that
would may be want a *gwal** of pzaties coming on the idle
season; and a hard and a bitter landlord he was to the
poor fellows that wouldn't have the rent agen the gale
day, and good care he took, I'll be bound, that not a single
connopp† ever left the airth ant'l every camack‡ was
paid, dead gale and all.   Signs on, it often chanced, as
most like it was, that the poor tinants, not having the
difference o' the rint, used to go into the pzatie fields at
night, pulling up the stalks and filling their little Jack

* Armful.   † Potato.   ‡ Penny token.

Daws* with what God sent up with the roots, which being
made known to John Finnane, yon see, he sat up a night
to know would he catch any of the plunderers at their
doings, which they having notice of, didn't come, as why
should they? being marked for the quarter sessions, surely.
"Well! 'twas coming on midnight, and Mr. Finnane
being as it were tired with himself, sat down on a ridge of
the pzaties, with his feet in the furrow, and he very sleepy,
it being Jerry Graham's quarter. 'Tis aisily known he
opened his eyes wide enough, whin he heard, what do you
think, only Jerry's white-eyes talking to one another in the
ground under him! He stooped his head down, and
began to hearken. 'Will you grow any more?' says a
little pzatie to a big one.—'No, a gra gal', says the big
pzatie, 'its big enough I am already'.—'Well, then', says
the other, 'move out o' the way with you a piece, and
let us grow for Jerry Graham and the craturs'.—'I'd be
happy to oblige you then', says the big pzatie, 'but sure
it's well you know none of us can stir from our places an
inch ontil John Finnane gets his rint'. 'Murther alive!'
says John, crossing himself and thumping his breast
about, 'are the pzaties themselves cryen out agen me?
Murther, but that's great intirely'. Home he went,
wondering, and people say Jerry Graham was bid to dig
his quarter and welcome next mornen".

"E'then, thanky for your parable, Sandy", said the
herdsman, "but may be we'd find one on the other side,
for an open hand isn't always the luckiest after all ".

Sandy suffered his arm to rest on the shoulder of the
animal he was tending, and placed himself in an attitude
of attention, while the other, throwing himself back in an
easy reclining posture, commenced his "fable".

"Mr. David Foy had a great heart, but, like the
master, there was too much of it, for there was no bounds
at all to his doings, when he took it into his head to spend

* John Doe, a small bag.

his money; an having no famaly nor air a wife that would
look after the house and things, every whole tote went
wrong intirely. Besides, he was great after the hounds;
and a fine rider he was, and with sech a dawny darland
of a horse, that he one day left the hounds, hunt, hare, an'
all behind him. On he went, an' he was goen, goen, goen
(as the ould gossips say), ont'l he came to a great valley
intirely. And there he saw THEMSELVES, in their little
red jackets, and with caps on their heads, and hurlies in
their hands, and they playen goal. Well, an ould hag
that was sitten as it might be this way like meself, see
David, and made to-*wards* him with a piggin of something
that's good, which he refused, and well became him,
knowen it was not good to take drink from the like.
'Take it, heart', says the ould hag, ' and don't spare. It's
David Foy's cider, and long may he live and reign ; we
don't want for the best he has, for it's we that get all
that's wasted in the house by bad looken after, and it's
good liven we have here, while the poor Christians are
starving at his door. Take the drop and be comfortable'.
' Thanky kindly, ma'am ', says David, ' but I rather not,
av you plase, wit the same thanks to you as if I did; my
stomach is not well indeed this mornen, saving your
favour'. ' No offince in life, sir ', says she. So they sat
down together. By an by, in comes a strappen young
Clooricaun with a pailful o' sweet milk. ' Where did you
get that, eroo?' says the hag. ' E'then long life to Davy
Foy, where should I get it only out of his dairy? He
was out hunten, an Bridget was in the haggart wit Tim
Fouloo, so I came in for my share wit the cat an the dog'.
' *Sha guthine!* is this the way of it ?' says Davy to himself. Then comes in another of the gentry with a firkin
o' butter, and another with a gammon o' bacon, and all in
the same story, and Davy himself by all the time, and not
one o' them knowen him, in rigard of his never being
about the house, hardly. ' 'Tis little admiration for ye to

be so fat, gintlemin ', says he at last, as he was wishen
'em a good mornen, at which they all laughed hearty, and
nodded and winked their little wicked eyes at him, mighty
merry intirely, as much as to say: ' True for you, lad '. In
a year after he came to the same place: the little goal-
players were nothen but skin and bone, and the old hag
was scrapen a raw pzatie agen a grater to make a cake for
their supper. ' Oh, then the Cromaylian curse upon your
head, David Foy, for we know you now!' says the whole
set of 'em together—' there's all we got losing after you
this twelvemonth ', showen the raw pzatie the same time.
' The more my luck', says David, 'wasn't it yer own
taiching ?'"

Having, as he believed, fully discomfited Sandy at his
own weapons, old Michael rose to depart, with the view
of instituting an inquiry at the neighbouring village
relative to the owner of the mysterious brogues and
pavers.

He was scarcely out of sight, when the back door of
the dwelling-house opened, and the stranger who had on
the preceding evening accosted Sandy in the avenue of
Kilavariga, made his appearance. The latter was busily
occupied in polishing a stubborn fetlock when the old man
hurried into the stable.

"Come, Sandy, saddle the horse, and lead him out
here", he exclaimed. "I have received a piece of intelligence from Mr. Evans which will render it necessary
for me to travel fifty miles before night fall. Is the
animal frost shod?"

"Quite complate, yer honour. But that's a thing o'
nothen. Mr. William Aylmer that bid me have the cratur
convanient for himself this morning ".

"Where is he going?"

" Sarrow a know do I know ".

" No matter. Give me the horse, and make out what
excuse you can for your young master ".

"The best I can offer, then", said Sandy as he assisted the stranger to mount, "will be to keep out of his way intirely, for indeed he's not over honest* when he do be crossed".

"Kind father for him", said the stranger laughing.

"Wonst in his day, sir", replied Sandy, "but time and trouble changes the people".

The expression of merriment was instantly quelled on the lip of the stranger. He fetched his breath hard, and, checking the bridle, rode through the yard gate just as Aylmer, wrapped in his great coat, and covered with snow-flakes, made his appearance on the avenue. The latter used a slight action of surprise, as the other passed him at a more rapid pace than he had before employed.

"He knows the horse!" said Sandy, "time for me to be moven". And he was about to depart, when the young gentleman's voice arrested his flight.

"Who is that man, Sandy?"

"That man sir? is it?——It's——Mick Donovan, sir, Mr. Fitzmaurice's herdsman".

"He looks more large, and rides better than he used".

"Thriving with him the place is, your honour.—Not a word about the horse!" he added, in some astonishment, as Aylmer, with a look of some disappointment, turned off in the direction of the house. "Some trouble at Kila-variga, I'll be bail".

————

The limits which we prescribed to ourselves at the commencement of this little tale, render it impossible for us to enter into a minute detail of many unimportant circumstances which occupied the principal personages during the several days which followed the eventful morning of Aylmer's discovery. It will save the reader a great deal

* *Honest* is a synonym for *mild* or *gentle*, in Ireland.

of heavy reading, and the historian of the parties a great deal of analyzing matter, of speculations on impulse and motive, and cloudy talking, if we proceed to the next situation of the story with as little preface as possible.

Fitzmaurice and his daughter having heard nothing more of Aylmer, concluded that his resolution was fixed, not to enter the house of his old benefactor from that time forward. Although the cause of this determination, and the apparent probability of her young friend's persevering in it, had produced a mournful change both in the heart and in the appearance of the lively Katharine, she had exerted a sufficient degree of mastery over her wounded feelings to conceal at least the voluntary expression of her suffering from the eye of her parent. Convinced as she now was of the depth and intensity of her love for the haughty fugitive, and satisfied, even to the very limit of utter hopelessness, that no chance or change of circumstances could ever again restore the hearts of both to the relative position which they had occupied from childhood—satisfied, in a word, that, loving as she did even to sickness of soul and frame, she yet loved in vain, it was touching to witness the quiet fortitude with which she disguised those feelings when in the presence of her parent. Frequently, indeed, in her wanderings about the lonely mansion, when a scattered remembrancer of " past, happy hours " caught her eye; when she looked from her window, in the calm and silent even-fall, on the scenes of their youthful sports; or when her hand, unconsciously straying over her neglected harp, happened to awaken a cadence of one of his favourite melodies, in those moments it was that her bosom would swell and tighten, while the sudden passion laboured in her throat, and relieved itself at length in bursts of overwhelming grief. But the moment her father's footstep sounded on the flagged hall without, these signs of anxiety disappeared, and the note of the harp was changed to one of a lesser interest and meaning.

The change which had taken place in the disposition and manner of the old man was still more striking and more rapid. It seemed as if, instead of experiencing any relief from the confidence he had made, it only added fresh terrors to those which he had so long confined in his own bosom, and multiplied the chances and fears of detection that had made the last years of his life one long and weary chain of anxiety and sorrow. His eye had lost its heaviness and gloom, while it assumed instead a restlessness of glance, and a wildness and distrust in its most ordinary expression, which furnished his now more than ever vigilant and affectionate daughter with a more startling subject for alarm, than even the increased paleness of his lips and brow and the rapid wasting of his sallow checks afforded. The sound of a strange footstep, the shutting of a door, the whistling of a sudden gust around the dreary mansion, any unexpected sight or sound, seemed to shake his being to the very centre. At those times, too, he was wont to receive the accustomed consolations of his daughter with expressions full of a sharp and pettish asperity, which, continued, repeated, and unatoned for, as they were, by any after-kindness, put the devotion of her filial love to a severer test than even the revolting cause in which they originated. With the fineness of perception which is so peculiarly the characteristic of her sex, she quickly arrived at the mode of treatment best adapted for the novel turn which the disease had taken. Like the minstrel of the Israelitish monarch, when the evil influence came over the mind of her patient, she abandoned all efforts to combat it by argument, or even condolence, and affected an air of perfect abstraction and security, while she ran, as if in careless practice, over the chords of her instrument, varying and accommodating the character of the melody to the changes which were visible in the countenance of the listener, with a tact and fidelity which would not have been

unworthy even of the mighty name which we have before
mentioned. Yet all this was far from being remedial,
and it was even palliative in a very inconsiderable degree.

They had been sitting together for some time, on the
morning of the eighth day from that of Aylmer's departure,
without interchanging a single sentence beyond the customary domestic greetings. The old man sat near the fire, his
head drooped upon his bosom, and his eyes fixed with a
melancholy expression on the clear light blaze of the turfen
fire before him, while Katharine, accompanying herself on
her harp, murmured over, *sotto voce*, the words of a
popular "keen-the-caun", the lament of a mother over
the grave of a beloved son. We give the stanzas :—

I.

The Christmas light* is burning bright
  In many a village pane ;
And many a cottage rings to night
  With many a merry strain.
Young boys and girls run laughing by,
  Their hearts and eyes elate—
I can but think on mine, and sigh,
  For I am desolate.

II.

There's none to watch in our old cot,
  Beside thy holy light ;
No tongue to bless the silent spot
  Against the parting night.†
I've closed the door, and hither come
  To mourn my lonely fate ;
I cannot bear my own old home,
  It is so desolate !

* The Christmas candle—a light, blest by the priest, and lighted
at sunset on Christmas-eve, in Irish houses. It is a kind of impiety
to snuff, touch, or use it for any profane purpose after.

† It is the custom, in Irish Catholic families, to sit up till midnight on Christmas-eve, in order to join in devotion at that hour.
Few ceremonies of the religion have a more splendid and imposing
effect than the morning mass, which, in cities, is celebrated soon
after the hour alluded to, and long before day-break.

III.

I saw my father's eyes grow dim,
   And clasped my mother's knee;
I saw my mother follow him,
   —My husband wept with me.
My husband did not long remain,
   —His child was left me yet;
But now my heart's last love is slain,
   And I am desolate!

The song was not concluded when both the melodist and
listener were startled by a quick and vehement knocking
at the chamber-door. The latter was the first to start
from his chair in a passion of terror. Before he could
recover the command of speech or action, the voice of the
little chambermaid was heard without, imploring instant
admission, in accents which showed that all the agitation
was not confined to the interior. Katharine hastily slipped
back the little bolt, and admitted the eager girl.

"What is the matter, Norry?" exclaimed her mistress.

"O ma'am we're all zuin'd intirely. O master! O ——"
pausing, as her eye fell on the ghastly figure of the con-
science-stricken Fitzmaurice, and fetching her breath for
a moment. "Come, come this way, Miss Kate, I want to
speak a piece wit you", beckoning the young lady after her.

"Stay!" cried the old man, hoarsely, "what have you
seen? Speak, quickly!"

"Oh, murder, sir?" Norry cried aloud, wringing her
hands in agony, "the army, the army,* intirely!"

"Coming hither?" inquired Kate.

"Two red coats, wit ould Hasset along wit 'em, miss.
Upon the aveny already".

The intelligence seemed almost to have paralysed both
the mind and frame of Fitzmaurice. He did nothing,
proposed nothing, and was even listless, helpless, and
passive, while plan after plan, both of escape and concealment, was suggested and rejected in rapid succession

---

* Any number of soldiers is so called by the Irish peasantry.

by the agonized daughter and her faithful and anxious attendant. "The back window", "the loft", "the turf-
rick", "between the bed-ticks", "the chimney", were all
cast aside as stale and hopeless, when, her eyes suddenly
flashing with a gleam of intelligence, Norry slapped the
palms of her tough hands together, so as to produce a
report that echoed through the house like a pistol-shot,
and startled the old man himself from his lethargy of
fear.

"The ould makings of a cupboard", she exclaimed,
pointing to the pier-glass, "the same place fare I hid the
little dog the day the taxman was here, whin he began
barken in the wall within".

The proposal was caught up and acted upon instantly.
The large glass was removed, and a square niche in the
solid wall, originally intended for a cupboard, was disclosed. Into this recess was the terrified old man hurried
by the two girls, himself too perfectly overwhelmed with
apprehension to offer either opposition or assistance to
their movements. The mirror was then carefully replaced,
and Katharine, after crossing her hands on her bosom for
one moment, in a strong effort to master her struggling
anxieties, and murmuring a brief and anxious petition to
the throne of mercy, prepared to act her part in the coming
emergency with the necessary firmness and composure.

"If he doesn't behave quieter than little Minos, there's
little chance for him", said Norry, as she left the room.

The recollection of this circumstance was a new subject
of alarm for the sensitive daughter. The story of Miss
Fitzmaurice's dog, concealed from a tax-gatherer in a
recess behind the pier-glass, and betrayed by his own
barking, at the very instant when the old steward was
leaving a blank for the article "dogs" in the inventory,
had been so generally circulated, and excited so much
amusement throughout the country, that there was little
hope of its having escaped the ears of Mr. Hasset. For

this, however, she had to trust to fortune, as it was now too late to alter the position of the old man.

In a few minutes the magistrate made his appearance. He had the delicacy, or the wariness, to forbid the approach of his armed attendants, and if it were not for the previous intimation of their approach, the young hostess would have had no reason to judge this other than a visit of mere ceremony. Katharine found herself, for the first time in her life, compelled to violate the truth, in the answers which she returned to this unwelcome guest. She did it, however, with tenderness.

Was her father at home?

He had ridden out (very frequently, understood).

Whither?

She had not asked him.

Did she soon expect him?

She believed his *return* was quite uncertain.

The magistrate was silent for a few seconds; then seeming to have formed a sudden resolution, he said:

"Miss Fitzmaurice will pardon me, but I have a very disagreeable duty to perform. The presence of her father is absolutely required—and that duty shall not be discharged until every possible means has been resorted to in order to secure it".

"The doors are open, sir", said Katharine, rising, with an assumed haughtiness in her carriage, while her heart bounded with terror; "you are at liberty to use your authority as you please".

The young lady left the room, and the soldiers were admitted. She remained in the next apartment, listening in an agony of the cruelest suspense to the movements of the searchers within. They prolonged their scrutiny in a manner that showed how little reliance their director placed on the equivocations of the fair hostess. At times, a thrill of fierce terror shot to the very centre of her heart, and suspended its pulsation, when the footsteps of

any of the party approached the hiding-place of the
criminal.

" To the next room ! " said the voice of the magistrate;
" don't mind the mouse-holes". Katharine felt relief.

" Easy, sir", exclaimed a fourth man, who had just entered, and in whose sharp, angular, cunning tones, the
trembling Kate recognized the voice of Hasset's clerk, a
gentleman who, to establish his qualifications for the
situation he held, would very gladly have hanged half the
parish, if necessary, " you have not done all the bizuiz
clean yet".

Kate grasped the back of a chair, and drew her light
handkerchief tightly around her neck, while her whole
frame shivered with a chilling anxiety.

" Well for ye", she heard the new comer continue, in a
jeering way, " to have a lad that know's what he's about
to guide ye. Did none o' ye hear the little matter about
the dog and the tax-gatherer? Puh !"

" I remember something of it, I confess, Linehan", said
Hasset, startled.

" Try it then now".

Almost delirious with fear and disappointment, the
miserable daughter fetched a quick and hoarse breath, and
bit her lip until the blood forsook it, to prevent her
screaming aloud. Her limbs shook convulsively, and her
eyes wandered with the wildness of despair around the
chamber, while she waited the next movement of the
inquirers.

" What are you about there?" exclaimed the informer.
" Is it going to pick yourself out o' the glass you are for a
prisoner? Behind the picktur is the place, you fool ! "

" Never fear, Miss !" whispered Norry, who had just
before slipped into the apartment, " that'll bother 'em.
They'll find nothen there, barring pusheen and her kittens,
for she has a way of her own up into it".

A suppressed burst of laughter among the men confirmed the truth of this anticipation; and the hissings, spittings, and growlings of the indignant occupier of the recess, as she placed herself in front of her squeaking brood, seemed to increase their merriment. The magistrate, however, quickly restored order.

"Hush! hush! come along, lads. Linehan, the place is there sure enough, and your hint was a good one: but Richard Hasset's name to a warrant for such a prisoner as this, would scarcely look well in the county calendar".

The discomfited wit made no reply, and the party left the room. As soon as she heard the door close after them, the daughter sunk exhausted into the chair beside which she had been standing, and gave vent to her excited feelings in bursts of mingled tears and laughter, while her hands clasped, and raised, all trembling as they were, to Heaven, gave all the evidence she could then furnish of her deep and burning gratitude.

Both mistress and attendant then returned to the parlour, where they were soon after rejoined by Mr. Hasset and his downcast secretary, the soldiers this time remaining without. It is needless to say their search had been unsuccessful. After apologizing for the uneasiness which he had given her in the performance of an unavoidable duty, etc., the former gentleman took his leave, and was followed by the clerk.

"I wonder what is it that thief o' the world, Linehan, is whisperen in ould Hasset's ear", said Norry, as she watched the party pacing slowly down the lawn.

"Are they returning hither?"

"They wor thinken of it, I'm thinken, but to change their mind they did".

After having watched them fairly out of sight, the victorious pair proceeded to release their captive. He had sufficiently recovered from the stunning effects of the first announcement of his danger, to be now fully aware of its extent, and he descended from his lurking-place, the most

perfect picture of guilt and horror that a stricken conscience ever made. Norry was extending one arm to
support him, and with the other whisking the dust and
mortar from his coat, when a deep and rapid inspiration of
the young lady near her startled them both. The principle of life had been strained to so extreme a degree of
excitement by the varying emotions of the last hour, that
it was proportionably depressed on the restoration of
security. The sight of her father, safely protected through
the imminent perils which had during that time surrounded him, effected more than the immediate presence of
those dangers themselves. In the effort which she made
to cast herself into her father's arms, her powers suddenly
failed her, and she sunk at his feet in an access of syncope.

The old man raised her from the ground, and supported her across his breast, while tears of grateful
affection fell down in rapid showers upon her neck and
bosom. The attendant, while she supplied the necessary
means for the revival of her mistress, did not refuse her
sympathy to the sufferings of the aged parent.

At that moment the door opened, and Mr. Secretary
Linehan reëntered.

"I beg pardon, but I dropped a *handkitcher* somewhere,——O, murder! what's this, intirely?" as his eye
fell on the group.

All were too completely absorbed in another matter to
observe the intruder. Taking a speedy advantage of this
circumstance, the honest limb of justice approached the
window, and beckoned to some persons without. In a few
minutes afterwards, and while he yet stood concealed in
the dark corner into which he had slunk, the whole party
were present at his side. Norry, hearing the clatter of
footsteps, looked over her shoulder, shrieked, started to her
feet, and dropping the stiff and clenched hand of her young
lady, began clapping her own, and repeating her doleful
cries in all the frenzy of Irish despair. The father turned

his wildered eyes on the strangers, and resigning his
daughter to the arms of her attendant—

"My child does not hear me", he said in a faint and
mournful accent, "but give her my blessings when she
wakes, and bid her pray for me. God bless you all!
One moment, sir————". As he spoke, he pressed his
lips to the cold and marble brow of his still unconscious
daughter, and untying the light silk handkerchief from her
neck, he placed it listlessly in his bosom. Then putting
himself in the custody of the magistrate, he was conducted
in silence to the carriage which awaited him at the avenue
gate.

Another actor was now added to the scene. William
Aylmer had joined the party at their return; but, unwilling, for many reasons, to encounter the unhappy object
of their pursuit, he had remained without until after their
departure, and now entered the room just as Katharine
began to revive.

"He is well. Be comforted, Katharine", were all the
answers which he returned to her first inquiries for her
parent. She was not, however, so easily to be satisfied.
She repeated her inquiries with an energy and determination of manner which made disguise hopeless.

"And what do *you* here?" she exclaimed, in a delirium of passion, so soon as she had collected from Norry's
"O-hones!" and Aylmer's silence, the truth of the event;
"you were not with them when they first arrived—he was
surprised—and you are his betrayer".

"You do me foul wrong. I endeavoured, perhaps
against my conscience, to dissuade the officers of justice
from entering here".

"Against your conscience!" she smiled with a ghastly
bitterness on him as she answered. "The conscience of
an ingrate who could turn against the life of an adopted
father; a man whose bread he ate, whose fire warmed
him, whose roof protected him, and whose heart loved

him for seventeen years! Justice! The justice of a law
that would spill the cold blood of age, to make a peace-
offering for the forgotten errors of youth! The law that
continues to persecute after God has forgiven! Go, go,
sir; you have less heart than I thought. Go, satisfy
your conscience, and be just".

"If my words must not be credited", said Aylmer, "I
have only to endure and to be silent".

"Answer one question. Have you not linked your
name with those of his accusers? Are you not numbered
on their list?"

Aylmer was silent.

"You have pledged yourself to take the old man's life!
Aylmer, do not say so. Think where you passed your
childhood. Look around you, and upon those scenes
where you first learned to enjoy life yourself. Will you
make them desolate? Oh! believe me, Aylmer, it is seldom, very seldom, that it is in the power of human judgment to decide between the right and the wrong in cases
so doubtful as this. The law of man that cries for 'blood'
to the last, may yet be wrong: laws as fierce and cruel
have been, and are no more in existence: and a more
merciful race of men may alter this. The law of God,
that commands mercy and holy forgiveness, *may* possibly
be right. Let your own grateful heart tell you to which
of these chances you should incline".

" Katharine——"

"Or let this consideration guide you. Suppose yourself lying to-morrow on your death-bed, and gathering
comfort to your soul from the memory of your past actions,
would you feel happier then in the thought that you had
forgiven a wrong, and saved your old friend, than if you
had gratified your irresolute thirst for vengeance, or justice, now?"

"The Almighty, that sees my heart, sees how clear it
is from the tainting sin that you impute to it", exclaimed

5*

the youth; " but I have swo:n to do what is just between
the accused, his country, and his God.   That oath I must
not break".

" May that God, then, be my poor father's help; for his
Earthly friends have forsaken him.   It is enough—Aylmer, farewell !"   She placed her hand in his.   " May he
or she who acts ill in this, find mercy and pardon at the
throne of grace.   I leave you without anger; for you and
I, whatever be the issue of this heavy trial, must never
meet again".

Before Aylmer could, by act or word, return any
answer to her farewell, Katharine had glided out of the
apartment.   Wishing, nevertheless, to leave some message
for her, which might possibly have the effect of vindicating him in some degree from the charge of wanton
ingratitude, which she had urged against him, he turned
towards Norry, who still remained, her back supported
against the wall, clearing away, with the corner of her
check apron, the tears that were pouring fast from her red
and heavy eyes.

" Norry—" he was about to proceed.

"Oh !   Go from me, sir !" cried the faithful attendant,
with a fresh burst of grief; " go from me, you contrairy
gentleman—I rise out o' you !"

And throwing her arms aloft, as if to give increased
force to the expression, the indignant *soubrette* followed
her mistress.

The next day's noon beheld the father and daughter inclosed within the prison doors of an inconsiderable assize-
town on the western coast.

The first month of a mild spring had passed away,
without inducing any material change in the condition of
the persons of our history, and the little town above
alluded to began to put on an appearance of life and
bustle as the assize-week drew nigh.   The generally silent
and sunshiny streets were now made to echo the frequent

tramp of the bespattered and reeking saddle-horse, and
the lumbering rattle of the car which brought its load of
corn (stacked until now, the season of scarcity) to the
store of the small dealer, a sort of Lilliputian merchant,
who made a new profit by shipping, or rather boating the
grain to the next trading city.   The fronts of the inns
and *shebeens* were screwed up, and the rooms made ready
for the temporary convenience of petty jurors, summoned
from the furthermost limits of the county; strong farmers
anxiously looking for the success of their road present-
ments; Palatines seeking compensation for burnt hay-
ricks and out-houses, fired by the hand of the ubiquitous
Whiteboy; rural practitioners demanding the legal grant
for the support of a dispensary; middlemen in the commission of the peace, eager to curry favour with the mighty
sojourners by the number and the importance of their
committals; gray-coated rustics, who had come up to
town to stand by a friend and relation, whose black-thorn
perhaps had been a little too fatal among the neighbours
at the last fair; country gentlemen willing to show off as
lords of the scene, and ambitioning a niche on the grand
jury list; and last and first and best, young and blooming
speculators of another order, armed with as many terrors,
bent up to as fatal a purpose, and with as fair and philosophical a principle for their motive, as that which governed
the awful sword-bearers of the law itself.

The concourse of in comers on this occasion was more
numerous than usual, a circumstance readily accounted for
by the singular case which was to be decided during the
ensuing week.   All intercourse with the prisoner was
interdicted, and even his daughter, in order to retain the
permission, which had in the first instance been granted
her, of attending to her father's wants in person, was
obliged to restrict her own movements to the limits of the
prison.

A calm, breathless morning beheld the small fishing-

smack in which Aylmer had taken his passage for the
town, drop her peak in the small inlet which glided by
the village of Blennerville, a kind of pigmy outpost to
the larger, or capital town. Nothing could be in more
perfect accordance with the state of the voyager's mind,
than the scene which was presented to his eyes when the
loud call of the boatman summoned him on deck. The
air, as before mentioned, was perfectly still and breathless,
and the clear sunless serenity of a spring forenoon rested
on the landscape. On his left hand lay a flat champaign
of grayish marl, covered with numbers of sea-birds, who
were busily angling in the little inequalities of the plain
for the juniors of the scaly tribe, deserted by the tide in
its retreat. Between him and the ocean, this marl or sand
elevated itself into mounds of so considerable an altitude,
as to leave only an occasional shimmering of the mighty
sea without visible between their obtunded summits. On
the right hand the bleak and barren chain of mountains,
which form the distance of the Killarney scenery on the other
side, rose suddenly in abrupt masses, to a height which left
the southern prospect entirely to the imagination, and
threw an air of softened gloom and solitude around the
handsome villas, which were scattered over the richly
wooded and improved country at their base. The faint
hum of the little town, in the distant inland, the twitter-
ing of the early swallow, the cry of the red-shank, the occasional wild scream of the horse-gull, the whistle of the
curlew, and the soft and plaintive cry of the green plover,
all heard singly, and at long intervals, formed a fitting ac-
companiment to the scene, unless when the report of a shore-
gun, directed by the murderous eye of some fustian-clad
prowling duck-shooter on the coast, reverberated like a
thunder-peal among the echoes of the mountain, and filled
the air with a thousand whirring wings, and cries of terror and reproach. Above the little bridge of Blennerville,
a group of boys stood knee-deep in the stream which

flowed from the town, groping for "*flukes*", while their occasional exclamations of success or disappointment, sounded as distinctly in Aylmer's ear as if they had been uttered by his side. Toward the offing of the little inlet, the drooping sails of the sloops and cutters, the sluggish heaving of the bulky ocean, and the jeering of the wits and master-spirits of the different crews, as they sat dangling their legs over the sides of their vessels, formed no unworthy balance to the inland portion of the picture.

" The two tin-pinnies, ye'r honour?" said the boatman, touching his hat, as Aylmer, with the privileged abstraction of melancholy, was turning off in the direction of the town, forgetful of his fare. Having rectified his error entirely to the satisfaction of the other party, he pursued his way to the town, which lay about a mile distant.

The flourishing of trumpets and the trampling of many feet, announced to him as he entered the suburbs of the place, that the judges were already on their way to the court. As he hurried along the crowded street, obstructed in his career by persons as eagerly bent to accomplish the same end as himself, he fell in with a scene which presented as singular a contrast to that which he had just been admiring, as his imagination could possibly have anticipated. The rushing of the anxious multitude in various directions, the rattling of outside jaunting-cars, empty turf-kishes, and grand jury men's decayed and mud covered carriages, the clattering of brogues and horse-hoofs, the shouting of one party at the release of a clans-man from the clutches of the law, the shrieking and cursing of another group, who saw in the drooping head and manacled hands of an equally valued kinsman the fearful announcement of a contrary judgment, the war-whoop of a drunken faction-leader, as he made an effort to caper in the air and wheel his seasoned black-thorn above his head, the yelping of dogs, the squalling of children, the shrill remonstrances of shrewish mothers, the yet

more hideous tones of a steam-engine ballad-singer, **whose**
awful lungs, victorious over the frantic uproar about him,
made most distinctly audible the burden of a song on the
woes of the then existing colonial war :

"And they powering down their chain balls for to sweep our min
    away,
  O wasn't that a could riciption in the North of Americay ?"

alternated now and then, in compliment to the naval
port'on of his auditory, to the more popular doggrel of,

"A sailor courted a farmer's daatur,
  Who lived convanient to the Isle of Man".

These, superadded to the ordinary bustle of the town,
formed a combination of sounds that would, had he been
present, have qualified Old Morose for Hoxton ; and
would have sounded strangely in the ears of an election
assessor, a common councilman, an M. P., or a writer of
overtures.

It was past noon when Aylmer, after bustling his way
through the narrow purlieus of the place, found himself
placed in the centre of a small, low-roofed, ill-lighted,
dingy court, on one side the bench, from which at that
moment the final sentence of the law was issuing ; on the
other the dock, over the bar of which leaned two or three
squalid looking, pale-faced creatures, listening with a stare
of wildered abstraction to the announcement of their fate.
The benches at either side were covered with counsel in
blue frock-coats and coloured handkerchiefs, the usual
forensic insignia being treated with philosophical indifference on a provincial circuit. In a small gallery at
one end Aylmer witnessed an infraction of the inviolable
rules of Irish female decorum, the presence of a woman
among the audience of a court of justice. She seemed
sensible herself of the singularity of her position, for her
face and person were completely enveloped in a hood and

cloak, and the place she occupied was the most unobtrusive that could have been selected.

"So the bills have been found against Cahil Fitzmaurice?" said a voice at Aylmer's side.

"Aye, have they, then", was the reply, "and it's
the next on the list. It's a droll* story: they say Counsellor—— has instructions to call up young Aylmer, in regard of a ghost appearing to him, and telling him the
whole tote, by which token he drew the confession out of
the old man next morning. It was a quare thing. They
say young Aylmer thrun holy-water on the sperit, but it
did not mind that no more than the devil would a parson,
until he threatened it with the sacrament, when it flew up
through the roof in a sheet of flame as big as a bonfire
of a St. John's Eve".

A whisper now passed from the clerk of the crown to
the judge, and was subsequently transmitted to the turnkey, who bowed and put himself in motion. The little
grating at the far end of the dock was thrown open, and
the rush which took place in the court showed that all present anticipated the meaning of the order. Heads were
thrust out, and eyes strained from their sockets to catch
the first glimpse of the aged prisoner.

The slow and uncertain footstep at length sounded on
the boarded ascent leading from the prison, and the form
of the accused emerging from the gloom of the outer dock,
was in a short time presented to the gaze of the multitude.
The old man bowed as he took his place, and passing his
hand once or twice over his eyes to relieve them from the
influence of the strong light which fell immediately around
him, he remained passively awaiting his fate. Although
he had been prepared to expect a considerable change in
the appearance of his old guardian, Aylmer experienced a
shock when he first looked upon his face and person, which
contributed very materially to shake his conviction of the

* Extraordinary.

fairness or the justice of the course which he was himself
pursuing. The pale and emaciated countenance of the
prisoner, the thin wrinkled cheeks, deeply indented temples,
eyes full of a morbid, sepulchral light, dry, staring hair,
wasted fingers, and short hectic cough, seemed to intimate,
that it was of little consequence to him, so far as life
was concerned, in what way the trial terminated. His
intellect, too, appeared to have suffered from the ravages
which disease had made on his frame and constitution.
It was some moments before his attention could be sufficiently aroused to enable him to give utterance to the
plea of "not guilty!" and attend to the opening statement of the king's counsel.

In Ireland, where, from a certain train of causes (the
origin of which we leave to weightier judgments to deter-
mine), it has been found necessary to appeal more to
the cowardice than the generosity of human nature, and
where the even-handed goddess, Justice, has been too
often accustomed to strike up her balance with her sword
—in this strange country, people are not surprised to
hear what is meant to be the opening statement of the
facts of a criminal case, made the vehicle of cruel, unrea-
soning, and inhuman invective against the accused. Whatever be the evidence in reserve against him, be it so heavy
and damning as to make any previous wordy accusation
needless and brutal, or be it so light as to leave the wild
and empty whirl of blackening assertions poured from
the crown lawyer's lip unauthorized and libelous, still
the malicious prosecutor has carried his point—he hears
his victim, whether innocent or guilty, branded with all
the diabolical epithets that a flowery vein of fancy, aided
by a tolerable acquaintance with the poets, can suggest.
The whole range of imaginative and real history is exhausted in search of monsters to serve for his parallel, and
every sly and subtle art by which the personal feelings
and prejudices of his judges can be enlisted against the

unhappy culprit is relentlessly put in execution. When we look at this fatal engine, which the law allows only to the accusing party, and consider that it is most frequently directed against some poor wretch who is not even acquainted with the language in which he is thus traduced in his own hearing, and consequently cannot avail himself of his privilege (!!) of reply, we may, perhaps, perceive why it is that persons once placed in the dock make their exit more frequently through the back than the front entrance, why ropemakers thrive at a certain season, why the hangman can endow his daughter so handsomely, and why the science of anatomy is so attainable and so practically understood in Ireland.

On this occasion, however, there was some degree of tenderness observed, and the detail of the case was straight forward, simple, and impartial. After going through the greater portion of the evidence which he had in reserve, the counsel was observed to pause as he came to that part of his brief which contained the deposition of William Aylmer. It was a difficult subject, and one which, if he had had a less credulous audience to deal with, the learned gentleman might have hesitated yet more about introducing. The deep silence, however,—the hush which his own pause occasioned among his auditory, showed him that they anticipated the tale (which was, indeed, already in circulation, with various embellishments similar to that overheard by Aylmer in the court), and that he would at lea t have to tell the story to grave and attentive ears. He was now coming, he said, to a portion of the evidence which would, perhaps, require a severer exercise of their judgments than any which had been hitherto submitted to their consideration. He believed—he knew, that he was addressing himself to Christian hearers, to men convinced as he was himself of the divine origin of those sacred records which told of the last warning of the buried Samuel, the supernatural re-

vealment of the murder of Uriah, and a thousand other
interpositions of the Almighty Being, setting aside, or
suspending, for some immediate end, the ordinary pro-
cesses of nature. Justice, he remarked, was the same
now as in those days—it was the same God who watched
over the actions of all generations, and although the
completion of the divine code, left perfect by the Founder
of the Christian religion, rendered those miraculous in-
terventions less needful for the interests of mankind than
they were while revelation was yet partial and defective,
still there was no ground on which a man could be
justified in declaring such occurrences out of the pale
of things possible. He admitted that nothing short of
evidence amounting almost to ocular demonstration—a
wonderful corroboration in circumstances—and, in short,
all the most powerful incentives to belief which could be
adduced—would be sufficient to persuade them to do so
much violence to their common experience ; but he trusted
he should be enabled to bring all the corroborative
testimony, which they could deem necessary, before
them in the course of the evening.

With this preamble, the learned counsel proceeded to a
detail of the deposition made by Aylmer; after which,
the examination of witnesses commenced. The listless
woman of the mountain, Vauria, was one of the first who
were called ; but her testimony went no further than to
the quarrel of the friends, its termination, and a subsequent muttered threat on the part of the prisoner, as he
followed the deceased up from the cabin. She admitted,
too, on her cross-examination, that she was instigated to
come forward now, after a long interval of silence, by the
desire of her kinsman, who had been imprisoned on the
information of young Aylmer, for plundering the prisoner's
sheep-walk.

Night had fallen before the case for the prosecution
closed. Numbers of the spectators, exhausted by the

length of the trial, had dropped off one after another,
leaving the audience now comparatively thin and meagre.
The voices of the counsel sounded more loudly, owing to
the emptiness of the adjacent hall and the silence of the
streets, while the dull, heavy light cast by the few tallow
candles which were placed in sconces against the walls
and about the bench, added considerably to the comfortless solemnity of the scene.

At length young Aylmer was called on to give his
evidence. A heavy moan from the prisoner, almost the
first audible sound which had broken from his lips during
the day, struck on the ear and on the heart of the youth,
as he ascended the steps leading to the witness-table. It
was too late, however, for pause or wavering. He
mustered his spirits, and bent up his soul to the duty
which he had to discharge.

At the moment he took the book in his hand, and proceeded to repeat the form of oath, a low, broken scream
of anguish, long suppressed, and now in its effort to
relieve itself seeming to rend the heart from which it
proceeded, rang through the building, and immediately
after, a well-known, though strangely altered voice, from
the now silent and nearly deserted gallery, exclaimed in a
tone of piteous entreaty:

"Aylmer! Aylmer! O Aylmer! mercy! for the sake
of old times, mercy! Do not swear away the old man's
life!"

The sensation which this singular appeal produced in
the court may be easily imagined. The softness and
tenderness of the tones brought tears into the eyes of
many of the hearers, and it was even with some difficulty that the judge could compel his features into an
expression of high indignation.

"Remove that person, Mr. Sheriff", he said, quietly.
"I know it, sir, and can make allowance for it", he continued, in answer to a whisper from one of the prisoner's

counsel, " but it is exceedingly indecorous.   It should **not**
have been permitted".

Order was again restored, and the witness, mastering,
by a violent effort, the convulsions of passion by which his
frame was shaken to the centre, proceeded to make his
deposition.   He went through all the circumstances of
his testimony with a plainness and feeling which won
irresistibly upon the sympathies of his audience, and
impressed even the most incredulous with the conviction,
that, however deluded his senses might have been, the
youth was saying only that which in his heart he
believed to be true.   The chief ground, however, upon
which the counsel for the crown rested his claim on the
credence of the jury, was the corroboration which the
prisoner's conduct, on the next morning, afforded to the
supernatural revelation of the night preceding.   The impression left on the minds of those who sat in the box was
striking and perceptible.

As Aylmer concluded his evidence, and prepared to
descend, a low whisper, addressed to the ear of the
prisoner's leading counsel, caught his ear.

"MUST IT BE, SIR?"

"IT MUST.   WE HAVE NO OTHER CHANCE, AND IT IS
AS WELL FIRST AS LAST", was the reply, also conveyed in
a whisper.

Aylmer, imagining that he recognized the voice of the
querist, turned quickly round, but saw no face that he
knew.   The counsel was already engaged in earnest conversation with a learned brother.

The case for the prosecution having terminated with the
evidence of William Aylmer, the gentleman who was
engaged on the other side was about to rise and proceed
with the defence, when he was interrupted by the court:—

" They had already", his lordship observed, "prolonged
the hearing of the case far into the night, and many
hours beyond the customary period of rising.   He was

far, however, from wishing either to cut short, or postpone the termination of the case, and he would suffer it
to proceed until the whole of the testimony had been laid
before the jury, if the counsel on either side desired it.
But it appeared to him that a more direct course might be
used, in order to arrive at a satisfactory decision. The
doubt which remained on his own mind, was so strong
as to induce him to hesitate a moment on the propriety
of sending the case to the jury, such as it was at that
moment. The evidence was of so peculiar a character,
that it required an exertion of reason, almost " beyond
the reaches" of that faculty in man, to form a conscientious judgment upon it. He admitted the force of
the learned counsel's argument, in his statement of the
case: he could not, no believer in Christianity could, deny
the possibility of such supernatural appearances; but there
was one short mode of deciding the question, as to the
reality of that which was here deposed to with so much
apparent sincerity. The only ground on which the jury
could reconcile to their own consciences the possibility of
the tale, was the necessity of such an intervention, the
dignus vindice nodus, for the ends of justice. " Let then",
his lordship continued, elevating his voice to a pitch of
sonorous gravity, " let the ghost of the murdered man (*if*
murdered) come forward, and tell his tale here in this
court, where his presence is much more necessary than in
the chamber of a single individual.— Crier, repeat the
form !"

A murmur of amazement ran through the court at this
extraordinary speech, and immediately after a silence
ensued, as breathless, anxious, and profound, as if the
spectators really imagined they were about to witness a
miracle. The crier twice went through the form, and
twice the call died away unheeded among the echoes of
the deserted halls. Aylmer, anxious to observe its effect
on the prisoner, turned round to gaze upon him, when a

startling change which took place in the whole appearance
of the man, riveted and fixed his eyes in the direction
they had taken. Fitzmaurice was elevating his head
from the stooping posture which he had maintained
during the period of the last witness's examination, and
casting a wild and wavering glance around him, when
those who, like Aylmer, had their eyes fixed on his, observed them to settle in a stare of frozen horror upon a
certain point. His lip grew white, quivered, and then
was still as marble—his hair stirred and separated—his
brow and cheek became yet more damp and death-like
than before—a slight shivering passed over his frame, and
then every member set and stiffened in a statue-like
repose. There was no start—no sudden change of
attitude; there was merely an interruption of the action
of the frame, as if some fearful shock had penetrated at
once to the principle of life, and left the will and the
power of motion paralyzed and helpless; with a suddenness similar to that of a cataleptic attack, in which the
patient seems to have

"——forgot himself to stone"

before any external change is visible. The eyes only of
the prisoner moved, following a certain object along the
entrance of the court and to the witness-table. Aylmer,
terrified by the action of the criminal, looked in the same
direction. An old white-haired man was in the act of
ascending the steps. Aylmer felt as if a bolt of ice had
been struck into his heart, when he recognized in the
equivocal and lurid candlelight, the features of his midnight visitor; while the gray frieze-coat and heavy
sounding tread of the figure, brought to his recollection
the strange letter-bearer of the Kerry mountains!

"You see before you, my lord", said the stranger, "an
unfortunate man, who has only within a few months returned to his native country, and has during that time

been wandering like a thief about the precincts of his own estate, in fear of a legal visitation on a charge of many years' standing. I am weary of a life of anxiety and concealment, and even if I were not called upon by the tongue of justice herself to come forward now, I would, before long, have gladly delivered myself up to the laws of my country".

" Your lordship will observe", quickly remarked the counsel for the prisoner, " that this gentleman, *Mr. Robert Aylmer of Bally-Aylmer*, does not make any confession or admission whatsoever of the truth of the charge to which he alludes ; he merely comes forward to meet inquiry, and redeem his forfeited place in society".

His lordship smiled as he nodded an acquiescence, and Mr. Aylmer smiled too, but in a more melancholy sort.

" Gentlemen", said the judge, addressing the jury, " I am glad to inform you that your business is over for this night. You will find a verdict of acquittal and attend to-morrow".

" This beats the witch of Endor hollow", said the crown lawyer, as he threw his brief to the solicitor; " your lordship may take place among the cabalists of Domdaniel after this".

Several other equally admirable witticisms passed among the junior counsel on the back benches ; such as that his lordship was a clever resurrection-man—that he had given a *grave* turn to the proceedings—that it was a dead-letter affair, with various inflictions of a similar nature, which we grieve to say our slippery memory will not enable us to lay before the reader.

No person had yet sufficiently abstracted their attention from the now engrossing point of interest, the resuscitated lord of Bally-Aylmer, to bestow a thought on the prisoner. It was with a general exclamation of surprise, therefore, that they perceived, when the court commanded his immediate discharge, that his place at the bar was empty

The turnkey, all confusion at this unaccountable disappearance, seized a candle and examined the dock, when
the unhappy man was found stretched on the floor, which
was flooded with blood around his head. He was raised
gently, and conveyed, while yet in a senseless state, to his
bed-chamber in the adjoining prison; Sandy Culhane, by
the direction of Mr. Aylmer, lending his assistance to the
officers of the place.

The court immediately after became astir with the bustle
of separation, and many a wondering hearer went home to
astonish the ears of his fire-side circle with a red-hot
narrative of the night's adventures, whi h have since been
transmitted, with sundry decorations and gratuitous incidents superadded, to their children's children.

The two Aylmers, thus strangely restored to each other,
proceeded together to a hotel, where the remainder of the
night was spent in mutual inquiries and explanations, with
an entire detail of which we shall not trouble the reader.
The old man would, he said, have prevented all necessity
for an investigation before it commenced, had he been
aware of the circumstances that had taken place; but a
communication from the Flushing contrabandist, who had
saved his life on the night of the quarrel with Fitzmaurice, and who was then sojourning at Waterford, had
called him suddenly away, the morning after he had
visited Aylmer at Kilavariga. He had been induced to
take this step by the information given him by Sandy
Culhane, that a marriage was contemplated by Fitzmaurice
between Aylmer and his daughter; a circumstance confirmed in some degree by the extraordinary care which he
observed had been taken of the Aylmer property. This
arrangement was not only unpleasing to him in itself, but
doubly so from its interference with a long and anxiously
cherished design of his own, with respect to the fasci-
nating and accomplished daughter of his foreign friend,
Miss Quisana Van Huggel Schneiderdrugger.

"I perceive", Mr. Aylmer continued, as a slight flush

passed over the brow and cheek of his son, at the allusion to Katharine Fitzmaurice, "I see that I was wrong in my calculation, and so there is an end of the scheme at once. Totally ignorant as I was of my son's character and disposition, and rather induced to believe, from his intimate connection with the family of Kilavariga, that I should at least have wounded feelings and severed and bleeding affections to contend with, it is hardly surprising that I should have preferred making a confidant of the ancient and faithful servant of our house, immediately on my arrival. All occasion for secrecy is now, however, done away with, as my old friend Evans of Evanstown informs me that I have nothing further to apprehend from the possibility of evidence being yet found to establish the charge once in existence against me".

The old man was correct in his anticipations on this head. The next morning he placed himself voluntarily under arrest, and was presently after discharged in consequence of the non-appearance of the prosecutors.

The shock which Fitzmaurice had received was not so immediately fatal as might have been expected. He lived long enough to be reëstablished in peace and good neighbourhood with the friend of his youth, and to join the hands of his daughter and her lover in the holy clasp of authorized affection.

"Well, Mick", said Culhane, addressing the aged herdsman, as the wedding party passed near them in their return, "there's the thief with the brogues and pavers, that you traced from Kilavariga the night of the great snow. Which o' the three now do you think will dance the best *moneen* at the hauling home?"

"The master thin, agen the world! Ah! the times for grinding and footing are gone by, but the Aylmers were always great hands at the feet, and av there's a relic of ould times in the country, it will be shown that night at Bally-Aylmer".

THE HAND AND WORD.

—— Porque ninguno
De mi venganza tome
Vengarme de mi procuro
Buscando desde esa torre
En el ancho mar sepulchro.

CALDERON'S El mayor Monstruo los Zeles

Vengeance is here the right of none—
My punishment be mine alone!
In the broad waves that heave and boom
Beneath this tower I seek my tomb.

THE village of Kilkee, on the south-western coast of Ireland, has been for many years to the city of Limerick (on a small scale) that which Brighton is to London. At the time, however, when the events which form the subject of the following little history took place, it had not yet begun to take precedence of a watering-place somewhat farther to the north on the same coast, called Miltown Malbay, which had been for a long time, and still was, a favourite summer resort with the fashionables of the county, such as they were. The village itself consists merely of six or eight streets, or straggling rows of houses, scattered irregularly enough over those waste banks of sand in which the land terminates as it approaches the Atlantic.

Those banks, or sandhills, as they are called, do not in this place slope gradually to the marge of the sea, but

form a kind of abrupt barrier or natural terrace around
the little bay, descending with such suddenness that the
ledges on the extreme verge completely overhang the
water, and with their snow-white fronts and neat green
lattices, produce a sufficiently picturesque effect when the
tide is at the full.

The little inlet which has been dignified with the title
of a bay, opens to the north-west by a narrow mouth,
rendered yet narrower in appearance by the Duggara
rocks, which stretch more than half-way across from the
southern extremity.   A bed of fine hard sand reaches as
far as low-water mark, and when the retiring waves have
left it visible, affords a pleasant promenade to the bathers.
Winding on either side towards the opening of the bay
and along the line of coast, are seen a number of broken
cliffs, which, rising to a considerable height, form to the
north a precipitous headland called Corballagh, and to the
southward they stretch away behind Duggara in a thousand fantastic shapes.   Close to the mouth or opening, on
this side, is the Amphitheatre, which has been so named
in later years, from the resemblance which instantly
suggests itself to the beholder.   Here the rocks lift
themselves above the level of the sea in regular grades,
bearing a kind of rude similitude to the benches of such
a theatre as that above-named, to the height of two or
three hundred feet.   In the bathing season this place is
seldom without a few groups or straggling figures, being
turned to account in a great many different ways, whether
as a resting-place to the wanderers on the cliffs, or a point
of rendezvous to the numerous pic-nic parties who come
here to enjoy a dinner *al fresco*, and luxuriate on the
grand and boundless ocean-prospect which lies beneath
and beyond them.

A waggish host of the village with whom I had the
honour to domiciliate during a brief sojourn in the place a
few years since, informed me that a number of serious

accidents had rendered the visitors to the Amphitheatre somewhat more cautious of suffering themselves to become entangled among the perils of the shelving and disjointed crags of which it was composed. Among many anecdotes of warning he mentioned one which occurred to a meditative guest of his own, for which I at first gave him credit for a poetical imagination, though I afterwards found he had spoken nothing more than a real fact.

"To take out his book" (he said in answer to a question from me, as to the manner of the occurrence), "and to sit down as it might be this way on a shelving rock, and the sea to be roaring, and he to be thinking of nothing, only what he was reading, when a swell riz and took him out a distins, as it might be to give him a good sea-view of the cliffs and the place, and turning again the same way it came, laid him up on the same stone, where, I'll be your bail, he was mighty scarce in less than no time".

Beyond the Amphitheatre, the cliff rises to a still greater height, forming an eminence called the Look-out. Shocking as the tale may appear to modern readers, it has been asserted, and but too many evidences remain to give weight and colour to the supposition, that in those barbarous (though not very distant) times, this place was employed as an observatory by the wild fishermen of the coast and neighbouring hamlets, the principal portion of whose livelihood was derived from the plunder of the unfortunate men who happened to be wrecked on this inhospitable shore; and it is even recorded, and generally believed, that fires were, on tempestuous nights, frequently lighted here, and in other dangerous parts of the coast, in order to allure the labouring vessel, already hardly set by the war of winds and waves, to a more certain and immediate destruction on the rocks and shoals beneath, a practice, it is said, which was often successful to a fearful extent.

The most remarkable point of scenery about the place, and one with which we shall close our perhaps not unneedful sketch of the little district, is the Puffing-hole, a cavern near the base of the cliff last-mentioned, which vaults the enormous mass of crag to a considerable distance inland, where it has a narrow opening, appearing to the eyes of a stranger like a deep natural well. When the tremendous sea from abroad rolls into this cavern, the effect is precisely the same as if water were forced into an inverted funnel, its impetus of course increasing as it ascends through the narrow neck, until at length reaching the perpendicular opening, or Puffing-hole, it jets frequently to an immense height into the air, and falls in rain on the mossy fields behind.

At a little distance from this singular phenomenon stood a rude cottage. It was tenanted by an aged woman of the place, the relict of one of the most daring plunderers of the coast, who was suspected to have been murdered by one of his own comrades a good many years before. The interior of the little building bore sufficient testimony to the unlawful habits of its former master. All, even the greater proportion of the domestic utensils, were formed of ship timbers: a rudder had been awkwardly hacked and hewed up into something bearing a resemblance to a table, which stood in the middle of the principal apartment; the rafters were made from the spars of boom, peek, and yard; a *settle bed* at the further end had been constructed from the ruins of a gallant ship; and the little boarded parlour inside was furnished in part from the same materials. A number of planks, carelessly fastened together by way of a dresser, stood against the wall, shining forth in all the glory of burnished pewter, wooden-platter, and gaudily painted earthenware the heir-looms of the house of Moran.

Terrified and shocked to the soul by the sudden fate of her late spouse, Mrs. Moran, the proprietress of the cottage, resolved that their boy, an only child, **should not** follow the dangerous courses of his father. In this **she** happened to be seconded by the youth's own disposition, which inclined to a quietude and gentleness of character. He was, at his sixteenth year, far beyond his compeers of the village in point of education, and not behind in beauty of person, and dexterity at all the manual exercises of *goal*, single-stick, etc., etc., accomplishments, however, which were doomed not to be wasted in the obscurity of his native wilderness, for before he had completed his seventeenth year, he was laid by the heels, one morning as he sat at breakfast, and pressed to sea.

One day was allowed him to take leave of old friends, and prepare to bid a long adieu to his native home. This day was a painful one, for more reasons than one.

Of course it is not to be supposed that so smart, handsome, clever, and well disposed a lad as Charlie Moran, should be unappreciated among the maidens of the district in which he vegetated. He had in short a lover; a fine flaxen-haired girl, with whom he had been intimate from infancy up to youth, when the wars (into the service of which he suspected he was betrayed by the agency of the girl's parent, a comfortable *Palatine* in the neighbourhood) called him away from his boyish sports to the exercise of a premature manhood. Their parting was by no means more agreeable to little Ellen Sparling than to himself, seeing that they were more fondly and deeply attached to one another, than is frequently the case with persons of their age and rank in life, and moreover that it would not have been the easiest matter possible to find a pair so well matched in temper and habits, as well as in personal loveliness (just then unfolding itself in each with a promise of perfect maturity) anywhere about the country-side.

The father of the girl, however, who, to say the truth, was indeed the contriver of Moran's impressment, looked forward to his absence with a great deal of joy. The old Palatine, who possessed all the prudence of parents in every soil and season, and all the natural obstinacy of disposition inherent in the national character of the land of his forefathers, had on this occasion his prejudices doubly strengthened, and rendered at last inveterate, by the differences of religion and education, as well as by that eternal, reciprocal, and indomitable hatred which invariably divides the usurping and favoured immigrant from the oppressed indigenous disinherited inheritor of the soil. Fond of his little girl, yet hating her friend, he took the part of weaning them asunder by long absence, a common mistake among more enlightened parents than Mr. Sparling.

On the day preceding that of young Moran's departure, when the weeping girl was hanging on his neck, and overwhelming him with conjurations to "prove true", an advice, to follow which, he assured her over and over again in his own way, he needed no exhortations, her lover proposed to her to walk (as it might be for the last time) towards a spot which had been the usual limit to their rambles, and their general rendezvous whenever her father thought proper to forbid their communing in his house, which was only done at intervals, his vigilance being a sort of chronic affection, sometimes rising to a height which seemed dangerous to their hopes, sometimes relapsing into a state of almost perfect indifference. To this spot the lovers now repaired.

It was a recess in the cliff that beetled over the caverns, and was so formed as to hold no more than three or four persons, who, when they occupied the rude seats naturally formed in the rock, were invisible to any human eye which might be directed otherwhere than from the sea. The approach to it was by a narrow footway, in ascending or descending which, one seemed almost to hang in air, so far did the cliff-head project over the waters, and so scanty

was the path of the descent on either side. Custom,
however, had rendered it a secure footing to the inhabitants of the village, and the lovers speedily found
themselves within the little nook, secluded from every
mortal eye.

It was a still autumn evening: there was no sunshine,
but the fixed splendour of the sky above and around
them, on which the lines, or rather waves, of thin vapour
extending from the north-west, and tinged on one side by
the red light of the sun, which had just gone down, presented the similitude of a sea frozen into a brilliant mass
in the act of undulation. Beyond them lay Bishop's
Island, a little spot of land, shooting up from the waves
in the form of a gigantic column, about three hundred
feet in height, the sides barren and perpendicular, and the
plain above covered with verdure to the marge itself.
Immediately above their heads was a blighted elder tree
(one of the most remarkable phenomena* of this woodless
district) which now hung, like a single gray hair, over the
bare and barren brow of the aged cliff.

The wanderers sat here in perfect security, although by
a step forward they might look upon a tremendous in-
slanting precipice beneath, against the base of which, at
times, the sea lashed itself with such fury, as to bound in
huge masses over the very summit, and to make the cliff
itself shake and tremble to a considerable distance inland.

"I have asked you to come here, Ellen", said her
lover, as he held her hand in one of his, while the other
was passed round her waist, "for a very solemn purpose.
It is a belief amongst us, and many have seen it come to
pass, that those who pledge themselves to any promise,
whether of hate or love, and who, with their hands

---

* A sufficiently characteristic observation of Cromwell on the
barrenness of the country inland, is preserved among the peasantry.
"There was", he observed, "neither a tree to hang a man, fire to
burn, nor water to drown him."

clasped together as ours are now, plight their faith and troth to perform that promise to one another—it is our belief, I say, that whether in the land of the living or the dead, they can never enjoy a quiet soul until that promise is made good. I must serve five years before I obtain my discharge ; when I get that, Ellen, I will return to this place, and let you know, by a token, that I am in the neighbourhood. Pledge me your hand and word, that when you receive that token, whether you are married or unmarried, whether it be dark, moon-light, or stormy, you will come out alone to meet me where I shall appoint, on the night when I shall send it".

Without much hesitation the young girl solemnly pledged herself to what he required. He then unbound from her hair a ribbon by which it was confined, kissed it, and placed it in his bosom, after which they ascended the cliff and separated.

After the departure of young Moran, his mother, to relieve her loneliness, opened a little place of entertainment for the *fish-jolters*, whose trade it was (and is) to carry the fish taken on the coast to the nearest market-town for sale, as also for the fishermen of the village and chance passengers. By this means she had accumulated a very considerable sum of money in a few years. Ellen Sparling observed this with the more satisfaction, as she felt it might remove the greatest bar that had hitherto opposed itself to her union with Charles Moran.

Five years and some months had rolled away since his departure, and he had not been heard of during that time in his native village. All things remained very nearly in the same state in which he had left them, with the exception of the increased prosperity of his mother's circumstances, and the matured beauty of Ellen, who was grown into a blooming woman, the admiration of all the men, and it is said, though I don't vouch for the fact, of all the women too, of her neighbourhood. There are

6*

limits of superiority beyond which envy cannot reach, and it might be said, perhaps, that Ellen was placed in this position of advantage above all her female acquaintances. It is not to be supposed that she was left untempted all this while, or at least unsought. On the contrary, a number of suitors had directly or indirectly presented themselves, with one of whom only, however, I have any business at present.

He was a young fisherman, and one of the most constant visitors at the elegant *soirées* of the widow Moran, where, however, he was by no means a very welcome guest, either to the good woman or her customers. He held, nevertheless, a high place at the board, and seemed to exercise a kind of dominion over the revellers, perhaps as much the consequence of his outward appearance, as of his life and habits. He was powerfully made, tall, and of a countenance which, even in his hours of comparative calmness and inaction, exhibited in the mere arrangement of its features, a brutal violence of expression which was exceedingly repugnant. The middle portion of his physiognomy was rather flat and sunken, and his mouth and forehead projecting much, rendered this deformity disgustingly apparent. Deep black, large glistening eyes glanced from beneath a pair of brows, which so nearly approached each other, as, on every movement of passion or impulse of suspicion, to form in all appearance one thick shaggy line across, and the unamiable effect of the countenance altogether was not improved by the temper of the man, who was feared throughout the neighbourhood, as well for his enormous strength, as for the violence, the suspicious tetchiness, and the habitual gloominess of his character, which was never more visible than when, as now, he affected the display of jollity and hearty good-fellowship. It was whispered, moreover, that he was visited, after some unusual excitement, with fits of wildness approaching to insanity, at

the accession of which he was wont to conceal himself
from all human intercourse for a period, until the evil
influence (originating, as it was asserted privately among
his old associates, in the remorse with which the recollection of his manifold crimes was accompanied) had
passed away—a circumstance which seemed to augur a
consciousness of this mental infirmity. At the end of
those periods of retirement, he was wont to return to his
companions with a haggard and jaded countenance, a dejected demeanour, and a sense of shame manifested in his
address, which, for a short space only, served to temper
the violence of his conduct. Robbers and murderers, as
all of his associates were, this evil-conditioned man had
gone so far beyond them in his total recklessness of crime,
that he had obtained for himself the distinguishing
appellative (like most nicknames in Irish low life, ironically
applied) of Yamon Macauntha, or Honest Ned; occasionally varied (after he had reached the estate of
manhood, and distinguished himself among the smugglers,
over whom he acquired a speedy mastery, by his daring
spirit, and almost invariable success in whatever he undertook) with that of Yamon Dhu, or Black Ned, a name
which applied as well to his dark complexion, long, matted,
coal-black hair and beard, as to the fierce and relentless
energy of his disposition.

One anecdote, which was told with suppressed breath
and involuntary shuddering, even among those who were
by his side in all his deeds of blood, may serve to illustrate
the terrific and savage cruelty of the man. A Dutch
vessel had gone to pieces on the rocks beneath the Look-
out. The waves rolled in like mountains, and lashed
themselves with such fury against the cliffs, that very
speedily nearly all those among the crew who clung to the
drifting fragments of the wreck, were dashed to atoms on
the projecting granite. A few only, among whom was the
captain of the vessel, who struggled with desperate

vigour against the dreadful element, succeeded in securing themselves on a projecting rock, from whence, feeble and exhausted as they were, the poor mariners endeavoured to hail a number of people, who were looking out on the wreck from the cliff-head above them. They succeeded in attracting attention, and the spectators prepared to lower a rope for their relief, which, as they were always provided against such accidents, they were not long in bringing to pass. It was first girded around the waist of the captain, and then fastened around that of his two companions, who, on giving a signal, were drawn into the air, the former holding in one hand a little casket, and with the other defending himself against the pointed projections of the cliff as he ascended. When very near the summit, which completely overhung the waves, he begged, in a faint tone, that some one would take the casket from his hands, as he feared it might be lost in the attempt to secure his own hold. Yamon was but too alert in acceding to the wretched man's request: he threw himself forward on the sand, with his breast across the rope, and took the casket from his uplifted hand.

"God's blessing on your souls, my deliverers", cried the poor man, wringing his clasped hands, with a gesture and look of fervent gratitude, "the casket is safe. thank God! and my faith to my employers——" he was yet speaking, when the rope severed under Black Yamon's breast, and the three men were precipitated into the yawning waters beneath. They were hurried out by the retiring waves, and the next moment their mangled bodies were left in the recesses of the cliff.

A cry of horror and of compassion burst even from the savage hearts of a crew of smugglers, who had been touched by the courage and constancy which was displayed by the brave unfortunates. Yamon alone remained unmoved (and hard must the heart have been which even the voice of gratitude, unmerited though it was, could not

soften or penetrate). He gave utterance to a burst of
hoarse, grumbling laughter, as he waved the casket in
triumph before the eyes of his comrades.

"Huh! huh!" he exclaimed, "she was a muthann—
why didn't she keep her casket till she drew her painther
ashore?"

One of the men, as if doubting the possibility of the
inhuman action, advanced to the edge of the cliff. He
found the rope had been evidently divided by some sharp
instrument; and observing something glittering where
Yamon lay, he stooped forward and picked up an open
clasp-knife, which was presently claimed by the unblushing
monster. However shocked they might have been at the
occurrence, it was no difficult matter for Yamon to
persuade his companions that it would be nowise convenient to let the manner of it transpire in the neighbourhood; and in a very few minutes the fate of the
Dutchmen seemed completely banished from their recollection (never very retentive of benevolent emotions),
and the only question held regarded the division of the
booty. They were disappointed, however, in their hopes
of spoil, for the casket which the faithful shipman was so
anxious to preserve, and to obtain which his murderer had
made sacrifice of so many lives, contained nothing more
than a few papers of bottomry and insurance, valueless to
all but the owners of the vessel. This circumstance
seemed to touch the villain more nearly than the wanton
cruelty of which he had been guilty; and his gang, who
were superstitious exactly in proportion to their want of
honesty and of all moral principle, looked upon it as a
supernatural occurrence, in which the judgment of an
offended Deity was made manifest.

This amiable person had a sufficiently good opinion of
himself to make one among the admirers of Ellen
Sparling. It is scarcely necessary to say that his suit was
unsuccessful. Indeed the maiden was heard privately to

declare her conviction that it was impossible there could be
found anywhere a more ugly and disagreeable man, in
every sense.

One fine frosty evening, the widow Moran's was more
than usually crowded. The fire blazed cheerfully on the
hearth, so as to render any other light unnecessary,
although the night had already begun to close in. The
mistress of the establishment was busily occupied in re-
plenishing the wooden *noggins*, or drinking vessels, with
which the board was covered; her glossy white hair
turned up under a clean kerchief, and a general gala
gladness spreading an unusual light over her shrivelled
and attenuated features, as by various courtesies, addressed to the company around her, she endeavoured to
make the gracious in her own house. Near the chimney-
corner sat Dora Keys, a dark featured, bright eyed girl,
who on account of her skill on the bagpipe, a rather un-
feminine accomplishment, and a rare one in this district
(where, however, as in most parts of Ireland, music of
some kind or another was constantly in high request)
filled a place of high consideration among the merry-
makers. The remainder of the scene was filled up with
the fishermen, smugglers, and fish-jolters; the latter wrapt
in their blue frieze coats, and occupying a more unobtrusive corner of the apartment, while Yamon, as noisy
and imperious as usual, sat at the head of the rude table,
giving the word to the whole assembly.

A knocking was heard at the slight hurdle-door. The
good woman went to open it, and a young man entered.
He was well formed, though rather thin and dark skinned,
and a profusion of black curled hair clustered about his
temples, corresponding finely with his glancing, dark,
fiery eye. An air of sadness, or of pensiveness, too, hung
about him, which gave an additional interest to his appearance, and impressed the spectator with an involuntary
respect. Mrs. Moran drew back with one of her lowest

curtsies. The stranger smiled sadly, and extended his hand. "Don't you know me, mother?" he asked. The poor woman sprung to his neck with a cry of joy.

All was confusion in an instant. "Charles"—"Charlie" —"Mr. Moran"—was echoed from lip to lip in proportion to the scale of intimacy which was enjoyed by the several speakers. Many a rough hand grasped his, and many a good-humoured buffet and malediction he had to endure before the tumultuous joy of his old friends had subsided. At length after all questions had been answered, and all old friends, the dead, the living, and the absent, had been tenderly inquired for, young Moran took his place among the guests; the amusements of the evening were renewed, and Yamon, who had felt his importance considerably diminished by the entrance of the young traveller, began to resume his self-constituted sovereignty.

Gambling, the great curse of society in all climes, classes, ages, and states of civilization, was not unknown or unpractised in this wild region. Neither was it here unattended with its usual effects upon the mind, heart, and happiness of its votaries. The eager manifestation of assent which passed round the circle, when the proposition of just "a hand o' five-and-forty" was made, showed that it was by no means an unusual or unacceptable resource to any person present. The young exile, in particular, seemed to catch at it with peculiar readiness; and, in a few minutes, places and partners being arranged, the old woman deposited in the middle of the table a pack of cards, approaching in shape more to the oval than the oblong square, and in colour scarcely distinguishable from the black oaken board on which they lay. Custom, however, had rendered the players particularly expert at their use, and they were dealt round with as much flippancy as the newest pack in the hands of a demon of St. James's in our own time. One advantage, certainly, the fashionable gamesters possessed over these primitive gamblers: the latter were perfectly ignorant of the useful niceties of play, so much in request among the former. *Old gentlemen, stags, bridges,* etc., were matters totally unknown among our coast friends, and the only necessary consequences of play, in which they (perhaps) excelled, were the outrageous violence, good mouth-filling oaths, and the ferocious triumph which followed the winnings or the losses of the several parties.

After he had become so far acquainted with the dingy pieces of pasteboard in his hand, as to distinguish the almost obliterated impressions upon them, the superior skill of the sea-farer became apparent. Yamon, who played against him, soon began to show symptoms of turbulence, which the other treated with the most perfect coolness and indifference, still persevering in his good play, until his opponent, after lavishing abundance of abuse on every body around him, especially on his unfortunate partner in the game, acknowledged that he had no more to lose. The night had now grown late, and the guests dropping off one by one, Moran and his mother were left alone in the cottage.

"Mother", said the young man, as he threw the little window-shutter open, and admitted a gush of moonlight which illumined the whole room, "will you keep the fire stirring till I return: the night is fine, and I must go over the cliffs".

"The cliffs! to-night, child!" ejaculated the old woman. "You don't think of it, my heart?"

"I must go", was the reply; "I have given a pledge that I dare not be false to".

"The cliffs!" continued the old woman. "The way is uncertain even to the feet that know it best, and sure you wouldn't try it in the night, and after being away till you don't know, may be, a foot o' the way".

"When I left Ellen Sparling, mother", said the young man, "I pledged her my faith, that I would meet her on

the night on which she should receive from me a token she
gave me. She, in like manner, gave me hers. That
token I sent to her before I entered your doors this evening,
and I appointed her father's ould house, where he lived in
his poor days, and where I first saw her, to meet me. I
must keep my word on all hazards". And he flung the
cottage-door open as he spoke.

"Then take care, take care", said the old woman,
clasping her hands and extending them towards him,
while she spoke in her native tongue. "The night, thank
God! is a fine night, and the sea is still at the bottom of
the cliffs, but it is an unsure path. I know the eyes that
will be red, and the cheeks that will be white, and the
young and fair ones too, if anything *contrary* should come
to you this holy evening". "I have given her my hand
and word", was Moran's reply as he closed the door, and
took the path over the sand hills.

The moon was shining brightly when he reached the
cliffs, and entered on the path leading to the old rendezvous of the lovers, and from thence to the ruined
building, where he expected to meet Ellen. He trudged
along in the light-heartedness of feeling inspired by the
conviction he felt, that the happiness of the times, which
every object he beheld brought to his recollection, had not
passed away with those days, and that a fair and pleasant
future yet lay before him. He turned off the sand-hills
while luxuriating in those visions of unchecked delight.

Passing the rocks of Duggara, he heard the plashing of
oars, and the rushing of a canoe through the water. It
seemed to make towards a landing-place further down,
and lying almost on his path. He pursued his course,
supposing, as in fact proved to be the case, that it was
one of the fishermen drawing his canoe nearer to the
caverns which were to be made the scene of a seal-hunt
on the following day. As the little vessel glided through
the water beneath him, a wild song, in the language of

the country, rose to the broken crag on which he now rested, chaunted by a powerful masculine voice, with all the monotonous and melancholy intonation to which the construction of the music is peculiarly favourable. The following may be taken as a translation of the stanzas :—

I.

The Priest stood at the marriage board,
  The marriage cake was made:
With meat the marriage chest was stored,
  Decked was the marriage bed.
The old man sat beside the fire,
  The mother sat by him,
The white bride was in gay attire
  But her dark eye was dim,
                  Ululah! Ululah!
The night falls quick—the sun is set,
Her love is on the water yet.

II.

I saw the red cloud in the west,
  Against the morning light,
Heaven shield the youth that she loves best
  From evil chance to-night.
The door flings wide! Loud moans the gale,
  Wild fear her bosom chills,
It is, it is the Banthee's wail,
  Over the darkened hills,
                  Ululah! Ululah!
The day is past! the night is dark!
The waves are mounting round his bark.

III.

The guests sit round the bridal bed,
  And break the bridal cake,
But they sit by the dead man's head,
  And hold his wedding-wake.
The bride is praying in her room,
  The place is silent all!
A fearful call! a sudden doom!
  Bridal and funeral!
                  Ululah! Ululah!
A youth to Kilfiehera's ta'en.
That never will return again.

Before Moran had descended much further on his way, he perceived that the canoe had reached a point of the rock close upon his route. The fisherman jumped to land, made fast the painter, and turning up the path by which Moran was descending, soon encountered him. It was Yamon Macauntha.

"Ho! Mr. Moran! Out on the cliffs this hour o' the night, sir?"

"Yes, I have a good way to go. Good by to you".

"Easy a while, sir", said Yamon; "that is the same way I'm going myself, and I'll be with you".

Moran had no objection to this arrangement, although it was not altogether pleasing to him. He knew enough of the temper and habits of the smuggler to believe him capable of any design, and although he had been a stronger built man than he was, yet the odds, in case of any hostile attempt, would be fearfully in Yamon's favour. He remembered, too, certain rumours which had reached him of the latter being occasionally subject to fits of gloom approaching in their strength and intensity to actual derangement, and began to hesitate as to the more advisable course to be pursued. However, not to mention the pusillanimity of anything having the appearance of retreat, such a step would in all probability have been attempted in vain, for Yamon stood directly behind him, and the path was too narrow to admit the possibility of a successful struggle. He had only to obey the motion of the fisherman and move on.

"You don't know", said the latter, "or may be you never heard of what I'm going to tell you now; but easy, and you'll know all in a minute. Do you see that sloping rock down by the sea, where the horse-gull is standing at this minute, the same we passed a while ago. When my mother was little *better* than seven months married, being living hard by on the sand-hills, she went many's the time down to that rock, to fetch home some of the salt-water for pickle and things, and never made any work of going down there late and early, and at all hours. Well, it was as it might be this way, on a fine bright night, that she took her can in her hand, and down with her to the rock. The tide was full in, and when she turned off o' the path, what should she see fronting her, out, and sitting quite erect intirely upon the rock, only a woman, and she having the tail of her gown turned up over her head, and she sitting quite still, and never spaking a word, and her back towards my mother. '*Dieu uth*', says my mother, careless and civil, thinking of nothing, and wanting her to move; but she took no notice. ' Would it be troubling you if I'd just step down to get a drop o' the salt-water?' says my mother. Still no answer. So thinking it might be one of the neighbours that was funning, or else that it might be asleep she was, she asked her very plain and loud to move out o' the way. When there wasn't ere a word come after this, my mother stooped forward a little, and lifted the *gownd* from the woman's forehead, and peeped under—and what do you think she seen in the dark within? Two eyes as red as fire, and a shrivelly old face without any lips hardly, and they drawn back, and teeth longer than lobster's claws, and as white as the bleached bones. Her heart was down in her brogue* when *it* started up from her, and with a screech that made two halves of my mother's brains, *it* flew out over the wide sea.

"My mother went home and took to her bed, from which she never stirred till 'twas to be taken to Kilfiehera church-yard. It was in that week I was born. I never pass that place at night alone, if I can help it—and that is partly the reason why I made so free to ask you to bear me company".

Moran had his confidence fully reëstablished by these words. He thought he saw in Yamon a wretch so

* Shoe.

preyed upon by remorse and superstition, as to be incapable of contemplating any deep crime, to which he had not a very great temptation. As Yamon still looked toward the rock beneath, the enormous horse-gull by which he had first indicated its position to Moran, took flight, and winged its way slowly to the elevation on which they stood. The bird rose above, wheeled round them, and with a shrill cry, that was repeated by a hundred echoes, dived again into the darkness underneath. Moran, at this instant, had his thoughts turned in another direction altogether, by the sight of the little recess in which Ellen and he had held their last conversation. He entered, followed by Yamon, who threw himself on the rude stone seat, observing that it was a place "for the phuka to make her bed in".

The young traveller folded his arms, and gazed around for a few minutes in silence, his heart striving beneath the load of recollections which came upon him at every glance and motion. On a sudden, a murmured sound of voices was heard underneath, and Moran stooped down, and overlooked the brink of the tremendous precipice. There was a flashing of lights on the calm waters beneath, and in a few minutes a canoe emerged from the great cavern, bearing three or four men, with lighted torches, which, however, they extinguished as soon as they came into the clear moonlight. He continued to mark them until they were lost behind a projecting crag. He then turned, and in removing his hand detached a pebble, which, falling after a long pause into the sea, formed what is called by the peasant children, who practise it in sport, "a dead man's skull". It is formed when a stone is cast into the water, so as to emit no spray, but cutting rapidly and keenly through, in its descent, produces a gurgling evolution, bearing a momentary resemblance to the tables of a human skull. The sound ceased, and all again was still and silent, with the exception of the sound which the stirring of the waters made in the mighty cavern beneath.

"I remember the time when that would have won a button* for me", said Moran, turning round. He at the same instant felt his shoulder grasped with a tremendous force. He looked quickly up, and beheld Yamon, his eyes staring and wild with some frantic purpose, bending over him. A half uttered exclamation of terror escaped him, and he endeavoured to spring towards the path which led from the place. The giant arm of Yamon, however, intercepted him.

"Give me, cheat and plunderer that you are", cried the fisherman, while his limbs trembled with emotion, "give me the money you robbed me of this night, or by the great light that's looking down on us, I'll shake you to pieces".

"There, Yamon, there: you have my life in your power—there is your money, and now—" He felt the grasp of the fisherman tightening upon his throat. He struggled, as a wretch might be expected to do, to whom life was new and dear; but he was as a child in the gripe of his enemy. There was a smothering shriek of entreaty —a wild attempt to twine himself in the limbs and frame of the murderer—and in the next instant he was hurled over the brow of the cliff.

"Another! another life!" said Yamon Dhu, as with hands stretched out, and fingers spread, as though yet in act to grasp, he looked out over the precipice. "The water is still again—Ha! who calls me?—From the caverns?—No.—Above?—Another life!—A deal of Christian's blood upon one man's soul!" and he rushed from the place.

About eleven o'clock on the following morning (as fine a day as could be), a young lad named Terry Mick (Terry,

* The practice of playing for *buttons* is very common among the peasant children.

the son of Mick, a species of patronymic very usual in
Ireland), entered, with considerable haste, the kitchen of
Mr. Morty Shannon, a gentleman farmer, besides being
coroner of the county, and as jolly a man as any in the
neighbourhood. Terry addressed a brief tale in the ear of
Aby Galaghar, Mr. Shannon's steward and fac-totum,
which induced the said Sandy to stretch his long, well-
seasoned neck, from the chimney-corner, and directing his
voice towards the door of an inner room, which was
complimented with the appellation of a parlour, exclaimed:
" Mr. Morty ! you're *calling*, sir ".

" Who am I *calling?*" asked a rich, waggish voice, from
within.

" Mr. Sparling, the Palatine's boy, sir ", replied Aby,
quite unconscious of the *quid pro quo.*

" Indeed ! More than I knew myself. Walk in, Terry ".

" Go in to him, Terry dear ", said Aby, resuming his
comfortable position in the chimney-corner, and fixing a
musing, contented eye upon a great cauldron of potatoes
that hung over the turf-fire, and on which the first sim-
mering froth, or *white horse* (as it is called in Irish
cottages), had begun to appear.

" The master sent me to you, sir ", said Terry, opening
the door, and protruding an eye, and half a face into the
sanctum sanctorum, " to know with his compliments——"

But first, I should let you have the glimpse that Terry
got of the company within. The person to whom he
immediately addressed himself sat at one end of a small
deal table, on which were placed a jug of cold water, a
broken bowl, half filled with coarse brown sugar, and a
little jar, which, by the frequent changes of position it
underwent, seemed to contain the favourite article of the
three. Imagine to yourself a middle sized man, with stout,
well-set limbs, a short and thick head of hair, an indented
forehead, eyes of a piercing gray, bright and sparkling, with
an expression between leer and satire, and a nose running in

a curvilineal direction toward the mouth. Nature had, in the first instance, given it a *sinister inclination*, and chance, wishing to rectify the *morals* of the feature, had by the agency of a black-thorn stick in the hands of a rebellious tenant, sent it again to the right. 'Twas kindly meant, as Mr. Morty himself used to say, though not dexterously executed.

" *The* master's compliments, sir", continued Terry, " to know if your honour would just step over to Kilkee, where there has been a bad business this morning—Charlie Moran being lying dead, on the broad of his back, at the house, over".

When I say that an expression of involuntary satisfaction, which he in vain endeavoured to conceal, diffused itself over the tortuous countenance of the listener at this intelligence, it is necessary I should save his character by reminding the reader that he was a county coroner, and in addition to the four pounds which he was to receive for the inquest, there was the chance of an invitation to stay and dine with the Sparlings, people whose mode of living Mr. Morty had before now tried and approved.

" Come here, Terry, and take your morning", said he, filling a glass of ardent spirits, which the youth immediately disposed of with a speed that showed a sufficient familiarity with its use, although some affectation of mincing decency induced him to colour the delicious relish with a grimace and shrug of comical dislike, as he replaced the glass on the table.

" E'then, that's good stuff, please your honour. Sure I'd know the master's anywhere over the world. This is some of the two year old, sir. 'Twas made the time Mr. Grady, the guager, was stationed below there, at the white house—and faix, many a drop he tasted of it himself, in the master's barn".

" And is the still so long at work, Terry?"

" Oh, long life to you, sir,—aye is it and longer too

The master has *sech* a 'cute way with him in managing
the still-hunters. 'Tis in vain for people to inform: to
be sure, two or three tried it, but got nothing by it,
barring a good lacing at the next fair-day. Mr. Grady
used regularly to send notice when he got an information,
to have him on his guard against he'd come with *the
army*—and they never found anything there, I'll be
your bail for it, more than what served to send 'em
home as drunk as pipers, every mother's son. To be
sure, that Mr. Grady was a pleasant man, and well liked
wherever he came, among high and low, rich and poor,
although being a guager and a Protestant. I remember
making him laugh hearty enough once. He asked me,
says he, as it might be funning: 'Terry', says he, ' I'm
very bad inwardly. How would you like to be walking
after a guager's funeral this morning?' 'Why thin. Mr.
Grady', says I, ' I'd rather see a thousand of your *religion*
dead than yourself, and meaning no love for *you*, neither'.
And poor man, he did laugh hearty, to be sure. He had
no pride in him—no pride, more than a child, had'nt Mr.
Grady. God's peace be with him wherever he is this day".

In a few minutes Mr. Shannon's blind mare was
saddled, and the head of the animal being directed
toward Kilkee, away went Terry, trotting by the coroner's
side, and shortening the road with his quaint talk. On
arriving at the Palatine's house, they found it crowded
with the inhabitants of the village. The fairy doctor of
the district sat near the door; his brown and weather-
beaten face wrapped in an extraordinary degree of mystery,
and his eyes fixed with the assumption of deep thought on
his twirling thumbs: in another part of the outer room
was the schoolmaster of the parish, discussing the
"crowner's quest law" to a circle of admiring listeners.
In the chimney-corner, on stools which were ranged for
the purpose, were congregated the "knowledgable" women
of the district. Two soldiers, detached from the nearest

7

guard, were stationed at the door, and at a little **distance** from them, seated at a table, and basking in the morning sunshine, might be seen a number of fishermen and others, all deeply engaged in converse upon the occurrence which had summoned them together. One of them **was** in the act of speaking when the coroner arrived:—

"We had been drawing the little canoe up hard by the cavern, seeing would we be the first to be in upon the seals when the hunt would begin, when I see a black thing lying on the shore among the sea-weed, about forty yards or upwards from the rock where I stood; and 'tisnt itself I see first, either, only two sea-gulls, and one of 'em perched upon it, while the other *kep* wheeling round above it, and screaming as nait'rel as a christen; and so I ran down to Phil, here, and says I: 'There's murder down upon the rocks, let us have it in from the fishes'. So we brought it ashore. 'Twas pale and stiff, but there was no great harm done to it, strange to say, in regard of the great rocks, and the place. We knew poor Moran's face, and we said nothing to one another, only wrapt the spritsail about it, and had it up here to Mr. Sparling's (being handier to us than his own mother's), where we told our story".

Passing into the house, Mr. Morty Shannon was received with all the respect due to his exalted station. The women curtsied low, and the men raised their hands to their foreheads with that courteous action which is familiar to all, even the most unenlightened of the peasantry of the south of Ireland. The master of the mansion, a comfortable-looking farmer-like sort of person, rose from his seat near the hearth, and greeted the man of office with an air of greater familiarity, yet with a reserve becoming the occasion. As the door of an inner apartment stood open, Mr. Shannon could see the corpse of the murdered man laid out on a table near the window. Close to the head stood the mother of the dead, hanging over the corpse in silent grief, swaying herself backward and forward with a gentle motion, and wringing her hands; yet with so noiseless an action, that the profound silence of the room was never broken. On the opposite side, her fine head resting against the bier—her white, wan fingers wreathed together in earnest prayer above the body, while a half-stifled sob occasionally shook her delicate frame —and her long and curling tresses fell in flaxen masses over the bosom of the murdered, knelt Moran's betrothed love, Ellen Sparling. As she prayed, a sudden thought seemed to rush upon her, she raised her head, took from her bosom a light green ribbon, and kissing it fervently and repeatedly, she folded and placed it in that of the murdered youth, after which she resumed her kneeling posture. There are few, I believe, who have lived among scenes of human suffering to so little purpose as not to be aware, that it is not the heaviness of a particular calamity, nor the violence of the sorrow which it produces, that is at any time most powerful in awakening the commiseration of an uninterested spectator. The capability of deep feeling may be more or less a property of all hearts, but the power of communicating it is a gift possessed by few. The murmur of a bruised heart, the faint sigh of a broken spirit, will often stir and thrill through all the strings of sympathy, while the frantic ravings of a wilder, though not less real woe, shall fail to excite any other sensation than that of pain and uneasiness. Perhaps it may be, that the selfishness of our nature is such, that we are alarmed and put on our guard, in proportion to the violence of the appeal which is made to us, and must be taken by surprise, before our benevolent emotions can be awakened. However all this might be, being no philosopher, I can only state the fact, that Mr. Morty Shannon, who had witnessed many a scene of frantic agony without ex-periencing any other feeling than that of impatience, was moved, even to a forgetfulness of his office, by the quiet, unobtrusive grief which he witnessed on entering this apartment.

It was the custom in those days, and is still the custom in most parts of Ireland, where any person is supposed to have "come by his end" unfairly, that all the inhabitants of his parish, or district, particularly those who, from any previous circumstances, may be rendered at all liable to suspicion, shall meet together and undergo a kind of ordeal, by touching the corpse, each in his turn. Among a superstitious people, such a regulation as this, simple though it was, had been frequently successful in betraying the guilty conscience; and it was a current belief among the peasantry, that in many instances where the perpetrator of the horrid deed possessed strength of mind or callousness of heart sufficient to subdue all appearance of emotion in the moment of trial, some miraculous change in the corpse itself had been known to indicate the evil doer. At all events, there was a degree of solemnity and importance attached to the test, which invested it with a strong interest in the minds of the multitude.

Suspicion was not idle on this occasion. The occurrences of the previous evening at the widow's house, and the loss there sustained by Yamon, contributed in no slight degree to fix the attention of the majority upon him. It did not pass without remark, neither, that he had not yet made his appearance at Mr. Sparling's house. Many wild tales, moreover, were afloat respecting Ellen Sparling, who had on that morning, before sunrise, been seen by a fish jolter, who was driving his mule loaded with fish along the road towards Kilrush, returning across the hills towards her father's house, more like a mad woman than a sober Christian. Before we proceed further in our tale, it is necessary we should say something of the circumstances which led to this appearance.

When Ellen received the token on the previous evening from young Moran's messenger, she tied her light chequered straw bonnet under her chin, and stole out by a back entrance, with a beating and anxious heart, to the appointed rendezvous. The old ruined house which had been named to her, was situated at the distance of a mile from her father's, and was at present tenanted only by an aged herdsman in his employment. Not finding Moran yet arrived, although the sun was already in the west, she sent the old man away on some pretext, and took his place in the little rush-bottomed chair by the fire-side. Two hours of a calm and silent evening had already passed away, and yet he came not. Wearied with the long expectation, and by the tumult of thoughts and feelings which agitated her, she arose, walked to a short distance from the cottage, and sitting on a little knoll in the vicinity, which commanded a wide prospect of the sea, she continued to await his arrival, now and then gazing in the direction of the cliffs by which the messenger told her he was to pass. No object, however, met her eye on that path, and no sound came to her ear but the loud, full-toned, and plaintive whistle of the ploughman, as he guided his horses over a solitary piece of stubble-ground, lightening his own and their labour by the wild modulations of the *Keen-the-cawn*, or death-wail; the effect of which, though it had often delighted her under other circumstances, fell now with an oppressive influence upon her spirits.

Night fell at length, and she returned to the old house. As she reached the neglected *haggart* on the approach, a light breeze sprang up inland, and rustling in the thatch of the ruined out-houses, startled her by its suddenness, almost as much as if it had been a living voice. She looked up an instant, drew her handkerchief closer around her neck, and hurried on towards the door. It might be he had arrived by another path during her absence! High as her heart bounded at the suggestion, it sunk in proportion as she lifted the latch, and entered the deserted room. The turf-embers were almost expiring on the hearth, and all was dark, cold, saddening, and comfortless. She felt vexed at the absence of the old servant, and regretted the caution which induced her to get rid of him. Amid all the intensity of her fondness, too, she could not check a feeling of displeasure at the apparent want of ardour on the part of her lover. It had an almost slighting look; she determined she would make it evident in her manner on his arrival. In the next moment the fancied sound of a footstep made her spring from her seat, and extend her arms in a perfect oblivion of all her stern resolutions. Quite beaten down in heart by constant disappointments, and made nervous and feverish by anxiety, the most fearful suggestions began now to take place of her pettishness and ill-humour. She was alarmed for his safety. It was a long time since he had trod the path over the cliffs. The possibility that here rushed upon her, made her cover her face with her hands, and bend forward in her chair in an agony of terror.

Midnight now came on. A short and heavy breathing at the door, as she supposed, startled her as she bent over the flame which she kept alive by placing fresh *sods* on the embers. She rose and went to the door. A large Newfoundland dog of her father's bounded by her as she opened it, and testified by the wildest gambols about the kitchen, the delight he felt in meeting her so unexpectedly, at such an hour, and so far from her home. She patted the faithful animal on the head, and felt restored in spirits by the presence even of this uncommunicative acquaintance. The sagacious servant had evidently traced her to the ruin by the fineness of its sense, and seemed overjoyed at the verification of his diagnostic. At length, after having sufficiently indulged the excitement of the moment, he took post before the fire, and after divers indecisive evolutions, he coiled himself up at her feet and slept. The maiden herself in a short time imitated the example.

The startling suggestions that had been crowding on her in her waking moments, now began to shape themselves in vivid and fearful visions to her sleeping fancy. As she lay back in her chair, her eyes not so entirely closed as to exclude the "lengthening rays" of the decaying fire before them, she became unaccountably oppressed by the sense of a person sitting close at her side. There was a hissing, as if of water falling on the embers just before the figure, and after a great effort she fancied that she could turn so far round as to recognise the face of her lover, pale, cold, with the long dark hair hanging drearily at each side, and as she supposed, dripping with moisture. She strove to move, but was perfectly unable to do so, and the figure continued to approach her, until at length, placing his chilling face so close to her cheek, that she thought she felt the damp upon her neck, he said gently: "Ellen, I have kept my hand and word: living, I would have done it; dead, I am permitted". At this moment a low grumbling bark from the dog Minos awoke her, and she started from her seat, in a state of nervousness which for a short time prevented a full conviction of the non-existence of the vision that had oppressed her slumber. The dog was sitting erect, and gazing with crouched head, fixed eyes, and lips upturned in the expression of canine fear, toward the door. Ellen listened attentively for a few minutes, and a gentle knocking was heard. She recognised too, or thought she recognised, a voice precisely similar to that of the figure in her dream, which pronounced her name with the gentlest tone in the world. What surprised her most, was that Minos, instead of starting fiercely up as was his wont on hearing an unusual sound at night, cowed, whimpered, and slunk back into the chimney-corner. Not in the least doubting that it was her lover, she rose and opened the door. The vividness of her dream, being yet fresh upon her, and perhaps the certainty she felt of seeing him, made her imagine for the instant that she beheld the same figure standing before her. It was but for an instant, however; on looking a second time, there was no person to be seen. An overwhelming sensation of terror now rushed upon her, and she fled from the place with the rapidity of madness. In a state half-frantic, half-fainting, she reached her father's house, and flung herself on her bed, where the news of Moran's death reached her next morning.

To return, however, to the present position of our tale. A certain number of the guests were now summoned into the room where the body lay, and all things were prepared for the ordeal. At a table near the window, with writing materials before him, was placed the worthy coroner, together with the lieutenant of the guard at the lighthouse, who had arrived a few minutes before. Mr. Sparling stood close by them, his face made up into an expression of wise abstraction, his hands thrust into his breeches pockets, and jingling some half-pence which they contained. The betrothed lover of the murdered man had arisen from her knees, and put on a completely altered manner. She now stood in silence, and with tearless eyes, at the head of the bier, gazing with an earnestness of purpose, which might have troubled the carriage even of diffident innocence itself, into the face of every one who approached to touch the body. Having been aware of the suspicions afloat against Yamon, and the grounds for those suspicions, she expected with impatience the arrival of that person.

He entered at length. All eyes were instantly turned on him. There was nothing unusual in the manner or appearance of the man. He glanced round the room, nodded to a few, touched his forehead to the coroner and the lieutenant, and then walking firmly and coolly to the centre of the apartment, awaited his turn for the trial. A very close observer might have detected a quivering and wincing of the eyelid, as he looked toward Ellen Sparling, but it was only momentary, and he did not glance in that direction a second time.

"Isn't that droll,* Shawl ?" whispered Terry in the ear of the fairy doctor, who stood near him. The latter did not deem it convenient to answer in words, but he compressed his lips, contracted his brows, and threw an additional portion of empty wisdom into his physiognomy.

"E'then", continued Terry, "only mark Tim Fouloo going to touch the dead corpse all a' one any body would sispect *him* to be taking the life of a chicken, the *lahu-muthawn*" (half-natural), as a foolish looking, open-mouthed, open-eyed young booby advanced in his turn in a slow waddling gait to the corpse, and passing his hand over the face, retired with a stare of comic stupidity, which, notwithstanding the awful occasion, provoked a smile from many of the spectators.

Yamon was the last person who approached the corpse. From the moment he entered, the eye of Ellen Sparling had never been withdrawn from him for an instant, and its expression now became vivid and intense. He walked to the place, however, with much indifference, and passed his hand slowly and repeatedly over the cheek and brow of the dead man. Many a head was thrust forward, as if in expectation that the inanimate lump of clay might stir beneath the feeler's touch. But no miracle took place, and they gazed on one another in silence as he slowly turned away, and folding his arms, resumed his place in the centre of the apartment.

"Well, Mr. Sparling", said his worship the coroner, "here is so much time lost : had we begun to take evidence at once, the business would be nearly at an end by this time ".

The old Palatine was about to reply, when their conversation was interrupted by an exclamation of surprise from Ellen Sparling. Turning quickly round, they beheld her with one of the clenched hands of the corpse between hers, gazing on it in stirless amazement. Between the

---

* " Droll", in Ireland, means simply, *extraordinary*, and does not necessarily excite a comic association.

dead-stiff fingers appeared something of a bluish colour slightly protruded. Using the utmost strength of which she was mistress, Ellen forced open the hand, and took from it a small part of the lappel of a coat, with a button attached. And letting the hand fall, she rushed through the crowd, putting all aside without looking at one, until she stood before Yamon. A glance was sufficient. In the death-struggle, the unhappy Moran had torn away this portion of his murderer's dress, and the rent was visible at the moment.

"The murderer! blood for blood!" shrieked the frantic girl, grasping his garment, and looking almost delirious with passion. All was confusion and uproar. Yamon darted one fierce glance around, and sprung toward the open door, but Ellen Sparling still clung as with a drowning grasp to her hold. He put forth the utmost of his giant strength to detach himself from her, but in vain. All his efforts seemed only to increase her strength, while they diminished his own. At last he bethought him of his fishing-knife; he plucked it from his belt and buried it in her bosom. The unfortunate girl relaxed her hold, reeled, and fell on the corpse of her lover, while Yamon bounded to the door. Poor Terry crossed his way, but one blow laid him sprawling senseless on the earth, and no one cared to tempt a second. The rifles of the guard were discharged after him, as he darted over the sand-hills; but just before the triggers were pulled, his foot tripped against a loose stone, he fell, and the circumstance perhaps saved his life (at least the marksmen said so). He was again in rapid flight before the smoke cleared away.

" *Shuil! Shuil!* The sand hills! the cliffs!" was now the general shout, and the chase immediately commenced. Many minutes elapsed ere they arrived at the cliffs, and half a dozen only of the most nimble-footed just reached the spot in time to witness the last desperate resource of

* Come! Come!

the murderer. He stood and looked over his shoulder for an instant, then rushing to the verge of the cliff, where it walled in the land to a height of forty feet, he waved his hand to his pursuers, and cast himself into the sea.

The general opinion was that he had perished, but there was no trace ever seen that could make such a consummation certain. The body was never found, and it was suspected by a few, that, incredible as the story might appear, he had survived the leap, and gained the little rocky island opposite.

The few who returned at dusk to Mr. Sparling's house, found it the abode of sorrow, of silence, and of death. Even the voice of the hired keener was not called in on this occasion to mock the real grief that sat on every brow and in every heart. The lovers were waked together, and buried in the same grave at Kilfiehera.

THE BARBER OF BANTRY.

CHAPTER I.

THERE is a small river which, rising amid the wildest and least cultivated upland of the county of Limerick in Ireland, pursues its lonesome course amid heath and bog, by cliff and quarry, through scenery of the bleakest and yet the most varied kinds, until it discharges its discoloured waters into the bosom of the Lower Shannon. Now gliding, deep and narrow, through some heathy plain, it presents a surface no wider than a meadow streamlet, and, like placid characters in the world, indicating its depth by its tranquillity ; anon, it falls in one white and foamy volume over the brow of some precipitous crag, at the foot of which it dilates into a pool of tolerable extent. Further down it may be traced through the intricacies of a stunted wood, now babbling in one broad sheet over the limestone shallow ; now rolling silent, deep, and dark, beneath the overhanging brier and hazel bushes that fling their tangled foliage across the waters from the indented bank. In another place, it may be found dashing noisily from ledge to ledge of some opposing mass of limestone, or pursuing its swift and gurgling course along the base of a perpendicular cliff, until, as it approaches the mighty river in which its waters are received, it acquires surface and depth sufficient to float the fisher's skiff, and the small cot or lighter that conveys a lading of marl or sea-weed to manure the little

potato garden of the humble agriculturist upon its banks.
Nor even in this dreary region is the wild streamlet wholly
destitute of animated figures to give a quickening interest
to the general loneliness of the scenery along its side.
The neighbouring cottager "snares" for pike and salmon
in its shallows; the cabin housewife beetles her linen in
the summer evening on its banks, and the barefoot and
bareheaded urchin, standing or sitting by the side of an
overhanging ash or elder, drops his pin-hook baited with
an earthworm into the deep and shaded corner which he
knows by profitable experience to be the favourite haunt
of the eel and trout; and in which it may be said, in
passing, his simple apparatus is often as destructive as all
the erudite machinery of Izaak Walton and his disciples.

In the summer season the appearance of this little river
is such as we have described. In the winter, however,
after the great rains, common in mountain scenery, have
set in, the shallow bed of the stream is often filled, in the
course of a few minutes, with a body of water, collected
from the heights around its source, that presents a
formidable contrast to the usually placid tenor of its course.
It is then seen roaring and foaming along in one huge,
yellow flood, inundating not unfrequently the cottages and
hamlets near its banks, and carrying dismay and death
among pigs, poultry, and other anti-aquatic animals, who
happen to stray within reach of its overflowing current,
and sometimes even placing life in jeopardy.

Not far from the banks of the river, and commanding a
full prospect of its windings through a varied and extensive, though wild and thinly populated landscape, may be
seen at this day the walls of a roofless mansion, which
bears in its decay the marks of having been once inhabited
by persons somewhat superior in rank to the "strong
farmers" who, with few exceptions, constitute at present
the sole aristocracy of the district. The style of the mason-
work (the sounding term architecture would be somewhat

misapplied to so simple an edifice) refers the date of its
erection, and indeed correctly, to the beginning of the last
century. The small windows are nearly square, and deep
set in the massy stonework, while the lofty gables, comprising more than half the height of the whole building,
present, when viewed from the end, an angle almost as
acute as that of a wedge. Around, in a still more dilapidated condition than the dwelling-house, may be traced
the ruins of numerous out-offices, the stable, the cow-house,
the turf-house, the piggery, the fowl-house, and even (a
contrast to the present poverty of the surrounding country)
the coach-house. At a little distance, the urchins of the
neighbourhood point out the remains of earthen fences, not
much more distinct than the immortal Roman entrenchment
of Monkbarns, as all that is left of what was once the
kitchen and flower-garden. Polyanthuses, almost dwindled
into primroses, bachelors'-buttons impoverished both in
size and colour, and a gooseberry or currant bush, choked
up in furze, furnish corroborative testimony to the tradition. The neighbouring peasantry still preserve the history
of the building from its earliest foundation, as well as of
its successive owners, who were persons of no little noto-
riety in their time.

In the beginning of the last century, the tract of land
on which the ruin stands was purchased by a certain Mr.
Patrick Moynehan (more commonly known by the familiar
diminutive Paddy Monehan, or Paddy the Lad). As,
although respectably descended, Mr. Moynehan was not
heir to any property whatever, and as his subsequent
habits did not furnish any indications of that thrift which
Shylock tells us,

" Is blessing, if men steal it not",

there was very general whispering, and great perplexity as
to how Paddy Moynehan could have acquired the means
of purchasing an estate, and building a handsome house.

As the stories circulated upon the subject were numerous, and characteristic both of the place and period, we will venture to relate a few.

It was said by some, that on an occasion, when yet a young man, Pat Moynehan went to attend the "berrin" of a friend. While the remainder of the crowd were occupied at their devotions in the place of death, young Moynehan, little impressed by the solemnity of the scene before him, rambled about among the graves, "funning" and amusing himself, and paying little attention to the severe glances that were occasionally directed towards him from the kneeling crowd. On one occasion, it happened that he found, placed upon the corner of a monument, a bleached skull, the eyeless sockets directed towards him, and seeming to convey a more terrible rebuke than ever could have proceeded from the eyes that once moved within their orbits. Moynehan, however, was nothing checked in his career of mirth.

"Look there!" he said, pointing out the skull to a companion, who in vain endeavoured to repress his unseasonable levity, "much as you think of yourself, that was once as fine a man as you are, and you'll have as ugly a grin upon your own face yet; he was just as good a gentleman, and as devout a Christian". Then turning to the skull, and taking off his hat with an air of mock politeness, he added: "I am happy, sir, to have the pleasure of making your acquaintance, and will feel obliged by your giving me the honour of your company at breakfast next Sunday". And off he turned with another bow of mock respect, and left the churchyard with his companion.

Before breakfast hour on the following Sunday (the legend still continues), young Moynehan went out to speak with a neighbour; while he was absent, and while the servant girl was occupied in preparing breakfast, the door was opened from without, and "a big man" entered. He did not say "God save you", nor "God bless you", as he

came in, and walked silently to a chair that stood near the
fire, and took his seat without speaking.   His singular
conduct was but the counterpart of his appearance.   His
dress was that of a gentleman, and rich, but so grotesque
in form, and strange in material, that it was impossible to
decide on the rank or country of the wearer.   A high
standing collar, a flowered silk waistcoat, ruffles at the
wrists, a handsome pair of plush under garments, with
golden knee-buckles, and silver ones of an enormous size
across the insteps of his square-toed shoes; these, together
with a well-powdered head of hair, brushed backward and
gathered behind into a handsome queue, a cocked hat,
which he carried under his arm, and a slender rapier by
his side, constituted the chief portion of that costume
which looked so perplexing in the eyes of the mountain
handmaiden.   With all this, there was in the expression
of his eyes, and in the mechanical regularity of his movements, an air of she knew not what, that chilled the spirit
of the young woman, and left her scarce the power to ask
his business.   Being, however, naturally of a free and
hearty disposition, she did not suffer herself to be altogether
daunted, but said, in a laughing manner, and after waiting
a considerable time to hear him speak :

"Why, then, sir, arn't you a droll gentleman, to walk
into a house in that kind o' way, an' sate yourself without
sayin' a ha'p'orth ?"

The stranger looked fixedly at her.   "It is a law where
I come from", says he, "that none of us shall speak until
we are spoken to; and if the same law prevailed among
people I know here, there are many of their friends that
would have reason to be glad of it.   But where's the man
o' the house? isn't it a shame for him to ask a gentleman to breakfast with him, and not to be at home
before him ?"

While he was speaking, Moynehan entered.

"Isn't it a burning shame for you", said the stranger,

in a loud voice, " to ask a gentleman to breakfast with you, and not to be at home before him?"

" Me ask you to breakfast!" exclaimed the astonished Moynehan; " I never laid eyes on you before; but you are as welcome as if you got fifty invitations".

" Indeed, but you did ask me", said the stranger, " and I'll tell you where, too";—and stooping over towards him, he whispered in his ear.

The instant Moynehan heard the whisper, he fell in a death-like faint upon the floor. The stranger showed not the least concern, nor made any effort to relieve him, but waited with the utmost indifference until he should revive. While he was yet insensible, the girl, standing in awe of this mysterious guest, requested him to sit down to breakfast.

" No, no", he answered; " I can eat nothing until your master sits with me; it was with him I came to breakfast".

When Moynehan came to himself, understanding from the girl what the stranger had said, he repeated the invitation, which was immediately accepted, and both sat down together. The effect of the first shock having passed away, Moynehan made up his mind to perform the part of host with true Irish hospitality. He laughed, talked, jested, told his best stories, shook his guest by both hands together, and protested that he was as welcome " as a rose in June". He ordered the freshest eggs, and fried the richest bacon, and treated the stranger with the most perfect hospitality.

They had scarcely done breakfast, when a bell was heard ringing at a distance.

" What's that bell?" asked the stranger, in a sharp tone.

" Oh, it's nothing", said Moynehan, with a careless air; " only the bell for chapel".

The stranger said nothing, but looked very serious. At

length, rising from his chair, he addressed his host as
follows :—

" You're an honest fellow, after all, and you may thank
your hearty, hospitable conduct that I do not make you
suffer severely for the trouble you gave me by your invitation ; however, you must not say that you gave your
breakfast for nothing. Meet me this evening by the elder
tree near the river side, and you shall hear something that
you will thank me for".

Moynehan kept the appointment, and those who gave
credit to the story (and they comprised no small portion
of the inhabitants of the surrounding cottages) asserted
that during their evening conference, his unearthly visitor
revealed to him a quantity of hidden treasure in a neighbouring ruin, more than sufficient to warrant the expensive
style in which he soon began to live ; others, while they
admitted the truth of the greater portion of the story,
denied that there was anything supernatural in the case.
They asserted that the whole was a *hoax* played upon
Moynehan, by a young man, a stranger in the place, who
observed his conduct at the funeral, and availed himself
of the mock invitation which he overheard, to read the
wag a lesson, and to help himself to a comfortable breakfast. It was certain, indeed, that Moynehan himself never
liked to have the story alluded to in his hearing, but this
circumstance was urged, by the advocates of the wonderful, as evidence in favour of their own version of the
tale. Those who contended for the common-place, were
in the habit of accounting for Moynehan's great accession
of wealth by other than supernatural means. He had
become engaged, they said, in common with many other
persons in his time, in a species of commerce which is
viewed with a jealous eye by all governments ; and by his
share in the disposal of two or three cargoes of tobacco
and other expensive luxuries, had amassed money enough
to rest on his oars for all his after life.

Other persons gave a different account of the manner in which Moynehan obtained his riches. This party seemed inclined to strike a medium between the supernatural and the common-place. Moynehan, they said, rented two or three small farms nearly adjoining that tract of mountain-land which subsequently became his estate. Neither providence nor settled and regular industry were amongst the qualities for which he was most remarkable. A man whose sole income was derived from his share in the profits of those small farms, he still maintained a style of living not surpassed by many who could boast of fee-simple patrimonies to support and palliate such ex-travagance. He kept a pack of hounds and a huntsman, and gave jovial entertainments to such of the neighbouring gentry as would condescend to accept his hospitality. His house was ever open; a family piper lent his music to the dance of ruin; there was nobody who did not look upon Moynehan as a paragon of good fellows, except his land-lord, and even he could scarcely find it in his heart to proceed to extremities with a person of so much spirit and goodnature. It is the fate of most goodnatured spend-thrifts, however, to tire out in the end the forbearance of even their most forbearing friends, and Moynehan formed no exception to the general rule. After running six years in arrear of rent, he was thunderstruck by the intelligence that Sir David Hartigan was on the eve of visiting his property in the county, and of course would not leave Mr. Patrick Moynehan without a call. This was the signal for consternation. Ejectments and executions floated before the eyes of Moynehan; and before he could collect even a moderate portion of the arrear last due, the baronet was on his way to his estate. It was (no uncommon case with Irish landowners, even at that period of home legislation) the first visit he had ever made to his paternal inheritance, and of this circumstance Moynehan determined to take advantage for his security. He called the tenants together, and harangued them in the most earnest manner on the propriety of giving their landlord a suitable reception.

"I need not tell you all", he said, " that Sir David has been a good landlord to us all—[hurra! hurra!] a man that gives the poor man time for his money—[hurra!]— that never yet *distressed** a tenant for his rent, nor bore hard on those that he knew to be well inclined if they had the means—[hurra! hurra!]—very well then, lads; you will remember that this is the first time he has ever shown himself amongst his tenants, and let us take care that he has no cause to complain of his reception".

A new volley of cordial " hurras" announced the acquiescence of the assembled tenants in this agreeable proposal, and preparations were immediately set on foot for receiving the baronet in the most splendid style. The demesnes and lawns of the small gentry within five miles round, were stripped of their fairest poplars and mountain ash, in order to form triumphal arches along the road which led to the village of * * * * *, where the great man was to reside during his stay. Hardy would have been the owner of a tapering fir or larch, who had dared to murmur at seeing his grounds invaded, and the pride of his shrubbery laid low for this festive purpose. The mothers, wives, and sisters of the cottiers lent their bright coloured shawls, ribands, and handkerchiefs, to flutter amid the foliage, and add new gaiety to the scene. There was one article of holiday splendour in which there was no stint. A great portion of Sir David's estate consisting of excellent bog, there was no lack of material for bonfires. Accordingly, at every cross road within half a mile round, and almost at every second cabin in the village itself, there was a pile of turf and bogwood, the contribution of the surrounding tenantry, ready for the torch the instant the carriage of the mountain sovereign should appear.

* Distrained.

But what exceeded all beside, was the zeal exhibited by
Mr. Patrick Moynehan himself, the instigator, in a great
degree, of the whole proceeding, and who was moved to
it, partly by real good-will towards his landlord, and in
part by certain undefined hopes and impulses, which we
will leave the knavish reader to divine. Before his door,
upon the bare and level green, was piled a circle of turf,
in the midst of which was suspended by machinery, which
had taxed the ingenuity of the whole district, a prime ox,
intended to be roasted whole. Besides this, were the
lesser fires, at which pigs, turkeys, geese, and other
inferior animals of culinary celebrity were prepared, each
by the persons who had contributed both fire and meat.

Above the gateway which led to this gala spot, was
suspended a painted board, surrounded by green boughs,
with, of course, what other inscription than " Cead millia
faltha", executed in the best manner that the village could
afford.

The day at length arrived, and the great man came. In
consequence of his continual absenteeism, he had certain
misgivings with respect to his popularity amongst his own
tenantry, which made him wholly unprepared for the enthusiastic reception with which he was now honoured.
Within half a mile of the village, he was met by a prodigious multitude of people, of both sexes, and of all
ages, shouting, laughing, and capering for joy. Flutes,
fiddles, bagpipes, and, in lieu of these, tin cans, dildorns,
and every other implement from which any sound could be
extracted that might bring the idea of music to the mind
of the rudest hearer, added their obstreperous harmony to
the general uproar. What need to pen our way through
all the glories of the feast that followed? Some idea may
be formed of the enjoyment of the worthy baronet (who
was amazingly fat), when we mention that he was placed
from noon to evening of a broiling day in June, in the
centre of between thirty and forty huge fires, the smoke of

which, settling low, in consequence of the calm and the
tenuity of the mountain air, had well nigh stifled him ; that
in addition to this, he had to dance (according to in-
dispensable custom) with almost all the young women in
the place; besides other duties of courtesy, so oppressive,
that he was afterwards heard to declare, that he had
almost as lief be a king, and go through all the labour of
a levee or drawing-room, as to spend such another day at
* * * * *. In addition to this, when it is remembered that
the gates were thrown open, and free admission given to
all travellers, comprising the numerous beggars, whom the
foregone fame of the feast had drawn together from the
distant parishes, it must be acknowledged that the situation
of the excellent Baronet was truly enviable. At all
events, he could not choose but feel the deepest gratitude
to Mr. Moynehan, at whose house he spent the ensuing
fortnight. The latter, however, seemed to think the glory
sufficient for his landlord, for by some means or other Sir
David never could find an opportunity of engaging him in
any serious conversation on the subject of his rent. If
he spoke of money, Moynehan talked of woodcocks,—if
he mentioned arrears, Moynehan could show him the
prettiest fly-fishing in Ireland,—or he had a present of
gray-hounds of the genuine old Irish stock,—known
relatives of those that were presented by Sir Somebody to
the Great Mogul,—or he insisted on his accepting a
beautiful mare of the most unblemished pedigree,—anything—everything he was ready to furnish him with
except the needful. And the issue was, that Sir David
returned to Dublin, looking upon Moynehan as one of the
most generous fellows and the most impracticable tenants
in the world.

However, such a state of things could not continue.
Year followed year, threat came on threat, and ruin
showed her hideous countenance at length in the shape
of a formal ejectment from his holding. He might still

(such were the times) have set the law at bay, and maintained possession for some years longer at least; but this he would not do. He must give up his farm, and the thought filled him with the deepest melancholy. At table, the huntsman cracked his joke in vain (for the huntsman, it should be understood, was a man of sufficient importance to occupy a small side table in the common dining room, and after dinner to take his seat by the ample fireside). It signified little that it was the same irresistible joke, or the same admirable anecdote which had shook his sides with laughter regularly once a day for half a score years before. He now listened to it with a vacant eye, and a countenance that plainly showed how far his thoughts were out of hearing.

What was to be done? Was he to bid farewell to his numerous domestics, and to tell his huntsman that he was to hunt no more for him, and to sell or give away the hounds, and to resign his flies and fishing-tackle, and to watch no more the beautiful motion of his grayhounds as they shot like ghosts across the mountain heath in March? The thought was dreadful. He wandered like a solitary being by the river side, and along the hedges which enclosed his lawn and paddock, and seemed to feel already the pressure of the abject poverty to which he must soon be reduced.

Amid all the faults which he now so bitterly regretted, if not for a better motive, yet for the ruin they had brought upon himself, there was one feature in his past conduct which he called to mind with pleasure. He never in a single instance had refused assistance to a fellow-creature in distress. No matter who the individual, how indifferent the character, or what his own circumstances at the moment, he never had withheld his aid where it was wanted. No consideration of inconvenience to himself, no dread of theft or lack of means in his own household, prevented his affording to every individual, without ex-

ception, high or low, great or little, who chose to apply
for it, a comfortable dinner and a night's lodging beneath
his roof. This indiscriminate charity, it is said, was not
wholly in accordance with the views of Mrs. Moynehan,
whose wardrobe and fowl-house had often suffered for her
husband's hospitality, but he would hear nothing of her
complaints. Giving was with him the easiest of all duties,
and as there were some others to which he did not
attend so closely, he seemed determined to practise this
in its perfection. The greater the loss and the greater
the inconvenience, he thought the greater the merit also ;
and he had an idea, that what is bestowed in this way is
not lost, but that merciful actions, beyond all others
whatsoever, buoy up the spirit at the hour of death and
after.

In his arguments with Mrs. Moynehan upon this subject,
he was in the habit of relating an anecdote for her
edification, which we will transcribe for that of the reader.

" 'There were two brothers, twin-brothers ", he said,
" who were so fervently attached, that each made the
other promise, in case he should die first, to return, if
possible, and let the survivor know how he had fared in

> 'That undiscovered country from whose bourne
> No traveller returns '.

Both, however, had passed the meridian of life without
meeting any serious illness, and both forgot a compact
which they had made in their youth, and which was blotted
from their memory by the cares of manhood and the new
engagements in which matrimony had involved them. On
a sudden one of them was stunned by the intelligence
that his brother had died of that species of brain fever
called a *coup de soleil.* The news filled him with grief.
In the evening he walked out to indulge his sorrow in a
neighbouring church-yard, and to relieve his mind by
prayer. While thus occupied, an oppressive sense of some

extraordinary presence fell upon his mind. He looked
up—his brother stood before him. His first feeling was an
emotion of ecstacy at the thought that the rumour of his
brother's death was false, and he ran to cast himself upon
his neck. But as he proceeded, the other retired, and
always, to his extreme astonishment, preserved exactly
the same distance at which he had at first beheld him.

" 'Why do you not speak to me?' said the surviving
brother; 'they told me you were dead, and that we should
meet no more'.

" 'Brother', said the figure, in an unearthly voice, 'do
you forget the agreement which we made near this spot
exactly twenty-five years since?'

" The hearer instantly understood the whole, and that
it was his brother's shade which he beheld. He trembled,
and a cold moisture settled on his forehead.

" 'I am allowed to come back', says he, 'for your
warning and for your consolation. Immediately after my
death, I found myself in the finest country I ever saw in
my life, with the richest demesnes and grandest houses
that ever were found, and millions of people walking
amongst the trees, and talking and laughing together, as
happy as the day is long. To my great surprise, I found
that almost all the ladies and gentlemen that owned the
fine houses were people that I remembered in this world
as poor beggars, and religious Christians, and persons of
that kind, that nobody cares about. I went from one to
another, but not one of them knew me, and the man that
had the charge of the place was going to turn me out,
when one of the gentlemen called to him and said he
knew me. I looked close at him, and at last remembered
the face of a poor blind man whom I had guided once on
a stormy night from a neighbouring village to his own
door; but he had now a pair of eyes as bright as stars.
That was the only act of real charity I ever recollected to
have done in my life, and it was the means of getting me

8

a handsome house and garden, where I live happier than
I can describe' ".

A celebrated Greek critic tells us that if we separate the
sublime from the allegorical, we shall often strip it of half
its excellence. If the axiom be applied in the case of
Moynehan's legend, even polished readers may find it not
wholly without meaning. From the fact, however, that
Mr. Moynehan was in the *habit* of repeating it for the improvement of his lady, it may be inferred that it had
not all the influence upon her conduct which he could
desire.

CHAPTER II.

A FEW evenings previous to the day on which he, Moynehan, was to give up possession of his house and lands, a
storm arose so terrible that it seemed doubtful whether the
building would survive the ownership of its present
master. The wind came howling and shrieking up the un-
sheltered heath, and through the close ravines in the
neighbourhood. Now it shook the window frames as if in
sudden passion at their obstinate resistance to its fury, now
it hissed and roared against the well-bound thatch—and
now wound its dismal horn in the lofty chimney-top. Mr.
Moynehan sat by his parlour-fire, comparing his past with
what must, in all probability, be his future style of living,
and the contrast was almost too much for his philosophy.
Suddenly the voice of Mrs. Moynehan, raised high in ob-
jurgation in the kitchen, attracted his attention. Half
opening the parlour door, he paused to ascertain the cause
of sounds " not unfamiliar to his ear".

"Out of my house—pack—out of my house this
instant", exclaimed the lady, in a voice scarce a note of
which was lower than C above the fifth over line. " It

was you, and the like of you, that brought ruin to our
door,—pack out!"

A shrill and querulous murmur was heard in answer.
" The storm !" continued Mrs. Moynehan ; " it is no
matter for the storm.   As well as you found your way
here, find your way back, for here you shall not stay an
hour.   Do you hear me talking to you?   Quit my house
this instant.   Aye—cough, cough—I dare say you know
how to do more than that when it serves your turn.
Out—pack at once !"

At this instant Mr. Moynehan entered the kitchen,
where he beheld a sight that filled him with indignation against the cruelty of his helpmate.   An old man,
shaking with palsy, and so worn down by age and its infirmities that it seemed as if his years could scarcely
number less than a century, was standing on the well-
flagged kitchen floor, and gazing on the stout and portly
Mrs. M. with a deprecating attitude.   It would be difficult to conceive a more complete picture of misery than
the old man presented.   A long staff, half again as high
as its possessor, and held in both hands, seemed all that
enabled him to keep his feet; his knees, his hands, his
head, his whole frame shook violently with his disease, so
that, had his features been less strongly marked, it would
be difficult to gather their expression in the continual and
rapid motion.   His dress was ragged in the extreme, and
so patched that it seemed as if he never had been the
master of another suit.   In addition to this, he had been
already drenched in rain from head to foot, and his long
white hair and the hanging fritters of his garment, still
dripped as if he were about to dissolve away upon the
floor, while his face, which looked as if the loose skin had
been drawn over without being attached to the fleshless
bones, was glistening with rain, and haggard with fear, at
the prospect of being again exposed to the horrors of the
storm.   Moynehan could not help thinking, however, as he

looked on the old man, that his terror seemed excessive for the occasion, and that his manner resembled that of one who feared some danger of a still more appalling kind than any which the storm could bring.

"Will you—turn out—the—poor old man in—the storm an' all?" he gasped forth word after word at long intervals, and with gestures of the most agonizing terror. "Give me a night's—lodg—in' an' I'll pray for—you for—ever an'—ever. Don't send me out to the robb—— storm, I mane".

"To the robbers? what robbers? What robbers do you expect to meet in ——? and if it was full of them, what have you to lose by robbers? eh?"

"Did I—say—robbers, a-gra?" said the old man—"don't mind me—I'm an ould fool that hasn't any sense. Sure enough, what robbing could they have upon me; a poor ould beggar that has nothin' only what rags is coverin' my ould bones—nothin' in life—nothin'—Ayeh—robbers—I don't know what I'm sayin' with the dint o' fear; but won't you, like a good Christian, gi' me a night's lodgin'—anywhere—upon these bare flags—I'm aisy, so as the robb——so as I'd have the roof betune me an'—an' the clouds to-night,—an' may the Heavens be your 'bed hereafter".

"She will—she will—come in and sit by the fire", exclaimed Moynehan, interposing just as his lady had opened her lips to give vent to a fresh volley of reproaches. "Get supper ready for that poor man", he added, to a servant—"and you, my dear, will not even affliction itself teach you to pity the afflicted? you don't know how long we may have a house ourselves".

"I know how long we're to have this house", answered Mrs. Moynehan, in a low growling tone, like that of an over zealous watch-dog, which has received a reprimand from its master for offering a too obstinate resistance to the entrance of a peaceable stranger.

"You don't know that neither", said Moynehan, "and no matter if it should be ours for no longer than an hour, I am determined to make a free use of it while it belongs to me. Walk in, good fellow".

The poor man, clapping his hands together, and muttering blessings, staggered forward to the fire-place, still casting a timid eye askance at the lady, as if he could have answered in the language of poor Buff—

"I dare not, sir,
For fear of your cur".

Mr. Moynehan having seen the beggar comfortably established by the fire-side, returned to the parlour. Here he began to meditate upon the difference between his own condition and that of the poor mendicant, and found so much that was preferable in the former that he began to recover his spirits.

"At the worst, my dear", said he, addressing Mrs. Moynehan, "we are not so badly off as that poor fellow. We will still have many friends, and we will not, in all probability, be without a house of some kind or another, and at all events we have each of us a decent suit of clothes, which is more than can be said for him. So that 'tis a great comfort to think our case is not so bad but that it might be worse".

Before Mrs. Moynehan could reply, the parlour-door was opened, and a face, distinguished by a gaping mouth and a pair of staring eyes, appeared at the aperture. It was that of Rick or Rickhard Lillis, the faithful groom and valet (not to mention fifty other offices which he filled with equal fidelity and skill) of Mr. Moynehan. He remained for a time in the same position, gaping and gazing as if, like a ghost, he could not speak until some living being had addressed him.

"Well, Rick, what ails you now?"

"The poor man, sir!"

"What of him?"

" He wants the priest, sir; I'm in dhread he's dyin'".

" Phoo, nonsense!" exclaimed Mr. Moynehan, snatching a light and hurrying from the room. Strange as it seemed, he found his servant's story true. The old beggar was lying in the kitchen, on the straw pallet which had been prepared for him, and gasping, as it appeared, almost in the agonies of death. By this the storm had in some degree abated, and Moynehan ordered Rick Lillis to tie a collar on the head of the working mare, and ride off at once for the clergyman and the neighbouring doctor. When both those functionaries had left the house (which was not for a few hours) he paid another visit to his miserable guest. The old man was lying on his back in a feeble condition, and still muttering some incoherent sentences about " robbers " and " down the glen of B———" and of " the storm ", and " his own cabin in the west ". On hearing Mr. Moynehan's voice, he looked fixedly upon him, and seemed making an effort to collect his scattered reason.

" You will have no raison, sir ", he said, " to repent your charity to me. The docthor tells me I can't live; so I must only see and make use o' the time that's left me.

" I was born westwards, near Dingle. My father thought to make a scholar of me, but from a child I never could take to the book. Neither birch nor masther could ever get any good o' me. No one could equal me for michin from school, and while I was there, I'd be at anything but the learnin'. So one day, afther a'most breakin' his heart to thry an' get good o' me, my father kem' out, an' he havin' a book in one hand and a spade in the other.

" ' Here, Tom', says he, ' take your choice between these ; if you choose the book, you may become a counsellor one time or other—if you take the spade, you'll die as you began '.

"I looked this way and that, and afther considherin' for a while, I took the spade. My father left me nothin' else, but I thought it enough, for I didu't know what it was to have more. I was light and happy; my conscience ga' me no throuble, an' I had no sort o' care upon my mind.

" Well, of a day, a burnin' day in June (I remember it well—it was the worst day to me that ever came out of the skies)—of a little St. John's eve, I was making a drain to clear a bog belongin' to a gentleman that used to gi' me work. I ought to think o' that day well, an' so I do, an' often did before. It was a fine bright day, but it darkened my mind for ever afther. The sun was shinin' all around, the birds were singin' in the little bushes, the cuckoo was cooin' at a distance in the wood, an' the young foals were gallopin' about upon the green fields like kittens at play. 'Twas a fine day to man an' beast, but 'twas a woful day to me. It was just then, as I was whistling an working in the thrench, I threw up somethin' upon the bank that sounded as it hit agin' a stone. I took it up au' looked at it. It was like a collar that would be round a person's neck, an' I was told afther-wards, that it was a kind o' collar the ould Irish knights or kings, or people o' that sort, used to wear as an ornament in former times. I scraped it a little, an' it was yellow inside; I took it to the docthor that lived in the same place, to see could he make anything of it. He dipped the top of a quill in a little bottle he had, an' touched it where I scraped it, au' afther lookin' at it again, he wiped it au' handed it back to me, an' tould me it was raal goold.

' Until that time the thoughts o' riches, nor money, nor anything o' the kind ever ga' me a day's unaisiness. I had my hire from one day to another, an' I had health, an' I cared for no more. But the minute he tould me it was raal goolJ, I felt as if my whole mind was changed within

me at once; I took home the goold, an' put it under **my**
head that night an' slep' upon it, an' in the mornin' I went
off to town, where I took it through all the gooldsmiths'
shops to see what they'd gi' me for it, and I sould it at last
for seven pounds, which was twelve times more money
than ever I had in my life before. From that day out, I
never knew an hour's pace o' mind; and for eighty-seven
years afther, that's to this present time, my whole end and
aim was to add as much as I could to the price of what I
found. I stinted my food, I stinted my clothin'; I never
laid out as much as one ha'penny in sport. I never yet
since that day, gave so much as one farthin' to a fellow
crathur—an' now I must part it all".

Here the unfortunate old man heaved a deep groan, and
his ghastly eyes rolled in their sockets with the agony.

"Bring witnesses if you have 'em", said he, in a feeble
tone, "so that the law can't come between my words and
their meaning afther I am gone".

Mr. Moynehan complied, and summoned Rick Lillis and
another servant to the mendicant's bedside.

"Ye are witnesses", said the old man, faintly, "that
out o' thanks to this gentleman for his charity to me, an'
having no kith nor kindred o' my own, an' bein' sure he'll
make a betther use o' what I have, than any body else I
know, I lave him my outside coat an' its contents, an' all I
have in the world besides".

The servants then retired, and the mendicant, taking a
small and rusty key from his bosom, where it was tied fast
with a piece of hempen twine, handed it to Moynehan, and
said:

"There's a small cabin without a stick o' furniture, on
the side of a hill by the ould bridge near Dingle. Any
body will tell you where Garret Casey, the miser, lives
when he's at home. There's a padlock on the doore, an'
this is the key of it. Whisper hether. When I'm gone,
go to that house, an' search in the corner near the cup-

board in the inner room, an' rise up a brick that's there, an' have what's undher it—but—but—not till I'm gone, you know", the old man added, with a sudden expression of alarm; "the mother never loved her child, nor the wife her husband, nor the glutton his food, nor the drunkard his glass, as I loved what's undher that stone; an' what good is it for me now? I fasted for it—I watched for it—I hungered and thirsted for it—and I bore the heat and the cold, an' thought nothing of any kind o' labour that could add the smallest trifle to it; an' now I must part it all. If I suffered as much for my sins, this would be a happy night to me. Many a mile I walked barefoot on many a flinty road, to add a little to it; an' all for you. If I loved the law o' God as well as I loved what's undher that brick, what a saint I'd be to night".

Soon after he began to rave in a distracted manner about robbers, and felt for his key, and missing it, burst, into feeble lamentations, and complained that he was un-done, and that his house was plundered. Before morning he expired, after recovering his reason sufficiently to request that his remains might be conveyed to his own parish. On examining his garments, they were found quilted with coins of every description, from gold to humble copper; guineas, dollars, shillings, pence, and halfpence, being stitched in indiscriminately between the lining and the cloth, to the amount of more than thirty pounds.

Mr. Moynehan complied with the last wishes of the dying man. He had the remains conveyed to the men-dicant's native parish, and having found the cabin, waited until night in order to examine it. He then went, accompanied by Rick Lillis, and bearing a dark lantern in his hand, to the miser's wretched dwelling. It was a hovel of the very vilest kind. A round stone near the chimney corner served for a seat. There was no ap-pearance of firing, no ashes on the hearth, nor even the

8*

least indication that any such luxury had brightened the
lonely spot for years before.   By the light of the lantern,
Moynehan searched the gloomy little inner room which
was partitioned off by a hurdle rudely smeared with clay.
He found the brick and raised it.   After clearing away a
quantity of loose earth, he found a bag of tanned calf-
skin, which, by its weight and bulk, he judged to be the
treasure sought.   It was nearly filled with gold, far more
at the first glance than would be sufficient to relieve the
legatee from all his difficulties.

When they had returned to the small inn at which
they slept, Moynehan charged his servant to say nothing
whatsoever when they should reach home of their good
fortune, judging of course that he might safely leave it to
his own discretion to keep silence while they were still in a
strange place.   Rick Lillis could not for a long time find
any form of expression in which to convey an idea of the
extraordinary thoughts that filled his mind since the completion of this adventure.   He remained sauntering from
corner to corner of the room in which his master sat
quietly musing by the fire-side, now looking down at his
feet, now directly up at the ceiling, now at every corner
above, and anon successively at every corner below, as
if he were looking out in all directions for suitable
expressions.

" Well, there's no use in talking, master, but this day
flogged Ireland.   See, for all, how 'tis no way foolish to
do a good turn to high or low.   Why then, I remember
of a time, my father tellin' me (rest his sowl!) of a thing
o' the kind that happened a first cousin of his own, one
Brien Sheehy, that lived estwards in the hills o' Knock-
aderry.   He was a very stupid man, sir, with submission
to you, an' hadn't as much sense as would carry him from
this to the bedpost ; but he had a wife that was just as
'cute as he was foolish, an' many's the time he'd be lost
only for her.   Well, 'tis innocent people, they say, mostly

gets the luck. Of a day Brien found a handful o' money in a field, where he was diggin', an' nobody lookin' at him the same time, so he went an' hid it in a ditch, makin' a hole for it with his spade, until he'd come an' take it away when it would be his convenience. Well, sir, he went home and tould his wife what he found. 'You done some good at last', says she; 'where's the money?' 'Oh, I have it a-hide', says he, 'in the field where I got it'. 'Well an' good', says the wife; 'I hope you have a mark upon it, the way you'll find it again; an' not to be like Pat Piercy, the cobbler, that hid his tools so well that he never could find 'em afther'. 'Oh, I'll find it asy enough', says Brien; 'for I took a fine big mark for it', says he, 'a gray horse that was feedin' a-near the place when I put it a-hide'. Well, the wife gev one screech that you'd hear a mile off. 'Oh, murther! you born *omodhaun*', says she; 'sure the horse was no mark for you to take. Sure he'll lave that to go elsewhere', says she, 'an then what'll become o' your mark? 'Twas an evil day', says she, I ever had anything to say to you; an' you'll bring us to beggary at last'. Well, poor Brien stood as if you shot him; an' then he darted out the doores, an' run for the bare life to the field where he left the money. An' sure enough the horse was clane at a conthrairy side o' the field. Poor Brien clapped his hands to his head, and was fit to be tied at the thoughts of it; but it was no use for him. He sarched the whole field; but he might just as well be lookin' for lobsters in the same place.

"Well, sir, as he was walkin' a few weeks afther on the high road, comin' from market, he met an ould beggar-man that axed him for an alms. 'Don't be talkin' to me, man', says Brien. 'I lost more money a month ago, than I'll ever have in my life again; but here's one penny for you any way'. 'Where did you lose it?' says the poor man. 'I lost it in such a field, where I had it a-hide in a ditch', says he. 'Well', says the beggar, 'one good turn

desarves another. If you'll step acrass the field, to Paul
Rahilly's, you'll hear somethin' of it', says he :   *I turned
in the *boreen*, 'while ago, au' I heard them talkin' of a
power o' money the childher found in a ditch, as they were
playin''.   Well, sir, sure enough, he went acrass to
Rahilly's, an', I declare, he got the money again.   The
Rahilly's were very honest people; an' the first token he
gev 'em o' the money bein' his, I'll engage they handed
it over to him.   So that even a poor beggar might have it
in his——.   Sonuhar to me", added Rick, as a loud,
sound, resembling the noise of a penny trumpet, cut short
the moral of his tale.   "Sonuhar* to me, but he's fast
asleep the whole time, an' I, like a fool, tellin' my story
to the four walls.   Well, an' some walls have ears, they
say, an' why shouldn't I ?   The masther is a made man,
any way, that's plain enough".

CHAPTER III.

It will be recollected that we do not relate the above as a
fact of which we have historical knowledge; but as one of
the explanations rumour gave of the way in which Mr.
Moynehan had obtained his sudden wealth.   His secret
was kept, and the day of sale arrived.   An auctioneer
from Limerick attended to put up the household furniture
and other articles to the highest bidder.   Many, however,
said it was folly to talk, that there would be no bidders
at all, the Moynehans were so hospitable, and so well
liked throughout the country.   Though the morning was
rainy, it did not prevent great crowds from attending,
and to the great astonishment of the whole world,
biddings were just as smart as if Mr. Moynehan
were a perfect stranger.   There was one circumstance,

* A good wife, or husband.

however, which occasioned universal amazement in the crowd.

Mr. Moynehan had taken his seat next the auctioneer, his hands resting on his walking cane, and his eyes fixed upon the various bidders, as if to be satisfied by ocular demonstration of the identity of the individuals who were now pouncing like hawks upon the spoils of the mansion, which had been for near a score of years as free to their use as to his own. The auction was about to commence, when in strutted Rick Lillis, with the air of a nobleman, and took his place amongst the aristocratic purchasers.

" Give me a chair, here!" he cried aloud, in a voice like thunder.

Three or four servants flew to execute his orders, and he placed himself in the seat with an air of surly dignity, as if he wished to see who would presume to meddle with him. The gentlemen and ladies around him began to whisper, and gather their brows, and seemed not altogether to like it, but Rick maintained his place unmoved.

" Gi' me a bottle o' wine !" he called aloud, in the same tone —" an' a glass for dhrinkin', an' a crust o' bread".

Again half a dozen attendants flew to execute his wishes with the same alacrity as before.

" That'll do", said Rick; " now, Misther Auctioneer, you can commence business : I'm quite ready".

The auctioneer bowed low with mock gravity, and proceeded to put up the articles of furniture in succession. Nothing could be more painful to Mr. Moynehan's friends than to bid at all; but *as the articles were going*, each thought he might as well have them as another. What was their astonishment, however, when Rick Lillis bid for every lot just as it was about to be knocked down to another ! Lot after lot, there was nothing too high nor too low for him; and he paid for every article in sterling gold upon the instant. Every article, without exception,

not a stick of furniture, nor of anything else, was carried
out by a stranger. The bidders now began to turn the
tables upon Rick, and many said that he was an ungrateful fellow, after having been able to save so much
money through the liberality of his master, to make so
thankless an use of it at the close. However, amid all
this generous zeal for the ruined Moynehan, none of the
jovial companions and old friends seemed to think of
asking him to his house, but, one after another, they
dropped away, and left him to confer alone with his
calamity.

Mr. Moynehan made no effort to retain his farms, but
settled honourably with his landlord. He then made the
purchase long since spoken of, and began to build the
house, the ruins of which have been described at the commencement of our narrative. It would be a vain attempt
to paint the consternation which was excited throughout
the country side by the news that Moynehan had purchased an estate, nor the celerity with which he had all
his friends about him once again, as officious and as
cordial as ever. The mystery of Rick Lillis's extraordinary wealth became clear when they found the
furniture of the old house appropriated to its accustomed
uses in the new.

Mr. Moynehan, however, did not reproach his old
neighbours with their ingratitude.

"How would I be the gainer, my dear", he would say
to his indignant helpmate, on perceiving her anger rise at
the approach of any of those worthy adherents, "how
would I be the gainer by declaring war against all my
neighbours, because they are not just the kind of people
I would have them?— If I were to wait for friends until
I should find them without fault, I might live to the age
of Methusalem without finding as much as would make a
hand at whist, and Dumby one of the party too. Sure
'tis the very fault I have to find with myself, that I'm not

just as I'd like to be. And, poor people! if they have
acted wrong, they will suffer enough for it hereafter,
without my endeavouring to make them uncomfortable at
present".

Accordingly, there was no one who was not invited to
the Housewarming. Now, if any uninitiated reader should
desire to kno v what an Irish Housewarming was in the
days of Mr. Moynehan, he must be content with our brief
description, seeing that no such entertainment is to be
found amongst the extravagancies of the present day.
The period was a century too late for the muse of DERRICK,
and a century too early for the bard of Ballyporeen, or we
would have considered it unnecessary to say more than
that a Housewarming had been given.

" Rick !" Mr. Moynehan exclaimed from the bed-room,
where he was occupied in an operation from which half the
human race are happily exempt—we mean that of
shaving—" Rick!" exclaimed Mr. Moynehan.

" Goin', masther !" The reader must understand that
Rick Lillis generally said *going*, when he meant *coming*.
"Goin', masther !" answered Rick, and his gaping mouth
and staring eyes were presently visible at the chamber
door.

" Rick, do you know that I am to give a Housewarming
on Thursday next?"

" Oyeh, iss, sir—long life to you. The missez tould us
ov it ".

" Well, Rick, you know we shall want music, so I leave
that part of the affair to your management".

" Ullilu! me, sir !" exclaimed Rick, in modest alarm.
" Sorrow tune did I ever play in my life upon anything,
exceptin' it was a little taste upon the jew's-harp, an' I'm
sure it is aisily known that wouldn't go far among a whole
housefull".

" You mistake me, Rick ; I have as little inclination to
listen to your music as you can have to furnish it. But I

mean that you shall find musicians; so mind what I tell
you: if I find that there is a man within three baronies
round us, that ever drew horsehair across catgut, or ever
danced the chanter of a bagpipe on his knee, or ever
whistled God save the King upon a pipolo, who shall not
be at the Housewarming on Thursday next—I'll—no I
can't hang you—ah, joy be with the times when I could—
before we ever had a law to interfere with us—but I'll be
tempted to go as near it as I can".

" Long life to your honour, sure I'll do my best".

" Take no excuse, as you value your head".

" Excuse!" exclaimed Rick, with a half shout of surprise; " I'll go bail, I'll make 'em come jumpin', an' glad
to be axed—I'll take my hazel stick in my hand, an' I'd
like to see the man among 'em that would daar say ' no'
to me, when I give the commands".

He left the room, and so punctually did he fulfil his
commission, that on the Thursday following a troop of
fiddlers, fifers, pipers, and other musicians, of all ages, and
of both sexes, had assembled at the new edifice, sufficient
of themselves to have constituted a numerous company.
But they were soon lost in the multitudes that followed.
Cars, horses, truckles (furnished with a bed-tick, to supply
the lack of springs and cushion), every species of vehicle,
and every beast of burden that the land afforded, were put
in requisition by the numerous guests who came with unblushing countenances to claim a share of Moynehan's
returning hospitality. Nor did he treat them to Timon's
feast of " smoke and lukewarm water". Moynehan never
expected much gratitude from his friends, so he was not
disappointed when he did not receive it. It was in
compliance with the promptings of his own heart, and not
in the wild-goose-chase of human gratitude, that he was
either hospitable or generous; so he felt no indignation at
being denied what he had never sought. Indeed, it is
most probable that if he had heard the story of Timon of

Athens, he would have thought him a selfish fellow, who
precisely met with his desert for affecting the name of
generosity, when in reality he gave nothing for which he
did not both expect and demand a return; and an exquisite temper he manifested, too, when he made that wonderful discovery, that it is not quite so easy to borrow as it is
to lend in this world. No: "uncover, dogs, and lap", was
not the welcome Moynehan gave his guests, but such a
banquet that it was "given up to it", such a "giving
out" was never known before in that side of the country,
any way. And he had the satisfaction, too, of finding
that it was all a mistake about the ingratitude of his
neighbours; for there was scarcely an individual amongst
them that did not before morning take an opportunity of
assuring their host, that all he had in the world was at
his service, and his life, if he wanted it, into the bargain;
a fact which shows how erroneous was the evil opinion
entertained of them by Mrs. Moynehan, and how cautious
we ought to be of judging by appearances.

And so the house was built and warmed.

CHAPTER IV.

DURING the life-time, or, as the peasantry on his estate
termed it, the "reign" of Mr. Moynehan, the affairs of
Tipsy Hall, as he named his new residence, "for raisons",
were managed with tolerable moderation. We have material enough to dwell at ample length on the subsequent
history of the edifice, before it came into the hands of the
individual whose earthly destinies were most intimately
interwoven with the subject of our tale. We might describe the feasting, the drinking, and, unhappily for the
credit of a portion of our ancestry, the duelling, the cock-
fighting, the horse-racing, the dissipation of every kind of
which it was once the scene; and some readers might find

so faithful a detail of manners, now, happily, almost forgotten, not wholly destitute of interest. We might dwell upon the unheard-of magnificence displayed at the funeral of the first Moynehau, who chose to be interred at his birth-place, which was "far up in the north", in the county of Donegal. We might follow the sable vehicle for eighteen days along the wild and varied road, attended as it was the whole way by near one thousand persons. We might describe the storm of rain that, for three long days, pouring down incessantly upon the mournful train, added unexpected dreariness and discomfort to a task already full of gloom and woe; we might tell (for the sources from which we draw our information faithfully record the number) how many, dying on the wayside of cold and of fatigue, how many, in a sudden feud arising between two hostile factions, who were included in the train, had given this testimony of their fidelity and zeal to the manes of their benefactor. For a whole day, it was said, the coffin halted in its progress, until this controversy was decided, and then the whole proceeded in the same order as before. We might dilate yet further on the extravagancies of the more unbridled spirits who succeeded the founder of the mansion in his possessions, and on the wilder orgies with which they made its walls reëcho through many a winter night. But we write to illustrate, not to satirise, human nature; and it is possible that if we were to transcribe all that is preserved amongst the neighbouring peasantry of the history of the ruin, the reader might hardly thank us for our preciseness. Add to this, that we must confess, at the risk of losing no matter how many of our readers, the subject has for us but little attraction. Boisterous, quarrelsome manners, habitual excesses, the manners, in a word, of the drinking table, have for us, whether in life or on paper, but little charm, even when dashed with gaiety and wit, and made interesting by personal daring and adventure. Our ancestors had their follies—we have

ours; and it is rather hard that we should laugh at their
manners, when they have not the opportunity of returning
the compliment.

We shall, therefore, suffer this portion of our history to
be gathered from the lips of no less a personage than Rick
Lillis himself, as, an old and crutch-borne man, he stood
amongst the ruins of the building on a summer day, de-
tailing with melancholy interest, to an inquisitive tourist,
the fortunes of the family he had survived.

" There was somethin' wrong about the house, sir, ever
from the very big'nin'. The dhrollest* *nizes* ever you
seen, used to be hard about the place at night, every day,
from the time the first stone was laid, until the roof an'
all came down.   In the dead o' the night time the people
used to be called out o' their sleep by sthrange voices, and
they never could find out who it was that called 'em.   It
bate all ever you hear.   For a time after the ould masther's death (rest his sowl!) there was no standin' the
place at all, with the stories they all had, that he used to
be seen risin'—himself an' the ould *bucogh*, that it was
known afther left him all the money.   Sometimes they
used to be seen walkin' together, lock-arms, in the moon-
shine; more times, they say, when the family would be
sittin' by the fireside, talkin', an' no light in the place only
the blaze o' the fire, they'd hear the doors open, an' they'd
look back this way over their shoulders, an' there they'd
see old Moynehan with his grave-clothes about him,
lookin' in upon 'em.   But there's one thing I was, as I
may say, present at myself, an' 'tis as thrue as you're
standin' there.

" You don't know, may be, the *dizaze* the ould masther
died of?   Asy, an' I'll tell you.   It was what they call a
stomach-wolf.   He was out of a day in harvest with the
men, an' bein' rather hot, an' the fresh hay convanient,
he sat down upon a cock of it, an' fell asleep.   Well, he

* Strangest.

knew nothin' of it, but it is then the rogue of a wolf took
an advantage of him to get into his mouth, so 'cute, an'
down his throath, an' into the stomach snug an' warm, an'
the masther nivir knowin' a word about it. When he woke
by an' by, an' went home to dinner, he felt so hungry that
you'd think he'd ate the world, an' dhrink the ocean dhry.
His dinner was no more to him than a boiled piatee. He
ate an' he ate, an' he dhrank an' he dhrank, an' he was
just as hungry an' as thirsty when he got up as he was
when he sat down. So it went on from day to day, an'
instead of being betther, 'tis worse and worse he was
gettin' ever an' always.

"One neighbour come in, an' another, an' not one of
'em could give the laste account of what aileded him. An'
what was worst of all was, that in place o' getting fat
with all he ate, 'tis laner an' laner he was gettin' every
day, till he was a complete nottomy. Not a ha'porth he
ett or dhrank done him any good.

"Still nobody could tell from Adam what was the
matther with him. The docthor that was in the place,
although bein' a very knowin' man, he knew nothin' whatever of this ailment, never meetin' a case o' the kind before.
One neighbour recommended one thing, and another another, but the masther didn't give in to any of 'em some
way, an' when they'd bring him any great physic, in place
o' takin' it, he'd give it to the missiz to keep for him.
Well, one day he came in, lookin' so pale and wake, that
he was ready to dhrop. 'There's no use in talkin', my
dear', says he to the missiz, 'but there's some bad work
goin' on inside in me'. 'Can't you take some of the mud-
dicines, my love?' says she. 'Rech 'em hether', says he,
'I believe I must do something'. So she rech'd 'em all
down. 'Why, then, the Heavens direct me now', says
the missiz, 'which o' these I'm to give you', says she,
lookin' at the hape. 'I'll tell you what', says the masther, 'if one o' them is good, the whole o' them must be

betther.   Make them get a saucepan', says he, 'an' a
dhrop o' wather'.   So she did.   The saucepan was brought,
and the masther haved 'em all into it headforcmost, bottles,
an' pills, an' powders, in as they wor, an' boiled 'em all
together with the dhrop o' wather.   When it was boiled
he dhrank it, an' little was wanten but it was the last
dhrop he ever dhrauk.   He *lost his walk** the same
day, an' before night it was all the same thing as over
with him.

"Well, nothin' would satisfy the missiz, but some docthor should see him, to keep people's tongues quiet.
While she was thinkin' who she'd send for, an ould *bucogh*
come to the doore axin' charity, an' he up an' tould her
where she'd get a rale docthor.   'There's a docthor', says
he, ' livin' upon the borders of Kerry, an' if there's any
man', says he, ' that's able to raise the dead to life, 'tis
he'.   So the missiz called Tim Dalton, or Tim Tcll-truth,
as we used all to call him, by raison he never would tell a
word o' thruth by his own good will, an' sent him off on
horseback for this great docthor.   I can only give you
Tim's word for what took place, until he came back next
day following.   He rode for a good part of a day, until he
come into the lonesomest mountain counthry he ever seen
in his life.   He made inquiries, and they showed him
where the docthor lived, in a loncsome house down
in a little glen, an' the smoke comin' out o' the chimney.
'Well', says Tim to me, an' he tellin' me the story, ' I
med for the house, an' if I did, there I seen all the place
sthrown all round with dead men's bones, an' the pathway
up to the hall-doore was paved with little white things
that looked just like knuckle-bones.   Well become me',
says Tim, ' I med for the hall doore, an' gev a great rap,
and axed for the docthor.   The sarvant girl showed me
into the kitchen, where there was a great pot bilin' on the
fire.   Thinks I to myself, I wondher what in the world is

_____
* The use of his limbs.

In the pot.   So while I was wondherin', the dochor come
ont an' axed me my business, which I up an' toult him.
" Well", says he, " stay asy a minute, an' I'll be with you ;
but for your life", says he, " take care you don't look after
me".   ' I'll engage', says Tim, ' I wasn't said by him, but
the instant he left the kitchen, I took an' opened the doore,
an' gave a dawny peep into the room that was inside it'.
Well, what Tim seen in that room, he never was very
ready to tell, only from that day out, he wouldn't take a
taste of muddicine if he was dyin'.   He used to say he seen
keelers all round the room, an' dead people hangin' up,
an' their blood dhroppin' into the keelers, to make muddi-
cines.   I'm sure, as for myself, I only hould it to be one
of Tim's stories.   But he brought the docthor away with
him, any way.

    " When the docthor come to the ould masther's room,
an' felt his pulse, he looked very sarious.   He began
makin' a cut jest anear the heart with his insthruments, an'
I declare you could hear the wolf barkin' inside, quite
plain, at every cut he made.   So he brought out the wolf,
an' showed it to us all—a little dawny thing not the length
o' my finger, but the tail going like a switch, an' the eyes
like little sparks of fire.   But howsomever it was, the
poor masther didn't get much good of it, an' 'twasn't long
afther that we had to lay him with his people.

    " Be coorse, the masther's son, Misther Henry, como
after him—an' a sore day it was for the estate, the day
it come into his hands.   If the ould masther was over
foolish in spendin', he was twice more so.   Cocks, an'
horses, an' hounds, an' every other ha'p'orth that the first
gentleman in the land could fancy, he had about him from
year to year.   But it wasn't that that broke him after all,
only I'll tell you.

    " There was a poor Dumby the ould masther kep, that
used to dhraw out anything in the whole world upon a
slate ; he was still in the house when the new masther

was goin' on this way. Well, of a day when Misther
Thomas was gettin' ready for the Curragh, sure the very
day before the jockey was to take her off, the mare was
found dead in the stable! The masther was fit to be tied
—so he sent off privately for Shaun Dooley, a knowledge-
able man that lived down near the *say*-side, that had a
great report for bein' thick with the good people. 'Tis
myself went for him, an' carried a led horse ready saddled
to bring him up to Tipsy Hall, not to spake of a goold
guinea I had for him at the first word. I waited till
night-fall, because the masther would be very unfond any
body should know he'd send for a fairy docthor.

"I brought Shaun Dooley up to the masther, and he
seemed for a while greatly puzzled to know what could
be the cause of it. ' Did you ever shoot a weazel?' says
Shaun Dooley. ' Not to my knowledge', says the masther. ' Or a magpie?' ' Not as I remember, indeed'.
' Do you be whistlin' when you do be out at night at all?'
' That can't be', says the masther, ' for I never turned a
tune'. ' Well, I don't know in the world what to think
of it', says Shaun. So while he was thinkin', there was
a great flutterin' outside. ' What's that noise?' says Shaun
Dooley. ' I suppose it's the pigeons that's comin' home',
says the masther. ' Pigeons!' cries Shaun, ' do you keep
pigeons about the house? It's plain to me now', says
he, ' what rason your mare died, an' I wouldn't wondher',
says he, ' if all belongin' to you was gone to rack and ruin'.
' What rason?' says the masther. ' I'll not tell you what
rason', says Shaun, ' but if you take my advice, you'll
not have one of 'em about the place'.

"He went, an' next mornin' airly the masther went
about shootin all the pigeons. There was one of em that
the Dumby had tamed, an' when he seen 'em all shootin',
he took an' hid it from the masther, poor crathur, it was so
quiet an' so fond of him. Well, sure enough, in less than
two mouths afther the ould missiz died, an' the masther

found out that the Dumby kept the pigeon. I never seen one
so wild. He turned the Dumby out o' doors (although
the crathur cried a gallon full, an' went on his knees to
ax pardon), an' twisted the head off o' the pigeon. But
it was no good for him. From that day out it seemed as
if the luck went out o' the doors with the Dumby. And
when the next Mr. Moynehan came into the property, he
found himself much in the situation of more jentlemen in
the country then an' now, that have 'pon my honour, and
nothing to back it ".

CHAPTER V.

But since the accession of this third Moynehan to the
proprietorship of Tipsy Hall brings us into the most important portion of our tale, we shall take the story out of
the hands of Rick Lillis, and resume our own task as
historians of the ruined building.

So indeed it was. In the course of less than half a
century, the fair estate which Mr. Moynehan was so
anxious should be long preserved in the hands of his
posterity, had melted away to a small remnant, which was
wholly inadequate to the maintenance of the family in the
style of splendid hospitality which they had always upheld.
What added to this embarrassment was that Mr. Thomas
Moynehan never could be prevailed upon to augment his
diminishing income by seeking some situation suitable to
his rank, which he might easily have procured amongst
his influential friends. Antiquarians tell us that among
the ancient Irish, all occupations of a commercial nature
were held in the highest scorn, and the term, *ceanuighe*,
or merchant, was considered wholly incompatible with
that of a gentleman. Until a very late period a strong
tincture of the same spirit appears to have influenced tho

conduct of our Irish gentry. Mr. Moynehan seemed to
think that his family would be disgraced if he were actually
to earn the bread which he had hitherto received as his
patrimonial right. A circumstance which took place while
affairs were in this condition is said to have had a strong
effect in withdrawing him from society, and indeed in
hastening his death.

The public road, which passed close by Mr. Moynehan's
gate, was the same by which the judges of assize were
accustomed to travel on their way to the western towns.
It happened one evening (so goes the tale) that one of
those personages who was about to open a commission in
Tralee, was overtaken by nightfall in the neighbourhood
of Tipsy Hall. As there was no inn within the distance
of several miles, and the judge and Mr. Moynehan were
well acquainted, the former determined to pass the night
at the house of his friend, and resume his journey on the
following morning. Accordingly, he directed his coach-
man to drive through the avenue gate, and he was received with a ready welcome at the open door.

Mr. Thomas Moynehan, notwithstanding those weaknesses which we have seen, and a certain violence of
temper, which was at times uncontrollable, was yet in
many things a man of a reflective and solemn turn of mind.
Much of his attention had been given occasionally to the
nature of human law and the extent of its power over
human life and liberty. It was his opinion that in most
governments too little regard was shown to human life;
and there was one point in particular which moved his
horror. This was the ease with which circumstantial
evidence was received in British courts of justice on
questions of a capital nature. Such convictions, taking
into account the many occasions on which the innocence
of the culprit had subsequently been manifested in time
to redeem his reputation, but not to save his life, appeared
to him in the light of so many formal and deliberate murders

9

On the present occasion, as the judge and he were sitting quietly together by the fire-side after dinner, he could not resist the opportunity of introducing his favourite topic. He found, as he had expected, his learned guest entirely of the other way of thinking. The judge said that it was true, circumstantial evidence might sometimes be merely specious, and undoubtedly in such cases it was wrong to convict; but that there were circumstances which were fully as demonstrative of the guilt or innocence of the accused as the most direct ocular testimony could be.

"For", said he, "Gentlemen of the Ju—Mr. Moynehan, I should say—we must remember that the degree of certainty is not altered by the nature of the evidence. Certainty is certainty still, by whatever means it is obtained. I am certain that two and two are the equation of four, and I am certain that this glass, if I drop it, will fall on the floor, and I am certain that King Charles the First lost his head. My certainty with regard to the three positions is the same, yet the means by which I arrive at it are different; for the last fact I have only on hearsay, whereas the others are physical and metaphysical truths. So I grant you circumstantial evidence can only give us moral certainty; yet moral certainty, when it is certainty at all, is fully equal to any other whatsoever. When people say they are *only* morally certain of anything, they use a vulgar expression, which means that they are not certain at all; for if they were morally certain, they would be perfectly so".

So saying, he hemmed, and looked as if he expected there should be no reply. Accordingly Mr. Moynehan, though he could not see what the lecture upon the nature of certainty had to do with his own assertion that circumstantial evidence could never produce it in a conscientious mind, did not conceive it prudent to urge the matter further, contenting himself with saying that perhaps the time might yet arrive when he would have an opportunity of furnishing his lordship with a case in point.

On the following day the judge continued his route, and Mr. Moynehan resumed his customary occupations. He still continued to reflect much upon the injustice of depriving a fellow-creature of life where there was even a possibility of his innocence. Even if there were cases, as he doubted not there might be some, in which circumstantial evidence might amount to certainty, he was yet convinced that no such strength of testimony was required in the great number of instances in which convictions had taken place. The more he thought upon it, the more he became assured of the correctness of his own views, and he only longed for an opportunity of converting the judge to his opinion.

In a few mornings afterwards he was preparing to take breakfast at an early hour, when Rick Lillis entered the parlour, to say, with a countenance aghast with horror, that some countrymen without had taken a murderer, and wanted that Mr. Moynehan (who was a justice of the peace) should commit him to the county gaol. Mr. Moynehan seemed deeply struck at the intelligence. It seemed as if he even felt a nearer interest in the case owing to his recent controversy with the judge.

"Let them wait outside", said he, "until I have done breakfast, and I will hear them".

In a short time after he ordered the men to be summoned into the office, where he usually took his examinations. Three countrymen entered, conducting a fourth, who by his pale and terrified countenance, his disordered appearance, and some reddish stains upon his garments, was evidently the person accused. One of the others held a pitchfork, the handle of which was dabbled with blood.

Mr. Moynehan, who knew the man perfectly well as one his own labourers, and one of the most peaceable cha-

racters in the conntry, seemed much concerned at beholding him in such a situation, but determined to give
the fullest hearing to all the parties.

"Plase your worship", said the eldest of the three
accusers, "this *boy* an' my son Ned were at work together yestherday, an' they *had some words* comin home,
which nobody then took much notice of. But this
morning it so happened that I went to work in your
honour's piatec garden agreeable to ordhers. It was early,
an' I expected to be first upon the ground, which I knew to
be plaisin' to your honour, but I was overtaken on the road
by these two neighbours; so the three of us went on together
with our spades in our hands. When we come into the field
it was just the dusk o' dawn. 'Stop', says this man here
to me, 'don't you hear groaning?' 'I hard something',
says I; 'but I made nothing of it, thinkin' it was the
wind'. ' 'Tis not the wind', says he, 'but some one
that got a bad hurt, an' there they are!' Sure enongh, at
that minute we seen this boy here thrying to make off
with a pitch-fork—this pitch-fork here—in his hand, but
we pinned him. Little I knew what use he was afther
puttin' it to. I wish I had no more to tell—it's dear I
airned your worship's piatees. We found my poor boy
a dead corpse in the furrow, an' there's the villian
that done it".

The two other witnesses being examined, corroborated
in all its circumstances the evidence given by the first.
Having patiently heard all they had to say, and finding
that they had not detected the man in the very act, Mr.
Moynehau seemed desirous to dismiss the case. It was
true, he said, they had found the man on the spot, and
with the bloody weapon in his hand, and with his hands
on the dead body. This and his precipitate flight when
seen, and the disagreement of the previous evening, were
strong circumstances; yet they did not amount to actual

evidence of guilt, and he called on the prisoner for his explanation.

The unhappy man turned pale and red alternately, and trembled as if his doom had been already fixed. He acknowledged the dispute, and indeed all the circumstances deposed by his accusers, yet he attested Heaven that he was wholly guiltless.

"I went into the field", said he, "to my work, an' I found the corpse before me in the furrow, an' the pitchfork lyin a-near it, an' while I was feelin' him to see had he any life, an' examinin' the spade, these people come upon me. I run, becase I was afeerd they'd say 'twas I done it, an' I took the pitch-fork with me in my fright".

Mr. Moynehan, who seemed affected in the strongest manner by the poor fellow's anxiety, was so far from judging him guilty, that he peremptorily refused to issue a warrant of committal, and used all his influence to dissuade the friends of the deceased from proceeding further against the prisoner. To this, however, they would by no means listen. They conveyed the accused before another magistrate, who committed him to gaol without hesitation.

The day of trial came, and Mr. Moynehan happened to be one of the jury. The evidence was the same as before—the judge his old acquaintance. To the whole court, except Mr. Moynehan, the testimony seemed conclusive. He, however, would not listen to the thought of a conviction. The arguments of his eleven fellow-jurors were in vain—he would not subscribe to their verdict. The foreman made his report to the judge, who reproached Mr. Moynehan severely with his obstinacy. The latter, however, was not to be moved, and the issue was (as the rumour goes) that the jury were *kished*, and the prisoner set at liberty.

When the judge had returned to his lodgings, he could

not avoid reflecting on the extraordinary character of this man, who had thus, to gratify a favourite theory, let a murderer loose upon society, and set up his own solitary judgment against the unanimous conviction of a crowded court. So deeply did it prey upon his mind, that he sent for Mr. Moynehan, in order that they might exchange some quiet conversation on the subject. The latter readily attended on his summons.

"My lord", said Mr. Moynehan, with a serious air, on hearing the cause of the judge's message, "you may remember a conversation which we had some time since on the subject of circumstantial evidence?"

"Perfectly well", replied the judge.

"I told your lordship then", said Mr. Moynehan, "that the time might yet arrive when I should have an opportunity of making you a convert to my own opinion".

"That time, Mr. Moynehan, is certainly yet to come; for I never knew a case so clearly against you, as that which we have tried to-day. May I request to know your reasons for such extraordinary—perseverance—to give it no harsher name?"

"My reasons are at your lordship's service", answered Mr. Moynehan, "provided that I have your solemn word of honour not to divulge them during my own lifetime".

The judge, without hesitation, gave him the promise he desired.

"I admit, my lord", said Mr. Moynehan, "that this case had all the strength of circumstantial testimony which you considered necessary; but I could not in conscience convict the prisoner, for I AM MYSELF the slayer of the deceased".

The judge started back in horror.

"Yes", said he, "it happened on that morning that I was in the field before any of my workmen. The deceased was the first who made his appearance, and I rebuked him for his neglect. Being a man of hot temper, he

answered me with more than equal warmth, and I lost all
command of mine. I struck him—he returned the blow
—I held the pitch-fork in my hand, and with one blow
more I felled him to the earth. I fled in terror, and in
less than one hour after, the prisoner was brought before
me. Judge whether I had not reason to be constant in
my verdict of acquittal".

The judge kept his promise, but from that day forward
he was more cautious in receiving circumstantial evidence
on a capital charge.

On the death of Mr. Thomas Moynehan (a considerable
portion of whose history might, perhaps, in the reader's
opinion, have been omitted with advantage) the estate
and mansion of Tipsy Hall fell into the hands of Edmond
Moynehan, his nephew, and the last of the iace who
held dominion beneath its roof.

CHAPTER VL

MR. EDMOND MOYNEHAN, though succeeding tc a diminished income, had been in some respects more fortunate
than any of his predecessors. He had received an excellent
education, in the truest sense of the word, and up to the
period of his accession to the estate of Tipsy Hall, had
used it, in all appearance, to the best advantage. As far
as any one could be said to enjoy happiness in a world
where people find no situation so good that they do not long
for better, Mr. Edmond Moynehan was a happy man. He
had a wife, who, whether as a doctress, counsellor, or
housewife, was without her equal in the country side. At
the time when they were suddenly called to the inheritance of Tipsy Hall, they inhabited a small cottage near
the romantic town where the Knights of the Valley once
held feudal sway. Their scanty income was derived from

their agricultural pursuits; and industry, united with
economy, euabled them to maintain a more respectable
station in their neighbourhood than many who were far
superior in fortune. For it must be understood, that all
this while it was not wholly for want of knowing better
that so much dissipation prevailed among the Irish country
squires, and instances might occasionally be found, of
families who fulfilled in every respect the duties of their
station. Of this description were Mr. Edmond Moynehan
and his wife ; they were examples of piety and of sobriety
to their humble neighbours ; they were active benefactors
of the poor around them ; and in a country where the
wealthier gentry seldom made their appearance, it was
an incalculable advantage to the peasantry to have even
one family who could in some degree supply their place
as counsellors and protectors. Fortunately kept at a
distance from the coarse corruption that surrounded them,
by their own good sense, they were still more fortunate in
living at a distance from the more dangerous, because
more subtle and less perceptible, corruption that prevailed
then, as at all times, in towns and cities. They were
happy even in their ignorance how far the human mind
and heart can go astray when they have forsaken the path
of simple truth. It was true they saw vice around them,
but they never yet had seen it justified : they saw the duties
of religion neglected, but they did not know that the mind
can even be brought to vindicate such neglect, and give
it specious names. They maintained their plain and simple
course, at peace with themselves and Heaven, and in good
will with the whole world. Of politics (in the angry sense
of the word) or of controversy, they heard and thought
but little, and maintained a primitive simplicity as well in
their mode of thinking as of living. They fasted on all the
fast days, and they kept all the holidays holy. They never
troubled their heads about new points of doctrine, and thus
were left more leisure to practise what they already believed.

Perhaps it would be difficult for a person engulfed in the vortex of the world and all its cares, absorbed by the anxieties of commerce, the intrigues of love or of ambition, or consumed by the devouring thirst of fame or power, to imagine the happiness which the Moynehans up to this period had enjoyed in their tranquil river-side life. It was not slothful, for the Moynehans were stirring with the dawn, and till sunset occupied in some charitable or useful avocation; Mr. Moynehan in the fields with his workmen, or on the road to some neighbouring fair, his fair help-mate in the dairy, or superintending her flax-dressers in the open barn, or hearing her son Edmond read aloud while she knitted a stocking at the parlour window. Neither was it a solici-tons life, for their attachment to the world or its posses-sions was not so strong as to awaken anxiety; the solitude in which they lived kept reflection awake, and no artificial rapidity of profit, or intoxicating violence of pleasure, ever seduced them into forgetfulness of the real value of mortal hope or joy. Even their love for each other was, we fear, such as would by no means satisfy a real votary of romance. That poetical gentleman, who said he knew only two places in the universe—viz., where his mistress was, and where she was not—would have looked with scorn upon Mrs. Moynehan; for she knew a great many places besides that where her husband was; and yet it was not saying a little to assert that, after ten years of wedded life, there was no other which she liked so well.

If, amongst the many who occasionally shared the hos-pitality of Moynehan's cottage, some votary of fashion made his appearance, the life of these simple people must have appeared to him insipid, dull, and monotonous in the extreme. There was nothing in their tranquil pastoral enjoyments at all so highly seasoned as to satisfy a devotee of pleasure, and he would have attributed to the nature of the life they led the insipidity which was wholly owing to the defect in his own sense. But to the Moynehans,

whose relish for the pleasures of innocence had never been
dulled by any acquaintance with those of vice, it did not
appear that there was anything so tasteless or so burdensome
in their daily life. They found health in the morning air,
that blew freshly from the sunlit river, and relief from
weariness of mind in the occupations of their farm. The
undecorated exhortation of their parish clergyman on
a Sunday, had with them more weight than all the
eloquence and learning of a metropolitan pulpit upon the
ears of metropolitan hearers. It might be said of them
with truth, that they thought more with the heart than
with the head, and if they had not the learning, neither
had they the pride, of the philosopher.

From this humble, simple life it was that the Moynehans
were called to the inheritance of Tipsy Hall. The news
came upon them somewhat unexpectedly, and it might be
almost said without a welcome. The cottage in which
they now lived had been their residence since they were
united. It was the birth-place of their only son, and the
scene of their calm and prosperous industry during so many
happy years. The accession, however, to such a property
as that of Tipsy Hall was too important an addition to
their fortune to be neglected, and they prepared for a
removal. Mrs. Moynehan, in particular, had a strong
misgiving with respect to this migration, and felt as if
every knock of the carpenters, as they were taking the
furniture to pieces for the purpose of conveyance, sounded
the knell of their departing happiness. There was no
use, however, indulging, much less communicating, such
fancies.

The day appointed for their removal came, and a number
of weeping friends and neighbours assembled to bid farewell
to their long-established associates and companions. An
elderly lady, who had often filled the office of counsellor
and instructor to Mrs. Moynehan on critical occasions,
and who had not been sparing of her rhetoric upon the

present, gave so many hints with respect to a family of the name of Tobin, living within the distance of two miles of Tipsy Hall, that Mrs. Moynehan became quite alarmed.

"I do not want to make you uneasy, my dear, by what I say", concluded this sagacious friend, "but to make you cautious in time. I know how little relish Mr. Moynehan has for such society—indeed he's an angel of a man—where will you meet such another?—but men are men after all—the best men are frail, and the Tobins are enough to corrupt a monastery".

"Is it possible?" said Mrs. Moynehan, astonished; "I thought Mr. Tobin was a magistrate of the county. Does he not sit at the Quarter Sessions?"

"He does—and a pretty magistrate he is; but I don't choose to say any more at present. I have said enough to put you on your guard, and that was my only reason for speaking at all. The Tobins are a very good family, no doubt, and have excellent connections, but it is a wild house!"

Mrs. Moynehan thanked her friend for those suggestions, which she promised to bear in mind. Soon after they set out for Tipsy Hall, their mode of conveyance being suited rather to their past than to their present fortunes. It consisted of a truckle or low cart with a block of timber for an axle-tree. On this were laid a feather bed and quilt, on which Mrs. Moynehan and her son Edmond, a child about six years of age, took their seat, while Neddy Shaughnessy, "the boy" who acted as charioteer to the group, sat with his legs dangling from a corner. Behind rode Mr. Moynehan on horseback, musing much upon their sudden change of fortune. Even already his helpmate could imagine that she beheld a shade of solicitude darkening over his features, which, until this unhoped improvement had taken place in their circumstances, were as clear and unruffled as a noontide lake.

It was evening when they entered the small demesne of
Tipsy Hall, Mr. Moynehan still looking more serious than
he had ever done in his life before, and his soft-hearted
companion crying as if some terrible misfortune had
befallen them both. Her grief attracted the interest of
Rick Lillis, who at first entertained some involuntary
prejudice against his new master and mistress. In the
course of the evening, while he was busy in arranging
some furniture under her directions, she took an opportunity
of making some inquiries about the Tobins.

"A family o' the name of Tobin, ma'am, please your
honour?" echoed Lillis, when he had heard her question.
"There is indeed then, an' there's none has betther rason to
know it than the masther's family; an' if you plase, ma'am,
plase your honour, Mrs. Moynehan, since you axed me
the word, I'll tell you my mind o' them people, not out of
any ill-will to them, but the way you'd put the masther
upon his guard again 'em, in case they'd be borrowin'
money or inveiglin' him any way to his hurt. Them
Tobins, ma'am, arn't right people, with submission to you.
They'd borry money, an' they wouldn't pay it, an' if they
couldn't borry, there's rason for sayin that they'd go some
other way about gettin' it besides what would be proper.
You'd lend em a hundhert pounds, an' when you'd go to ax
for your money, afther, in place o' gettin' it or thanks,
instead of it may be 'tis to challenge you to fight 'em they
would — they're such *jewellers*, Lord save us! There isn't
such *jew'lyery* goin' on all over Ireland, ma'am, as
what they goes on with; a very black, terrible family,
ma'am".

In the course of the ensuing fortnight, nearly all the
families within three miles round, who had any pretensions
to gentility, had visited the new proprietors of Tipsy Hall.
The Moynehans had never before received so much attention, or had to digest so large a quantity of civil flattery.
The Tobins were almost the only family that might have

been expected, and yet did not make their appearance. Never, for a considerable time, was there so thorough a revolution effected in any establishment as in that of Tipsy Hall. During the ensuing two years, the mansion hardly knew itself; every thing was done in order; the traces of a sober and careful management were visible in all quarters. They did not here consider it a part of hospitality to make their guests drunk at their table, and it was remarked by Rick Lillis, that it was the first time since the foundation-stone of the building had been laid, that two successive years had rolled over the roof of Tipsy Hall, without its being possible for any body to say with truth that he had seen a human being "tossicated" within its walls, or a tradesman leave the door with his bill unpaid.

Notwithstanding all that Mrs. Moynehan could do to prevent such an occurrence, her husband became acquainted with the Tobins, and relished their acquaintance. Their wit, their fun, their show of good-nature and of hospitality, could not fail to win some favour from one who really was what they affected to be. There are many persons whose very virtues, or at least dispositions for virtue, are often sources of strong temptation to themselves. Mr. Moynehan's frank and unsuspecting nature and social temperament were to him occasions of imminent danger. The Tobins talked so pleasantly, and so good-humouredly, and so good-naturedly, that he found it impossible not to like their company. Of the justice of this opinion, Mrs. Moynehan could not form any correct idea, for as there were no females amongst the family at Castle Tobin, she had never set her foot within its precincts. Her opinion, at first so unfavourable, became something more tolerant, however, when, after several months had passed, she could not recollect that her husband had once returned home with any symptom of those excesses about him, which she had been taught to apprehend at Castle Tobin.

In another way, however, their acquaintance was not so

advantageous. On two or three occasions, old **Mr. Tobin**
had found it necessary to trespass on his friend Moynehan's
purse, to an amount already rather embarrassing; and
with what the latter could not help thinking the best
intentions in the world, these moneys had never been
repaid. Mrs. Moynehan, however, as soon as she understood
what had taken place, was determined to provide against
a recurrence of the same misfortune. She entered upon
the subject one morning at the breakfast table, and after
a severe lecture on the injustice he was committing towards
their child, as well as those who had better claims on his
assistance, obliged him to "make a vow" that he never
again would lend money to the Tobins without her concurrence. He did so, and all was peace for some time
after.

All hitherto was well with Mr. Moynehan. He had a
property, moderate, it is true, but to which his industry
was daily adding something; a wife who knew Buchan's
Domestic Medicine, in the country phrase, from cover to
cover; and in whose eyes he was, without exception, the
greatest man in Ireland; a promising boy, acknowledged
on all hands to be the "living image" of himself, and a
tenantry who looked up to him for assistance and protection,
and were never disappointed. He rose at morning with
the sun, dressed himself briskly, was not ashamed to
go down on his knees to return thanks for the past, and
petition for the future; nor did he think himself a whit the
worse for never omitting this duty either at night or morning.
He kept a hospitable board; a door "that opened with a
latch"; a bed for the traveller; a warm fire-side and a wholesome dinner for the humble mendicant. When he had discharged his duties his conscience was at rest, and if any of his
neighbours at such a time sought to make amends for their
own delinquencies by lecturing him, he would listen in
silence, contented with having done what other people only
seemed to talk about.

This life of tranquillity and goodness, however, was doomed to meet with a singular reverse. The fiend,

——grown wiser than of yore,
Who tempts by making rich, not making poor,

put it into the head of some official functionary of the state to appoint Mr. Moynehan a collector of assessed taxes i: his district, and into Mr. Moynehan's to accept it. What the publicans were in the ancient Roman provinces, the tax-collectors were at a certain period in " our own green isle", that is to say, persons well paid for taking pains to make their own fortunes. A few years before, the proprietor of Tipsy Hall might have thought such a situation not worthy of his acceptance, but a considerable alteration had taken place in the affairs of that establishment. It was therefore with no little satisfaction that Mr. Moynehan received the appointment, wholly ignorant as he was of the innumerable risks by which it was attended. He had heretofore been honest, and he did not see why a man might not be an honest tax-gatherer as well as an honest farmer. Accordingly he set about the duties of his new office with alacrity.

An eminent statesman, some years since, when about to announce the intention of government to repeal the assessed taxes in Ireland, assigned as one of the motives which influenced ministers in coming to such a resolution —" that they were found to fall very heavy upon those country gentlemen *who were kind enough to pay them*". Mr. Moynehan found few of his neighbours so disposed. It was true, nothing could be more frank and hospitable than the manner in which they all received him when he came to their houses. They loaded him with attentions. The best bed in the house and the best wine in the cellar were at his service. They had company to meet him, and they had a thousand little things which he might want, and which they would find an opportunity to send him. But few articles liable to king's taxes could he find in their

possession. They had no windows—no hearths—no cows
—no carriages; all the wealth which on the previous
evening had been displayed with so much munificence,
had dwindled on the following morning into absolute
poverty. Mr. Moynehan was thunderstruck; but he could
not help himself. His predecessors in office, he was told,
had pursued a certain line of conduct, and he must not
make himself singular. On one occasion his preciseness
was near involving him in a serious affair. There was no
carriage, he was told; and as he knew that truth towards
a tax-gatherer was not here regarded with much scru-
pulosity, he asked to see the coach-house. The gentleman
bowed in assent, but signified at the same time that he
considered such conduct as an impeachment of his veracity.
Mr. Moynehan did not persist, and he was favoured in a
few days with a cordial salute from this veracious gentleman
as he passed him in a dashing cabriolet. It was indeed
a thing almost impossible (so irresistible is the influence
of bad example) to hold the office and to keep the hands
untainted—

> And things impossible can't be,
> And never, never come to pass.

Temptation effected for Mr. Moynehan what it has effected
for millions. It wrought his fall. Bribes were poured in
upon him from all quarters. One supplied his table—one
his manger—another his binn—a fourth his cellar—a
hundred his pantry. Every house in the country had a
convivial board, a comfortable chamber, and a blazing fire
for the tax-gatherer. The least he felt to be expected for
these civilities was (like the unjust steward), where one
owed a hundred bushels to the state, to take his pen and
write down fifty, or perhaps not a fifth of that, and it often
happened that even that fifth remained unpaid.

  Those who have once enjoyed the peace of a pure conscience, cannot find repose in its opposite. Neither the

influence of an example that seemed almost universal, not
the stunted maxims of convenience by which the tax-
gatherer sought to satisfy his mind, could make his new
life happy. " What signifies it! when the loss is divided
amongst so many that they can't feel it?"—" Sure every
body is doing it".—" What good would it do to have one
out of a thousand go against all the rest?" Such were the
arguments by which at moments of reflection he resisted
the warnings of conscience, but which could not wholly
silence its reproaches. We grieve to relate the issue.
When peace of mind is lost, men generally seek to supply
its place by false excitement, and so did Mr. Moynehan.
He found it easier to divert his attention from the consideration of his evil ways, than to take up a vigorous resolution and amend them. Accordingly, Moynehan, the
pattern of sobriety and decorum to his neighbourhood, fell
by degrees into habits of vulgar dissipation. He seldom
now returned sober to his home. His rational hours were
hours of hurry, and fretfulness, and impatience, and he
now was only mirthful when reason had been drowned in
whisky punch.

It must not be supposed, however, that this course was
deliberately chosen by Mr. Moynehan; on the contrary,
there was scarcely a morning on which he did not renew
his determination of altering his life, and scarce an evening
after which this determination did not require a renewal.

" Say no more, Mary, say no more", he said, after
Mrs. Moynehan had given utterance to one of her customary
morning counsels; " I tell you this is the last night I will
ever dine away from home".

" You have often said that".

" Well, I will fulfil it now".

" Take my advice, Edmond, and do not dine to-night at
Castle Tobin. You know that you no longer leave that
house in the condition that you ought. The place and the
company would overcome all the resolutions that were

ever made. Oh, my dear husband, you are putting an
end to all our happiness, and, what is worse, you are
securing your own destruction. Do, Edmond, be guided
at last by one who loves you better than ever the Tobins
did. Do not continue to destroy our comfort and the
hopes of our poor child; I wish we had never left our
little cottage on the Shannon side; I wish we had never
heard of this estate, that has brought sin and ruin to our
doors. Will you not grant me this request, my dear
husband? Will you not look to yourself before it is too
late? You dare not think of continuing such a life, and
how can you tell what time may be given you for amend-
ing it?"

"Say no more, now, Mary,—say no more".

"But I must say more, Edmond, until I have your
promise. I am more than ever anxious on this morning,
for I had the most dreadful dreams last night about you
and the Tobins".

"Pooh, pooh, nonsense".

"It may be so, and I trust it is so; but I can't help
thinking of it. I thought that they made you stay to dine
at Castle Tobin, and that after making you drunk, they
were murdering you in a private room, while you cried out
to them to give you time for repentance, but they refused
it". As she said this, she cast herself weeping upon her
husband's neck.

"What folly, my dear!" exclaimed Moynehan in an
angry tone. "I wonder you could pay attention to such
silly thoughts; to talk in that manner of the Tobins! some
of the best fellows breathing, and the warmest friends
I have".

"If they were your real friends", said Mrs. Moynehan,
"they would not do so much as they are doing to bring
about your ruin. We were happy until we knew them.
Listen to me, Edmond. You have already done us
grievous injury—to me and to your child, and, worst of all,

to yourself. Stop where you are, and go no farther on the road to ruin. Begin this instant, by resolving not to go to-night to Castle Tobin, and by keeping that good resolution ".

" But I promised Tobin, my dear ".

" Break that promise, and come home ", said Mrs. Moynehan. " If you expect to change your whole plan of life without meeting any difficulties, or without being obliged to use any violence to your own wishes, or to those of others, you are mistaken, I can assure you. Make this one effort resolutely, and the next will be easy ".

" Pooh, my dear; is it not a great deal better to keep this one promise, since I have made it, and to-morrow, and for the future, to take care to make no promise at all?"

" It is not", said Mrs. Moynehan. " Every new sin makes the bad habit twice as strong; you will find it harder to refuse promising to-morrow, than you do to break the promise you have made to-day. Remain at home this evening, Edmond, and begin what you dare not think of leaving unbegun for ever".

The tax-gatherer paused to meditate. Reform and be at peace! A happy prospect; but how enormous was the mountain of guilt that now lay between him and his past condition. All that he had ever pilfered from the public purse must be restored. That awful word " Restitution" had more of terror in it than all besides. What! condemn himself to poverty and want for all future life, in order to refund the thousands at the embezzlement of which he had connived. Why, two long lives, spent in the closest economy, would not enable him to repay one half the amount. Still, justice confronted him with her immutable countenance; it must be done, or he was lost for ever.

May one be pardoned, and retain the offence?

He struggled with the uncomfortable conviction; and

while he did so, the prospect of Mr. Tobin's jovial board,
the pleasant laughing faces and inspiring cheer by which
it was to be enlivened, came before him, and the words
"lost for ever!" died away on the horizon of his thought
with a faint and feeble echo.

While he was deliberating, the hour arrived for his departure.

"No", he said to his wife, "I cannot and I will not
break my promise of dining with Tobin; but this is the
last evening I will ever dine away from home. Mind
now—I have said it, and you shall find that I will keep
my word".

Mrs. Moynehan said no more, but a look of agony told
her disappointment. On entering the hall he found a
number of people assembled at his levee as usual.

"My master's compliments, Sir, with a pair of young
turkeys for Mrs. Moynehan".

"My master's compliments, Sir, with a bag of oats".

"My master's compliments, Sir, an' he has the grass o'
the cow ready now, that he was talkin of".

"My master's compliments, Sir——"

And a dozen other presents, which there was no re-
fusing. The messengers were dismissed with suitable
answers, and the state was defrauded of a fresh portion
of its revenue. Open-eyed, Mr. Moynehan consented to
the peculation of some fifty or sixty pounds additional
from his Majesty's exchequer. And his only apology was
custom. Every body did it! Devouring custom!

But all was now ready for his departure, and Mrs. Moynehan's deeper anxieties were swallowed up in providing
for his personal comfort.

"Remember, Edmond, if anything *should* oblige you to
spend the night at Castle Tobin, to look well to the sheets.
You remember the last night you slept there that you were
near bringing home your death of cold. If you just
hold the sheet that way to your cheek for half a minute

(taking a corner of her apron to suit the action to tho
word), you can tell at once whether it is damp or not.
Here's the opodeldoc—and the thing for the tooth-ache.
Nelly! Nel—ly!"

"Goin', goin', ma'am".

"Where's the comforter?"

"Tis in the pocket o' the masther's *loody*, ma'am".

"That terrible stumbling mare! I don't know how you
can trust your life to her. But you men absolutely don't
know what fear is. Nelly! Nel—ly!"

"Goin', ma'am, goin'!"

"Where's the child?"

"Masther Mun, where are you, sir? Dont you hear
yourself callin'?"

The child was brought out to receive his father's customary parting caress. Many further additions were made
to those

> ———lengthened sage advices
> The husband fra the wife despises,

before the tax-gatherer mounted his horse and rode away.
Trotting briskly down the avenue which led to the high
road, a few hours' easy riding brought him to the district
in which his business for the day was principally cast. It
is not necessary to follow him through the detail of all his
occupations. He collected a tolerable sum at the houses
of the neighbouring gentry, and in disregard of Mrs. Moynehan's "counsels sweet", took the road to Castle Tobin.

For a long time after they had left the main road, he
was accompanied by Rick Lillis, who still filled the same
situation in the employment of Mr. Moynehan that Faustulus
did in that of the Latin monarch. The evening had a
menacing look, and both occasionally glanced at the
gathering masses of vapour over head, without venturing
to exchange their apprehensions. At length, the following
conversation arose between them.

" Masther ".

" Well, Rick ?"

" Will you tell me, sir, if you plase, how much money you may have about you at this pras'nt moment ?"

" Why do you ask ?"

" Oh, for rasons o' my own ".

" I have near five hundred pounds ".

" 'Tis a dale o' money ", said Rick.

" It is, indeed ".

" This is a lonesome road, masther ".

" 'Tis, Rick ".

" An' do you mane to come back this way to-night from Castle Tobin, sir ?"

" If I should not be prevailed upon to remain for the night ".

Rick looked dissatisfied.

" 'Twas but a poor choice ", said he, " between the bog and the cliff. I'm not over satisfied, master, about the *propriety* of your having so much money about you late at night, an' goin' such a lonesome road. Sure you know, sir, 'twouldn't be wishin' to you for a dale, you lost that money to-night ".

" 'Twould not *be wishing* to me, Rick, for near five hundred pounds ".

" Ayah, it's no joke at all, masther, nor no laughin' matther either. I declare I don't like the thoughts of it, at all. I tell you there's bad boys about these mountains. I'd just as soon expect that one o' them lads would let a handful o' money that way pass him by, as I would to see a cat left alone with a pail o' milk, an' to have no call to it ".

" Don't you know, Rick, that in the reign of Brian Boroimhe, a young lady travelled on foot through Ireland, with a gold ring on the top of a long wand, to show that there was no such thing as a rogue in the whole island ?"

" Why then, sir, *sonuher* to the bit of that lady ever
let foot in these mountains, or if she did, it's more than
she could do these times. Be said by me, sir, an' go home
safe an' sound with your money, while you have it ".

" There is no danger, Rick ", said his master, " for if I
should not choose to encounter the midnight journey, I can
take a bed at Castle Tobin ".

" Why then, I'll tell you my mind out o' the face ",
said Rick; " that's a plan I don't like one bit betther
than the other. The Lord forgive us, 'tisn't in my way,
nor any one else's, to be spakin' ill o' those that arn't *convanient* to defend themselves; but there's rasons for what
I say. I'd be very unfond, if I had it, to pass the night
at Castle Tobin with such a sum o' money as that. Them
Tobins have a bad report in the counthry: they're needy,
bould, daarin young men (an' Heaven forgive me if I
belies 'em), that would a'most rob a priest. I declare, I'd
rather of the two take the road itself, bad as it is. An' see,
along with that, the night is threat'nin' ".

Mr. Moynehan could not help feeling struck, in spite of
himself, with the double warning that was given him by
both his wife and servant. The reports of robberies, and
even worse, among these lonesome hills were not unfrequent;
and it would, he knew, be certain and total ruin to him
and to his family to lose such a sum as he at present held
in his saddle-bags. Such, however, is the infatuation of
habit, that he could not reist the temptation of spending
a jovial evening with the Tobins, renewing, nevertheless,
his determination not to suffer any persuasion to lead him,
on this night at least, beyond the bounds of perfect moderation. It was true he felt some uncomfortable twinges
of conscience when he recollected certain immutable
truths which he was in the habit of hearing more
frequently than he heeded their significance; such as that
he who wills the cause, wills the effect, and that *he who
would fly the fault must fly the temptation*, and that *it is*

impossible to court the occasion and avoid the consequence; with other maxims of the kind, which, when they pressed in too troublesome a manner upon his recollection, he strove to banish by putting spurs to his mare, or entering into further conversation with Rick Lillis, as he strove to keep pace with his master.

By this time the night had begun to put its menaces into execution. The wind, now risen high, came howling up the mountain road behind them, and rustling in the fields of rushes and bog myrtle which skirted the lonesome track. The clouds, with outline faintly visible in the gathering darkness, drove rapidly over head, as if scared by some terrific power rising far behind on the horizon. Large drops of rain gave warning of the approaching deluge, and both travellers fastened a few additional buttons, and put their horses to a quicker pace. Before the storm had burst in all its terror, they had reached a crossway where it had been arranged that Lillis should take the homeward road, while Mr. Moynehau continued his route to Castle Tobin.

CHAPTER VI.

IT is necessary that we anticipate the arrival of the tax-gatherer, in order to give with all the brevity consistent with clearness of narrative, an account of the company who awaited him.

There was, in the first place, Mr. Tobin, the first of the family who had made his appearance in the country, and who had built the Castle to which he gave his family name. This castle, it should be stated, was no castle at all, but a plain house, dignified with that sounding name, from its occupying what was once the site of a strong-hold of the old Earls of Desmoud. Busy and malicious tongues asserted that Mr. Tobin had left his native country charged with the crime of Marmion, but nothing positive was ever known upon the subject.

One of his first acts was not calculated to conciliate the good will of the country people. In order to procure materials for the building, he took down the remaining walls of an old monastery, which stood at a little distance, rather than, at a slight increase of expense, be at the pains of drawing stones from a neighbouring quarry. And it was told of him as an instance of retributive justice, that in giving directions respecting the shaping of one of those stones, a splinter flew off, and, striking him in the right eye, deprived him for ever of the benefit of that organ.

There was one peculiarity in the site chosen for the edifice which is worth observing. It was so constructed that both the principal sitting-room and bed-room were in no less than three different counties, so that in case a bailiff should make his way unexpectedly into either apartment, Mr. Tobin, by shifting his chair from one side of the parlour fire-place to another, could plead an illegal caption, or if invaded at his dressing table, might jump into bed and defy the law and its officer together.

He had two sons, who were not blessed with an equal share of the parental affection. The idea had got into the heads of Mr. Tobin and his lady that the eldest boy was not their son, but a changeling, and the unhappy child was a sufferer to this wretched prejudice. They made him do the work of a menial in their kitchen, while the second was elevated to the place and privileges of the first born. It was perhaps fortunate for the elder in some respects, as he became the only amiable member of his family. Wisdom, like grief, says somebody, is an affection of the mind, and not a thing to be taught by lectures. It was so the elder Tobin learnt it, but the

10

unkindness of his friends affected his health, and he died young.

He was much missed at Castle Tobin, but the wicked preference of the parents was not left without some punishment. Young Tobin grew up to be a fine young man, and fought, and hunted, and drank, and gambled, and showed himself in every way a real son of his father, and no changeling whatsoever. And accordingly the father doted on him.

One morning, say the historians of the neighbourhood, Mr. Tobin saw his son going out at a very early hour. He asked him where he was going, and the young man answered carelessly " *nowhere*, only up the mountains to fight a duel". Whether through recklessness, or that he disbelieved the young scapegrace, the father is reported to have recommended him to " take the grayhounds with him, and that he might have a very pretty course when it was over". The son adopted the suggestion, but there was no occasion for the dogs. He was brought home, in less than two hours after, a corpse, to Castle Tobin.

It was on the death of his wife, which followed soon after, that old Tobin adopted Frank, his nephew, to whom, as he was one of the company on this occasion, it is necessary that we direct our attention for a little time.

Frank Tobin had the misfortune of being

"A self-willed imp, a grandame's child",

and was left for his education altogether to the system of society in which he grew up. As to restraint, he never knew what it was to have his wishes contradicted in a single instance in which it was physically possible to comply with them. His grandmamma, it should be known, was a great lady, and had spent many years abroad, where she had picked up several notions which it was very hard to understand. She hated anything that people were used to. Nothing would do for her either in the way of ribands or principles, except it was spick-and-span new.   If it were possible to administer nourishment at the ears, Mrs. Tobin never would have wished to see the mouth employed for that purpose ; and one would think, to hear her speak, that it was mere prejudice made all mankind persevere in walking erect instead of creeping on all-fours.   In a word, good Mrs. Tobin was rather a charlatan in her notions about educating children, and Master Frank Tobin was not five years old before he began to turn her foible to his own account; for none are more quicksighted than children in perceiving whether the individual entrusted with their instruction is a quack or a person of common sense.   Though not altogether an ill-natured child, he became, from Mrs. Tobin's system of passive compliance, one of the greatest pests and tyrants that ever plagued a household.   His father and mother, who had never travelled, did not altogether relish Mrs. Tobin's plans, but they were afraid to interfere.   His grandmother was rich, and they thought she would make Frank her heir.

But she died and disappointed them, as Frank had disappointed her.   And what was now to be done ?   Here was Frank, a fine gentleman, too proud to take any situation, and too poor to do without it.   His mode of life was now somewhat curious.   He used to spend a great part of the day fishing, or shooting, or coursing, and the produce of his sport he forwarded to the different families in the neighbourhood with whom he was connected by affinity or by liking.   He could glaze windows, and cement broken china, and mend old furniture, and tune pianos, and play a little on the flute, and execute sundry little offices of that kind, which made him a welcome visitor at the houses of most of his country friends.   And if he had confined his accomplishments to such matters as these, all would have been well ; but it was far otherwise.   Although very good-humoured at a

convivial meeting, and capable of singing a hearty song
and passing a merry joke, he was plagued with an unfortunate temper, which was continually involving him in
disputes. He had, however, by some means got the name
of an humourist, and his last adventure was circulated as
regularly in his own circle as the last *bon mot* of a legal
functionary in our own day. There was scarce an Assize
or Quarter Sessions at which Frank Tobin had not to
answer some score of charges for assault and battery. A
child of liberty, Frank could not, from his boyhood,
endure any system of human law, which he conceived
wholly unnecessary for the maintenance of society. All
law and government, he used to say, *was a job;* a mere
trick, intended for the purpose of putting money into the
pockets of lawyers, and throwing impediments in the way
of young fellows who were "inclined for fun". It was
all an invention of roguish attorneys and counsellors. This
theoretical antipathy to the entire system was not without
its practical effects; for Frank Tobin visited severely on
the persons of the individual professors, when they
happened to fall in his way, his abstract dislike of the profession. His highest game, however, in this way, were
the bailiffs and tipstaffs, who were sent to apprehend him
for his misdemeanours, or at best some Special Sessions
Attorney, and with these he waged perpetual and im-
placable war.

He was first recommended to the notice of his uncle by
a characteristic incident. He was sauntering one day
through the mountains in the neighbourhood of Castle
Tobin, when he saw a countryman at a little distance
walking to and fro upon a field and looking very disconsolate.

"Well, my good man", said Frank, "what's the
matter with you?"

"Ah, plase your honour, I'm destroyed. I have a *latificat* again' that man over, an' I don't know from Adam
how will I take him".

He pointed to a house about twenty yards distant. On the half door, which was closed, rested the muzzle of a blunderbuss, and behind sat the proprietor, quietly seated in his chair, and seeming to wait the first hostile movement on the part of his adversary. Having ascertained from the man that the case was one of peculiar hardship, Frank Tobin, who was a kind of knight errant in a small way, and quite as ready to encounter danger in another's behalf as in his own, determined to assist him. He bade the man continue to walk up and down while he went to seek assistance. He had not gone far before he met one of his companions.

" Tom", said he, " have you got a stick?"

" I have, sir".

" Do you see that house over ?"

" I do, sir".

" Well, go round and stand o' one side the back door, and when you see a man running out there, knock him down".

" I will, sir".

Away went Tom, while Frank, slipping close along the front of the house, laid both hands upon the muzzle of the blunderbuss and effectually secured it. The fellow, as he had anticipated, ran for the back door, where Tom with great punctuality knocked him down. Both then delivered their prisoner into the hands of the man who had got what he called the "latificat", while Frank said:

" 'That's the way to do business, my lad, and not to be looking for any of your latitats nor rattle-traps neither. If you take my advice, you never will have any call to the law. It would be long before one of your three-and-nine-penny schemers would show you how to serve that bit of paper after you had got it".

It happened that the man was a tenant of his uncle, who, on hearing of the affair, took Frank under his patronage, which he still continued to afford him, with some restraint, however, on his favourite inclinations, as **Mr.** Tobin's character obliged him to maintain some degree of decorum towards his old foes, a circumstance which many thought would prey upon his health.

Besides these were Will Buffer, so named for his prodigious strength of limb and wonderful agility of muscle, which almost enabled him to realise the fables of Fleetfoot in the fairy tale; and Mr. Dungan, Frank's old tutor, whom his grandmother had engaged for no other reasons, according to their humble neighbours, who are often as shrewd as their superiors, than that "he was just as cracked as she was herself". He had some strange notions about the pronunciation of the letter C, which had gone against him all through life, but which he would rather die than surrender.

Such were the principal individuals of the company, whom Mr. Moynehan was asked to meet to-night at **Castle Tobin.**

l,e was received with a tumult of delight, Frank Tobin undertaking, when they had sat down, to make him acquainted with the people in the room.

"That's Will Buffer sitting near my uncle. Did you ever meet Will Buffer before? He's one of the ablest fellows in Ireland. I saw him lift a deal table with his teeth. He can somerset over his horse. You never saw such a smart fellow. He can run like the wind".

" And who is that next your father?"

"That! Oh, that's Tom Goggin. You'll soon know who Tom Goggin is. He's a great wit. You never heard a fellow tell such stories, nor say such good things, as Tom. He'd make you split your sides laughing, listening to him".

There was something in the appearance of Tom Goggin and the Buffer, which Mr. Moynehan did not altogether relish, nor was his prejudice removed by the manners of both in the course of the evening. The Buffer was one of

those characters occasionally to be met in the Ireland of
that day—rare, we believe, in our own. He had just
enough of the gentleman in his appearance to form a convenient mask for the bully, which was his real character.
With an appearance of hot-headed impetuosity, he had underneath a low and selfish cunning. He knew perfectly to
whom he might be rude, and in what quarter his ignorant
contradictions might be hurled with impunity; but no one
had ever caught him playing off the bully towards any one
who was capable of affording him a dinner and bed, or
from whom he might at any time calculate upon a season-
able loan of money. With such persons he was content
to be a good-humoured and unresisting companion;—a
degree of servility for which he compensated to his wounded
pride by unprovoked and invariable insolence to all those
individuals from whom he expected nothing, because they
had nothing to afford. Incapable, either by any natural
or acquired superiority of mind, of attracting the attention
of a well-educated circle, he usually opened his conversation by a direct contradiction of the last speaker, always
provided the last speaker were not a person from whom he
had anything to hope for.

Nor was the wit in the least degree more prepossessing.
Tom Goggin's forte was a horse-laugh; it was almost all
that he could do in the way of social communion, and,
accordingly, his single faculty was put to frequent use. He
might be said to have laughed his way through life.
Whenever he said what he meant for a good thing, he
chorused the effort with a hearty laugh, and his companions
had gradually fallen into the habit of joining him, until at
length he got the reputation of a wit. Probably his hearers
thought no one had a better right to know what a joke
was worth than the man who had made it. But Tom
Goggin's faculty of laughing served him in many other
ways. It was just as useful to him in applauding another's
joke as in procuring sympathy for his own. If Tom had

injured your reputation, and that you remonstrated with
him about it, he laughed until it became almost impossible
to avoid joining him.   If he had purloined your great coat
or umbrella by way of joke, and you reclaimed your property, he would laugh, and laugh, and laugh, until you
gave up all hope of getting an answer from him.   If you
were fool enough to lose temper, and set about chastising
him, Tom would still laugh, and it was ten to one, if you
were not on your guard, but he would have the whole
country laughing at you too.

Notwithstanding all this fun, there was something, as
we have said, in Tom's countenance which the tax-gatherer
did not relish.   There was more, he thought, of meanness,
than of either good-humour or good-nature, in all his
laughter, and whilst he observed the half-knowing leer
which he sent around the room as he gave vent to one of his
good things, he felt less inclined to laugh, than to exclaim
with honest Dogberry: "Friend, hold thy peace; I do not
like thy look, I promise thee".

The evening, nevertheless, rolled pleasantly away, and
the tax-gatherer was tempted more than once to overstep
the bounds which he had prescribed to himself on leaving
home.   For a long time, however, he restrained himself,
nor was it until late that habit and the occasion overcame
his prudence.   It was observed that when he had done so,
although he soon entered fully, and even wildly, into the
revel spirit of the night, there was something strange and
peculiar in his manner during the whole evening.   He was
fitful in his mirth, and his loudest and most boisterous
bursts of hilarity were succeeded by long fits of absence
and absorbing silence, as if he were on the eve of some
enterprise, in which the fortunes of his life were interested.

The truth was, that the recollection of his gold, the
warnings of his wife and Rick, and his prejudice against
the new guests, to whom he had to-night been introduced,
made Moynehan anxious to see the money safe at Tipsy

Hall. Accordingly, about midnight, and in the midst of a wild bacchanalian uproar, he astonished his host and bottle-companions by suddenly rising, and declaring his intention of going home. Never did a proposition excite more general indignation. Never had so pleasant a party been so unexpectedly broken up. Tom Goggin had never been so happy; Will Buffer had given three somersets, and kicked the ceiling with his heels; and Ned Stokes, a capital fellow, who was at every party because he knew how to sing a comic song, was just going to give them "The Irish Schoolmaster". He had actually begun,

> Misther Byrne was a man
> Of a very grate big knollidge,
> An' behind a quickset hedge
> In a bog he kept his college,

when the tax-gatherer rose. Everybody strove to dissuade him.

"Why, 'tis blowing a perfect storm", said Mr. Tobin.

"And that mountain road", exclaimed Frank, "where robberies are as common as—as—anything".

"I —ca—can't help it—I must be home to-night", exclaimed Moynehan, endeavouring to resist the rising delirium that was already making inroads on his reason, and affecting an air of great industry and seriousness. "I have some accounts to make up that must be ready for the post to-morrow".

"If you have any loose cash about you, sir", said Goggin, rolling his eye about the room, and winking on the company, "I'd advise you to let me take care of it for you".

In the burst of laughter which followed this effusion Mr. Moynehan left the room, followed by the Tobins, who continued in vain to represent to him, with all the force of language and of argument which the glass had left them, the dangers of a solitary journey through the mountains at so late an hour. It was in vain, likewise, that the wind

10*

dashed in the door as soon as the latch was raised, with
such force as to extinguish all the lights they had brought
into the hall, and almost to destroy the tottering equili-
brium of the tax-gatherer. He seemed determined to
make up by obstinacy for the deficiency of argument, and
resolved, at all events, to undertake the journey. But-
toning up his great coat to his chin, and shaking the
hands of his companions and his host with vehement cor-
diality, he sprung upon his mare, and with a wild halloo,
dashed forward through the stormy night gloom. For
some minutes the revellers stood to hear the shout repeated,
and the tramp of the horse's hoofs growing fainter in the
distance, until it had ceased to reach their ears. Soon
after the company broke up, the Buffer and Tom Goggin
riding off together.

The next morning the tax-gatherer's horse was found
without a rider, at a little distance from his house, and the
saddle-cloth and bridle had the marks of blood. The truth
was at once disclosed to the perplexed and agonised widow,
for so she was already deemed. Mrs. Moynehan acted on
the occasion with more firmness and resignation than
might have been expected from her. She caused the
most thorough search to be made along the line of roads,
and through the fields and bogs, that lay between their
house and Castle Tobin. Every bog-hole was dragged,
and every corner ransacked, but in vain. A woman of
strong mind and deep affections, the shock to Mrs. Moynehan was proportionably violent.

"Look, Edmond", she said, holding up the bloody
housing, and looking with agony on her orphan child as
he entered her apartment, "look at all that is left us of
your father".

The boy started for a moment, as if at a loss to comprehend her meaning.

"My dear child", said the widow, "let what is our
ruin be at least your warning. Your father, who left

home yesterday in perfect health, will never now return to us again. He has been murdered on his road".

The boy turned pale and red by turns, as he looked from the saddle-cloth to his mother's countenance, and said at last in a whisper:

" By whom, mother?"

" Heaven only can tell that, and he who did it", said the widow. " Oh, it was an evil day for us all, when he accepted that situation. Till then he was happy, good, and virtuous—he made all happy round him. But now—"

At these words, and at the recollection of the altered life which her husband had been leading during his latter years, the unhappy woman swooned away, and was conveyed to her apartment. Years rolled away, and the circumstances attending the disappearance of the tax-gatherer remained enveloped in a darkness as deep as that in which he had set out on his last journey. A proclamation was issued from Dublin Castle, commencing with the usual: " Whereas, some evil-minded person or persons, etc.": and offering a reward of two hundred guineas for the detection of the murderer, but in vain. Whether he had been struck by lightning, stifled in a bog, torn to pieces (as some sage fair ones hinted) by evil spirits, or destroyed by beings no less malignant of his own form and species, were questions that exhausted speculation and remained unsolved. The broken-hearted widow sought some consolation for the terrible stroke in devoting herself to the education of her son, whom she determined to bring up in the strictest principles of religion and virtue.

CHAPTER VII.

ABOUT fifteen years before this period, there stood, within a hundred paces of the outskirts of B——, a house of moderate size, of which no living eye has seen a trace. It

was tenanted by an humble barber of the name of O'Berne.
Beside the dwelling stood a lofty elder, in which the magpie and the goldfinch built their nests. Behind was a
garden, stocked with heads of cabbage, some rows of
gooseberry and currant trees, with a few wall-flowers and
marigolds of flaming yellow. A handsome pole, rising
obliquely from the doorway, and bearing at its summit a
tuft of hair that streamed upon the wind, announced to
passengers the vocation of the owner. On either side of
the entrance, two small plots sprinkled with the commonest
flowers, and fringed with rows of London pride or bachelors' buttons, gave grace and fragrance to the decent tenement. The thievish sparrow reared his noisy brood beneath the eaves, and at evening, the robin would often
sing his short and plaintive song amongst the elder boughs.

The house of the barber, on Saturday evenings, afforded
a lounge to many of the neighbouring villagers. Here,
while O'Berne stropped his razors, or tucked a snow-white
napkin under the grisly chin of some unwashed artizan,
the many who waited to undergo a similar operation would
lean against the well-scoured dresser, or take a hay-
bottomed chair near the door, discussing politics, foreign
and domestic, circulating the easy jest, or listening to the
piquant anecdote. Amongst these persons there were few
subjects on which the opinion of O'Berne had not considerable weight; and few ventured to interrupt the current
of his speech, while, as he raised the mollient foam, he
would reveal to his wondering hearers the designs of many
a potentate and minister, who fondly deemed them a secret
to the world.

The barber, as it was generally said, had migrated to
this village from the south-western town of Bantry. It
was in the tenth year of his only son, Godfrey, this removal took place. Soon after, chance threw the latter in the
way of a singular education. One evening, during the
first year of their residence at B——, the barber was

busy, as usual, in preparing his shop for the customers who generally dropped in when the business of the day was over. While thus engaged, an old gentleman entered, a white-haired, venerable looking man, but with eyebrows black as coal, and something in the expression of his dry and shrivelled features that was unaccountably repulsive and forbidding. It was not that he was morose, for his countenance wore a continual smile, and he seemed ever on the watch for something to jest about; but sternness itself would have been more agreeable than this uncordial mirth. It was a dry and heart'ess levity, not genuine good humour; and evidently indulged in, rather for the gratification of his own vanity than from a desire of affording pleasure to others. Seeing little Godfrey playing on the floor, he began to question him, and was so much entertained with the thoughtful solemnity of his answers, that he proposed, if the barber would allow it, to take him into his household. O'Berne feared to miss an offer of patronage which promised so much advantage to his son, and promised with many expressions of gratitude, to take him to the gentleman's house on the following day.

The mansion was situated in a lonely and barren heath, about seven miles from the village. It was a bare, wild looking edifice, occupying the centre of an enclosure (it could hardly be called a demesne), on which not a single branch of foliage was to be seen, east or west, north or south, that could qualify in the least degree the natural dreariness of the place. The first impression of the scene sunk down like lead upon the mind of the younger Godfrey. A peasant, whom they overtook upon the road, and from whom they made inquiries respecting the proprietor, told them "that very little was known about him at all in them parts; that he had no one livin' with him, only an ould woman that used to dress his food and do the kitchen work, and that it was said he was a foreigner; but

he was livin' there a good long while, and nothing was
ever known to his disparagement".

They found the old gentleman within. Seeing little
Godfrey rather low-spirited at the prospect before him, he
took him into the library, which was pretty well furnished,
and took some pains to reconcile him to his new abode.

Here young Godfrey remained for six years, during
which time his only companions, except when he went to
spend a day at his father's, were the proprietor of the
mansion, the old woman, and, far more entertaining and
interesting to him than either, the books which burdened
the shelves of the small library. Reading, likewise, was
the constant occupation of his master. Seldom did he
favour Godfrey with any conversation, and when he did,
it was in such a brief and half-sneering style, that the
latter did not lament his general taciturnity. Never had
he heard of a man who lived so isolated—so entirely centred in himself—as his new master. Nor while he secluded
himself from all ordinary intercourse with the world in
which he lived, was it for the purpose of devoting himself
with more freedom to the concerns of another; for Godfrey
never observed in his master any of those actions or expressions, by which men are accustomed to intimate their
recollections of a higher allegiance than any they owe on
Earth. His patronage, however, and the leisure which he
here enjoyed, enabled Godfrey O'Berne to lay up a store
of information, which, though nearly useless, and in some
points worse than useless, from want of method, was far
more extensive than was usual in his station. The sudden
death of his patron deprived him unexpectedly of those
brilliant hopes to which his father looked forward with
a sanguine eye. The recluse was found one morning in
his bed a corpse, and Godfrey was recalled to the paternal
threshold, as much in mystery with respect to the character and history of his late master as when first he
entered his house.

In about a year after, the elder O'Berne himself being struck with his death sickness, sent for his son, who was at this time the only living member of his family. The latter, who was on a visit at the house of a friend in the neighbouring city, came without loss of time to receive the dying injunctions of his only parent. He found the latter seated in the arm-chair which was usually allotted to his customers, apparently awaiting the last stroke of death, and surrounded by a numerous crowd of relatives and friends. On seeing his son approach, he bade one of the men who stood near him, to unfix the pole, which was made fast at the front door, and to bring it into the house. His wishes being complied with, he took the pole in his right hand, causing it to stand erect upon the floor at his side, and addressed his son in the following words :—

"This painted pole, Godfrey, is one o' the most ancient marks of our profession. It signifies that stick which, when the barber and the surgeon were the same, used to be held in their hands by the customers, and worked this way to make the blood come freer from the vein. This riband, that's tied at the top, signifies the bandage, and this stripe of red paint that goes coiling down the pole, the blood, as it were, flowing from the arm. This pole, Godfrey, has stood at my door, winter and summer, for five-and-forty years. I never possessed a half-penny but what it brought me, and I never wished for an estate beyond it. If you are satisfied with it, you are as rich as an emperor; if not, the riches of an emperor would not make you so. Keep it, then, and be contented with it, and you will be happy".

So saying, he placed the pole in the hand of his son, and soon after gave up the ghost. The latter interred the remains of his parent with all demonstrations of filial respect and piety, and entered presently afterwards upon the business and possessions he had left behind him.

The younger Godfrey O'Berne had always been looked

upon in his neighbourhood as a kind of oddity. Tall and
ungainly in his figure, in his manner abrupt and sheepish,
he was to far the greater number of his companions a subject of jest and ridicule rather than admiration. There
was, however, another circumstance which counteracted
the effect of Godfrey's manner and appearance. He was
a great student, and from various sources had contrived to
amass a quantity of knowledge in a mind of no ordinary
force.

Were we to take opinions on the cause of O'Berne's reserve and awkwardness, it is probable that we should find
a great variety. Some would call it pride—some sensibi-
lity—some modesty—and some, by way of being wiser
than all the rest, might say, "it was a mixture of all
these". Whatever was the cause, the young barber, unlike his fellow in the Arabian Nights, was reserved and
meditative. He courted no friendships, sought no society,
and seemed even impatient of that which he could not
avoid. Still he bore in mind his father's dying counsel,
and, while he courted solitude as much as possible, he
gave no one any actual reason to complain of him.

The young barber felt a want which none of us, in
whatever rank or station we may be placed, have failed to
experience at some portion of our lives—the want of mental
sympathy. There was no one in the village who shared
his information, or who could understand his thoughts on
any subject; and it was not contempt, but the actual
difference of mind, that made him unwilling to mingle in
societies where he could find nothing of considerable
interest to him. It so happened that the train of his
reading was one peculiarly adapted to foster such con-
templative habits. The works which fell into his hands
related principally to moral and metaphysical subjects, and
the barber, who had an acute, intelligent spirit, was deeply
caught by the profound and absorbing disquisitions which
those books contained. How could he who had been all

the preceding evening engaged in arduous endeavours to comprehend the reasonings of various philosophers on the connection of mind with matter, and the mysterious manner in which both seem blended in the human individual, be expected on the following day to take an active interest in the labours of a mechanical vocation, or in the vulgar sports that made the village echo near his dwelling? There is no fact, however, more notorious than the possibility of uniting an extensive knowledge of, and the liveliest interest in, moral studies with a very inferior course of moral practice. The pleasure which Godfrey took in such pursuits as we have described was one of a purely intellectual character; the heart had little or nothing to do with it. He pleased himself with the noble exercise which the subject afforded to the faculties of his understanding, and thought little of deducing rules of practice from the sublime and immutable truths which he contemplated. Satisfied to let his imagination roam through the boundless sea of being, he bestowed comparatively little thought on the necessity of fulfilling with exactness the part allotted to himself in the universal scheme, and used the light afforded him, rather for the gratification of an active spirit than for the direction of his course through life. His silence, however, and his habits of application, produced a strong impression of his learning on the rustics in his neighbourhood, and they looked on him as one of the profoundest scholars in the world.

There lived at this time in B—————, a family of the name of Renahan, who were looked upon as amongst the leading denizens of the place. Mary, the eldest daughter of the house, was, in her seventeenth year, considered one of the wonders of the village. Her beauty was the subject of praise amongst the young, and her genuine piety and modesty amongst the old. Of the former, all had not the opportunity of judging, for Mary Renahan (who was too humble to aspire to the magnificence of a

bonnet) took care never to appear unhooded in the public
streets: and he who by any chance had seen her countenance,
was accustomed to tell it as an adventure worth recording
to his companions in the evening. Mary was rich, cheerful,
and handsome; it was therefore the subject of general
amazement, when the rumour spread that she was about
to become the bride of the poor, the melancholy, and the
ungainly Godfrey O'Berne.

Such, however, was the truth. Let who will divine the
cause, the gay and gentle Mary Renahan gave up, without
hesitation, her liberty and her affections into the hand of
one who was regarded by the rest of her companions
either with ridicule or fear.

From the day of his marriage, Godfrey O'Berne seemed
to have renounced his speculative habits, and became
practically industrious. He was attentive to his business,
and began to laugh and jest with his customers in such a
manner as to remind them of his father. To him belonged
the economy of the basin and the strop, the scissors and
the curling iron. His part it was to amuse the m'nds,
while he trimmed the whiskers of his customers; and to
enlighten the interior of the heads that came beneath his
hand, while he reduced the outside to the standard of
fashion and of grace. The regulation of the domestic de-
partment was committed exclusively to the management
of Mrs. O'Berne, who was as attentive to the minor
affairs of the little establishment as she was to the
happiness and comfort of her lord. An over-rigid
economy, however, was not the fault of either master or
mistress; and while custom increased, and comforts multiplied, the case was exactly the reverse with the hundred
pounds which the latter had brought her husband as a
dowry, and which they had set apart at first, in order
that it might perform for their eldest daughter the same
good office which it had done for Mrs. O'Berne.

Still all was gay and happy at the barber's. As a

husband and a father he had more than the average share
of happiness, and less than the average share of care.
His wife seemed well contented with the portion of enjoyment which their means afforded her; and his three
children were promising in mind and frame. Mortimer,
the eldest, could already make a decent "pothook" in his
copy-book, and the others knew as much of letters as
Cadmus himself at twice their age, or as Charlemagne is
said to have done while he was shaking Europe from the
Baltic to the Alps.

Occasionally, in the long summer evenings, Godfrey
would take down his violin, on which he was a tolerable
proficient, and in the absence of professional employment,
enliven the house with some old national air, to which his
wife would sometimes add the melody of a tolerable voice.
More frequently they would devote the evening to a walk
through the village, where their decent appearance attracted general notice. Indeed they were not without
being censured for over daintiness of dress by some of
those sharp-eyed individuals, who, when they can discover
nothing to ridicule in a neighbour's meanness, had rather
find the contrary fault than let him pass unwounded.

Nor were these the only annoyances from which the
comforts of the barber received a slight alloy. That class
of young persons inhabiting the purlieus of most towns
and villages, who are emphatically distinguished by the
epithet of "the blackguards", seemed, with that mis-
chievous instinct which enables men to distinguish what
is ludicrous in human avocations, to have marked out
O'Berne for their special amusement. Sometimes they
would snatch a new toy or wedge of bread from the hands
of his children as they stood gaping at the open door; at
others, they chalked uncivil nick-names on his pannels; or
else (and this was the unkindest cut of all) a whole gang
of them would watch an opportunity when he and his wife
were walking in all their finest through the village on a

Sunday evening, and set up in full chorus the popular
ballad :—

> Mullins the barber grew so grand,
> He listed in the Sligo band ;
> Mullins the barber grew so great,
> He knocked his nose against the gate, etc.

But notwithstanding these unavoidable mortifications,
peace still abode on the household of O'Berne, and the
tranquillity of his mind received no worldly shock that
could bear an instant's comparison with the sum of his
enjoyments.

CHAPTER VIII.

IT was on Saturday evening, and the shop was thronged,
as usual, with a crowd of hairy heads, and chins as rough
as hedge-hogs with the stubble of the week. On the
operating chair sat Molony, the blacksmith, the napkin
tucked beneath his massive jaws, and his chin already
white from ear to ear, adding a twofold grimness to the
smoke and ashes that encased the upper portion of his
countenance. A thoughtful silence for some time prevailed, while the eyes of all watched with a lazy admiration the skill with which the barber's razor flew along
the blacksmith's spacious jaws, demolishing, at every
stroke, a long flourishing harvest, and leaving behind it a
fair and glossy surface. At length, Mac Namara the
carpenter, who was one of the village dandies, and waited
to have his hair brought into form, broke silence as
follows :

"Well, of all de tings dat ever was done to me, dat's
de last I could ever bear—to have anoder man shave me.
Not meanin' de laste asparagement to Mr. O'Berne, nor to
his profession eider—but de iday of anoder man takin'

me be de nose, an' sweepin' a razhure up me troat, is
what I never could abide de toughts o' doin' ".

"When you have a beard at all, Tom Mac", said
O'Reilly the cooper, taking a pipe from his mouth, and
looking over his shoulder at the speaker, "it may come
to your turn to talk of shaving it".

"Surely, surely, Ned. Well den, it's come to your
turn to talk of it, any way, and to do it—for I declare
dere isn't a chin in B——— stands more in need o' de
razhure".

"Thrue for you, Tom. There's this difference betune
you an' me,—that you shave to get a beard, an' I shave to
get rid of it".

The conversation dropped, but there was a portion of it
which was not forgotten. A weak imagination is easily
impressed. With all his learning and capacity, it was
long before O'Berne could get rid of the horrid idea which
was suggested by the carpenter's random words. His
mind, though well enough supplied with knowledge, was
not subdued to any wholesome discipline; and such minds
are often the prey of every wandering fancy. From
time to time he would start as the foolish thought suggested itself to his imagination, and shudder, as if the
carpenter's words showed anything more than an extravagant caprice.

Still these were weaknesses known only to himself, and
his general prosperity continued unabated. Most minds,
as well as bodies, have their peculiar constitution, and
their peculiar ailment or "idiosyncrasy", which it requires
the hand of a nice and delicate counsellor to deal with.
Instead of despising the crowd of morbid thoughts, which,
arising like clouds, would gradually overshadow his whole
imagination, as he dwelt on those expressions of the carpenter, O'Berne encouraged, examined, and brooded on
them, until at length they communicated something like
a settled tinge to his whole character. Could such

individuals be brought to understand how much of misery
they might avoid by a moderate degree of habitual and
generous self-restraint, the world would be spared a great
deal of woe, and more, perhaps, of crime.

To this state of mind an accidental circumstance added
a prodigious force. At a little distance from B————,
there resided a family of the name of Danaher, hovering
between the frontiers of gentility and of that rank to
which the O'Bernes belonged. They lived in an equivocal
looking house which they dignified with the title of Rath
Danaher, held a pew at the chapel, and were looked upon
as a kind of "half-quality". As they were near relations
of Mrs. O'Berne, the latter and her husband were occasionally guests at the Rath, and contributed on festival
days to make the evening pass merrily away. At this
period the clouds of superstition still rested like a gloomy
fog upon the minds of the poorer peasantry (as they do in
all countries where education is retarded), nor were there
wanting some in the rank immediately above them who
participated in their credulity. In all such fancies, the
Danahers were, from first to last, profoundly versed.
They wore charms and spells; they never began a journey,
or a new piece of work, on a Saturday; they kept no
pigeons about the house; they would not hurt a weazel
for the world; they always took off their hats when a
cloud of dust went by them on the road; they read
"dhrame-books" and consulted fortune-tellers, and prac-
tised numberless rites of the most absurd and unmeaning
kind. Night after night, when the fire blazed cheerfully
upon the hearth, it was their wont to gather round it in
a circle, and interchange their gloomy tales of supernatural
agency, while even the youngest members of the group
were suffered to drink, undisturbed, at the foul and soul-
empoisoning stream, that flowed from the hag-ridden ima-
ginations of the story-tellers. Ghosts, fairies, witches,

murderers, and demons, glided with a horrid and hair
stiffening influence through all their narratives, and when
the listeners retired for the night. it was to hurry to their
beds with alarmed and shuddering nerves, and to supply
the frightful fancies of their waking moments by still more
frightful dreams.

One evening, while a conversation of this kind pro
ceeded at the fireside of Rath Danaher, the O'Bernes were
of the company. Godfrey, surprised at the extent to
which they carried their superstitious credulity, undertook
to disabuse them of their fears. He talked learnedly of
the nature of spirit and of matter of second causes, and
of the absurdity of supposing that the Divine Being would
suffer the ordinary laws of nature to be violated on occasions so fantastical and useless.

"I do not know how to make you understand", said he,
"that such an event could not happen without a direct
infraction of the present order of things, which is a
miracle to be wrought by the hand of Omnipotence alone.
That it may happen, as He who made the law can alter
it, I do not offer to deny ; but to believe that it does
commonly happen, and without cause or meaning, is to
turn the exception into the rule. Spirit, as it is an immaterial substance, has neither colour, nor sound, nor
smell, nor any quality which can make it perceptible to
our senses. Granting that they exist in myriads around
us, it is still impossible, according to the ordinary laws of
nature, that they can do us either physical injury or
physical good. What communion they may hold with
the mind, as that is likewise immaterial, has nothing to
say to the purpose. It is possible they may suggest either
good or evil to the soul (as religion even teaches us they
do); but that, without supposing a miracle, they can
pinch the body black and blue, transport it from place to
place, affright the senses with extraordinary sights and
sounds, is against the common order of nature. The

Deity must clothe them with material faculties before they can produce material effects".

"Well, Mr. O'Berne", said Robert Danaher, a young man, who, having attended a course of surgical lectures in Dublin, conceived himself entitled to his share of authority on metaphysical questions, and who was, moreover, perhaps the only person present who understood half what the barber said—"I do not know that any miracle at all is necessary to the purpose. It is an undisputed fact, that spirit does act on matter. The Deity, who is a pure spirit, sustains all things, both material and the contrary, in their daily courses—and we know that in the human being, the mind directs and regulates the movements of the body at its pleasure. Why may not the spirit, separated from its clay, possess the same influence over the matter that surrounds it, which it once held over that with which it was united in the human frame? For my part, as it is a mystery to me by what means my will directs my arm to extend or to contract itself, I would not presume to say that the same spiritual will, when separated by death from this frame of flesh and blood, may not possess a similar influence over the wind that moans by my window, the candle that is burning on my table, or the silent air that favours my midnight slumbers. I know not how the effect is produced in the one case any more than in the other; but when I know that the one effect does take place, I should be far from asserting that it would require an infraction of the natural harmony to produce the other".

"Ye may talk as ye will", said Kitty Danaher, "but fractions or no fractions, the spirits are abroad as regular as the sun goes down. Our John can tell you that, on a market night last year, after selling some cattle in New Auburn, he was mounting his horse at the door of the Harp and Shamrock, when three times, one after another, he fell over on the other side, without one near (that he

could see) to give him a shove, and the poor old mare
standing as quiet as a lamb".

O'Berne, who supposed that there might be reasons for
John's unsteadiness after leaving the Harp and Shamrock,
a; art from outward agents, either spiritual or material,
was not so much struck by this example, as he was by
the argument which it seemed intended to illustrate. He
remained for a long time silent, while each of the family
in turn poured out some fearful tale of supernatural agency
in order to subdue his incredulity. They did not, however,
succeed in convincing him. He continued to express his
contempt for the ridiculous legends that they sought to
thrust upon him, admitting only the possibility of such
appearances as formed their leading subject.

"I can assure you of one circumstance, at all events",
said Mrs. Danaher, "which took place beneath this very
roof. Mr. Andrew Finncane the apothecary, to whom
Robert served his time, was speaking one night, as you
are, of the folly of believing in such stories, when we all
warned him to be careful of what he said, as he did not
know the moment he might have reason to change his
mind. He laughed, but when he woke next morning he
found himself lying with his head where his heels ought
to be".

This tale brought on a fresh torrent of similar anecdotes. The evening passed away, and the barber and his
wife returned home. It was in some weeks after, that the
former, returning late from the neighbouring city, was obliged to take a bed for the night at an inn on the roadside.
The stillness of the night and the loneliness of the place,
for it was situate in one of those dreary flats which the
road traversed on its way to the western coast, and
tenanted only by an old woman and her son, brought to
his recollection the discourse which had passed in his
presence at Rath Danaher. The instinct of the supernatural is one, which perhaps nobody, except some

11

conscience-scared criminal, whose heart is hard to every natural feeling, can ever wholly lay aside. It is implanted in us for the best of purposes, and though we may abuse it, as we do the best emotions, to our ruin, it is not the less intended for our good. O'Berne, though he had his weakness, was by no means superstitious; yet he could not avo'd bearing testimony in his own heart to the existence of the universal instinct as he gazed through his small window upon the wide and starlit heath that lay before it, and which was, in itself, a prospect sufficient to have awakened lonesome and melancholy thoughts. Still feeling a contempt for such terrors as those which preyed upon the household of Rath Danaher, he confessed, however, a sufficient degree of nervousness to lock the door of his sleeping room inside, and to make fast the window, to make "assurance doubly sure". He then knelt down, as usual, prayed with somewhat more than usual earnestness, and went to rest. His sleep was sound and dreamless as the sleep of a weary man is wont to be, but a surprise awaited him in the morning which made him almost doubt the evidence of his senses. On opening his eyes, he was astonished to perceive that the window which, when he went to rest, stood behind the head of his bed, and a little at the side, stood now directly opposite, as if it had made a circuit of the chamber in the night! He rose, and his perplexity increased. He found himself now lying with his feet towards the head of the bed, the pillow and all the bed furniture being reversed in the same way, and even his silver watch still lying as he had placed it under the bolster, but having participated in the general change of position. His astonishment was excessive. The bed had no appearance of the disturbance which such a change might be expected to make. It even seemed as if he had slept without motion through the night; and but that his recollection of the contrary was distinct, he would have been persuaded that the whole must be an error of his own. The door was locked, and the window fastened, as he had left them, but in no place could he find his clothes, which he had laid on the preceding night upon the chair at his bedside. After thoroughly searching the room without success, he was about to summon the people of the house, in order to make inquiries from them, when his eye fell upon the old portmanteau which he had brought with him from home. It seemed more full than it had been when he took it off his horse on the preceding eve. He opened it. Wonder on wonder! There was the suit folded, brushed, and made up with an exactness that was admirable! Every article was in its place, and every buckle made fast with just the proper degree of tightness. The barber was perfectly bewildered. The mysterious agent, whose prerogative he had disputed in the case of Mr. Andrew Finucane, had sought an opportunity of vindicating, in his case also, the slighted power that was allotted him. So would the Danahers have construed the story; and for that reason, the barber determined for the present to say nothing of the circumstance to them or to any body else.

For many months the circumstance continued unexplained, and its impression, from the very force of constant thinking on it, began to grow faint on the barber's mind. Again there was a party at Rath Danaher, and again the barber and his wife were of the number of the guests. The conversation on this evening happened to turn on the superstition of the Fetch, or warning spirit, which shows itself, say the country people, in the likeness of some person doomed to die, at some short period before his death.* Numberless instances were related of such appearances, and again Mr. O'Berne expressed his total incredulity. In a fortnight after, as he was passing

---

* Our friend Mr. Barnes O'Hara has given such celebrity to this superstition, that there is no need of a more particular description.

through B——, he was met by Mr. Guerin (the **father** of Peter Guerin, whose exploits at "the great House' the reader will find in another volume). He was surprised to see that Mr. Guerin, with whom he was always on the most friendly terms, now passed him by with an offended air. Nor did he make his appearance as usual on Saturday evening at the barber's shop, in order to have his beard and hair made decent for the ensuing Sabbath. A neighbour solved the mystery.

"Why, Mr. O'Berne", said he, "Peter Guerin says there's no spakin' to you now, you're grown so grand".

"I had much the same complaint to make of himself", replied the barber. "He wouldn't speak to me in the street when I saluted him".

"That's dhroll!" said the peace-maker. "It's the very account he gives o' you. He says that he was standin' at his shop doore th' other morning about six o'clock, just afther day brake, an' that you walked by, lookin' him straight in the face, an' without ever takin' any notice, although he axed you how you was as plain as could be".

The instant the man had concluded his account, O'Berne recollected the recent conversation at Rath Danaher. He had not, he knew, for years before been in B——, or any where outside his own door at so early an hour as six in the morning; and he had not the slightest recollection of the rencontre to which Mr. Guerin referred. What was it then that the latter had seen? The Danahers would have found a ready answer, and in spite of himself he felt a creeping through his nerves as he remembered the prediction with which the appearance was supposed to be associated. He had sufficient promptitude of mind, however, to keep his secret from transpiring.

"Mr. Guerin may be sure", said he, "that he is the last man in B—— I would think of treating in that way. I have no recollection whatever of passing him by at any time in that manner, and I'm sure I never had the least idea of doing such a thing".

The village Mr. Harmony, who received this explanation, lost no time in conveying it to the proper quarter, and peace was reëstablished between the barber and his friend. In spite of himself, some occasional qualms respecting the state of his health, would cross the mind of the former, and this new adventure gave threefold strength to that already related. As time rolled by, however, and he found his bodily vigour undiminished, his courage rose, and he began to make inquiry respecting the nature of the superstition. It was then he learned for the first time, that the appearance, when seen early in the morning, was supposed *to predict a long life to the individual whose semblance is assumed.*

There is no time when one is more inclined to admit the truth of a supernatural prediction than when it coincides exactly with one's own desire. The barber would not directly admit, even to himself, that his incredulity was shaken in the least degree, but it was certain that his repugnance to conviction in this instance was not so vivid as in the former.

Half a year had passed away, before the spirit which had tormented him at the lonely inn on the roadside took any pains to confirm the impression which had been made by its first essay. It happened one night that the barber slept at Ruth Danaher, where he had turned in from a violent storm of rain and wind. The chamber which was allotted to him commanded a lonely prospect of the river and distant mountains, and the barber was forcibly reminded of the adventures of the last night he had spent away from home. In the same manner as he had done on the former night, he fastened the door and window-frame before he went to rest. Whether it was owing to a growing doubt of the reality of such appearances, or a state of bodily indisposition, it was a long time now before he could sleep. When he did so, however, his sleep, as usual, was sound and dreamless.

After midnight, he awoke with a sense of cold. The bed-clothes had all disappeared! Nothing but the gray striped tick remained upon the bedstead, and on that he lay, exposed to the sharp cold of a November night. By the aid of some embers which still were burning on the hearth, he was enabled to light a small candle, which he had extinguished on going to rest. He searched the room, but the fugitive bed-clothes were nowhere to be seen. It was impossible that this could be a trick of any human being. The door and window were fast as he had left them, and even if it were possible for any body to have got in, the fact that he should have been thus annoyed, at two different houses, of which no one member perhaps knew even the existence of the other, was in itself incredible. He was on the point once more of giving up the search, when his attention was directed to an old oak press which stood in a corner of the room; it was locked, but the key was in the lock. The barber opened it, and could scarcely believe his eyes; there lay the objects of his search, folded and laid upon the shelves with as much order and exactness as if they had never left the draper's counter. The barber was thunderstricken. He felt no terror, but he was stunned to the very soul; he walked, he struck his breast, he moved the candle to and fro, in order to be satisfied that it was not all a dream. But nothing could change the facts, and with a bewildered mind he laid the clothes upon the bed again, and passed the remainder of the night in troubled and interrupted slumbers.

In the meantime, perplexities of a less metaphysical kind began to darken on the fortunes of the barber; and in common with his species he felt in his turn the influence of those inferior causes, to which for its own wise ends all-curbing Providence seems often to abandon human in-

forests. A handsome house had been erected on the
opposite side of the road, about half-way between the
barber's dwelling and the village, and speculation was
exhausted as to its probable use; some said it was
intended for a toll-house, others for a shrine of Bacchus.
Before the point could be decided a typhus fever confined
O'Berne to his apartment and his bed, from which he was
unable to rise during the space of a summer month.
During this time (the first period of affliction which they
had ever known), his wife attended him with a tenderness
and care that excited in his mind a deeper sentiment of
affection and respect towards her than he had ever felt
before. What heart, be it high or low, that ever yielded
to affection, has not, like that of the poor barber, experienced, either in its bitterness or in its consolation, the truth
so delightfully sung since then by our national poet?

When we first see the charms of our youth pass us by,
    Like a leaf on the stream that will never return,
When our cup, which had sparkled with pleasure so high,
    First tastes of the *other*—the dark flowing urn;
Then, then is the moment affection can sway,
    With a depth and a tenderness joy never knew.
Love nursed among pleasures is faithless as they;
    But the love born of sorrow, like sorrow is true.

Nor was the gratitude of O'Berne on first making this
discovery, in its happier sense, less tender or less true that
he was but a village barber.

On the first day of his convalescence, a new, and it
must be confessed, an unwelcome surprise awaited the
invalid. Walking with difficulty to the low window, where
his wife had placed a chair, he looked out with strange
and altered eyes upon the healthy active world, that still
continued its career of growth, of bloom, and of decay,
unchanging in design, though for ever varying in effects.
The sun still smote the ripening grain; the fresh wind
shook the boughs; the noisy carmen rattled by to

market, and the smaller birds, which least of Nature's
children seem known to sickness or to pain, fluttered with
vigorous wing and frequent twitter about the leaves, and
amid the branches of the rustling elder.

But there was one sight, which, from the moment when
it first had caught the barber's eye, diverted him from
every other thought.   The new house, above alluded to,
had been completed and inhabited during his illness, and
it was with astonishment and dismay he perceived that
the inmate was no other than a rival barber.   He could
not without anxiety contemplate the superior splendour
displayed by this new competitor.   The front of the house
was handsomely dashed; the pole, exceeding at least by
half the size of O'Berne's, was surmounted by a gilded
ball that shone like another sun, while close beneath was
fastened a long banner of hair that floated the winds as
if anticipating triumph.   Above the lintel of the door
was a sign board, executed in metropolitan style, which
announced the proprietors (for it seemed to be a partnership) as " Fitzgerald and O'Hanlon, late from Paris
and Dublin, professors of hair-cutting and perfuming", etc.

"Mary", said the convalescent to his wife, as he surveyed this great display, "why didn't you tell me there
was a new barber set up since I lay down?"

" I didn't think of it", replied the wife; " what matter
can it be to us?"

"I'm afraid time will show us that", said O'Berne.
" Wasn't Ireland big enough without their coming to
plant themselves, and their pole, over-right my very
door?"

" What signifies themselves and their great pole?"
replied the wife.   " You have your custom made, and the
neighbours will stand by you, I'll engage".

" That's not the way of the world", replied the barber,
"and I'd be a fool if I thought it would be the way with
me; there are some I know I can count upon.   There's

the blacksmith, because he has no capers that way, and he says no one knows the sweep of his jaws but myself· he'll stick to me; and there's my third cousin, Pat Sheehy, the weaver, will stay by me for blood's sake; and a few more friends I may be sure of; and perhaps others that will be honest, as some will be rogues, without expecting it; but the rest, you'll find, will have their notions. The golden ball will draw many an eye away, and where the eye goes, the chin and head will follow. But where's the use of talking?"

The event even outstripped the anticipations of the barber. The time lost by his own illness and that of his wife, who fell ill of the same disease immediately on his recovery, accelerated a catastrophe which he had too much cause to fear. The villagers were unwilling to frequent a house which I ad now for two months been the seat of contagion. Party spirit also lent its influence to the success of the new-comers, and O'Berne lost many a head and chin to political differences.

In fine, before the lapse of many years, extreme and squalid misery descended on the dwelling of the barber. By degrees, retrenchment followed retrenchment, until what once were necessaries, assumed the character of luxuries too costly to be thought of. The barber and his wife no longer appeared abroad except when it could not be avoided, and at length that day was one of joy to the family which saw them supplied with a bare sufficiency of food.

From circle to circle, however, they descended in the region of adversity, nor had they yet arrived at the depths of the abyss. The rent of their tenement ran into arrear, and they were menaced more than once with an ejectment. This was the only event which began to strike a real gloom into the mind of the barber, already weakened by misfortune and tre effects of sickness. While it startled every affection of his heart, it awoke in all its force (as the

11*

heart in its alarm will often do) the full power of an imagination that prosperity had lulled into comparative inaction.
The barber, though he had received the same education, did not use it to the same advantage as his wife. It
perplexed, while it soothed him, to observe the serenity
with which his wife sustained the adverse change in their
circumstances. She, who had sacrificed so much for him,
did not even seem to be conscious that she had made any
sacrifice whatever. Her wealthy relatives were now all
scattered and burdened with their own separate claims,
and could do nothing to assist the barber. Still, in their
distress, her concern seemed all for her husband and her
children. The sea is not more necessarily agitated by the
sighing of the winter winds, than is a generous and religious bosom by the accents of distress and sorrow in a
fellow being. So natural, so free from effort or reluctance,
appeared the affectionate concern with which the gentle
Mary exerted herself to alleviate the sufferings of her
husband and her children.

At different times her gentle uncomplaining conduct
produced varying effects upon her husband's mind. Sometimes, when his reflections took a gloomy turn, the clear
angelic serenity of her looks would, with an influence like
that of gentle music, subdue his discontent, and restore his
thoughts to calmness and to order; at others, when he
beheld her sharing in their common want, and remembered what she was when she resigned abundance and
respectability to unite her earthly lot to his, his anguish
far exceeded what it was when he thought only of his own
privations.

"We are worse off now", he said to her, one summer
evening, as they sat before the open window which looked
upon their little orchard, and watched the crows winging
high above them to the distant wood ; "our case is worse
than that of even the animals that are left without reason.
The face of the round world is free to them ; from the worm

to the eagle, all are well provided for. The crow has his nest upon the bough, and the hare has her form in the furze, and their food is ready for them at morning in the fields, or by the river, for no trouble but the pains of seeking it. In the water, in the air, or on the earth, food, clothing, and a home, are ready found for all. The goldfinch has his painted feathers, and the robin his grain of seed, while our poor babes are perishing with cold and hunger".

"For every pain we bear with true patience in this life", said his wife, " we shall receive an age of glory and of happiness in the next".

"Yet who would murmur at a Providence that is inscrutable", resumed O'Berne, in a fit of sombre musing; "if men would only do their duty by each other? But it is not, and it never will be so. They say that if you take a young bird unfledged from the nest, and set it down alone in some field far away, where the parents cannot find it, and leave it there and watch it, they say there is no bird that passes, of whatever kind, and hears its lonesome chirp, that will not bring it a worm, or a mouthful of some other food, until it gets strength to shift for itself. But men! men must have laws to force them even to do so much as will keep the breath of life within the lips of their own kind".

"All is well", said Mary, "while we keep our own fidelity. Let the storm blow as it will, let all our prospects and our possessions go to ruin; all still is well while Heaven is not offended. Let us keep our hands unstained, and in His name who distributed suffering and joy, let the worst that will befall us. It is not want nor plenty that can either give or take away our peace of mind. To be contented with the will of Heaven, and to strive to put it into practice, is always in our power, and if we are not so disposed in our distress, we may be certain that we should not be so under any change whatever. Let us preserve our innocence, and all is well".

"You are very easily contented", said the barber with
an angry look. "What were your thoughts, two months
since, when the fire seized on the grocer's house next
door, and we saw, with our own eyes, the remains of an
unhappy infant dug out of the ruins?"

"I will tell you, Godfrey, what I thought", replied his
wife; "I trembled for myself when I beheld it. He,
said I, who has created the world so fair, and filled it
with so many blessings, who has made that beautiful sun,
and those millions of shining stars, and who daily and
hourly shows his goodness and his mercy in new acts of
kindness to his creatures; he too it is who has permitted
that sinless child to perish by a frightful death. Let me
therefore take the warning, and beware in what condition
I fall into his hands; for if he thus afflicts the innocent
and good on Earth, what should be done with us? I
speak to you in this way, dear Godfrey, because I see you
are beginning to sink in spirits. Beware, my dear, dear
husband; it is in our moments of gloom and melancholy,
as well as in those of thoughtless gaiety, that the enemy
of our souls endeavours to seduce us into crime or
madness".

As she said these words she laid her hand caressingly
upon her husband's shoulder. Moved by the action as
well as by the words with which it was accompanied,
O'Berne was softened, and melted slowly into tears.

"Read to me", said he, "and it may be better".

His wife complied, and taking from the drawer a copy
of the scriptures, began to read a portion of the New
Testament. Godfrey listened, and it seemed to him as if
he had never heard the words before. For several days
after he became totally absorbed in the perusal of the
volume; the profound wisdom of its counsels, the majestic
simplicity of its narrative, and the stupendous nature of
the events which it recorded, the heartfelt spirit of prayer
with which it was pervaded, the terrible solemnity of its

wa,nings, the melting tenderness of its promises, and the
striking nature of the examples by which both were illus-
trated, made a deep and strong impression on the mind
of the village philosopher. It seemed to him as if he
never before had heard how all things were first called
into existence; how murder entered first into the world,
which, until then, was the abode of love and happiness.
He there heard the Deity delivering his law to man, amid
the lightnings and the thunders of Mount Sinai; he saw
in the fate of Eli and his sons, an example of the divine
justice against neglectful parents; he dwelt with enchant-
ment on the mystical beauties of the story of Ruth and
the marriage of Rebecca: and he traced with astonishment and awe, the tremendous and affecting history of the
origin, the fall, and restoration of his species, detailed in
language worthy of a subject so sublime. He read, and it
astonished him to think how mechanical till now had been
the nature of his feelings and his practice. What! was
he then one of those who really believed that the Divinity
himself had come on Earth to teach his creatures, both
by word and by example, the real nature of moral
goodness; to overthrow the worldly error which ascribed
to human pride the honours due to virtue; and to introduce
modesty, humility, patience, and mildness, to the same
rank in human estimation which they had ever held in
the divine, and which men till then accorded to false
glory, ambition, revenge, and haughtiness of soul?

The philosophic barber, however, while he wondered
how little hitherto he had felt the real nature of the character he professed in society, rather revolved these
wonders in his intellect than let them sink into his heart.
His imagination became deeply impressed, and he brooded
by day and dreamed by night on what he had been
studying, until his whole mind became absorbed with the
one engrossing subject. To change the heart, it is not
sufficient that the mind should be excited. To create a

spirit ot tenderness and love is of far greater importance in the way of virtue, than to captivate the fancy or amaze the understanding.

The impatience, therefore, with which he bore the increasing perplexity in his affairs, was not in any permanent degree diminished. A week of extreme misery and privation was closed by a formal ejectment from the house in which he lived. We pledge ourselves not to the truth of the events of a few days and nights immediately succeeding, but relate them as they are told in the neighbourhood, reserving all comment to the conclusion of the tale. It was a Friday evening, and the family were to give up possession before twelve on the following Monday. With a mind weakened by distress and apprehension, the barber spent the day pacing alone from room to room of the little dwelling, like one distracted in his thoughts.

"If it be true", said he, striking his forehead with a burst of anger,—"if it be true, that immaterial things can hourly, as young Danaher asserted, exert an influence over what is possible and material, why will they not interfere to serve as well as to perplex and to annoy us? Why will not that power, whatever it may have been, that visited me for my discomfort in that lonely inn and at Rath Danaher, present itself again for my assistance, at a time when human aid has left me at my last extremity?"

His wife, who overheard those words, was afraid that her husband's misfortunes were beginning to affect his reason.

"Remember , she said, 'that apart from human aid we have but one source of power to which we can apply".

"I would apply to ANY"", cried her husband with a burst of frenzy; "from whatever source assistance comes, I am ready to receive it".

Saying this, he rushed rom the room. The fit of passion having passed away, he was able to reflect with

more distinctness on the nature of what he had said, and
his imagination froze at the thought that it was possible
he might yet be taken at his word. Terror, in addition
to the former excitement, now seized upon his nerves, and
unfitted him for any settled thought. He could only wait
in hopeless silence the passing of the shocking gloom
that seized upon his mind, without knowing how to
quicken its departure.

In this mood, say the story-tellers, he retired to rest.
The chamber in which he slept looked out upon the
orchard, at the door of which, some evenings before, the
conversation already recorded had taken place between
the barber and his wife. The bed was so placed that the
former could see as he lay down, on a moonlight night, a
considerable portion of the orchard and the country lying
far beyond it. Such a night was that of which we speak;
it was between one and two o'clock, and in mid-winter,
when after a few hours' slumber, the view of the orchard,
with its moonlight paths, crossed by the sharply defined
shadows of the trees, came slowly on his sight through
the uncurtained window.

For a time as he looked out upon the scene, the barber
could not tell if he were waking or asleep, so indistinct
and floating was the consciousness that existed in his
mind. All doubt, however, ceased, or rather he ceased to
question what his actual condition was, when he beheld a
figure dressed in a grotesque suit of black, advancing
through the trees and approaching the windows with a
slow but steady pace. An unaccountable influence held
the barber motionless, until the stranger approached so
near that his singular drapery almost appeared to touch
the glass. It seemed to the former as if an iron hand
were laid upon his breast and pressed him to the bed.
The moonlight falling on the back of the figure prevented
him from seeing with distinctness what the features were
of this unknown intruder, but the sense of horror which

his presence excited was almost insupportable. After a
little time the figure slowly raised one hand, and retiring
a little from the window, waved it gracefully as a sign
for Godfrey to arise and follow. The sequel is gathered
from Godfrey's own indistinct recollection of what took
place. He could not, he said, resist the summons; he got
up like one under the influence of some necromantic
power, hastily drew on his clothes, and proceeding to the
window, opened the sash and stepped out into the orchard.
The figure retired, still turning at intervals, and beckoning
with one hand until they had passed into the open country.

On a sloping hill at the eastern side of the village stood
a grove of firs, shadowing a tract of soil which once had
been a burying-ground, but in which no interment had
taken place for centuries before. Tradition only, and the
half-obliterated remains that were sometimes dug out of
the soil, supplied the history of its former uses, for
neither monument nor grave-stone had for a long period
been discernible upon the slope. Near the borders of
this sombre grove it was that O'Berne beheld the figure
panse and seem to wait his arrival. Still moved by the
same irresistible influence, the barber pressed forward up
the slope, fixing his eye upon the stranger, and even
eager for the conference. which he anticipated with a
dizzy sense of terror. Nor were his wonder and his awe
diminished, when, on turning round to address him, the
stranger revealed the countenance and figure of his old
master!

CHAPTER IX

WE pursue the barber's narrative as he is said to have
delivered it

"You said" (the stranger slowly and calmly enun-
ciated each syllable, like one who utters words of the last

importance), "that you were ready to receive assistance
from ANY source. I am one who have both the will and
the power to afford it".

"And who are you?" the barber would have said in
turn, but his jaws, locked fast as if by a fit ... tetanus,
refused to articulate the words. His guide, however,
seemed to understand his thought.

"Who I am", said he, with a voice so inexpressibly
mournful that it penetrated to the hearer's soul, "is of
no importance to your present views or mine. Let it be
enough for you to know, and for me to tell you, that I
can procure you the assistance you require. Speak therefore, and tell what thou wouldst have".

The barber replied at once :—

"Food for my family and a certain home. They are
miserable. If thou canst secure them sustenance and
shelter, thou shalt have my gratitude".

"I require it not", replied the figure with a smile of
subtle scorn. "I seek not love but service. I have it in
my power to do all and more for thee than thou requirest,
but no one offers wages without requiring a return. I
offer then to relieve you from your present difficulty, but
it is on one condition".

"Name it", cried the barber.

"It is a simple one", replied the spirit. "Those who
are at war do not use to pay the servants of their Enemy.
You must be one of us, if you would receive our aid".

"What! become like you an open enemy to the
Divinity?"

"Become like us".

"There is no step in crime or in calamity", replied the
barber, "beyond an express and formal hatred of the
Deity. I dare not accept of the condition".

"Remain then as thou art, and serve in wretchedness",
replied the fiend. "He whom thou servest has abandoned
thee to want and woe Continue if thou wilt to worship

a neglectful master instead of one who is willing to repay
thee with abundance".

"It may be", said the barber, "that he does but try
my patience and my loyalty.   This life is short : he may
be bounteous in the next".

"Feed on that painted hope if thou wilt", replied the
fiend, " and see if it will satisfy thy present misery. Did
He not tell thee likewise that whosoever should forsake all
things for Him in this world, should receive an hundred-
fold even in the present life ?"

"Aye", said the barber with a sigh, "but he meant in
the sweets of a good conscience, which is a treasure
beyond all that kings or emperors enjoy".

"Well", said the spirit, " be content with that, if thou
prefer it.   If thou accept my offer, happiness and peace
and plenty shall surround thee for the term of thy mortal
life; if not, affliction, trouble, and necessity".

"For my mortal life perhaps", replied the barber, "but
how shall it be after ?"

"Why", said the fiend, "thou wouldst not look to be
better than thy master".

Godfrey was silent, and the spirit, after a pause,
resumed :

"To-morrow thou shalt have the choice of misery or
joy.   I do not press thee to decide at once.   Whenever
the extremity may be at hand, my power will not be
distant".

With these strange words he vanished, and the barber
returned to his dwelling.   Of his adventures on the way
home, or the manner in which he obtained an entrance
into his own house, he had no recollection.   On the following morning he found himself in his bed as usual, but
could remember nothing of what took place from the
moment of the spirit's disappearance.   There were no cor-
roborating signs in the position of his dress or in the state
of the window, that bore testimony to the reality of his

midnight excursion ; and he would have been inclined, notwithstanding the regular train of the occurrences, and the vivid impression he retained of what had passed, to pronounce the whole a dream, if it were not that the two former mysterious events which had befallen him, left his reason far more open to an admission of supernatural agency.

The day which followed was the same in which, as set forth in a preceding portion of this narrative, Mr. Moynehan the tax-gatherer left home to dine at Castle Tobin. It was a trying one to Godfrey, on more than one account. Not one of the inmates of the dwelling had tasted food since they arose, and at night the cries of the younger children rent the father's breast. To complete the dreariness and discomfort of the scene, the night was gusty and full of showers, and the sound of the inclement weather breaking against the doors and windows, seemed to give promise of the destitution which awaited them when they should no longer own the shelter of a roof.

Emaciated even more by wasting thoughts than by the want of necessary food, the barber sat in the chair, which now but rarely held a customer, attending in silence (if he attended at all) to the consolatory expressions that were now and then addressed to him by his wife, and weaving vain conjectures on the future.

"Talk you of comfort ?" he said, looking backward on the latter with a ghastly smile. " Have you the wallet ready, then? and the wattle and tin can? and the slate and voster for Mortimer to study in the dyke on summer days, when we all sit down together by the roadside in the shade, away from the dust of the horses' feet and the carriage wheels, while we ask the gentlefolks for charity as they roll by ? not forgetting the linen caps for the girls, and all the beggar's furniture? Have you all that ready, since you talk of comfort ?"

" Even if it came to that", replied his wife, with a tone

of slight severity mingled with affection, "I trust we all have resignation to endure it".

"It would be less a burden to my mind", said the barber, "that you had asked me 'why I brought you to this misery?' rather than to hear you speak so kindly. And why, why did I do so? Why did I not leave you where I found you, happy and prosperous in your father's house?"

At this moment one of the younger children which had crept from its pallet of straw, took Godfrey by the coat, and looking up with a pallid face and crying accent, said :—

"Father, Ellen is hungry".

If those who make themselves miserable about fancied evils, could know the pangs that rent the heart of O'Berne at this instant, it is probable they would look upon their own condition with a more contented eye. In the agony of his soul the unhappy man bent down his head, and half murmured between his teeth :—

"If the opportunity now were offered me again, I would not, I think, reject it".

He had scarcely framed these words in his own mind, when the tramp of horse's hoofs was heard approaching the door, and soon after a loud knocking with a whip handle made the panel echo through the house.

"Hollo! ho! ho! Who's within? Open, I say! O'Berne, where are you? Are your razors ready?"

> "They have got a new method of shaving,
> They have got a new method of shaving—
> Oh, I wouldn't lie under that razor,
> For all that lies under the sun.

"O'Berne, I say! Godfrey, bring out the light!"

"'Tis Mr. Moynehan the tax-gatherer's voice", said Mary.

"And drunk", added the barber,

"May Heaven forgive him!"

" Why—O'Berne, I say! Are you asleep or dead?
Open! open the door!

> " Over the mountain and over the moor,
> Barefoot and wretched I wander forlorn,
> My father is dead, and my mother is poor,
> And I weep for the days that will never return.
> Pity, kind gentlefolks ——

" Come—come—barber, this is no joke".

The door was opened, and Mr. Moynehan made his appearance, wrapped in a dark frieze travelling coat, which glistened with rain, as did the fresh and well-nurtured countenance of the owner. In one hand he held the bridle of his horse, which seemed inclined to follow him into the house.

" How are you? how are you?" said the tax-gatherer, as he staggered forwards,—" no compliments at all at present, do you see? I'm come to stay the night with you, for 'tis rather late and windy".

" You have chosen but a poor house for your lodging, sir", said the barber.

" No matter for that; many a better fellow often slept in a worse. So that you find a dry corner for my horse, you may put myself anywhere, do you see?"

" Mortimer", said the barber, " take the gentleman's horse round to the little cow-house, and see him well rubbed for the night".

" And hark you!" said the tax-gatherer, setting his arms akimbo, and endeavouring to keep his balance while he gazed on Mortimer, " before you do so, my young hero, give me that portmanteau that's fastened behind the saddle. That's right", he added, as the boy complied, " King George would have a crow to pluck with me if I let anything happen to them. And hark in your ear— another thing—I took a glass too much at Castle Tobin : no matter—a set of rogues—They have their reasons for tempting me to exceed".

"Mary", said the barber, "put the children to bed, and shut the door".

"Good night, Mrs. O'Berne—good night—And hark you—Mrs. O'Berne, I see you're shocked to see me as I am, but 'tis my weakness, that and a little tender-heartedness about the making out of an inventory—I confess it —if an honest, hospitable country gentleman sends me, in a goodnatured sort of way, a sack of corn for that poor animal abroad, and then omits all mention of his own neat riding nag, I haven't the heart to charge him with it. Good Mrs. O'Berne, I protest to you, there is not a single four-wheeled carriage, nor a gig, nor a riding horse in the whole neighbourhood of B——. Those are all phantoms that we meet every day upon the roads—phantoms, madam.—I have the best authority for it—the word of the owners themselves—all ghosts of grayhounds, ghosts of pointers, ghosts of spaniels, terriers, servants, and all. Oh! Mrs. O'Berne, there's nothing in the island but ghosts and rogues! There's that attorney—no matter who—he's an honest fellow to be sure, and keeps a capital bottle of whisky: he had the assurance, last week, after putting blank, blank, blank, against horses, carriages, and servants, to turn about as he handed me the paper, and offer me a ride in his own curricle as far as the village. And I protest to you, the ghost of a curricle carried us both uncommonly well. As for the great men of the county, I can't for the life of me tell how they manage with two hearths and six windows. There's a place that shall be nameless — I don't say 'tis Castle Tobin now—where I can count four-and-twenty windows as I ride up the avenue; but on entering I cannot persuade Tob the owner I mean—that it is more than quarter the number. Assessed taxes! assessed rogues and swindlers! But good night, these things must not continue—Pray for me,—your prayers, I think, are heard. As for that husband of yours—he deals in witchcraft".

"Who?—I?" cried the barber, starting from a fit of gloomy musing.

"Ha, ha, ha! observe how he starts. Look at him, Mrs. O'Berne. I would not trust my life with that fellow across the street".

Godfrey gathered his brows and looked darkly on the ground.

"Look at him", continued the tax-gatherer, laying his hand on Mrs. O'Berne's arm, and pointing with the other to her husband, who, in an attitude of ghastly anger, looked backward in his face. "There are men who go through life straight, like the handle of my whip; and there are others that, like the lash, will take any crooked bend you give it. Look at him, how he eyes the portmanteau!"

Again the barber started.

"Ha, ha! Come, come, O'Berne, I did but jest. You must learn to take a joke".

Mrs. O'Berne retired, and the tax-gatherer remained with her husband in the kitchen. During the foregoing conversation, a dreadful struggle had been taking place within the mind of the latter. The gold! Mr. Moynehan, in his random jest, had harped his thought aright. That portmanteau would secure his family for ever against all fear of indigence. Terrified by the workings of his own breast, and desirous to remove a temptation which he feared might grow too strong for his already flickering virtue, he approached the tax-gatherer, and said, with a hoarse and mournful energy of voice and manner:

"Mr. Moynehan, it is as your friend I advise you to return home to-night. There are evil minds abroad, hearts weakened by affliction, and unable to resist the deadly thoughts that want and melancholy whisper to them in the silence of the night. Be wise, therefore, and return to your house at once".

"Return to my house!" cried the tax-gatherer, setting

both his hands upon his sides, and looking on the barber with a stare of high defiance. "And who are you, sir, that order me to return to my house? I shall stay where I am, sir, and you may frown and grind your teeth as you will, sir, but I shall not be ordered off by you. And I will tell yon more, I'll have myself shaved to-night; so get your apparatus ready on the instant".

"To-night", said O'Berne, "pray do not say to-night. It is already one o'clock".

But Mr. Moynehan, like many who have not a perfect possession of their reason, was obstinate. He insisted on being shaved, and took his seat in the centre of the room, while the barber, with trembling knees, and a mind shaken to its foundation by its own internal struggles, prepared the implements necessary to the task allotted to him.

"These things must have an end, O'Berne", the tax-gatherer resumed, as he loosened his neck-cloth and laid it on the back of the chair. "I cannot continue long to lead this life—'tis bad—'tis wicked—'tis unchristian. My good lady is for ever lecturing me about it, and I believe she's right. I promised her this morning that this should be the last time I would ever dine from home again, and I am resolved to keep my word, I am resolved to——"

Here he began to grow drowsy as he sat, and continued nodding in his chair, while he spoke in interrupted sentences:

"Yes—she's right—the women are right after all about these matters—they are more doc—do—docile—well—I'll mend. She hinted that I might begin too late—but no—to-morrow morning will be time enough—to-night it would be late indeed—Cas—Ca—Castle To— Tob--Tobin—farewell—I'll mend—I'll---re—form—I'll —I'll—To-morrow I'll begin—I'll——"

He dropped his head upon his breast and fell fast asleep. The storm had now subsided, and the moon by fits, as on the preceding night, gleamed brightly on the

hearth. The barber opened the door, which looked into
the orchard. The picture was one which might have
made a spectator tremble, if there had been a spectator
there. O'Berne, with his worn and haggard countenance,
standing at the open door, and looking with wild eyes and
ghastly teeth into the moonlit orchard. The tax-gatherer
sleeping, with his neck-cloth laid aside, and his head
hanging back in the profound repose of drunkenness—
the hour late—the night favourable—and the instruments,
which might as readily be made to serve the purposes of
destruction as of utility, lying open on the barber's table.
Let us close the scene upon this horrible tableau.

CHAPTER X.

In less than two hours after she had first retired to rest,
the sleep of Mrs. O'Berne, which had been disturbed by
frightful dreams, was altogether broken by the sound of
a foot-step in her room. Looking up, she beheld her husband, with an end of candle lighted in his hand, looking
pale and terrified. In answer to her question, he said,
that the tax-gatherer had not yet retired to rest. She
fell asleep again and did not wake till morning. Her husband then informed her, that Mr. Moynehan, notwithstanding all his persuasions, had insisted on leaving the
house on the preceding night, and taking the road to his
own residence, which was well known to be infested by
footpads. But he had good news also for her ear.
Before leaving the house, he had lent him a sum which
would be more than sufficient to reëstablish them
in all their former comfort. But this was to be kept a
secret.

There was something in the manner of her husband, as
he gave her this account, which perplexed and pained her.

12

It was not gloomy, as before, but unequally and fitfully joyous. He laughed, and his laughter was broken by a spasmodic action of the frame, as if a searing iron had suddenly been applied to a part of it. Mrs. O'Berne now feared, from many things her husband said, that the un-expected generosity of the tax-gatherer might produce an effect as dangerous to her husband's mind as his previous poverty.

In the evening, while Mary sat musing on what had passed, her husband, who had gone out on business, suddenly entered the house with a hurried and agitated look.

"I was right", said he, "in warning Mr. Moynehan not to take that road last night".

" Why so ?"

" His horse was found this morning near the village, but without a rider".

Mrs. O'Berne clasped her hands with a silent gesture of affright.

"I tell you truth—and there was blood upon the saddle-cloth—blood, Mary".

" He was murdered then ?"

"Why so? Who told you that? How do you know it?"

"What else does it look like? What else do they think of it?"

"Think! Oh, they think as you do—but it is all conjecture".

" Let him have perished as he may", said Mary, hurried onward by the dreadful tidings into an energy unusual to her disposition, "it is certain at least that he has per-ished. O fearful Providence! It was a heart of stone that took him in his fit of sin !"

" Be charitable, wife", said the barber angrily.

" I should be so, indeed. I thank you for the counsel. If he was murdered, then, may Heaven forgive his murderer !"

"Pray for him", said the barber, "but not that way. Perhaps the wretch was crazed with want or hunger—perhaps he was strongly tempted—and that when ruin was threatening him on one side and the temptation assailed him on the other – and the opportunity—and the silence—and the night—perhaps he could not hold his hand—but what of that?— Our children shall not starve, at all events—I have the gold—the gold".

And he laughed with a shocking levity.

"Yes, we have reason to rejoice", replied his wife, with calmness—"but the widow—the poor widow! To-night, while the wind is howling about her house, how lonesome is her heart, and low within her! They had one child, a boy; and she is often looking at him how, and asking herself if the story can be true. Oh, wretched man! Had he, who did the deed, no wife, no family, to care for. when he made a widow and an orphan at a blow? And all for a little dross!"

"Well—well", said the barber hurriedly, "perhaps he means to pay it back again as soon as he can, and to lay the bones in consecrated ground. What more can the poor wretch do now? Oh, wife, they say such money is easily earned, but he who did it knows better".

"To-night", continued Mary, following up her own train of thought, "while the servants are whispering in the kitchen, she is lying on her bed, with the child close by her, and listening to every fresh account they bring her of her loss. To see a husband or a wife go calmly to their doom—to tend them in their last sickness— to read them holy lessons—to pray for them aloud when they are dying or when they are dead—that's happiness to what she feels to-night, although when you were sick I thought it would be misery. She must not even know that he lies in holy ground".

"But perhaps he shall in time. Let us talk no more of this, to-night, at least".

"Aye, Godfrey, it is test; blood will speak, if it should burst the grave for it".

There was a cobbler in B———————, who, like our barber, could scarcely obtain as many half-pence by his awl as might procure him a sufficiency of the cheapest food. Yet, however he was enabled to procure the means, the fellow was a habitual drunkard. It was his practice when intoxicated, to take his post at the village cross, and, putting his hands under his leather apron, to commence a string of vociferous abuse against all the inhabitants of the place without exception. The out-pouring usually continued five or six hours without intermission, from ex-ordium to peroration, greatly to the scandal of the regular inhabitants, and to the entertainment of the little urchins of the place, who gathered round him in a circle in order to chorus his monologue with their shrill hurras. Yet, at other times, the unfortunate wretch could be as decent and well conducted as any individual in the place, and he might have been, as the world goes, an estimable cha-racter, if the fascination of strong drink had not an in-fluence over him which it appeared almost impossible for him to resist.

Within a fortnight after the occurrence just related, it happened that this cobbler was sitting at work in his miserable hut, and singing, as he made his lapstone ring, when he was surprised to see the barber cross his thres-hold. The latter having closed the door behind him, and shoved in the bolt, approached the man of patches with a serious countenance.

"Shanahan", said he, "I have something serious to say to you, and it may be for your advantage, provided you promise to keep it secret".

"Sacret, Mr. O'Berne? As to keepin' a sacret, providin' its nothin' agin law or conscience, I'll keep a sacret with any man brathin', though 'tis I says it, that oughtn't".

" It is not against law or conscience. Listen then. For three nights successively, within the last fortnight, I dreamed of money in a certain place, that I will name to you, provided you promise to assist me in obtaining it".

" Assist you! I'll engage I will so, an' welcome. An' is this what you call something sarious to say to me? Now I call it something pleasant—an' joyful—an' delightful!" exclaimed the cobbler, springing from his seat as he completed the climax. " Come away, au' let us lay hands on it at once".

" No—no—" said the barber, " not so fast. The search must be made at night. I will call on you myself about eleven o'clock, and be ready to come with me. I have not even mentioned it to my wife, for fear she might have some scruples about using the money. The spot is not far distant, though lonesome enough. I will tell you where it is when I come at night".

O'Berne was true to his appointment; and on this night it was, that in the presence of the cobbler, he dug up in a lonesome ruin, within less than a quarter of a mile of the village, that treasure, for the possession of which he accounted to his wife in a very different manner. A moderate portion of the prize easily bribed the cobbler to keep silence until it should suit O'Berne's convenience to call on him to give testimony of the manner in which he had obtained the money.

Soon after, the barber and his family left the neighbourhood of B————, where they were not heard again of for more than a score of years.

CHAPTER XI.

Young Edmund Moynehan was brought up with all the care that could possibly be bestowed on the education of a child. He was carefully preserved, in his early years,

from all access of superstition. He heard none of those
garrulous tales which too often haunt the nursery, and be-
speak future victims to weakness of mind, almost in the
very cradle. In the mean time, the true spirit of religion
was deeply impressed upon his heart; and his practice
was the more fervent in proportion as it was more enlightened. He grew apace, and in time inherited the office
which had proved so fatal to his father. He exercised it,
however, in a very different manner. He took no bribes,
and he allowed no false returns. The astonishment which
such a line of conduct excited about B———— was
proportioned to the novelty of the provocation. Almost
every tax-payer joined in abuse of Edmund Moynehau.
Many called him a mean, exact, prying fellow; and a few
of the more fiery gentry even talked of "calling him out";
but he did not alter his course, and they found themselves
under the necessity of being as exact as himself. In all
other respects, he was what his father had been in his
earlier and happier days.

He had reached his three-and-twentieth year without
meeting any adventure out of the ordinary course of rural
life in the rank in which he moved. He yet retained a
strong recollection of his parent, and he felt, without the
least emotion of revenge, a strong desire to investigate the
mystery of his disappearance.

One evening, he was standing at the window of the
small parlour which looked out (for he now occupied the
dwelling first owned by his father) on the waters of the
Shannon. Although the sun shone bright, a westerly gale
drove fiercely along the surface of the stream, and confined the fishing craft to their moorings by the windward
beach. The narrow-pinioned fishers hovering above the
broken waves, by their screams and rapid motion added
much to the interest of the scene. Occasionally a bulky
cormorant flew with outstretched neck along the surface of
the bay, while the pleasure boat (which Moynehan some-

times used in his days of leisure), tossed and tugged at
her anchor by the shore.

Living, notwithstanding his occupation, in comparative
solitude, with few objects to interest his thoughts in any
remarkable degree, it is not surprising that young Moynehan often dwelt with undiminished interest upon the
mystery of his father's fate.   That violence, and human
violence, had been employed in his destruction, he entertained no doubt.   Of greater enterprise and firmness
than his father had been, he only wanted footing for the
inquiry, and the total absence of this was what often lay
heavy at his heart.

A portrait of his father, rudely finished, yet with
sufficient resemblance to correspond with his recollection
of the original, was suspended against the wall.   Oppressed with the reflections which crowded on his mind
as he gazed on the familiar features, he left the house and
hurried to the strand, where he paced for some time in
silence along the margin of the water.   His boatman was
employed in repairing the keel of a small skiff, which was
used as a kind of tender on the pleasure boat.   Near him,
Rick Lillis, grown gray with years, and somewhat bowed
by care, was leaning against a huge block of stone, and
observing the boatman at work.

" The young masther looks as if he was put out a
-little", said the boatman.

" Ah, little admiration he should", replied the old herdsman.   " It is fourteen years and better now since we lost
the ould one.   Many's the time since I repented that I
didn't go with him that night, or make him go with me.
But when a man's hour's come they say the world wouldn't
put it off.   I might well know them hills were no place
for any one to be thravelling at night, let alone such a
night as that ; but he wouldn't be said by me.   I hard of
a thing happening among them hills before, that was

enough to make anybody look about him before he'd venture among 'em late at night".

" What was that ?"

" I'll tell you. You know Jerry Lacey, the pedlar, that used to go through the counthry formerly sellin' ribbons, an' rings, an' snuff-boxes, an' things that way, at the great houses an' places along the road ?"

" You mean him that has a shop now overright where O'Berne the barber lived formerly at B——— ?"

" I do—the very man. He was thravellin' from Cork, an' he took the conthrary way through the same mountains that my master (rest his sowl!) an' myself went that night. Well, if he did, it come late upon him, an' he turned off the road, thinkin' to make a short cut, an' he lost his way in the mountains, an' it was midnight before he met a human christian, or one ha'p'orth. ' What'll become o' me at all, I wondher', says Jerry ; ' 'twas the misforthinate hour I ever turned off o' you, for one road', says he. Well, on he went, an' in place o' comin' to any place, 'tis lonesomer an' lonesomer the road was gettin' upon him, till at last he hard a *nize*, as it were o' somebody hammerin' at a little distance. So he med towards the *nize*. Well, 'tisn't long till he comes to a little lonesome cabin without e'er a windy in front, and a rish light burnin' within, an' the doore half open, an' the ugliest man ever you see sittin' upon a stool in the middle of the floore, and he havin' a tinker's anvil on his lap, an' he makin' saucepans.

" ' Bless all here', says Jerry, pushing in the door.

" The little man made him no answer, only looked up sthraight in his face, an' tould him to come in au' shet the doore.

" ' An' what do you want now ?' says the little tinker, when Jerry done what he bid him.

" ' Shelther, then, for the night, plase your lordship, says Jerry, thinkin' it betther to be civil.

"'Take a sate by the fire', says the tinker, 'an' we'll see what's to be done'.

"'That your reverence may lose nothin' by it', says Jerry, dhrawin' a chair. 'Them that give the stranger shelter in this world, won't be left without it themselves in the next'.

"Well, there they sat. There was a pot boiling over the fire, au' it had a smell o' mait, which, I'll be bail, Jerry wasn't sorry to find. So afther a while, the tinker went out, as he said, to dig a handful o' pzaties, to have with the mait, au' tould Jerry for his life not to touch one ha'p'orth about the place, au' above all things, not to look into the pot, for if he'd daar do it, the mutton 'ud be spiled. Well, hardly was he outside the doore, when Jerry was a'most ready to faint, wantin' to know what was in the pot. So as there was ne'er a windee, and the doore fast shet, he thought he'd take one dawny peep. 'Never welcome himself an' his pot', says Jerry, 'if he hadn't to say anything about it, sure I wouldn't care one bane what was in it. I'm kilt from it, for a pot', says he, fixin' his two eyes upou it. 'I won't look at it at all', says he, ''tis up at the dhresser I'll look, an' I'll whistle the Humours o' Glin, an' who knows but I'd slhkame away the thoughts of it 'till himself 'ud come in'. So he turned his back to the fire, and began whistling. ''Tis bilin' greatly, whatsomever it is', says he by au' by. 'Ah sure what hurt is there in one peep? How will he ever find it out? A likely story indeed, that the mutton 'ud be spiled by one look. He's an ould rogue, that's what he is, an' I'll have a peep in spite o' the Danes'. So he went to the fireside, and he *ruz* the lid. There was a great steam, an' the wather bilin' tantivity. 'I'm in dhread o' my life', says Jerry. "What'll I do at all, if he pins me in the fact? No matther, here goes, any way', an' he struck down a fleshfork into the wather. Well, I'll go bail he opened his eyes wide enough, when

12*

he drew up upon the points of the fork a collop of a
man's hand ——"

"Eyeh, Rick, howl!"

"I'm only tellin' you the story as I hard it myself.
Sure I wasn't by".

"Do you mane to persuade me a thing o' that kind
ever happened?"

"Can't you hear my story? what do I know only as I
hear? 'Well', says Jerry, an' he lookin' at his prize,
'here's a state', says he; 'here's purty work; what in the
world will become o' me now at all?' says he: 'I'll let
down the pot-lid any way'.

"Well hardly all was right, when the tinker come in.

"'Did you look in the pot?' says he.

"'Oh my lord', says Jerry, "what for 'ud I be lookin'
in it?'

"'Are you hungry?'

"'Not much, my lord'.

"'Will you take a cup o the broth?'

"Well, Jerry thought he'd dhrop, when he hard him
axin' him to take a cup o' the broth.

"'Not any, we're obleest to your reverence', says he,
bowin' very polite.

"'What'll you do then?' says the tinker.

"'I'll stay as I am, with your lordship's good will'.

"'There's a bed within in the room, there; may be
you like to take a stretch on it?'

"Why then I believe I will, plase your reverence',
says Jerry, as I'm tired'.

"So he took his pack, an' away with him into the room,
as if he was walkin' into the mouth of a tiger. He didn't
like to go to bed, although there was the nicest bedstead
in a corner, with white dimity curtains, an' a fine soft
tick, an' the room nately boorded an' soundid as if there
was a kitchen under it. So he rowled himself in his
great coat, an' sat down in a corner waitin' to see what

'ud happen, bein' in dhread he'd fall asleep, if he stretched
upon the bed. The moon was shinin' in the windee, when,
about twelve o'clock, as sure as you're standin' there, he
tould my father, he seen the bed sinkin' in the ground.
Oh, his heart was below in his shoe! ' Wasn't it the good
thought o' me', says he, ' not to go to bed ? I declare to
my heart', says he, ' I'll make a race while he's below !'
So out he started, an I'll engage 'tis long till he was caught
goin' through the mountains at night again".

"Dear knows, that's a wondherful story", said the
boatman. "But asy! what boat is that I wondher,
runnin' in for the little creek? Some *jot* or another,
may be dhruv in by the wind, an' she comin' in from
Cove".

On nearer approach, however, the vessel seemed too
small to answer this conjecture. She was a little cutter,
of about ten or twelve tons burden, with snow white
sails, close-reefed, and drenched to the peak with spray.
Casting anchor near the shore, a small boat was lowered
from the stern, into which two persons entered, and proceeded to land. On reaching the shore, one left the boat,
while the other, pushing off into the breakers, which even
here ran high, returned to the cutter. The stranger, who
remained, was a man deeply " declined into the vale of
years", wrapped in an old plaid cloak, and wearing a cap
of seal-skin. He stooped much, and walked with so
much difficulty, that but for a stick, on which he leaned,
it would have been impossible for him to have maintained
his upright position. Perceiving him about to take the
road leading to the interior, young Moynehan approached,
and politely asked him to his house for the night, as it was
usual to do with any stranger who travelled in these lonely
districts. The only inn, he informed him, at which he
could obtain accommodation, was at such a distance that it
would fatigue him extremely to reach it on foot that day.
The same accommodation he offered for his boatman.

There was in the stranger's manner of accepting the courtesy, an air of deep humility and deprecation, that indicated habitual suffering. He trembled like one in a fit of palsy, and bowed low, supporting himself by grasping his stick with both hands, while he murmured forth his thanks. The same deep gratitude he showed for every trivial attention that was paid him on his entering the house. It seemed as if he thought the humblest attitude he could assume was far above his pretensions, and no exertions that either the widow or her son could make, were sufficient to draw him into free and unembarrassed conversation throughout the evening. He sat as far apart as possible from every individual that was present, bowed with the utmost respect at every word that was addressed to him, as if it were a favour of the last importance. Two or three times, Edmund Moynehan saw, or fancied he saw, the eyes of the stranger rest upon his features with an expression of inquiry, which, however, instantly disappeared as soon as their glances met. After Mrs. Moynehan had retired for the night, he endeavoured to lead their guest into more familiar dialogue, and to invite him to confidence by showing him an example.

"You must excuse my mother's retiring so early", said Edmund; "she always does so, since my father's death. We are rather a lonely family at present".

"Indeed, sir?" said the stranger with a smile.

"You are probably new to this country?" asked Edmund.

"Indeed, sir, much the same. It is now so long since I left it, that I may well be called a stranger".

"Ah, then it is not likely that you are acquainted with our misfortune. I never like, of course, to allude to it in the presence of my mother, but now that she is gone, it may furnish you with some kind of apology for the sorry entertainment you have met to-night".

The stranger bowed low, but made no reply, and Edmund

(who loved to talk of his father's unaccountable disappearance) gave him a full detail of all the circumstances
respecting it which had come to his knowledge. The
stranger seemed to listen with the deepest interest, but
like one who was habituated to feelings of a still deeper
kind than any which the narrative was calculated to excite
in the mind of an uninterested person.

"There are few circumstances attending my father's
death", said Edmund, "supposing him to have perished,
and indeed it would be idle to think otherwise, which are
to my mind so painful as its suddenness. Even at this
distance of time, and with my slight remembrance of my
father, it is surprising to myself what slight circumstances
will bring his fate, in all its force, upon my mind. The
other day, I happened to be present in the cottage of a
tenant, who lay in his death-sickness, endeavouring with
all the power of his heart and mind to review and anticipate the coming judgment on the whole. When I saw
him piously receiving the rites of his religion, and dying
at last amid the audible prayers of his family, how keenly
did the thought of my father's murder penetrate my soul,
when I compare it with this peaceful parting!"

Edmund paused, but the stranger made no remark.

"Still", continued Edmund, "I would not exchange his
lot with that of his murderer".

"No, no—oh, no", replied the stranger.

"To be sure", said Edmund, "I can but guess what the
remorse attending such a crime should be, but even from
conjecture, I wonder how a human being could prefer the
custody of such a torturing secret, even to detection and
ignominy".

"Hanging", said the stranger, "is such a horrid
death".

"But can it, short as the anguish is, be anything so
horrible as the remorse for such a deed?"

"Oh, no, I said not that", replied the stranger, "for

16

sure I am—at least I think—that were the innocent truly
to know what it is to feel remorse, they would never steep
their hands in crime. But they know nothing of it—
books—legends—all are painted flame to the fire of
genuine remorse in a bosom that is capable of feeling it".

"If such be your opinion", said Edmund, "how do you
account for the apparent indifference in which many live
who are known to have perpetrated the most appalling
crimes?"

"I know not", said the stranger; "that such is the
fact appears indisputable, but I cannot account for it on
natural reasons. Yet dreadful as it is to feel remorse, so
far at least as one may guess, to do nothing but tremble
for the future, and nothing but shudder at the past; to lie
on a restless bed, and find no comfort in the daylight, nor
in the sight of friends' faces or the hearing of familiar
conversation; I should still prefer remorse in its most
poignant form, to the dreadful insensibility that you
describe".

"You, then", said Edmund, "would not be one of
those who prefer remorse to reparation?"

"How can I answer you?" replied the stranger,
"Death, certain death is a thing so terrible to contemplate with a steady eye".

"It would appear indeed", said Edmund, "as if there
were persons who could find it easier to inflict than to
endure it".

At this moment the stranger, who scarcely seemed to
be in health during the whole conversation, complained of
fatigue, and expressed a wish to go to rest. Edmund
ordered a light, and the servant went before to prepare
the room.

"'There's no sin, I hope, sir", said the old man, turning
round with difficulty as he slowly walked towards the
chamber door. "'There's no sin after all, I hope, that
may not meet forgiveness. Even you, sir, I am sure,

could forgive the man who has injured you so nearly, provided he were humbly to beg forgiveness at your feet?
How much more reasonably might he hope for mercy al
its very source?"

"The difference is essential", answered Edmund.   "1
am far from feeling personal resentment against the author
of my father's death.   I do not mean to boast that I am
free from even the first impulses of passions that are
common to our nature ; but as there are pangs that pierce
too deep for tears—as there is bliss too exquisite for
laughter—so also there are injuries that in their very
magnitude exclude all thought of self-redress—that
in a peculiar manner seem to make vengeance (as
sure it is in every case) an usurpation of the divine
prerogative".

The stranger retired, and Edmund soon after followed
his example.   He had not yet, however, closed his eyes,
when the door opened, and a head was protruded into the
apartment.   It was that of old Rick Lillis.

"Whist! Misther Edmund!"

"Well, Rick?"

"Are you asleep, sir?"

"How could I answer your call if I were?"

"Sure enough, sir", said Rick, coming in and closing
the door behind him.   "Do you know that sthrauge
jettleman, sir?"

"Not I.   Do *you* know anything of him?"

"Oh, no, sir, only I just stepped in to mention a
dhroll thing I seen him doing that surprised me".

"Doing?   When?   Is he not in his room?"

"He was, sir, an' I seen the candle shinin' there when
I was walkin' down the lawn to go home for the nigh',
but of a sudden it moved, au' out it come to the parlour.
'I declare to my heart', says I, 'I'll go back an' see
what that lad wants out in the parlour again'.   So I crep
up to the windee, an' I jest tuk off my hat this way an'

peeped in, and sure there I seen him plain enough. An what do you think he was doin', sir ?"

" How can I tell ?"

"Sure enough. Well, he had the candle ruz up in his hand, an' he viewin' the pecthur—your poor father's pecthur this was—again the wall, an' if he did, afther viewin' it all over, he med towards the table, an' down he sat, an' covered his face this way with his two hands for as good as a quarter of an hour; an' when he done thinkin', or whatsomever he was doin', he ruz up again an' tuk out a little pocket-book, an' wrote something; but, just at that moment, it so happened that I hot the pane o' glass with the lafe o' my hat unknownst, an' he started like a little robineen, which I did also, an' run for the bare life, round by the haggart an' in the kitchen doore, in dhread o' my life he'd ketch me. An' that's my story."

" It's curious," said Moynehan. " Were you able to learn from his boatman who they were ?"

" Not a word, sir. Many an offer I med, but it's no use for me."

On the following morning to the astonishment of all the family, the stranger was nowhere to be found. The bed appeared as if it had been slept in, but there was no other trace remaining of their visitor. All inquiry was vain ; and they ceased at length to speak of what had taken place.

CHAPTER XII.

WHAT was more singular, the manner of the stranger's disappearance was as much a secret to himself as to anybody else. He had gone to rest on the preceding night in the bed which was assigned to him, nor did he wake 'till after sunrise on the following morning. What then was his astonishment and terror to find himself fully dressed, wrapped in his cloak, and lying in a meadow on the roadside, within more than a mile from the river, and in sight of the village of B————! Ashamed, however, to return to his hostess and her son after so singular an adventure, and not knowing how he could obtain credit for the truth, he pursued his way without interruption.

It happened in a few months after, that Edmund Moynehan, returning late from a journey, called into Rath Danaher, where he was acquainted. In the course of the evening, the conversation turned upon a report then prevalent about B————, respecting a " haunted house" in the outskirts of the place, which had once, they said, been tenanted by a barber of the name of O'Berne, but in consequence of having got an ill name, had for a long time continued uninhabited. The barber and his wife, they understood, had died abroad, but more than once of late strange noises had been heard about the place at night, and one person in particular distinctly averred that he had seen the ghost of the barber himself, with a light in his hand, going through all his professional evolutions as if attending and entertaining customers. One or two, they said, on the strength of this report, had had the courage to sit up alone at night to question the phantom, but in vain, for they had neither seen nor heard anything supernatural.

So highly was Edmund's curiosity excited by this account, that he immediately formed the resolution to watch with Lillis for the appearance of the phantom. The moment he announced this determination, he became, as may be supposed, the hero of the company. All crowded about him describing the fearful nature of the sounds which had been heard, and advising him to give up the idea as rash and foolish. At one time, they said, steps as of hoofs iron-shod were heard resounding through

the house; at another, whispers and sighs were audibly
breathed in the very face of the listener; while at other
times, a heavy pace was heard descending the stairs, and
at every landing-place a leap that shook the walls to their
foundation and made every door upon that story fly open
open as if burst by lightning.

It may be easily supposed that, of the two, Rick Lillis
was not the more desirous to put this audacious ex-
periment in execution. He was encouraged, however, on
understanding that the boatman was to be of the party.
On the following evening, the three set out together to the
barber's house. The night was falling fast, but a bright
crescent supplied the place of the declining day-light.
The barber's house had all the appearance of a long-
deserted tenement. The windows were broken, the
shutters shut, the little flower-plots overgrown with weeds,
and the wood-work of the building crushed and worm-
eaten. On entering the house, Rick and the boatman
proceeded to make two large fires, one for themselves in
an inner room, the other for Edmund Moynehan in that
which had heretofore served the purpose of a kitchen.
In each there was a table laid with lights and materials
for supper. In what had been the kitchen, young Moynehan remained alone, having given directions to his two
attendants, whatever they might see or hear, not to
intrude on him uncalled. As this was the chamber which
had especially the fame of being "haunted", Rick felt no
inclination whatever to dispute his commands, and would
even have been better pleased that the prohibition had
been wholly unconditional.

Night had long fallen, and the two fellow-servants, encouraged by the absence of any thing which could give
countenance to the awful rumours they had heard, began
to converse with freedom, while they laid hands on the
cheer which had been laid before them. Rick, in the
meantime, exerted all his eloquence and all his ghostly

lore in labouring to shake the obstinate incredulity of his companion, who could and would admit no possibility of the truth of such a rumour.

" Tell me", he said, at last, in indignation, "if you were to see it yourself, would you believe it?"

" I would".

" 'Tis a wondher. An' you won't believe other people when they sees it. Don't they say many a time, that if a man buries money, or if he didn't pay his debts before he died, or wronged any body, he'll be troubled that way, an' risin' ever an' always till——"

He paused, for at this moment a noise was heard at the door of the room in which they sat. It opened, and a sight appeared which froze the very heart of Rick, and even appalled for a time the incredulous mind of the boatman. A figure wearing a barber's apron, and bearing in its hands a basin and other professional implements, was seen distinctly to advance into the lighted room, and slowly moved towards where the watchers sat. Rick muttered a fervent ejaculation.

" I'll spake to it", said the boatman.

" A' Tim, eroo! Tim a-vourneen!"

" Do you mind his eyes?" said Tim.

" Blazin' like two coals o' fire", said Rick. " A' Tim, what'll become of us!—Oh, wisha, wisha!'

" I'll spake to it", said Tim.

" A' Tim, don't asthore! The less you say to it the betther, 'till the third time of it comin', an' if I wait for the third time, I'll give you leave to say my name isn't Rick Lillis".

The figure passed slowly by, and into the room in which young Moynehan sat. While this event proceeded, the latter was occupied with thoughts of an absorbing kind. The loneliness of the place and the purpose for which he had come thither, threw him naturally into a mood of melancholy reflection, and his thoughts gradually fixed themselves upon his father's story, which always occupied the deepest place in his mind. He regretted extremely that he had not taken greater pains to search after their strange guest, whose conduct respecting the portrait, together with his unceremonious departure, had indicated something more than an accidental interest. While he pursued these thoughts, the door of the inner room was opened, and it required all his presence of mind to enable him to maintain his resolution. The barber's ghost was there indeed before his eyes! One glance, however, at the old man's countenance was sufficient to reassure him, while at the same time it touched as if with an electric tangent the deepest feelings of his nature. The figure, differing only in attire, was that of the old man to whom they had given a night's lodging a short time before!

Edmund paused; he held his very breath with caution, while the figure, with dreamy eyes and measured thoughtful action, set about the task which he seemed to have in hand. His motion, however, although soft, was not so noiseless as to intimate the presence of a spiritual being. He laid aside the basin, took out a razor which appeared covered with rust, and seemed to whet it for some moments. He then paused for a long time, and seemed to suffer under the infliction of some excruciating doubt.

"Thou shalt not steal!"—he said in a whisper, "that's true. But must our children perish?"

He paused, and Edmund bent his whole mind to listen.

"Mary!" continued the barber, "lay by that prayer book, and attend to me. Mary, I say! True—true! she is asleep—they are all asleep but he and I. Who'll find it out? None—none—there is no fear".

Here he set a chair, and seemed as if watching the movements of another person.

"Honesty?" said he, still speaking in broken whispers,

"what's that? Is it justice? That my babes should starve while he—besides—'tis public—the public money— a mere grain—a drop—Oh! all the gold! what a heap! what a heap of gold! Here's riches! Where's the evil! 'Tis nothing to the state, and we shall never want again".

It then suddenly appeared as if his thoughts had taken a wholly new direction, for he put on a hurried manner, and exclaimed with great rapidity, but yet in whispered accents—

"What's to be done?—He wakes! He will search the house, and all will be discovered. I know it—the pear-tree in the orchard—Is it locked again, and the stones as heavy as the gold?—Thief?—hark! Who calls me thief?"

Here he shrunk upon himself with so much terror as to contract his figure to nearly half its usual height. "Oh, yes—all that is past! I can no longer look them in the face". Again his manner changed, and sinking on his knees, he fixed his eyes upon the ground, as if arrested by some object of riveting interest. "Who has done this?" he said in a whisper. "Quite stiff and cold! and the portmanteau gone! Oh, misery! what a night! how ill begun, and ended immeasurably worse—let him lie there awhile—we'll find a time to bury it. But the gold! yes! yes!—the gold! the gold! the gold! We are safe at last—our children shall not starve".

Here he held up his hands as if in exultation, and burst into a loud and lengthened fit of laughter, while he hugged his arms close, as if they held a treasure, and his countenance was convulsed between delight and biting agony. After a little time, he started as if some new thought had struck him.

"The razor—" he said, "the razor—where did I leave it?"

Edmund, however, had secured what he now considered the dumb but fatal witness of its owner's guilt. The

distress of the sleeper seemed extreme at not finding it,
but again his thoughts appeared to run into a new
direction, and after muttering something more about the
orchard and the pear-tree, he advanced to the kitchen
door and opened it. Edmund quickly followed, but the
door was fast before he reached it, nor could all his
strength or dexterity avail to open it. Conceiving the
quantity of evidence hardly sufficient to take any decided
step upon the instant, he waited until morning, when he
hastened to lay the whole before a neighbouring magistrate. It was determined, in order, by the number of
witnesses, to add as much as possible to the evidence
already procured, to watch for another night in the deserted house, in the expectation of a second ghostly visit
from its former owner. The police supplied by the magistrate were stationed in the garden, while Edmund, now
without light or fire, awaited, in a secret corner of the
kitchen, the appearance of him whom he strongly suspected to be his father's murderer. He was not disappointed. About midnight the barber came, but not, as
on the preceding night, a walking sleeper. He entered
wide awake—wrapt in his cloak, and followed by a man
whom Edmund easily recognized as the boatman who had
spent the night with him at their house.

"You shall be well rewarded", said the barber, "but
be secret. I will show you where the body lies that I
told you of—but remember there are the deepest reasons
for keeping secret the whole story of my friend's death,
and though I wish to have him laid in holy ground, it
would be evil and not good to have it talked of".

"Never fear", said the boatman, "only show the spot".
The barber accordingly led the way to the garden.
Edmund followed to the pear-tree, at the root of which
they dug up the soil, setting their spades in the direction
indicated by the old man. In a short time he saw them
raise from the earth the bones of a human figure, which

they placed upon the ground. Closing in the grave, they took the cloth between them, and were in the act of retiring from the orchard, when Edmund advanced upon the path before them, and commanded them to halt.

"Who's there?" exclaimed the barber.

"The son of your victim", answered Edmund; "of him whom you murdered with this razor, and whose bones you are conveying hence. You are our prisoner".

The barber had scarcely heard these words when he sunk, overpowered by terror, at the feet of his accuser. The assistant, affrighted at what was said, was about to fly, when he was intercepted by the magistrate's police, who brought the whole party before that functionary on the following morning. The latter, having heard the whole of the circumstances, was about to issue a warrant of committal, when the barber, who had not said a word in his own defence during the whole of the proceedings, requested at length to be heard in explanation. His wish was instantly complied with, and the deepest silence and attention prevailed while he spoke as follows:—

"It will surprise you, Mr. Magistrate, and you, Mr. Moynehan, to learn, that notwithstanding all this weight of circumstance, I am not guilty of the offence with which you charge me. When I have proved my innocence, as I shall do, my case will furnish a strong instance of the fallibility of any evidence that is indirect in a case where human life is interested. All the circumstances are true— my extreme necessity—his midnight visit to my house— his disappearance on that night, accompanied by signs of violence—my subsequent increase of wealth—and the seeming revelation of my waking dream, as overheard by Mr. Moynehan : and yet I am not guilty of this crime. If you will have patience to listen, I will tell you how far my guilt extended, and where it stopped".

He then detailed the circumstances preceding the nocturnal visit of the deceased tax-gatherer, disguising

nothing of his poverty, nor the many temptations by which
he was beset.

"Still", said he, "I tell you a simple truth when I
assert that, during the whole time of this visit, while he
lay sleeping in his chair, and while I held the razor in my
hand, so shocking a thought as that of taking a fellow-
creature's life never once, even for an instant, crossed my
mind. But there was another temptation which *did*
suggest itself, and to which I did give way. The portmanteau containing the money, lay on a chair near the
window—he slept profoundly—I took the key from his
pocket—I removed the money, which was chiefly in gold
and silver, and filling the two bags in which it was contained with small pebbles of about an equal weight, I
replaced the portmanteau as it was before. I then awoke
him with difficulty, and fearful of being discovered if he
remained till morning, persuaded him to resume his
journey.

"He had scarcely left the house when I found myself
seized with an unaccountable terror at the idea of detection and ignominy. Accordingly, abstracting from the
sum a few pieces of silver for present uses, I made fast
the remainder in a bag, and hurried out into the air, uncertain whither to direct my steps. I ran across the
neighbouring fields with the design of seeking out some
place of concealment for my treasure. An old ruin within
a short distance of the village suggested itself as a
favourable spot for my design, and thither accordingly I
hastened. In an obscure corner of the building I deposited the money, and returned to my own house with a
mind distracted by anxiety and remorse.

"On my way home, I heard voices, and the sound of
horses' feet, in a field upon my right. I listened, and the
words I caught seemed to be those of people who were
exercising and leaping horses. Soon after, a horse without
a rider left the field at full gallop. The sounds ceased,

and in a short time I saw two horsemen galloping from
the place.   Strange as it may seem, I have the proof of
what I am about to state, and let it warn you, sir, and
all who are in power, to weigh well the grounds on which
they decide the guilt or innocence of the wretches whom
they judge.   I entered the field, and found there, lying at
a distance from the ditch, the body of the tax-collector,
newly dead, with a dreadful wound upon the head, and
the portmanteau gone!   My first impulse—I know not
wherefore—was to conceal the work of murder.   Favoured
by the night, which still continued stormy, I conveyed
the body to my own orchard, where I gave it temporary
interment in the spot from which I was last night detected
in the act of seeing it removed.   It would be vain to tell
what poignancy this dreadful addition to the terrors of the
night imparted to my remorse.   I felt almost as if I had
been myself the author of his destruction; and the apparent
certainty, likewise, that the detection of the crime which
I *had* committed, would be sufficient to convict me also in
the eyes of all judges of that which I had *not*, made my
life one protracted thought of fear and misery".

Here the barber related, with feelings of the deepest
shame, the device which he had adopted of digging up the
treasure in the presence of the cobbler, in order to throw
a veil over the real origin of his new prosperity.

"Still", said he, "I could not be at rest amid the
scenes which continually reminded me of that terrible
event.   The consciousness of meanness joined to guilt
added the poignancy of self-contempt to the deeper anguish of remorse.   I fled the country, and sought refuge in
change of scene from my fears and my remembrances.

"But it was in vain.   I could not fin l repose, for I
carried my violated conscience still about me.   Every
new article I purchased for the use of my family—every
fresh morsel of food that I lifted to my lips, seemed like a
new and aggravated theft.   I would at this time have

13

given the whole world for a friend to whom I could confide
the secret that destroyed me. I thought of making a full
disclosure to my wife, but she was far too good and holy
to be the depositary of such a confidence.

"I entered into trade, and was successful, and in my
success, for a time, I lost something of my inward agony.
' will not weary you, gentlemen, by a long detail of the
means by which I became acquainted with many of the real
perpetrators of the more heinous offence. They were two
persons who dined in company with Mr. Moynehan at
Castle Tobin, on the evening previous to his disappearance.
One died in Ireland soon after the occurrence—the other,
William Cusack (commonly called Buffer), died abroad,
and left this written confession of their common guilt,
which I obtained as you shall hear.

"The hand of Providence began to press upon my house.
One member after another of my family dropped into the
grave, until I remained alone in the world with my remorse
for a companion. Misfortune humbled me : I sought relief
at length at the right source, and revealed the whole to a
clergyman who attended me in a dangerous illness. It
was through his means that document came into my
possession—and it is in fulfilment of his injunction that I
have now come to the restitution of the money which I
have so long retained".

Strange as the barber's defence appeared to Edmund
and the magistrate, it was fully substantiated in the sequel
by the testimony of the clergyman who had placed the
confession, for his security, in the hands of O'Berne. The
mode of his detection by Edmund Moynehan relieved the
barber from an apprehension which had long sat next to
his remorse upon his mind. This was the fancy that he
had been haunted by an evil spirit, who disturbed him in
his sleep, and had on one occasion engaged him in a fatal
compact. It now appeared that himself, in his somnam-
bulism, had performed all those feats which had so much

perplexed him, and that his midnight excursion to the fir-grove was but a dream, to which he never would have paid attention, but for the corroboration afforded to it by the other mysterious occurrences. There was no prosecution instituted on the minor offence, and the barber continued long after to lead a penitential life in the neighbourhood. The house, however, has long been razed (as we have already mentioned) to the earth, and it is legend alone that preserves the memory of its situation amongst the neighbouring villagers.

THE BROWN MAN.

All sorts of cattle he did eat :
    Some say he eat up trees,
And that the forest sure he would
    Devour up by degrees.
For houses and churches were to him geese and turkeys ;
    He ate all, and left none behind,
But such stones, dear Jack, which he could not crack,
    Which on the hills you'll find.
                    Dragon of Wantley

THE common Irish expression of "the seven devils" does not, it would appear, owe its origin to the supernatural influences ascribed to that numeral, from its frequent associations with the greatest and most solemn occasions of theological history. If one were disposed to be fancifully metaphysical upon the subject, it might not be amiss to compare credulity to a sort of mental prism, by which the great volume of the light of speculative superstition is refracted in a manner precisely similar to that of the material, every-day sun, the great refractor thus showing only *blue* devils to the dwellers in the good city of London, *orange* and *green* devils to the inhabitants of the sister (or rather step-daughter) island, and so forward until the seven component hues are made out through the other nations of the Earth. But what has this to do with the story ? In order to answer that question, the story must be told.

In a lonely cabin, in a lonely glen, on the shores of a
lonely lough, in one of the most lonesome districts of west
Munster, lived a lone woman named Guare. She had a
beautiful girl, a daughter named Nora. Their cabin was
the only one within three miles round them every way.
As to their mode of living, it was simple enough. for all
they had was one little garden of white cabbage, and they
had eaten that down to a few heads between them; a sorry
prospect in a place where even a handful of *prishoc* weed
was not to be had without sowing it.

It was a very fine morning in those parts, for it was
only snowing and hailing, when Nora and her mother were
sitting at the door of their little cottage, and laying out
plans for the next day's dinner. On a sudden, a strange
horseman rode up to the door. He was strange in more
ways than one. He was dressed in brown, his hair was
brown, his eyes were brown, his boots were brown, he
rode a brown horse, and he was followed by a brown dog.

" I'm come to marry you, Nora Guare ", said the
Brown Man.

" Ax my mother fust, if you plaise, sir", said Nora
dropping him a curtsey.

" You'll not refuse, ma'am", said the Brown Man to the
old mother. " I have money enough, and I'll make your
daughter a lady, with servants at her call, and all manner
of fine doings about her". And so saying, he flung a
purse of gold into the widow's lap.

" Why then the Heavens speed you and her together,
take her away with you, and make much of her", said the
old mother, quite bewildered with all the money.

" Agh, agh", said the Brown Man, as he placed her on
his horse behind him without more ado. " Are you all
ready now ?"

" I am !" said the bride. The horse snorted, and the
dog barked, and almost before the word was out of her
mouth, they were all whisked away out of sight. After

travelling a day and a night, faster than the wind itself,
the Brown Man pulled up his horse in the middle of the
Mangerton mountain, in one of the most lonesome places
that eye ever looked on.

"Here is my estate", said the Brown Man.

"A'then, is it this wild bog you call an estate ?" said
the bride.

"Come in, wife ; this is my palace", said the bridegroom.

"What ! a clay hovel, worse than my mother's ?"

They dismounted, and the horse and the dog disappeared in an instant, with a horrible noise, which the girl
did not know whether to call snorting, barking, or laughing.

"Are you hungry ?" said the Brown Man. "If so,
there is your dinner".

"A handful of raw white-eyes,* and a grain of salt !"

"And when you are sleepy, here is your bed", he continued, pointing to a little straw in a corner, at sight of
which Nora's limbs shivered and trembled again. It may
be easily supposed that she did not make a very hearty
dinner that evening, nor did her husband neither.

In the dead of the night, when the clock of Mucruss
Abbey had just tolled one, a low neighing at the door,
and a soft barking at the window, were heard. Nora
feigned sleep. The Brown Man passed his hands over her
eyes and face. She snored. "I'm coming", said he, and
he rose gently from her side. In half an hour after, she
felt him by her side again. He was cold as ice.

The next night the same summons came. The Brown
Man rose. The wife feigned sleep. He returned cold.
The morning came.

The next night came. The bell tolled at Mucruss,
and was heard across the lakes. The Brown Man rose

* A kind of potato.

again, and passed a light before the eyes of the feigning
sleeper. None slumber so sound as they who *will* not
wake. Her heart trembled; but her frame was quiet
and firm. A voice at the door summoned the husband.

" You are very long coming. The earth is tossed up,
and I am hungry. Hurry! Hurry! Hurry! if you would
not lose all".

" I'm coming", said the Brown Man. Nora rose and
followed instantly. She beheld him at a distance winding
through a lane of frost-nipt sallow trees. He often paused
and looked back, and once or twice retraced his steps to
within a few yards of the tree, behind which she had
shrunk. The moon-light, cutting the shadow close and
dark about her, afforded the best concealment. He again
proceeded, and she followed. In a few minutes they
reached the old Abbey of Mucruss. With a sickening
heart she saw him enter the church-yard. The wind
rushed through the huge yew-tree and startled her. She
mustered courage enough, however, to reach the gate of
the church-yard and look in. The Brown Man, the horse,
and the dog, were there by an open grave, eating something, and glancing their brown, fiery eyes about in every
direction. The moon-light shone full on them and her.
Looking down towards her shadow on the earth, she
stared with horror to observe it move, although she was
herself perfectly still. It waved its black arms and motioned her back. What the feasters said, she understood
not, but she seemed still fixed in the spot. She looked
once more on her shadow; it raised one hand, and pointed
the way to the lane; slowly rising from the ground, and
confronting her, it walked rapidly off in that direction. She
followed as quickly as might be.

She was scarcely in her straw, when the door creaked
behind, and her husband entered. He lay down by her
side, and started.

" Uf! Uf!" said she, pretending to be just awakened,
" how cold you are, my love !"

" Cold, inagh? Indeed you're not very warm yourself, my dear, I'm thinking".

" Little admiration I should'nt be warm, and you laving
me alone this way at night, till my blood is snow broth,
no less".

" Umph !" said the Brown Man, as he passed his arm
round her waist. " Ha! your heart is beating fast?"

" Little admiration it should. I am not well, indeed.
Them pzaties and salt don't agree with me at all".

" Umph !" said the Brown Man.

The next morning as they were sitting at the break-
fast-table together, Nora plucked up a heart, and asked
leave to go to her mother. The Brown Man, who eat
nothing, looked at her in a way that made her think he
knew all. She felt her spirit die away within her.

" If you only want to see your mother", said he, " there
is no occasion for your going home. I will bring her to
you here. I didn't marry you to be keeping you gadding".

The Brown Man then went out and whistled for his
dog and his horse. They both came; and in a very few
minutes they pulled up at the old widow's cabin-door.

The poor woman was very glad to see her son-in-law,
though she did not know what could bring him so soon.

" Your daughter sends her love to you, mother", says
the Brown Man, the villain, " and she'd be obliged to you
for a *loand* of a *shoot* of your best clothes, as she's
going to give a grand party, and the dress-maker has
disappointed her".

" To be sure and welcome", said the mother; and
making up a bundle of the clothes, she put them into his
hands.

" Whogh! whogh!" said the horse as they drove off,
" that was well done. Are we to have a meal of her ?"

" Easy, ma-coppuleen, and you'll get your 'nough

before night," said the Brown Man, " and you likewise, my little dog."

" Boh ?" cried the dog, " I'm in no hurry—I hunted down a doe this morning that was fed with milk from the horns of the moon."

Often in the course of that day did Nora Guare go to the door, and cast her eye over the weary flat before it, to discern, if possible, the distant figures of her bridegroom and mother. The dusk of the second evening found her alone in the desolate cot. She listened to every sound. At length the door opened, and an old woman, dressed in a new *jock*, and leaning on a staff, entered the hut. " O mother, are you come ?" said Nora, and was about to rush into her arms, when the old woman stopped her.

" Whist ! whist ! my child !—I only stepped in before the man to know how you like him ? Speak softly in dread he'd hear you—he's turning the horse loose in the swamp abroad, over."

" O mother, mother ! such a story !"

" Whist ! easy again—how does he use you ?"

" Sorrow worse. That straw my bed, and them white-eyes—and bad ones they are—all my diet. And 'tisn't that same, only——"

" Whist ! easy, again ! He'll hear you, may be—Well ?"

" I'd be easy enough, only for his own doings. Listen, mother. The fust night I came, about twelve o'clock——"

" Easy, speak easy, eroo !"

" He got up at the call of the horse and the dog, and staid out a good hour. He ate nothing next day. The second night, and the second day, it was the same story. The third——"

" Husht ! husht ! Well the third night ?"

" The third night I said I'd watch him. Mother, don't hold my hand so hard——He got up, and I got up after him——Oh, don't laugh, mother, for 'tis frightful——I

13*

followed him to Mucruss church-yard——Mother, mother
you hurt my hand——I looked in at the gate—there was
great moonlight there, and I could see everything as plain
as day."

"Well, darling—husht! softly! What did you see?"

"My husband by the grave, and the horse,——
Turn your head aside, mother, for your breath is very
hot——and the dog, and they eating.——Ah, you are
not my mother!" shrieked the miserable girl, as the Brown
Man flung off his disguise, and stood before her, grinning
worse than a blacksmith's face through a horse-collar.
He just looked at her one moment, and then darted his
long fingers into her bosom, from which the red blood
spouted in so many streams. She was very soon out of
all pain, and a merry supper the horse, the dog, and the
Brown Man had that night by all accounts.

OWNEY AND OWNEY-NA-PEAK.

Ay, marry, sir, there's mettle in this young fellow ;
What a sheep's look his elder brother has !
FLETCHER's *Elder Brother.*

WHEN Ireland had kings of her own—when there was no such thing as a coat made of red cloth in the country—when there was plenty in men's houses, and peace and quietness at men's doors (and that is a long time since)—there lived, in a village not far from the great city of Lumneach,* two young men, cousins : one of them named Owney, a smart, kind-hearted, handsome youth, with limb of a delicate form, and a very good understanding. His cousin's name was Owney too, and the neighbours christened him Owney-na-peak (Owney of the nose), on account of a long nose he had got—a thing so out of all proportion, that after looking at one side of his face, it was a smart morning's walk to get round the nose and take a view of the other (at least, so the people used to say). He was a stout, able-bodied fellow, as stupid as a beaten hound, and he was, moreover, a cruel tyrant to his young cousin, with whom he lived in a kind of partnership.

Both these were of an humble station. They were smiths—whitesmiths—and they got a good deal of business to do from the lords of the court, and the

* The present Limerick.

knights, and all the grand people of the city. But one
day young Owney was in town, he saw a great pro-
cession of lords, and ladies, and generals, and great people,
among whom was the king's daughter of the court—and
surely it is not possible for the young rose itself to be so
beautiful as she was. His heart fainted at her sight, and
he went home desperately in love, and not at all disposed
to business.

Money, he was told, was the surest way of getting acquainted with the king, and so he began saving until he
had put together a few *hogs*,* but Owney-na-peak finding
where he had hid them, seized on the whole, as he used
to do on all young Owney's earnings.

One evening young Owney's mother found herself
about to die, so she called her son to her bed-side and
said to him : " You have been a most dutiful good son,
and 'tis proper you should be rewarded for it. Take this
china cup to the fair—there is a fairy gift upon it—use
your own wit—look about you, and let the highest bidder
have it—and so, my white-headed boy, God bless you !"

The young man drew the little bed-curtain down over
his dead mother, and in a few days after, with a heavy
heart, he took his china cup, and set off to the fair of
Garryowen.

The place was merry enough. The field that is called
Gallows Green now, was covered with tents. There was
plenty of wine (potteen not being known in these days, let
alone *parliament*)—a great many handsome girls—and 'tis
unknown all the *keoh* that was with the boys and themselves. Poor Owney walked all the day through the fair,
wishing to try his luck, but ashamed to offer his china cup
among all the fine things that were there for sale.
Evening was drawing on at last, and he was thinking of
going home, when a strange man tapped him on the
shoulder, and said : " My good youth, I have been marking

*A *hog.* 1s. 1d.

you through the fair the whole day, going about with that cup in your hand, speaking to nobody, and looking as if you would be wanting something or another."

" I'm for selling it," said Owney.

" What is it you're for selling, you say ?" said a second man, coming up, and looking at the cup.

" Why then," said the first man, "and what's that to you, for a prying meddler, what do you want to know is it he's for selling ?"

" Bad manners to you (and where's the use of my wishing you what you have already ?) haven't I a right to ask the price of what's in the fair ?"

" E'then, the knowledge o' the price is all you'll have for it," says the first. " Here, my lad, is a golden piece for your cup."

" That cup shall never hold drink or diet in your house, please Heaven," says the second ; " here's two gold pieces for the cup, lad".

" Why, then, see this now—if I was forced to fill it to the rim with gold before I could call it mine, you shall never hold that cup between your fingers. Here, boy, do you mind me, give me that, once for all, and here's ten gold pieces for it, and say no more".

" Ten gold pieces for a china cup !" said a great lord of the court, that just rode up at that minute, " it must surely be a valuable article. Here, boy, here's twenty pieces for it, and give it to my servant".

" Give it to mine", cried another lord of the party, " and here's my purse, where you will find ten more And if any man offers another fraction for it to outbid that, I'll spit him on my sword like a snipe".

" I outbid him", said a fair young lady in a veil, by his side, flinging twenty golden pieces more on the ground.

There was no voice to outbid the lady, and young Owney, kneeling, gave the cup into her hands.

" Fifty gold pieces for a china cup !" said Owney to

himself, as he plodded on home, "that was not worth two! Ah! mother, you knew that vanity had an open hand."

But as he drew near home, he determined to hide his money somewhere, knowing, as he well did, that his cousin would not leave him a single cross to bless himself with. So he dug a little pit, and buried all but two pieces, which he brought to the house. His cousin, knowing the business on which he had gone, laughed heartily when he saw him enter, and asked him what luck he had got with his punch-bowl.

"Not so bad, neither," says Owney. "Two pieces of gold is not a bad price for an article of old china."

"Two gold pieces, Owney, honey! erra, let us see 'em, may be you would?" He took the cash from Owney's hand, and after opening his eyes in great astonishment at the sight of so much money, he put them into his pocket.

"Well, Owney, I'll keep them safe for you, in my pocket within. But tell us, may be you would, how come you to get such a *mort* o' money for an old cup o' painted chaney, that wasn't worth, may be, a fi'penny bit?"

"To get into the heart o' the fair, then, free and easy, and to look about me, and to cry old china, and the first man that *come* up, he to ask me, what is it I'd be asking for the cup, and I to say out bold: ' A hundred pieces of gold,' and he to laugh hearty, and we to huxter together till he beat me down to two, and there's the whole way of it all."

Owney-na-peak made as if he took no note of this, but next morning early he took an old china saucer himself had in his cupboard, and off he set, without saying a word to anybody, to the fair. You may easily imagine that it created no small surprise in the place, when they heard a great big fellow, with a china saucer in his hand, crying out: "A raal *chaney* saucer going for a hundred pieces of goold! raal chaney—who'll be buying?"

"Erra. what's that you're saying, you great gomeril?" says a man, coming up to him, and looking first at the saucer, and then in his face. "Is it thinking any body would go make a *muthaun* of himself to give the like for that saucer?" But Owney-na-peak had no answer to make, only to cry out: "Raal chaney! one hundred pieces of goold!"

A crowd soon collected about him, and finding he would give no account of himself, they all fell upon him, beat him within an inch of his life, and after having satisfied themselves upon him, they went their way laughing and shouting. Towards sunset he got up, and crawled home as well as he could, without cup or money. As soon as Owney saw him, he helped him into the forge, looking very mournful, although, if the truth must be told, it was to revenge himself for former good deeds of his cousin, that he set him about this foolish business.

"Come here, Owney, eroo", said his cousin, after he had fastened the forge door, and heated two irons in the fire. "You child of mischief!" said he when he had caught him, "you shall never see the fruits of your roguery again, for I will put out your eyes". And so saying, he snatched one of the red-hot irons from the fire.

It was all in vain for poor Owney to throw himself on his knees, and ask mercy, and beg and implore forgiveness: he was weak, and Owney-na-peak was strong: he held him fast, and burned out both his eyes. Then taking him, while he was yet fainting from the pain, upon his back, he carried him off to the bleak hill of Knockpatrick,* a great distance, and there laid him under a tombstone, and went his ways. In a little time after, Owney came to himself.

"O sweet light of day! what is to become of me now?"

* A hill in the west of the County of Limerick, on the summit of which are the ruins of an old church, with a burying-ground still in use. The situation is exceedingly singular and bleak.

thought the poor lad, as he lay on his back under the
tomb. " Is this to be the fruit of that unhappy present ?
Must I be dark for ever and ever ? and am I never more
to look upon that sweet countenance, that even in my
blindness is not entirely shut out from me ?" He would
have said a great deal more in this way, and perhaps more
pathetic still, but just then he heard a great mewing, as if
all the cats in the world wer^ coming up the hill together
in one faction. He gathered himself up, and drew back
under the stone, and remained quite still, expecting what
would come next. In a very short time he heard all the
cats purring and mewing about the yard, whisking over
the tombstones, and playing all sorts of pranks among the
graves. He felt the tails of one or two brush his nose ;
and well for him it was that they did not discover him
there, as he afterwards found. At last—

" Silence !" said one of the cats, and they were all as
mute as so many mice in an instant. " Now, all you cats
of this great county, small and large, gray, red, yellow,
black, brown, mottled, and white, attend to what I'm
going to tell you in the name of your king and the master
of all the cats. The sun is down, and the moon is up, and
the night is silent, and no mortal hears us, and I may tell
you a secret. You know the king of Munster's daughter ?"

" O yes, to be sure, and why wouldn't we ? Go on
with your story", said all the cats together.

" I have heard of her for one", said a little dirty-faced
black cat, speaking after they had all done, " for I'm the
cat that sits upon the hob of Owney and Owney-na-peak,
the whitesmiths, and I know many's the time young
Owney does be talking of her, when he sits by the fire
alone, rubbing me down and planning how he can get
into her father's court".

" Whist ! you natural !" says the cat that was making
the speech, " what do you think we care for your Owney,
or Owney-na-peak ?"

"Murther, murther!" thinks Owney to himself, "did any body ever hear the aiqual of this?"

"Well, gentlemen", says the cat again, "what I have to say is this. The king was last week struck with blindness, and you all know well, how and by what means any blindness may be cured. You know there is no disorder that can ail mortal frame, that may not be removed by paying a round at the well of Barrygowen* yonder, and the king's disorder is such, that no other cure whatever can be had for it. Now, beware, don't let the secret pass one o' yer lips, for there's a great-grandson of Simon Magus, that is coming down to try his skill, and he it is that must use the water and marry the princess, who is to be given to any one so fortunate as to heal her father's eyes; and on that day, gentlemen, we are all promised a feast of the fattest mice that ever walked the ground". This speech was wonderfully applauded by all the cats, and presently after, the whole crew scampered off, jumping, and mewing, and purring, down the hill.

Owney, being sensible that they were all gone, came from his hiding place, and knowing the road to Barrygowen well, he set off, and groped his way out, and shortly knew, by the roaring of the waves,† rolling in from the point of Foynes, that he was near the place. He got to the well, and making a round like a good Christian, he rubbed his eyes with the well-water, and looking up, saw day dawning in the east. Giving thanks, he jumped up on his feet, and you may say that Owney-na-peak was much astonished on opening the door of the forge to find him there, his eyes as well or better than ever, and his face as merry as a dance.

* The superstitious practice of paying rounds, with the view of healing diseases, at Barrygowen well, in the County of Limerick, is still continued, notwithstanding the exertions of the neighbouring Catholic priesthood, which have diminished, but not abolished it.

* Of the Shannon.

"Well, cousin", said Owney, smiling, "you have done me the greatest service that one man can do another; you put me in the way of getting two pieces of gold", said he showing two he had taken from his hiding place. "If you could only bear the pain of suffering me just to put out your eyes, and lay you in the same place as you laid me, who knows what luck you'd have?"

"No, there's no occasion for putting out eyes at all, but could not you lay me, just as I am, to-night, in that place, and let me try my own fortune, if it be a thing you tell thruth; and what else could put the eyes in your head, after I burning them out with the irons?"

"You'll know all that in time", says Owney, stopping him in his speech, for just at that minute, casting his eye towards the hob, he saw the cat sitting upon it, and looking very hard at him. So he made a sign to Owney-na-peak to be silent, or talk of something else; at which the cat turned away her eyes, and began washing her face, quite simple, with her two paws, looking now and then sideways into Owney's face, just like a Christian. By and by, when she had walked out of the forge, he shut the door after her, and finished what he was going to say, which made Owney-na-peak still more anxious than before to be placed under the tombstone. Owney agreed to it very readily, and just as they were done speaking, cast a glance towards the forge window, where he saw the imp of a cat, just with her nose and one eye peeping in through a broken pane. He said nothing, however, but prepared to carry his cousin to the place; where, towards nightfall, he laid him as he had been laid himself, snug under the tombstone, and went his way down the hill, resting in Shanagolden that night, to see what would come of it in the morning.

Owney-na-peak had not been more than two or three hours or so lying down, when he heard the very same noises coming up the hill, that had puzzled Owney the night before. Seeing the cats enter the church-yard, he began to grow very uneasy, and strove to hide himself as well as he could, which was tolerably well too, all being covered by the tombstone excepting part of the nose, which was so long that he could not get it to fit by any means. You may say to yourself, that he was not a little surprised, when he saw the cats all assemble like a congregation going to hear mass, some sitting, some walking about, and asking one another after the kittens and the like, and more of them stretching themselves upon the tombstones, and waiting the speech of their commander.

Silence was proclaimed at length, and he spoke: "Now all you cats of this great county, small and large, gray, red, yellow, black, brown, mottled, or white, attend—"

"Stay! stay!" said a little cat with a dirty face, that just then came running into the yard. "Be silent, for there are mortal ears listening to what you say. I have run hard and fast to say that your words were overheard last night. I am the cat that sits upon the hob of Owney and Owney-na-peak, and I saw a bottle of the water of Barrygowen hanging up over the chimbley this morning in their house".

In an instant all the cats began screaming, and mewing, and flying, as if they were mad, about the yard, searching every corner, and peeping under every tombstone. Poor Owney-na-peak endeavoured as well as he could to hide himself from them, and began to thump his breast and cross himself, but it was all in vain, for one of the cats saw the long nose peeping from under the stone, and in a minute they dragged him, roaring and bawling, into the very middle of the church-yard, where they flew upon him all together, and made *smithereens* of him, from the crown of his head to the sole of his feet.

The next morning very early, young Owney came to the church-yard, to see what had become of his cousin.

He called over and over again upon his name, but there was no answer given. At last, entering the place of tombs, he found his limbs scattered over the earth.

"So that is the way with you, is it?" said he, clasping his hands, and looking down on the bloody fragments: "why then, though you were no great things in the way of kindness to me when your bones were together, that isn't the reason why I'd be glad to see them torn asunder this morning early". So gathering up all the pieces that he could find, he put them into a bag he had with him, and away with him to the well of Barrygowen, where he lost no time in making a round, and throwing them in, all in a heap. In an instant, he saw Owney-na-peak as well as ever, scrambling out of the well, and helping him to get up, he asked him how he felt himself.

"Oh! is it how I'd feel myself you'd want to know?" said the other; "easy and I'll tell you. Take that for a specimen!" giving him at the same time a blow on the head, which you may say was'nt long in laying Owney sprawling on the ground. Then without giving him a minute's time to recover, he thrust him into the very bag from which he had been just shook himself, resolving within himself to drown him in the Shannon at once, and put an end to him for ever.

Growing weary by the way, he stopped at a shebeen house *overright* Robertstown Castle, to refresh himself with a *morning*, before he'd go any further. Poor Owney did not know what to do when he came to himself, if it might be rightly called coming to himself, and the great bag tied up about him. His wicked cousin shot him down behind the door in the kitchen, and telling him he'd have his life surely if he stirred, he walked in to take something that's good in the little parlour.

Owney could not for the life of him avoid cutting a hole in the bag, to have a peep about the kitchen, and see whether he had no means of escape. He could see only one person, a simple looking man, that was nnting his beads in the chimney-corner, and now and then striking his breast, and looking up as if he was praying greatly.

"Lord", says he, "only give me death, death, and a favourable judgment! I haven't any body now to look after, nor any body to look after me. What's a few tin-pennies to save a man from want? Only a quiet grave is all I ask".

"Murther, murther!" says Owney to himself, "here's a man wants death and can't have it, and here am I going to have it, and, in troth, I don't want it at all, see". So, after thinking a little what he had best do, he began to sing out very merrily, but lowering his voice, for fear he should be heard in the next room:

> "To him that tied me here,
>   Be thanks and praises given!
> I'll bless him night and day,
>   For packing me to Heaven.
> Of all the roads you'll name,
>   He surely will not lag,
> Who takes his way to Heaven
>   By travelling in a bag!"

"To Heaven *ershishin?*"* said the man in the chimney-corner, opening his mouth and his eyes; "why then, you'd be doing a Christian turn, if you'd take a neighbour with you, that's tired of this bad and villainous world".

"You're a fool, you're a fool!" said Owney.

"I know I am, at least so the neighbours always tell me—but what hurt? May-be I have a Christian soul as well as another; and fool or no fool, in a bag or out of a bag, I'd be glad and happy to go the same road it is you are talking of".

After seeming to make a great favour of it, in order to allure him the more to the bargain, Owney agreed to put him into the bag instead of himself; and cautioning him against saying a word, he was just going to tie him, when

* Does he say?

he was touched with a little remorse for going to have the innocent man's life taken : and seeing a slip of a pig that was killed the day before, in a corner, hanging up, the thought struck him that it would do just as well to put it in the bag in their place.   No sooner said than done, to the great surprise of the natural, he popped the pig into the bag, and tied it up.

"Now", says he, "my good friend, go home, say nothing, but bless the name in Heaven for saving your life ; and you were as near losing it this morning, as ever man was that did'nt, now".

They left the house together. Presently out comes Owney-na-peak, very hearty ; and being so, he was not able to perceive the difference in the contents of the bag, but hoisting it upon his back, he sallied out of the house. Before he had gone far, he came to the rock of Foynes, from the top of which he flung his burden into the salt waters.

Away he went home, and knocked at the door of the forge, which was opened to him by Owney. You may fancy him to yourself crossing and blessing himself over and over again, when he saw, as he thought, the ghost standing before him.   But Owney looked very merry, and told him not to be afraid.   "You did many is the good turn in your life", says he, "but the equal of this never". So he up and told him that he found the finest place in the world at the bottom of the waters, and plenty of money. "See these four pieces for a specimen", showing him some he had taken from his own hiding hole : "what do you think of that for a story?"

"Why then that it's a dhroll one, no less ; sorrow bit av I wouldn't have a mind to try my luck in the same way ; how did you come home here before me that took the straight road, and didn't stop for so much as my *gusthak** since I left Knockpatrick ?"

* Literally—*walk in.*

"Oh, there's a short cut under the waters", said Owney. "Mind and only be civil while you're in Thiernaoge, and you'll make a sight o' money".

Well became Owney, he thrust his cousin into the bag, tied it about him, and putting it into a car that was returning after leaving a load of oats at a corn-store in the city, it was not long before he was at Foynes again. Here he dismounted, and going to the rock, he was, I am afraid, half inclined to start his burden into the wide water, when he saw a small skiff making towards the point. He hailed her, and learned that she was about to board a great vessel from foreign parts, that was sailing out of the river. So he went with his bag on board, and making his bargain with the captain of the ship, he left Owney-na-peak along with the crew, and never was troubled with him after, from that day to this.

As he was passing by Barrygowen well, he filled a bottle with the water; and going home, he bought a fine suit of clothes with the rest of the money he had buried, and away he set off in the morning to the city of Lumneach. He walked through the town, admiring everything he saw, until he came before the palace of the king. Over the gates of this he saw a number of spikes, with a head of a man stuck upon each, grinning in the sunshine.

Not at all daunted, he knocked very boldly at the gate, which was opened by one of the guards of the palace. "Well! who are you, friend?"

"I am a great doctor that's come from foreign parts to cure the king's eyesight. Lead me to his presence this minute".

"Fair and softly", said the soldier. "Do you see all those heads that are stuck up there? Your's is very likely to be keeping company by them, if you are so foolish as to come inside those walls. They are the heads of all the doctors in the land that came before you; and that's

what makes the town so fine and healthy this time past,
praised be Heaven for the same!"

"Don't be talking, you great gomeril", says Owney,
"only bring me to the king at once".

He was brought before the king. After being warned
of his fate if he should fail to do all that he undertook,
the place was made clear of all but a few guards, and
Owney was informed once more, that if he should restore the king's eyes, he should wed with the princess,
and have the crown after her father's death. This put
him in great spirits, and after making a round upon his
bare knees about the bottle, he took a little of the water,
and rubbed it into the king's eyes. In a minute he
jumped up from his throne and looked about him as well
as ever. He ordered Owney to be dressed out like a king's
son, and sent word to his daughter that she should receive
him that instant for her husband.

You may say to yourself that the princess, glad as she
was of her father's recovery, did not like this message.
Small blame to her, when it is considered that she never
set her eyes upon the man himself. However, her mind
was changed wonderfully when he was brought before her,
covered with gold and diamonds, and all sorts of grand
things. Wishing, however, to know whether he had as
good a wit as he had a person, she told him that he
should give her, on the next morning, an answer to two
questions, otherwise she would not hold him worthy of her
hand. Owney bowed, and she put the questions as
follows:

"What is that which is the sweetest thing in the
world?"

"What are the three most beautiful objects in the
creation?"

These were puzzling questions; but Owney having a
small share of brains of his own, was not long in forming
an opinion upon the matter. He was very impatient for

the morning; but it came just as slow and regular as if he were not in the world. In a short time he was summoned to the court-yard, where all the nobles of the land assembled, with flags waving, and trumpets sounding, and all manner of glorious doings going on. The princess was placed on a throne of gold near her father, and there was a beautiful carpet spread for Owney to stand upon while he answered her questions. After the trumpets were silenced, she put the first, with a clear sweet voice, and he replied :

"It's salt !" says he, very stout, out.

There was a great applause at the answer; and the princess owned, smiling, that he had judged right.

"But now", said she, "for the second. What are the three most beautiful things in the creation ?"

"Why", answered the young man, "here they are. A ship in full sail—a field of wheat in ear—and——"

What the third most beautiful thing was, all the people didn't hear; but there was a great blushing and laughing among the ladies, and the princess smiled and nodded at him, quite pleased with his wit. Indeed, many said that the judges of the land themselves could not have answered better, had they been in Owney's place; nor could there be anywhere found a more likely or well-spoken young man. He was brought first to the king, who took him in his arms, and presented him to the princess. She could not help acknowledging to herself that his understanding was quite worthy of his handsome person. Orders being immediately given for the marriage to proceed, they were made one with all speed ; and it it is said, that before another year came round, the fair princess was one of the most beautiful objects in the creation.

14

THE VILLAGE RUIN.

THE lake which washes the orchards of the village of ——————, divides it from an abbey now in ruins, but associated with the recollection of one of those few glorious events which shed a scanty and occasional lustre on the dark and mournful tide of Irish history. At this foundation was educated, a century or two before the English conquest, Melcha, the beautiful daughter of O'Melachlin, a prince, whose character and conduct even yet afford room for speculation to the historians of his country. Not like the maids of our degenerate days, who are scarce exceeded by the men in their effeminate vanity and love of ornament, young Melcha joined to the tenderness and beauty of a virgin the austerity and piety of a hermit. The simplest roots that fed the lowest of her father's subjects, were the accustomed food of Melcha; a couch of heath refreshed her delicate limbs; and the lark did not arise earlier at morn to sing the praises of his Maker than did the daughter of O'Melachlin.

One subject had a large proportion of her thoughts, her tears and prayers—the misery of her afflicted country, for she had not fallen on happy days for Ireland. Some years before her birth, a swarm of savages from the north of Europe had landed on the eastern coast of the island, and in despite of the gallant resistance of her father (who then possessed the crown) and of the other chiefs, succeeded in establishing their power throughout the country. Thorgills, the barbarian chief who had led them on, assumed the sovereignty of the conquered isle, leaving, however, to O'Melachlin the name and insignia of royalty, while all the power of government was centred in himself. The history of tyranny scarcely furnishes a more appalling picture of devastation and oppressive cruelty than that which followed the success of this invasion. Monasteries were destroyed, monks slaughtered in the shelter of their cloisters ; cities laid waste and burnt; learning almost exterminated; and religion persecuted with a virulence peculiar to the gloomy and superstitious character of the oppressors. Historians present a minute and affecting detail of the enormities which were perpetrated in the shape of taxation, restriction, and direct aggression. The single word TYRANNY, however, may convey an idea of the whole.

Astonished at these terrible events, O'Melachlin, though once a valiant general, seemed struck with some base palsy of the soul that rendered him insensible to the groans and tortures of his subjects, or to the barbarous cruelty of the monster who was nominally leagued with him in power. Apparently content with the shadow of dominion left him, and with the security afforded to those of his own household, he slept upon his duties as a king and as a man, and thirty years of misery rolled by without his striking a blow, or even to all appearance forming a wish for the deliverance of his afflicted country. It was not till he was menaced with the danger of sharing the affliction of his people that he endeavoured to remove it.

Such apathy it was which pressed upon the mind of Melcha, and filled her heart with shame and with affliction. A weak and helpless maid, she had, however, nothing but her prayers to bestow upon her country, nor were those bestowed in vain. At the age of fifteen, rich in virtue as in beauty and in talent, she was recalled from those cloisters whose shadows still are seen at evenfall reflected in the waters of the lake, to grace the

phantom court of her degenerate father. The latter, proud
of his child, gave a splendid feast in honour of her return,
to which he was not ashamed to invite the oppressor of
his subjects and the usurper of his own authority. The
coarser vices are the usual concomitants of cruelty. Thorgills beheld the saintly daughter of his host with other
eyes than those of admiration. Accustomed to mould the
wishes of the puppet monarch to his own, he tarried
not even the conclusion of the feast, but desiring the
company of O'Melachlin on the green without the palace,
he there disclosed to him, with the bluntness of a barbarian
and the insolence of a conqueror, his infamous wishes.

Struck to the soul at what he heard, O'Melachlin was
deprived of the power of reply or utterance. For the
first time since he had resigned to the invader the power
which had fallen so heavy on the land, his feelings
were awakened to a sense of sympathy, and self-interest
made him pitiful. The cries of bereaved parents, to
which till now his heart had been impenetrable as a wall
of brass, found sudden entrance to its inmost folds, and a
responsive echo amid its tenderest strings. He sat for a
time upon a bench close by, with his forehead resting on
his hand, and a torrent of tempestuous feelings rushing
through his bosom.

" What sayest thou?" asked the tyrant, after a long
silence. "Shall I have my wish? No answer! Hearest
thou, slave? What insolence keeps thee silent?"

"I pray you, pardon me", replied the monarch, "I
was thinking then of a sore annoyance that has lately bred
about our castle. I mean that rookery yonder, the din of
which even now confounds the music of our feast, and
invades with its untimely harshness our cheering and
most singular discourse. I would I had some mode of
banishing that pest—I would I had some mode—I would
I had".

" Ho! was that all the subject of thy thought?" said

Thorgills—" why, fool! thou never wilt be rid of them till thou hast burned the nests wherein they breed "

" I thank thee ", answered the insulted parent; " I'll take thy counsel. I'll burn the nests. Will you walk into the house ?"

" What first of my request ?" said Thorgills. " Tell me that ".

" If thou hadst asked of me ", replied the king, " a favourite hobby for the chase, or a hound to guard thy threshold, thou wouldst not think it much to grant a week at least for preparing my heart to part with what it loved. How much more, when thy demand reaches to the child of my heart, the only offspring of a mother who died before she had beheld her offspring ".

" A week, then let it be ", said Thorgills, looking with contempt upon the starting tears of the applicant.

" A week would scarce suffice ", replied the monarch, " to teach my tongue in what language it should communicate a destiny like this to Melcha ".

" What time wouldst thou require, then ?" cried the tyrant hastily.

" Thou seest", replied the king, pointing to the new moon, which showed its slender crescent above the wood-crowned hills that bounded in the prospect. " Before that thread of light that g immers now upon the distant lake, like chastity on beauty, has fulfilled its changes, thou shalt receive my answer to this proffer".

" Be it so", said Thorgills ; and the conversation ended. When the guests had all departed, the wretched monarch went into his oratory, where he bade one of his followers order Melcha to attend him. She found him utterly depressed, and almost incapable of forming a design. Having commanded the attendants to withdraw, he endeavoured, but in vain, to make known to the astonished princess the demand of the usurper. He remembered her departed mother, and he thought of her own

sanctity, and more than all, he remembered his helpless
condition, and the seeming impossibility of doing anything
within the time to remove from his own doors the misery
which had already befallen so many of his subjects, without
meeting any active sympathy from him. Was this the
form which he was to resign into a ruffian's hands? Was
it for such an end he had instilled into her delicate mind the
principles of early virtue and Christian piety? By degrees.
as he contemplated his situation, his mind was roused by
the very nature of the exigency to devise the means of its
removal. He communicated both to Melcha, and was not
disappointed in her firmness. With a zeal beyond her
sex, she prepared to take a part in the desperate counsels
of her father, and the still more desperate means by which
he proposed to put them into execution. Assembling the
officers of his court, he made known to all, in the presence
of his daughter, the flagrant insult which had been offered
to their sovereign, and obtained the ready pledge of all to
peril their existence in the furtherance of his wishes. He
unfolded in their sight the green banner of their country,
which had now for more than thirty years lain hid
amongst the wrecks of their departed freedom, and while
the memory of former glories shone warmly on their
minds through the gloom of recent shame and recent injuries, the monarch easily directed their enthusiasm to the
point where he would have it fall, the tyranny of Thorgills
and his countrymen.

On the following day, the latter departed for the capital,
where he was to await the determination of his colleague.
Accustomed to hold in contempt the imbecility of the conquered king, and hard himself at heart, he knew not what
prodigious actions may take their rise from the impulse of
paternal love. That rapid month was fruitful in exertion.
Couriers were dispatched from the palace of O'Melachlin to
many of those princes, whose suggestions for the deliverance of the isle he had long since received with apathy

or disregard. Plans were arranged, troops organized, and a general system of intelligence established throughout the island. It is easy to unite the oppressed against the oppressor. All seemed almost to anticipate the wishes of the sovereign, so suddenly his scheme was spread through-out the country. The moon rolled by, and by its latest glimmer a messenger was dispatched to the capital to inform the tyrant that O'Melachlin would send his daughter to meet him at whatever place he should appoint.

There was an island on the lake in Meath, in which Thorgills had erected a lordly palace, surrounded by the richest woods, and affording a delicious prospect of the lake and the surrounding country. Hither the luxurious monarch directed that the daughter of O'Melachlin should be sent, together with her train of fifteen noble maidens of the court of O'Melachlin. The address of the latter in seeming to accede to the wishes of the tyrant, is preserved amongst the annals of the isle. It requested him to con-sider whether he might not find elsewhere some object more deserving of his favour than "that brown girl", and besought him to remember "whose father's child she was".

Far from being touched by this appeal, the usurper, on the appointed day, selected in the capital fifteen of the most dissolute and brutal of his followers, with whom he arrived at evening at the rendezvous. It was a portentous night for Ireland. Even to the eyes of the tyrant and his gang, half blinded as they were to all but their own hideous thoughts, there appeared something gloomy and foreboding in the stillness of nature, and seemed even to pervade the manners of the people. The villages were silent as they passed, and there appeared in the greeting of the few they met upon the route an air of deep-seated and almost menacing intelligence.

Meantime, with feelings widely different and an anxiety that even the greatness of the enterprize and the awakened spirit of heroism could not wholly subdue, O'Melachlin

prepared himself for the painful task of bidding farewell
to his beloved daughter. Melcha, already aware of his
design, awaited with the deepest anxiety, yet mingled
with a thrilling hope, the approach of the auspicious
moment that was to crown her ardent and long-
cherished wishes or to dash them to the earth for ever.
Alone, in her royal father's oratory, she lay prostrate
before the marble altar, and wet with floods of tears the
solid pavement at its base. She prayed not like a fanatic
or a worldling, but like one who understood with a feeling
mind the real miseries of her country, and knew that she
addressed a power capable of removing them. The step
of her father at the porch of the oratory aroused the
princess from her attitude of devotion. She stood up
hastily upon her feet, like one prepared for enterprise, and
waited the speech of O'Melachlin. He came to inform
her that all was ready for her departure, and conducted
her into an adjoining chamber, that he might bid her
farewell. The father and daughter embraced in silence
and with tears. Believing from the error of the light
that she looked pale as she stood before him, he took her
hand and pressed it in an encouraging manner.

"Follow me", he said, "my child, and thou shalt see
how little cause thou hast to fear the power of this Nor-
wegian Holofernes".

The king conducted her into another room, where stood
fifteen young maidens, as it seemed, and richly attired.

"Thou seest these virgins, Melcha", said the monarch.

"Their years are like thine own, but under every cloak
is a warrior's sword, and they do not want a warrior's
hand to wield it, for all that is woman of them is their
dress. Dost thou think", he added tenderly, "that thou
hast firmness for such a task as this?"

"I have no fear", replied his daughter. "He who put
strength into the arm of Judith can give courage to the
heart of Melcha".

They departed from the palace, where the anxious father remained a little longer, until the fast advancing shades of night should enable him to put the first steps of his design into effect. As soon as the earliest stars began to glimmer on the woods of Meath, he took from its recess the banner which so long had rested idle and inglorious in his hall, and the brazen sword which was once the constant companion of his early successes and defeats, but which now had not left its sheath since he received a visionary crown from Thorgills. Girding the weapon to his side, he drew the blade with tears of shame and sorrow, imprinted a kiss upon the tempered metal, and hastened with reviving hope and energy to seek the troop who awaited him in the adjoining wood. Mounting in haste, they hurried along through forests and defiles which were in many places thronged with silent multitudes, armed, and waiting but the signal word to rush to action. They halted near the borders of the lake of Thorgills, where a number of currachs, or basket boats, were moored under shelter of the wood. After holding a council of war, and allotting to the several princes engaged their parts in the approaching enterprise, O'Melachlin remained on the shore, casting from time to time an anxious eye to the usurper's isle, and awaiting the expected signal of his daughter.

The princess, in the meantime, pursued her hazardous journey to the abode of Thorgills. The sun had already set before they reached the shores of the lake which surrounded the castle of the tyrant, and the silver bow of the expiring moon was glimmering in its pure and tranquil waters. A barge, allotted by Thorgills for the purpose, was sent to convey them to the island, and they were welcomed with soft music at the entrance of the palace. The place was lonely, the guards were few, and the blind security of the monarch was only equalled by his weakness. Besides, the revel spirit had descended from the chieftain to his train, and most, even of those who were in arms,

14*

had incapacitated themselves for using them **with any**
energy.

Melcha and her train were conducted by a half-intoxi-
cated slave to an extensive hall, where they were commanded to await the orders of the conqueror.   The guide
disappeared, and the princess prepared for the issue.   In
a little time, the hangings at one side of the apartment
were drawn back, and the usurper, accompanied by his
ruffian band, made his appearance, hot with the fumes of
intoxication, and staggering from the late debauch.   The
entrance of Thorgills was the signal for Melcha to prepare
her part.   All remained still while Thorgills passed from
one to another of the silent band of maidens, and paused
at length before the "brown girl", for whom O'Melachlin
had besought his pity.   A thrill of terror shot through the
heart of Melcha as she beheld the hand of the wretch
about to grasp her arm.

"Down with the tyrant!" she exclaimed, in a voice
that rung like a bugle call.   "Upon him, warriors, in the
name of Erin! Bind him, but slay him not!"

With a wild "Farrah!" that shook the roof and walls
of the abhorred dwelling, the youths obeyed the summons
of the heroine.   The tornado bursts not sooner from the
bosom of an eastern calm, than did the band of warriors
from their delicate disguise at the sound of those beloved
accents.   Their swords for an instant gleamed unstained
on high, but when next they rose into the air they smoked
with the streaming gore of the oppressors.   Struck powerless by the charge, the tyrant and his dissolute crew were
disabled before they had even time to draw a sword.
Thorgills was seized alive, and bound with their scarfs
and bands, while the rest were hewed to pieces, without
pity, on the spot.   While this was done, the heroic
Melcha, seizing a torch which burned in the apartment,
rushed swiftly from the palace.   The affrighted guards
believing it to be some apparition, gave way as she ap-

proached, and suffered her to reach the borders of the
lake, where she waved the brand on high, forgetting in
the zeal of liberty her feminine character, and more resembling one of their own war-goddesses than the peaceful Christian maiden, whose prayers and tears, till now,
had been her only weapons.   Like a train to which a
spark has been applied, a chain of beacon-fires sprang up
from hill to hill of the surrounding country, amid the
shouts of thousands gasping for the breath of freedom,
and hailing that feeble light as its arising star.   The boats
of O'Melachlin, shooting like arrows from the surrounding
shores, darkened the surface of the lake, and the foremost
reached the isle before the guards of the tyrant, stupefied
by wine and fear, had yet recovered courage to resist.
They were an easy prey to O'Melachlin and his followers;
nor was the enterprise thus auspiciously commenced, permitted to grow cold until the power of the invaders was
destroyed throughout the isle, and Melcha had the happiness to see peace and liberty restored to her afflicted
country.

In the waters of that lake which so often had borne the
usurper to the lonely scene of his debaucheries, he was con-
signed amidst the acclamations of a liberated people to a
nameless sepulchre, and the power he had abused once
more reverted to its rightful owner.

In one thing only did the too confiding islanders neglect
to profit by the advice of Thorgills himself.   *They did not
burn the nests.*   They suffered the strangers still to possess
the sea-port towns and other important holds throughout
the isle; an imprudence, however, the effect of which did
not appear till the reign of O'Melachlin was ended by his
death.

The reader may desire to know what became of the
beautiful and heroic princess who had so considerable a
share in the restoration of her country's freedom.   As this
had been the only Earthly object of her wishes, even from

childhood, with its accomplishment was en led all that she
desired on Earth. Rejecting the crowds of noble and
wealthy suitors who ardently sought her hand, and pre-
ferring the solitude of her own heart to the splendours and
allurements of a court, she besought her father, as a re-
compense for her ready compliance with his wishes, that
he would allow her once more to retire into the convent
where she had received her education, to consume her days
in exercises of piety and virtue. Pained at her choice,
the king, however, did not seek to thwart it; and after
playing her brief but brilliant part upon the theatre of the
world, she devoted in those holy shades her virgin love
and the residue of her days to Heaven.

Such are the recollections that hallow the Village Ruin,
and dignify its vicinity with the majesty of historical association. The peasantry choose the grave of the royal nun
as the scene of their devotions; and even those who look
with contempt upon their humble piety, and regard as
superstition the religion of the buried princess, feel the
genial current gush within their bosoms as they pass the
spot at evening, and think upon her sing'eness of heart
and her devoted zeal. Long may it be before feelings
such as these shall be extinguished.

THE KNIGHT OF THE SHEEP

CHAPTER 1.

In the days of our ancestors it was the custom, when "strong farmer" had arrived at a certain degree of inde pendence by his agricultural pursuits, to confer upon him a title in the Irish language, which is literally translated, " The Knight of the Sheep." Though not commonly of noble origin, those persons often exercised a kind of patriarchal sway, scarce less extensive than that of many a feudal descendent of the Butlers or the Geraldines.

In one of the most fertile townlands in one of our inland counties, lived a person of this class, bearing the name of Bryan Taafe. No less than three spacious tenements acknowledged his sway, by the culture of which he had acquired, in the course of a long life, a quantity of wealth more than sufficient for any purpose to which he might wish to apply it.

Mr. Taafe had three sons, on whose education he had lavished all the care and expense which could have been expected from the most affectionate father in his walk of life. He had a great opinion of learning, and had frequently in his mouth, for the instruction of his children, such snatches of old wisdom as " Learning is better than houses or land," and

> " A man without learning, and wearing fine clothes,
> Is like a pig with a gold ring in his nose."

Accordingly, the best teachers that Kerry and Limerick could afford were employed to teach them the classics.

mathematics, and such other branches of science and letters as were current in those parts. The two elder sons showed a remarkable quickness in all their studies; but the youngest, though his favourite, disappointed both him and his instructors. So heavy was he at his book, that neither threats nor caresses could have any effect in making him arrive at anything like proficiency. However, as it did not proceed from absolute indolence or obstinacy, his father was content to bear with his backwardness in this respect, although it in some degree diminished the especial affection with which he once regarded him.

One day as Mr. Taafe was walking in his garden, taking the air before breakfast in the morning, he called Jerry Fogarty, his steward, and told him he wanted to speak with him.

"Jerry," says Mr. Taafe, after they had taken two or three turns on the walk together, "I don't know in the world what'll I do with Garret."

"Why so, masther?"

"Ah, I'm kilt from him. You know yourself what a great opinion I always had o' the learning. A man, in fact, isn't considhered worth spakin' to in these times that hasn't it. 'Tis for the same raison I went to so much cost and trouble to get schoolin' for them three boys; and to be sure as for Shamus and Guillaum, I haven't any cause to complain, but the world wouldn't get good o' Garret. It was only the other mornin' I asked him who it was discovered America, and the answer he made me was, that he believed it was Nebuchodonezzar."

"A' no?"

" 'Tis as thrue as you're standin' there. What's to be done with a man o' that kind? Sure, as I often represented to himself, it would be a disgrace to me if he was ever to go abroad in foreign parts, or any place o' the kind, and to make such an answer as that to any gentleman or lady, afther all I lost by him. 'Tisn't so with

Shamus and Guillaum. There isn't many goin' that could thrace histhory with them boys. I'd give a dale, out o' regard for the poor woman that's gone, if Garret could come any way near 'em".

" I'll tell you what it is, masther", said Jerry , "there's a dale that's not over bright at the book, an' that would be very 'cute for all in their own minds. May be Master Garret would be one o' them, an' we not to know it. I remember myself one Motry Hierlohee, that not one ha'- p'orth o' good could be got of him goin' to school, an' he turned out one of the greatest janiuses in the parish afther. There isn't his aiquals in Munsther now at a lamentation or the likes. Them raal janiuses does be always so full of their own thoughts, they can't bring themselves, as it were, to take notice of those of other people".

" Maybe you're right, Jerry", answered Mr. Taafe ; " I'll take an opportunity of trying".

He said no more, but in a few days after he gave a great entertainment to all his acquaintances, rich and poor, that were within a morning's ride of his own house, taking particular care to have every one present that had any name at all for "the learning". Mr. Taafe was so rich and so popular amongst his neighbours, that his house was crowded on the day appointed with all the scholars in the country, and they had no reason to complain of the enter- tainment they received from Mr. Taafe. Everything good and wholesome that his sheep-walk, his paddock, his orchard, his kitchen-garden, his pantry, and his cellar, could afford, was placed before them in abundance; and seldom did a merrier company assemble together to enjoy the hospitality of an Irish farmer.

When the dinner was over, and the guests busily occu- pied in conversation, the Knight of the Sheep, who sat at the head of the table, stood up with a grave air, as if he were about to address something of importance to the company. His venerable appearance, as he remained standing, a courteous smile shedding its light over his aged countenance, and his snowy hair descending almost to his shoulders, occasioned a respectful silence amongst the guests, while he addressed them in the following words :—

" In the first place, gentlemen, I have to return you all thanks for giving me the pleasure of your company here to-day, which I do with all my heart. And I feel the more honoured and gratified because I take it for granted you have come here, not so much from any personal feeling towards myself, but because you know that I have always endeavoured, so far as my poor means would enable me, to show my respect for men of parts and learning. Well, then, here you are all met, grammarians, geometricians, arithmeticians, geographers, astronomers, philosophers, Latinists, Grecians, and men of more sciences than perhaps I ever heard the names of. Now there's no doubt learning is a fine thing, but what good is all the learning in the world without what they call mother-wit to make use of it ? An ounce o' mother-wit would buy an' sell a stone-weight of learning at any fair in Munster. Now there are you all scholars, an' here am I a poor country farmer that hardly ever got more teaching than to read and write, and maybe a course of Voster, and yet I'll be bound I'll lay down a problem that maybe some o' ye wouldn't find it easy to make out".

At this preamble, the curiosity of the company was raised to the highest degree, and the Knight of the Sheep resumed, after a brief pause :

" At a farm of mine, about a dozen miles from this, I have four fields of precisely the same soil ; one square, another oblong, another partly round, and another triangular. Now, what is the reason that, while I have an excellent crop of white eyes this year out of the square, the oblong, and the round field, not a single stalk would grow in the triangular one ?"

This problem produced a dead silence amongst the guests, and all exerted their understandings to discover the solution, but without avail, although many of their conjectures showed the deepest ingenuity. Some traced out a mysterious connection between the triangular boundary, and the lines of the celestial hemisphere; others said, probably from the shape of the field an equal portion of nutrition did not flow on all sides to the seed so as to favour its growth. Others attributed the failure to the effect of the angular hedges upon the atmosphere, which, collecting the wind, as it were, into corners, caused such an obstruction to the warmth necessary to vegetation, that the seed perished in the earth. But all their theories were beside the mark.

"Gentlemen", said Mr. Taafe, "ye're all too clever—that's the only fault I have to find with ye'r answers. Shamus", he continued, addressing his eldest son, "can you tell the raison?"

"Why, then, father", said Shamus, "they didn't grow there, I suppose, because you didn't plant them there".

"You have it, Shamus", said the knight; "I declare you took the ball from all the philosophers. Well, gentlemen, can any o' ye tell me, now, if you wished to travel all over the world, from whom would you ask a passport?"

This question seemed as puzzling as the former. Some said the Great Mogul, others the Grand Signior, others the Pope, others the Lord Lieutenant. and some the Emperor of Austria; but all were wrong.

"What do you say, Guillaum?" asked the knight, addressing his second son.

"From Civility, father", answered Guillaum; "for that's a gentleman that has acquaintances everywhere"

"You're right, Guillaum", replied the knight. "Well, I have one more question for the company. Can any one

tell me in what country the women are the best housekeepers ?"

Again the company exhausted all their efforts in con
jecture, and the geographers showed their learning by
naming all the countries in the world, one after another,
but to no purpose. The Knight now turned with a fond
look towards his youngest son.

"Garret", said he, "can you tell where the women are
good housekeepers ?"

Garret rubbed his forehead for a while, and smiled, and
shook his head, but could get nothing out of it.

"I declare to my heart, father", said he, "I can't tell
from Adam. Where the women are good housekeepers?
—stay a minute. Maybe", said he, with a knowing look,
" maybe 'tis in America?"

"Shamus, do you answer," said the knight, in a disappointed tone.

"In the grave, father", answered Shamus, "for there
they never gad abroad".

Mr. Taafe acknowledged that his eldest son had once
more judged right; and the entertainments of the night
proceeded without further interruption, until, wearied with
feasting and music, such of the company as could not be
accommodated with beds, took their departure, each in the
direction of his own home.

CHAPTER II.

On the following morning, in the presence of his household, Mr. Taafe made a present to his two eldest sons of
one hundred pounds each, and was induced to bestow the
same sum on Garret, although he by no means thought he
deserved it after disgracing him as he had done before his
guests. He signified to the young men at the same time,

that he gave them the money as a free gift, to lay out in any way they pleased, and that he never should ask them to repay it.

After breakfast, the old knight, as usual, went to take a few turns in the garden.

" Well, Jerry ", said he, when the steward had joined him according to his orders; " well, Jerry, Garret is no genius ".

A groan from Jerry seemed to announce his acquiescence in this decision. He did not, however, resign all hope.

"With submission to your honour", said he, "I wouldn't call that a fair thrial of a man's parts. A man mightn't be able to answer a little *cran* o' that kind, au' to have more sense for all than those that would. Wait a while until you'll see what use he'll make o' the hundred pounds, an' that'll show his sinse betther than all the riddles in Europe".

Mr. Taafe acknowledged that Jerry's proposition was but reasonable ; and, accordingly, at the end of a twelvemonth, he called his three sons before him, and examined them one after another.

" Well, Shamus ", said he, " what did you do with your hundred pounds?"

" I bought stock with it, father ".

"Very good. And you, Guillaum?"

"I laid it out, father, in the intherest of a little farm westwards".

" Very well managed again. Well, Garret, let us hear what you did with the hundred pounds ".

" I spent it, father ", said Garret.

" Spent it! Is it the whole hundred pounds?"

" Sure, I thought you told us we might lay it out as we liked, sir ?"

" Is that the raison you should be such a prodigal as to waste the whole of it in a year? Well, hear to me, now, the three o' ye, and listen to the raison why I put ye to these trials. I'm an ould man, my children; my hair is white on my head, an' it's time for me to think of turning the few days that are left me to the best account. I wish to separate myself from the world before the world separates itself from me. For this cause I had resolved, these six months back, to give up all my property to ye three that are young an' hearty, an' to keep nothing for myself but a bed under my old roof, an' a sate at the table and by the fire-place, an' so to end my ould days in peace an' quiet. To you, Shamus, I meant to give the dairy-farm up in the mountains; the Corcasses and all the meadowing to you, Guillaum; and for you, Garret, I had the best of the whole,—that is, the house we're living in, and the farm belonging to it. But for what would I give it to you, after what you just tould me? Is it to make ducks and drakes of it, as you did o' the hundhred pounds? Here, Garret", said he, going to a corner of the room and bringing out a small bag and a long hazel stick; "here's the legacy I have to leave you—that, an' the king's high road, an' my liberty to go wherever it best plases you. Hard enough I airned that hundhred pounds that you spent so aisily. And as for the farm I meant to give you, I give it to these two boys, an' my blessing along with it, since 'tis they that know how to take care of it".

At this speech the two elder sons cast themselves at their father's feet with tears of gratitude.

" Yes", said he, " my dear boys, I'm rewarded for all the pains I ever took with ye, to make ye industrious, and thrifty, and everything that way. I'm satisfied, under Heaven, that all will go right with ye, but as for this boy, I have nothing to say to him. Betther for me I never saw his face".

Poor Garret turned aside his head, but he made no attempt to excuse himself, nor to obtain any favour from his rigid father. After wishing them all a timid farewell, which was but slightingly returned, he took the bag and staff, and went about his business.

His departure seemed to give little pain to his relatives. They lived merrily and prosperously, and even the old knight himself showed no anxiety to know what had become of Garret. In the meantime, the two elder sons got married; and Mr. Taafe, in the course of a few years, had the satisfaction to see his grandchildren seated on his knee.

We are often widely mistaken in our estimate of generosity. It may appear a very noble thing to bestow largely; but, before we give it the praise of generosity, we must be sure that the motive is as good as the deed. Mr. Taafe began, in the course of time, to show that his views in bestowing his property on his two sons were not wholly free from selfishness. They found it harder to please him now that they were masters of all, than when they were wholly dependent on his will. His jealousies and murmurs were interminable. There was no providing against them beforehand, nor any allaying them when they did arise. The consequence was, the young men, who never really felt anything like the gratitude they had professed, began to consider the task of pleasing him altogether burdensome. In this feeling they were encouraged by their wives, who never ceased murmuring at the cost and trouble of entertaining him.

Accordingly, one night while the aged knight was murmuring at some inattention which was shown him at table, Shamus and Guillaum Taafe walked into the room, determined to put an end for ever to his complaints.

" I'd like to know what would plaise you !" exclaimed Shamus. " I suppose you won't stop until you'll take house and all from us, an' turn us out, as you did Garret, to beg from doore to doore ?"

" If I did itself, Shamus", said the knight, looking at him for some moments with surprise. " I'd get no more than I gave".

" What good was your giving it", cried Guillaum,
" when you wou't let us enjoy it with a moment's comfort ?"

" Do you talk that way to me, too, Guillaum ?   If it
was poor Garret I had, he wouldn't use me so".

" Great thanks he got from you for any good that was
in him", cried one of the women.

" Let him take his stick and pack out to look for
Garret", said the second woman, " since he is so fond of
him".

The old knight turned and looked at the women.

" I don't wondher", said he, " at anything I'd hear *ye*
say.   You never yet heard of anything great or good, or
for the public advantage, that a woman would have a
hand in,—only mischief always.   If you ask who made
such a road, or who built such a bridge, or wrote such a
great histhory, or did any other good action o' the kind,
I'll engage 'tis seldom you'll hear that it is a woman done
it ; but if you ask who is it that set such and such a pair
fightin', or who is it that caused such a *jewel*, or who is it
that let out such a sacret, or ran down such a man's
character, or occasioned such a war, or brought such a
man to the gallows, or caused diversion in such a family,
or anything o' that kind, then, I'll engage, you'll hear that
a woman had some call to it.   We needn't have recoorse
to histhory to know ye'r doins.   'Tis undher our eyes.
'Twas the likes o' ye two that burned Throy, an' made the
King o' Leinstlier rebel again' Brian Born".

At this the two women pulled the caps off their heads,
and set up such a screaming and shrieking as might be
heard from thence to Cork.

" Oh, murther ! murther !" says one of them, " was it
for this I married you, tc be compared to people o' that
kind ?"

" What raison has he to me", cried the other, " that
he'd compare me to them that would rebel again' Brian

Boru? Would I rebel again' Brian Boru, Shamus, a' ra gal?"

"Don't heed him, a-vourneen, he's an ould man".

"Oh, vo! vo! if ever I thought the likes o' thai would be said o' me, that I'd rebel again' Brian Boru!"

"There's no use in talking, Guillaum", cried the second, who probably took the allusion to the fate of Troy as a slight on her own personal attractions; "there's no use in talkin', but I never'll stay a day undher your roof with anybody that would say I'd burn Throy. Does he forget that ever he had a mother himself? Ah, 'tis a bad apple, that's what it is, that despises the three it sprung from".

"Well, I'll tell you what it is, now", said the eldest son, "since 'tis come to that with you, that you won't let the women alone, I won't put up with any more from you. I believe, if I didn't show you the outside o' the doore, you'd show it to me before long. There, now, the world is free to you to look out for people that'll plaise you betther, since you say we can't do it".

"A', Shamus, agra", said the old knight, looking at his son with astonishment; "is that my thanks afther all?"

"Your thanks for what?" cried Guillaum; "is it for plasin' your own fancy? or for makin' our lives miserable ever siuce, an' to give crossness to the women?"

"Let him go look for Garret, now", cried one of the women, "an' see whether they'll agree betther than they did before".

"Ah—Shamus—Guillaum—a chree", said the poor old man, trembling with terror at sight of the open door, "let ye have it as ye will; I am sorry for what I said, a'ra gal! Don't turn me out on the high road in my ould days! I'll engage, I never'll open my mouth again' one o' ye again the longest day I live. A', Shamus, a-vich,

it isn't long I have to stay wid ye. Your own nair will
he as white as mine yet, plaise God, an' 'twouldn't be
wishin' to you then for a dale that you showed any dis-
respect to mine".

His entreaties, however, were all to no purpose. They
turned him out, and made fast the door behind him.

Imagine an old man of sixty and upwards turned out
on the high road on a cold and rainy night, the north
wind beating on his feeble breast, and without the
prospect of relief before him. For a time he could not
believe that the occurrence was real; and it was only
when he felt the rain already penetrating through his thin
dress that he became convinced it was but too true.

" Well", said the old man, lifting up his hands as he
crept out on the high road, " is this what all the teaching
come to? Is this the cleverness an' the learning?
Well, if it was to do again! No matther. They say
there's two bad pays in the world—the man that pays
beforehand, an' the man that doesn't pay at all. In like
manner, there's two kinds of people that wrong their
lawful heirs—those that give them their inheritance before
death, and those that will it away from them afther.
What'll I do now at all? or where'll I turn to? a poor
old man o' my kind that isn't able to do a sthroke o' work
if I was ever so fain! An' the night gettin' worse an'
worse! Easy!—Isn't that a light I see westwards?—
There's no one, surely, except an unnatural son or
daughter that would refuse to give an old man shelter on
such a night as this. I'll see if all men's hearts are as
hard as my two sons'".

He went to the house, which was situated at the
distance of a quarter of a mile from that which he so
lately looked on as his own. As he tottered along the
dark and miry *borheen* which led to the cottage door, the
barking of a dog inside aroused the attention of the
inmates. Being already in bed, however, before he had

arrived there, none of them were very willing to give admission to a stranger.

" Who's there ?" cried the man of the house, as the old knight knocked timidly at the door. " Do you think we have nothing else to do at this time o' night but to be gettin' up an' openin' the doore to every sthroller that goes the road ?"

" Ah! if you knew who it was you had there", said the knight, " you wouldn't be so slow of openin' the doore".

" Who is it I have there, then ?"

" The Knight of the Sheep".

" The Knight of the Sheep! Oh, you born villyan! 'Twas your son Shamus that chated me out o' thirty good pounds by a horse he sould me at the fair o' Killeedy—an animal that wasn't worth five! Go along this minute with you: or if you make me get up, 'tis to give you something that you wouldn't bargain for".

The poor old man hurried away from the door, fearing that the farmer would be but too ready to put his threat into execution. The night was growing worse and worse. He knocked at another door; but the proprietor of this in like manner had suffered to the extreme cleverness of Guillaum Taafe, and refused to give him shelter. The whole night was spent in going from door to door, and finding in every place where he applied that the great ability of his two sons had been beforehand with him in getting a bad name for the whole family. At last, as the morning began to dawn, he found himself unable to proceed further, and was obliged to lie down in a little paddock close to a very handsome farm-house. Here the coldness of the morning air and the keenness of his grief at the recollection of his children's ingratitude had such an effect upon him that he swooned away, and lay for a long time insensible upon the grass. In this condition he was found by the people of the house, who soon after came out to look after the bounds and do their usual

15

farming work.   They had the humanity to take him into
the house, and to put him into a warm bed, where they
used all proper means for his recovery.

When he had come to himself, they asked him who he
was, and how he had fallen into so unhappy a condition.
For a time the old knight was afraid to answer, lest these
charitable people, like so many others, might have been at
one time sufferers to the roguery of his two eldest sons,
and thus be tempted to repent of their kindness the instant they had heard on whom it had been bestowed.
However, fearing lest they should accuse him of duplicity
in case they might afterwards learn the truth, he at
length confessed his name.

"The Knight of the Sheep!" exclaimed the woman of
the house, with a look of the utmost surprise and joy.

"Oh, Tom, Tom!" she continued, calling out to her
husband, who was in another room.   "A', come here,
asthore, until you see Misther Taafe, the father o' young
Masther Garret, the darlin' that saved us all from ruin".

The man of the house came in as fast as he could run.

"Are you Garret Taafe's father?" said he, looking
surprised at the old knight.

"I had a son of that name", said Mr. Taafe, "though
all I know of him now is, that I used him worse than I
would if it was to happen again".

"Well, then", said the farmer, "my blessing on that
day that ever you set foot within these doores.   The rose
in May was never half so welcome, an' I'm betther
plaised than I'll tell you, that I have you undher my
roof".

"I'm obliged to you", said the knight, "but what's
the raison o' that?"

"Your son Garret", replied the man, "of a day when
every whole ha'p'orth we had in the world was going to
be canted for the rent, put a hand in his pocket an' lent
us thirty pounds till we'd be able to pay him again, an' we

not knowin' who in the world he was, nor he us, I'm sure. It was only a long time afther that we found it out by others in various parts that he had served in like manner, and they told us who he was. We never seen him since; but I'm sure it would be the joyful day to us that we'd see him coming back to get his thirty pounds".

When the old knight heard this, he felt as .. somebody wa running him through with a sword.

'. And this", said he, " was the way poor Garret spent the hundhred pounds! Oh, murther! murther! my poor boy, what had I to do at all, to go turn you adhrift as I done, for no raison! I took the wrong for the right, an' the right for the wrong! No matther! That's the way the whole world is blinded. That's the way death will show us the differ of many a thing. O murther! Garret! Garret! What'll I do at all with the thoughts of it! An' them two villyans that I gave it all to, an' that turned me out afther in my ould days, as I done by you! No matther".

He turned into the wall for fear the people would hear him groaning; but the remorse, added to all his other sufferings, had almost killed him.

In a little time the old knight began to recover something of his former strength under the care of his new acquaintances, who continued to show him the most devoted attention. One morning the farmer came into his room with a large purse full of gold in his hand, and said :

" I told you, sir, I owed your son thirty pounds; an' since he's not comin' to ax for it, you're heartily welcome to the use of it until he does, an' I'm sure he wouldn't wish to see it betther employed".

" No, no", replied Mr. Taafe, " I'll not take the money from you ; but I'll borrow the whole purse for a week, an' at the end o' that time I'll return it safe to you".

The farmer lent him the purse, and the knight waited for a fine day, when he set off again in the morning, and took the road leading to the dwelling from which he had been expelled. It was noon, and the sun was shining bright, when he arrived upon the little lawn before the door. Sitting down in the sunshine by the kitchen-garden wall, he began counting the gold, and arranging it in a number of little heaps, so that it had a most imposing effect. While he was thus occupied, one of his young daughters-in-law—the same whose beauty had drawn upon her the unhappy allusion to the mischief-making spouse of Menelaus—happened to make her appearance at the front door, and looking around, saw the old knight in the act of counting his gold in the sunshine. Overwhelmed with astonishment, she ran to her husband, and told him what she had seen.

"Nonsense, woman!" said Shamus; "you don't mean to persuade me to a thing o' that kind"

"Very well", replied the woman, " I'm sure, if you don't believe me, 'tis asy for ye all to go an' see ye'rselves".

So they all went, and peeping through the little window one afther another, were dazzled by the sight of so much gold.

"You done very wrong, Shamus", said Guillaum, " ever to turn out the ould father as you done. See, now, what we all lost by it. That's a part o' the money he laid by from year to year, an' we never'll see a penny of it".

At this they all felt the greatest remorse for the manner in which they had acted to the old man. However. they were not so much discouraged but that some of them ventured to approach and salute him. On seeing them draw nigh, he hastily concealed the gold and returned their greeting with an appearance of displeasure. It was by much persuasion, and after many assurances of their regret for what had passed, that he consented once more

to come and take up his abode beneath their roof, desiring
at the same time that an ass and cart might be sent to the
farmer's for a strong box which he had left there.

At the mention of a *strong box*, it may easily be imagined what were the sensations of his hearers. The ass
and cart were procured without delay, and, before evening,
those grateful children had the satisfaction to behold a
heavy box, of very promising dimensions, deposited in a
corner of the small chamber which was to be reserved for
the future use of their aged parent.

In the meanwhile, nothing could exceed the attention
which he now received from the young people. They
seemed only unhappy when not occupied in contributing
in some way to his comfort, and perceiving his remorse
for the manner in which Garret had been treated, used
all the means in their power to discover whither he had
gone. But it is not always in this life that one false step
can be retraced. The old knight was not destined to see
his son again, and his grief at this disappointment had
no slight effect in aggravating the infirmities of his old age.

At length, perceiving that he was near his end, he
called his sons and daughters to his bedside, and addressed
them in the following words :—

" Whatever cause I had once to complain of ye, Shamus
and Guillaum, that's all past and gone now, and it is right
that I should leave you some little remembrance for all
the trouble I gave you since my comin' home. Do you
see that chest over there ?"

" Ah, father! what chest ?" cried the sons. " Don't
be talkin' of it for a chest".

" Well, my good boys", said the knight, " my will is
in that chest, so I need tell ye no more".

" Don't speak of it, father", said Shamus, " for. as the
Latin poet says :—

       ' Non possidentem molia
       Recte beatum'

Only as you're talkin' of it at all for a chest, where's the key, father?"

"Ah, Shamus!" said the knight, "you were always great at the Latin. The key is in my waistcoat pocket".

Soon after he expired. The two sons, impatient to inspect their treasure, could hardly wait until the old man ceased to breathe. While Shamus unlocked the box, Guillaum remained to keep the door fast.

"Well, Shamus", said his brother, "what do you find there?"

"A parcel of stones, Guillaum!"

"Nonsense, man! try what's undher 'em."

Shamus complied, and found at the bottom of the box a rope with a running noose at the end, and a scroll of paper, from which Shamus read the following sentence aloud, for the information of his brother:—

"THE LAST WILL AND TESTAMENT OF BRYAN TAAFE, COMMONLY CALLED THE KNIGHT OF THE SHEEP.

"*Imprimis.* To my two sons, Shamus and Guillaum, I bequeath the whole of the limestones contained in this box, in return for their disinterested love and care of me ever since the day when they saw me counting the gold near the kitchen-garden.

"Item. *I bequeath the rope herein contained for any father to hang himself, who is so foolish as to give away his property to his heirs before his death*".

"Well, Shamus", said Guillaum, "the poor father laid out a dale on our education, but I declare all the taichin' he ever gave us was nothing to that".

THE ROCK OF THE CANDLE.

Soldiers.—Room, ho!—tell Antony Brutus is ta'en
Antony.—This is not Brutus, friends; but, I assure you,
A prize no less in worth. Keep this man safe,
Give him all kindness. I had rather have
Such men my friends than enemies.
Julius Cæsar.

REMEMBER ye not, my fair young friend, in one of those
excursions which rendered the summer of the past year
so sweet in the enjoyment and so mournful in the
recollection—remember ye not my having pointed out to
your observation the ruined battlements of Carrigogunniel
(the Rock of the Candle), which shoot upward from a
craggy hillock on the Shannon side, within view of the
ancient city of Limerick? I told you the legend from
which the place originally derived its name—a legend
which I thought was distinguished (especially in the
closing incident) by a tenderness and delicacy of imagination, worthy of a Grecian origin. You, too, acknowledged the simple beauty of that incident; and your
approval induces me to hope for that of the world.
On a misty evening in spring, when all the west is
filled with a hazy sunshine, and the low clouds stoop and
cling around the hill tops, there are few nobler spectacles

o contemplate, than the ruins of Carrigogunniel Castle
This fine building, which was dismantled by one of
William's generals, stands on the very brink of a broken
hill, which, toward the water, looks bare and craggy, but
on the landward side slopes gently down under a close
and verdant cover of elms and underwood. It is when
seen from this side, standing high above the trees, and
against the red and broken clouds that are gathered
in the west, that the ruin assumes its most imposing
aspect.

Such was the look it wore on the evening of an autumn
day when the village beauty, young Minny O'Donnell, put
aside the woodbines from her window, and looked out upon
the Rock. Her father's cottage was situated close to the
foot of the hill, and the battlements seemed to frown
downward upon it with a royal and overtopping haughtiness.

"Hoo! murder, Minny honey, what is that you're
doing? Looking out at the Rock at this hour, and the
sun just going down behind the turret?"

"Why not, aunt?"

"Why not?—Do you remember nothing of the candle?"

"Oh, I don't know what to think of it; I am inclined
to doubt the story very much; I have been listening to
that frightful tale of the Death Light since I was born,
and I have never seen it yet".

"You may consider yourself fortunate in that, child,
and I advise you not to be too anxious to prove the truth
of the story. I was standing by the side of poor young
Dillon myself, on the very day of his marriage, when he
looked out upon it through the wicket, and was blasted as
if by a thunder-stroke. I never will forget the anguish
of the dear young bride: it was heart breaking to see
her torn from his side when the life had left him. Poor
creature! her shrieks are piercing my ears at this very
moment".

" That story terrifies me, aunt.   Speak of it no more,
and I will leave the window.   I wonder if Cormac knows
this story of the Fatal Candle".

The good old woman smiled knowingly on her pretty
niece, as, instead of answering her half query, she asked
—" Do you not expect him here before sunset ?"

Minny turned hastily round, and seated herself opposite
a small mirror, adorned by one of those highly carved
frames which were popular at the toilets of our grand-
mammas.   She did so with a double view of completing
her evening toilet, and at the same time screening herself from the inquisitive glances of her sharp old relative,
while she continued the conversation.

" He promised to be here before", she replied , " but it
is a long way".

" I hope he will not turn his eyes upon the Rock, if he
should be detained after nightfall.   I suspect, Minny
that his eyes will be wandering in another direction.   I
think he will be safe, after all".

" For shame, aunt Norry.   You ought to be ashamed
of yourself, an old woman of your kind to speak in that
way.   Come now, and tell me something funny, while I
am dressing my hair, to put the recollection of that frightful adventure of the Candle out of my head.   Would not
that be a good figure for a Banthee ?" she added, shaking
out her long bright hair with one hand, in the manner
which is often attributed to the warning spirit, and casting
at the same time a not indifferent glance at the mirror
above mentioned.

" Partly, indeed,—but the Banthee (meaning no offence
at the same time) is far from being so young—or so
blooming in the cheeks; and by all accounts, the eyes
tell a different story from yours—a story of death, and
not of marriage.   Merry would the Banthee be, that
would be going to get young Mr. Cormac for a husband
to-morrow morning early ".
                                    15*

" I'll go look at the Rock again, if you continue to talk such nonsense".

" Oh, bubboo!—rest easy, darling, and I'll say no-thing.—Well, what story is it I'm to be telling you ?"

" Something funny".

" Oyeh, my heart is bothered with 'em for stories. I don't know what I'll tell you. Are you 'cute at all ?"

" I don't know. Only middling, I believe".

" Well—I'll tell you a story of a boy that flogged Europe for 'cuteness, so that if you have a mind to be ready with an answer for every cross question that'll be put to you, you can learn it after him ;—a thing that may be useful to you one time or another, when the charge of the house is left in your hands".

" Well, let me hear it".

" I will, then, do that. Go on with your dress, and I'll have my story done before you are ready to receive Mr. Cormac".

So saying, she drew a stool near her niece, and leaning forward with her chin on her hand, commenced the fol-lowing tale.

" There was a couple there, long ago, and they had a son that they didn't know rightly what was it they'd do with him, for they had not money to get him Latin enough for a priest, and there was only poor call for day labourers in the country. ' I'll tell you what I'll do', says the father, says he ; ' I'll make a thief of him', says he ; ' sorrow a better trade there is going than the roguery, or more money-making for a boy that would be industrious'. ' It's true for you', says the wife, making answer to him ; ' but where will you get a master for him, or who'll take him for an apprentice in such a business ?' ' I'll tell you that', says the husband to her again. ' I'll send him to Kerry. Sorrow better hand would you get at the business anywhere, than there are about the moun-tains there—and I'll be bound he'll come home to us a

good hand at his business', says he. Well and good, they
sent off the boy to Kerry, and bound him for seven years
to a thief that was well-known in these parts, and counted
a very clever man in his line. They heard no more of
him for the seven years, nor hardly knew that they were
out, when he walked into them one morning, with his
'Save all here!' and took his seat at the table along with
them—a fine, handsome lad, and mighty well spoken.
'Well, Mun,' says the father, 'I hope you're master o'
your business?' 'Pretty well for that, father', says he;
'wait till we can have a trial of it'. 'With all my heart',
says the father; 'and I hope to see that you haven't been
making a bad use o' your time while you were away!'
Well, the news ran among the neighbours, what a fine able
thief Mun had come home, and the landlord himself came
to hear of it among the rest. So when the father went to
his work the next morning, he made up to him, and—
'Well', says he, 'this is a queer thing I'm told about you,
that you had your son bound to a thief in Kerry, and that
he's come home to you a great hand at the business'.
'Passable, indeed, he tells me, sir', says the father, quite
proud in himself. 'Well, I'll tell you what it is', says the
gentleman; 'I have a fine horse in my stable, and I'll
put a guard upon him to-night, and if your son be that
great hand that he's reported to be, let him come and steal
him out from among the people to-night; and if he does,
he shall have my daughter in marriage, and my estate
when I die,' says he. 'A great offer, surely', says the
poor man. 'But if he fails', says the gentleman, 'I'll
prosecute him, and have him hanged, and you along with
him, for serving his time to a thief—a thing that's clearly
again' all law', says he. Well, 'tis unknown what a
whilliloo the father set up when he heard this. 'O
murther, sir,' says he, 'and sure 'tis well you know that
if a spirit itself was there he couldn't steal the horse that
would be guarded that way, let alone my poor boy', says

he; 'and how will it be with us, or what did we ever do
to you, sir, that you'd hang us that way?' 'I have my
own reasons for it', says the gentleman, 'and you'd better
go home at once, and tell the boy about it, if you have a
mind he should try his chance'. Well, the father went
home crying and bawling, as if all belonging to him were
dead. 'E', what ails you, father', says the son, 'or what
is it makes you be bawling that way?' says he. So he
up and told him the whole business, how they were to be
hanged, the two of them, in the morning, if he wouldn't
have the racer stolen. 'That beats Ireland', says the
son; 'to hang a man for not stealing a thing is droll,
surely; but make your mind easy, father, my master
would think no more of doing that than he would of eating
a boiled potato'. Well, the old man was in great spirits
when he heard the boy talk so stout, although he wasn't
without having his doubts upon the business for all that.
The boy set to work when the evening drew on, and dressed
himself like an old *bucaugh*,* with a tattered frieze coat
about him, and stockings without any soles to 'em, with an
old *caubean* of a straw hat upon the side of his head, and
the tin can under his arm. 'Tis what he had in the tin can,
I tell you, was a good sup of spirits, with a little poppy
juice squeezed into it to make them sleepy that would be
after drinking it. Well and good, Minny, my child, he
made towards the gentleman's house, and when he was
passing the parlour window, he saw a beautiful young
lady, as fair as a lily, and with a fine blush entirely,
sitting and looking out about the country for herself. So
he took off his hat, and turned out his toes, and made her
a low bow, quite elegant. 'I declare to my heart', says
the young lady, speaking to her servant that stood behind
her, 'I wouldn't desire to see a handsomer man than that.
If he had a better *shoot* of clothes upon him, he'd be
equal to any gentleman, he's so slim and delicate'. And

* A lame man—idiomatically, beggar-man.

who was this but the gentleman's daughter all the while! Well, 'tis well became Mun, he went on to the stable door, and there he found the lads all watching the racer. I'll tell you the way they watched her. They had one upon her back, and another at her head, where she was tied to the manger, and a great number of them about the place, sitting down between her and the door. 'Save all here!' says Mun, putting in his head at the door. 'E', what are ye doing here, boys?' says he. So they up and told him they were guarding the racer from a great Kerry thief they expected to be stealing her that night. 'Why then he'll be a smart fellow, if he gets her out of that', says Mun, making as if he knew nothing. 'I'd be for ever obliged to ye, if ye'd let me light a pipe and sit down awile with ye, and I'll do my part to make the company agreeable'. 'Why then,' says they, 'we have but poor treatment to offer you, for though there's plenty to eat here, we have nothing to drink—the master wouldn't allow us a hap'orth in dread we'd get sleepy, and let the horse go.' 'Oh! the nourishment is all I want', says Mun, 'I'm no way dry at all'. Well and good, in he came, and he sat among them telling stories until past midnight, eating and laughing ; and every now and then, when he'd stop in the story, he'd turn about and make as if he was taking a good drink out of the can. 'You seem to be very fond of that tin can, whatever you have in it', says one of the men that was sitting near him. 'Oh, its no signify', says Mun, shutting it up as if not anxious to share it. Well they got the smell of it about the place, and 'tis little pleasure they took in the stories after, only every now and then throwing an eye at the can, and snuffing with their noses, like pointers when game is in the wind. ''Tisn't any spring water you'd have in that, I believe', says one of them. 'You're welcome to try it', says Mun, 'only I thought you might have some objection in regard of what you said when I

came in'. 'None in the world', says they. So he filled a
few little noggins for 'em, and for the man on the horse
and the man near the manger, and they all drank until
they slept like troopers. When they were all fast, up got
the youth, and he drew on a pair of worsted stockings
over every one of the horse's legs, so they wouldn't make
any noise, and he got a rope and fastened the man I tell
you was upon the racer's back, by the shoulders, up to the
rafters, when he drew the horse from under him, and
left him hanging fast asleep. Well became him, he led
the horse out of the stable, and had him home at his
father's while a cat would be shaking his ears, and
made up comfortably in a little out-house. 'Well', says
the old man when he woke in the morning and saw the
horse sto'en—'if it was an angel was there', says he, 'he
could n't do the business cleverer than that'. And the
same thing he said to the landloid, when he met him in
the field the same morning. 'It's true for you, indeed',
said the gentleman, 'nothing could be better done, and
I'll take it as an honour if your son and yourself will give
me your company at dinner to-day, and I'll have the
pleasure of introducing him to my daughter'. 'E', is it
me dine at your honour's table?' says the old man, looking
down at his dress. ''Tis just', says the gentleman again,
'and I'll take no apology whatever'. Well and good,
they made themselves ready, the two of them, and young
Mun came riding upon the racer, covered all over with
the best of wearables, and looking like a real gentleman.
'E', what's that there, my child?' says the father, pointing
to a gallows, that was planted right opposite the gentleman's hall door. 'I don't know—a gallows, I'm thinking', says the son,—'sure 'tisn't to hang us he would be,
after asking us to his house, unless it be a thing he means
to give us our dinner first, and our *dessert* after, as the
fashion goes', says he. Well in with them, and they
found the company all waiting, a power of ladies and lords,

and great people entirely. ' I'm sorry to keep you waiting', says Mun, making up to them, quite free and easy, ' but the time stole upon us'. ' You couldn't blame the time for taking after yourself', says the gentleman. ' It's true, indeed', says Mun, ' l stole many is the thing in my time, but there's one thing I'd rather thieve than all the rest—the good will o' the ladies', says he, smiling, and looking round at them. ' Why, then, I wouldn't trust you very far with that either', says the young lady of the house.　Well and good, they sat down, and they ate their dinner, and after the cloth was removed, there was a covered dish laid upon the table.　' Well', says the gentleman, ' I have one trial more to make of your wit—and I'll tell you what it is :—let me know what is it I have in this covered dish ; and if you don't, I'll hang you and your father upon that gallows over, for stealing my racer'. ' O murther ! d'ye hear this ?' says the father,—' and wasn't it your honour's bidding to steal her, or you'd hang us ?　Sure we're to be pitied with your honour', says the poor old man.　' Very well', says the gentleman, ' I tell you a fact, and your only chance is to answer my question'. ' Well, sir', says Mun, giving all up for lost, ' I have nothing to say to you—although far the fox may go, he'll be caught by the tail at last'. ' I declare you have it', says the gentleman, uncovering the dish, and what should be in it only a fox's tail !　Well, they gave it up to Mun, that he was the greatest rogue going, and the young lady married him upon the spot.　They had the master's estate when he died ; and if they didn't live happy, I wish that you and I may".

"Amen to that, aunt.　Will you lay the mirror aside for a moment.—Ha ! whose fault was that ?"

"Oh, Minny, you have broken the mirror—O, my child ! my child !"

" Why so !　It is not so valuable".

" Valuable !　It is not the worth of the paltry glass,

darling—but don't you know it is *not good*? It is not lucky—and the night before your bridal, too!"

" I am very sorry for it", said the girl, bending a some-what serious gaze on the shattered fragments of the antique looking-glass. Then, by a transition which it would require some knowledge of the maiden's history to account for, she said, " I wonder if Cormac was with the Knight, when he made the sally at the castle, yesterday".

The answer of the elderly lady was interrupted by the sound of several voices in an outer apartment exclaiming, " Cormac! Cormac! Welcome, Cormac! It is Cormac!"

" And it is Cormac!" echoed Minny, starting from her seat, and glancing at the spot where the mirror ought to have been. " You were right, aunt", she added, in a dis-appointed tone, as she bounded out of the room, " it was unlucky to break the mirror".

" It might for them that would want it", replied the old lady, following at a lively pace ; " but for you, I hope it will bring nothing worse than the loss of it for this night".

She found Minny seated, with one hand clasped in those of a young soldier, dressed in the uniform of the White Knight, smiling and blushing with all the artlessness in the world. The young man wore a close fitting *truis*, which displayed a handsome form to the best advan-tage, and contrasted well with the loose and flowing dra-pery of his mantle. The *birrede* of green cloth, which had confined his hair, was laid aside ; and a leathern girdle appeared at his waist, which held a bright skene and pistol. The appearance of both figures, the expression of both countenances, secure of present, and confident of future happiness, formed a picture

Which some would smile, and more perhaps would sigh at;

a picture which would bring back pleasing recollections enough to sweeten the temper of the sourest pair that

Hymen ever disunited, and to move the spleen of the best natured old bachelor that ever dedicated his hearth to Dian and solitude.

The evening proceeded as the eve of a bridal might be supposed to do, with its proportion of mirth and mischief. The lovers had been acquainted from childhood ; and every one who knew them felt an interest in their fortunes, and a share in the happiness which they enjoyed. The sun had been already long gone down, when Minny, in compliance with the wish of her old aunt, sang the following words to an air, which was only remarkable for its simplicity and tenderness :—

I.

I love my love in the morning,
    For she, like morn, is fair ·
Her blushing cheek, its crimson streak ;
    Its clouds, her golden hair ;
Her glance, its beam, so soft and kind ;
    Her tears, its dewy showers,
And her voice, the tender whispering wind
    That stirs the early bowers

II.

I love my love in the morning,
    I love my love at noon ;
For she is bright as the lord of light,
    Yet mild as autumn's moon.
Her beauty is my bosom's sun,
    Her faith my fostering shade ;
And I will love my darling one
    Till even sun shall fade.

III.

I love my love in the morning,
    I love my love at even ;
Her smile's soft play is like the ray
    That lights the western Heaven.
I loved her when the sun was high,
    I loved her when he rose,
But best of all, when evening's sigh
    Was murmuring at its close.

The song was scarcely ended, when Minny felt her arm
grasped with an unusual force by the young soldier.
Turning round, in some alarm, she beheld a sight which
filled her with fear and anxiety. Her lover sat erect in
his chair, gazing fixedly on the open casement, through
which a strong and whitish light shone full upon his face
and person. It was an interlunar night, and Minny felt
at a loss to conjecture what the cause could be of this extraordinary appearance.

"Minny", said her lover, "look yonder! I see a
candle burning on the very summit of the rock above us!
Although the wind is bending every tree upon the hill-
side, the flame does not flicker or change in the slightest
degree. Look on it!"

"Do not look!" exclaimed the old aunt, with a shrill
cry. "May Heaven be about us! Do not glance at the
window. It is the death light!"

Minny clasped her hands, and sank back into her chair.

"Let some one close the window", said the young
soldier, speaking in a faint tone. "I am growing ill; let
some one close the window".

The old woman advanced cautiously towards the casement, and extending the handle of a broom stick at
the utmost stretch of her arm, was endeavouring to push
the shutter to, when Minny, recovering from her astonishment, darted at her an indignant look, ran to the window,
closed it, and left the room in darkness deeper than that
of night.

"What was that strange light?" asked the young soldier, looking somewhat relieved.

With some hesitation, and a few prophetic groans and
oscillations of the head, the old story-teller informed him
that it was a light, whose appearance was commemorial
with the rock itself, and that it usually foreboded considerable danger or misfortune, if not death, to any unhappy
being on whom its beams might chance to fall. It ap-

peared, indeed, but rarely ; yet, there never was instance known in which the indication proved fallacious.

The soldier recovered heart to laugh away the anxiety which had begun to creep upon the company ; and, in a little time, the mirthful tone of the assemblage was fully restored. Lights of a more terrestrial description than that which figured on the haunted rock, were introduced ; songs were sung ; jests echoed from lip to lip ; and merry feet pattered against the earthen floor, to the air of the national *rinceadh fadha.* The merriment of the little party was at its highest point, when a galloping of horses, intermingled with a distant rolling of musketry, was heard outside the cottage.

"My fears were just !" exclaimed Cormac, stopping short in the dance, while he still retained the hand of his lovely partner: "the English have taken the castle, and the White Knight is flying for his life !"

His surmise was confirmed by the occurrence which instantly followed. The door was dashed back upon its hinges, and the White Knight, accompanied by two of his retainers, rushed into the house. The chieftain's face was pale and anxious, and his dress was bespattered with blood and mire. Three figures remained in a group near the door, as if listening for the sounds of pursuit ; while the revellers hurried together like startled fawns, and gazed, with countenances indicative of strong interest or wild alarm, upon the baffled warriors.

" Cormac !" cried the Knight, perceiving the bridegroom among the company, " my good fellow, I missed you in an unlucky hour. These English dogs have worried us from our hold, and are still hot upon our scent. I have only time to bid my stout soldiers farewell, and go to meet them, for I will not have this happy floor stained with blood to-night".

"That shall not be, Knight", exclaimed the bride-

groom; "we will meet them, or fly together. You were
my father's foster-child".

" It is in vain—look there!" He laid bare his left arm,
which was severely gashed on one side.—" They have had
a taste of me already, and the bloodhounds will never tire
till they have tracked me home.   And yet, if I had only
one day's space —Kavanagh and his followers are at
Kilmallock, and the castle might be mine again before the
moon rises to-morrow evening".

"Kavanagh at Kilmallock!" exclaimed Cormac. "O
my chieftain! what do you do here? Fly, while you have
time, and leave us to deal with the foe".

" It were idle", repeated the Knight, " their horses are
fresher than ours, and my dress would betray me".

" My mare will bear you safe", cried the young soldier,
with a burst of enthusiasm ; "and for your dress, take
mine, and let me play the White Knight for once"

The chieftain's eyes brightened at the word, and a
hope seemed to bloom out upon his cheek,—but a low
sound of suppressed agony from the bride checked it in
the spring.

" No, Cormac", he said, " I will not be your murderer".

"There is no fear", said Cormac, warmly, " you will
be back in time to prevent mischief; and if you remain,
it will be only to see me share your fate. This is my only
chance for life ; for I will give the world leave to cry shame
upon my head, if ever I outlive my master".

" What says the bride?" inquired the Knight, bending
on her a look of mingled pity and admiration.

" I will answer for her", said Cormac;. "she had rather
be the widow of a true Irishman, than the wife of a false
one'.

" O allilu? we'll all be murthered if you don't hurry",
said the aunt. " What do you say, Minny, my child?"

" Cormac speaks the truth", replied the trembling girl,

hanging in her weakness on his shoulder; "if there be no other way, I am content it should be so".

She was rewarded for this effort of heroism by a fervent pressure of the hand from her betrothed, and the exchange of accoutrements was presently effected. The Knight mounted Cormac's mare, and prepared to depart.

"My gallant fellow", he said, holding out his hand to the generous bridegroom, "you do not mock the part you act, for nobility is stamped npon your soul. If you suffer for this, I have a vow, that I will never more wear any other garb than yours; for you are the knightlier of the two. Let me clasp your hand, than which a nobler never closed on gauntlet".

They joined hands in silence, and the chieftain galloped away with his retainers. When they were out of hearing, Cormac turned to his bride, and again pressing her hand, while he looked fixedly into her eyes, he said : "Now, Minny, you will show that you are fit for a soldier's wife. Go. with your aunt Norry, into your room. No one here will be molested but those who are in arms for the Knight; and I will contrive to postpone any violence, for a day, at least".

"I will not leave you, Cormac", said Minny, speaking more firmly than she had done since the interruption of the festivity. "I am somewhat more to you than you are to the White Knight".

Cormac smiled, and seemed to acquiesce for some time in her wishes. He took his seat at the hearth with the bespattered garb and sullied weapon of the knight, and awaited in silence the approach of the pursuers, while Minny occupied a chair as near him as might be decorous, taking his new rank into consideration. They listened for a considerable time to the changeful rushing of the night wind among the trees that clothed the hill-side, and the howling of the wolves, that were disturbed in their retreats by the sounds of combat. Those sounds, renewed after

long intervals and in an irregular manner, gradually approached more near, and they could plainly distinguish the
trampling of horses' feet over the beaten track that
winded among the crags as far as the cottage door.
Again, and with great eagerness, Cormac entreated his
love to secure herself from the chances of their first encounter, by joining the family in the inner room; but she
refused in a resolute tone, and on persisting, she assumed
an impatience, and even a desperation of manner, which
showed that her purpose was not to be shaken.

"Ask me not to leave you", she said; "any other
command I am ready to obey. I will be silent; I will
not shriek, nor murmur, even though ——" She shuddered, and let her head droop upon his hand. "I will
not leave you, Cormac. Whatever your fate shall be, I
must remain to witness it. Do not doubt my firmness;
only say that you will freely trust me, and 1 am ready for
the worst that can happen. I feel that I can be calm, if
you will only give me your confidence".

There are some spirits which, like the myrtle, require to
be bruised and broken by affliction, before their sweetness
can be discovered. The young bride of Cormac might
now have exhibited an instance of this moral truth. So
perfectly did her manner indicate the degree of self-possession which she promised to maintain, that Cormac yielded
without further argument to her entreaty, and resumed his
place at the fireside.

Scarcely had he performed this movement when a loud
knocking was again heard at the door; and immediately
after, as if this slight ceremony were only used in mockery,
the frail barrier was once more dashed inward on its
hinges. A crowd of soldiers rushed into the apartment,
and stopped short on seeing the bridegroom habited in the
accoutrements of the White Knight, and standing in a
posture of defence between his foes and the young girl,
who seemed to be restrained, rather by her deference to

his wishes, than by any personal apprehension, from pres·
sing forward to his side.

"Stand back!" said Cormac, levelling his blade at the
foremost of the throng. "Before you advance further,
say what it is you seek. The inmates of this house (all
but one) are under the protection of the English law, and
can only be molested at your great peril".

"If you be the White Knight, as your dress bespeaks
you", returned an English officer, "surrender your sword
and person into our hands. It is only him we seek, and
no one else shall be disturbed, further than to answer our
claim of *bonaght bor*—rest and refreshment for our small
troop until the morning breaks".

"I am not so thirsty of blood for the sake of shedding
it merely", returned the pseudo knight, "that I would
destroy a life of Heaven's bestowing in a vain encounter.
Here is my sword, although I am well aware that in yield-
ing it without a struggle, I do not add a single one to my
chances (if any I had) of safety in the hands of my Lord
President".

"It would be dishonourable in me to deceive you", said
the Englishman : "your ready, though late, surrender can
avail you little. I have here the warrant, which commands that the execution of the rebel captain should not
be deferred longer than six hours after his arrest. I am
not disposed, however, to be more rigid than my instructions compel me to be, so that you may call the whole six
hours your own, if you can find use for so much time in
this world".

Cormac turned pale, and thought of Minny ; but he
dared not look at her. The poor girl endeavoured to support herself against the chair which her lover had left
vacant, and retired a little, lest he should observe and par-
ticipate in the agitation which this fatal announcement had
occasioned.

"I thought it probable", said Cormac, with some hesita

tion, "that I might have had a day, at all events, to prepare for my fate ; but my Lord President is a pious man,
and must be better aware than I, how much time a sinner
under arms might require to collect his evidence for that
last and fearful court-martial, whose decision is irrevo-
cable. A soldier's conscience, sir officer, is too often the
only thing about him which he allows to gather rust. If
I had been careful to preserve that as unsullied as my
sword, I would not esteem your six hours so short a space
as they now appear".

"The gift of grace, sir knight", said a solemn-looking
sergeant, "is not like an Earthly plant, which requires
much time and toil to bring its blossom forth. Heard ye
not of the graceless traveller, who, riding somewhat more
than a Sabbath-day's journey on the seventh, was thrown
from his horse and killed near a place of worship ? The
congregation thought his doom was sealed for both worlds,
and yet,

> Between the stirrup and the ground,
> Mercy he sought and mercy he found"

"Aye", said the captive ; "there are some persons
who look on this world as mere billeting quarters, and
require no more time to prepare for the eternal route than
they might to brace up a havresac ; but my memory is not
so light of carriage. I remember to have heard at Mung-
harid, a Latin adage, which might shake the courage of
any one who was inclined to rely venturously on his
powers of spiritual dispatch :—

> Unus erat—ne desperes :
> Unus tantum—ne presumas.

However, I shall be as far wide of the first peril as I
should wish to be of the last. Come, sirs, you forget your
supper ; leave me to my own thoughts, and pray respect
this maiden, who will attend to your wants while I rest".

"She seems as if she would more willingly omit that

office", said the Englishman. " The maiden
for your misfortune, Knight".

" Poor girl !" Cormac exclaimed, venturing to look
round upon her for the first time since his capture. " It
is little wonder that she should wear a troubled brow.
You have disturbed her bridal feast". Then taking her
hand, and pressing it significantly while he spoke, he
added : " Your husband was reckoned a true man, and I
know him well enough to be convinced that he would not
place his heart in the keeping of an unworthy or a selfish
love. I know, therefore, that you could not make him
happier than by acting on this occasion with that firmness
which he expects from you. Tell him, I knew better the
value of life than to lament my fate, at least for my own
sake : and remember, likewise, Minny (is not that your
name ?) if ever Cormac should, like me, be hurried off by
an untimely stroke of fate—if ever"—he renewed the
pressure of the hand, which he still held in his—" if ever
you should see him led, as I must now be, to an early
death, remember, my girl, that none but the craven-
hearted are short-lived on Earth. A brave man, who had
fulfilled all his duties, can never die untimely ; but a
coward would, though every hair were gray upon his
brow".

He strove to withdraw his hand ; but Minny, who felt
as if he were tearing her heart away from her, held it fast
between both hers, and pressed it with the grasp of a
drowning person. Cormac felt, by the trembling and
moistness of her hand, that she was on the point of
placing all in danger by bursting into a passion of grief.
He lowered his voice to a tone of grave reproof, and said :

" Remember, Minny, let him not find that he has been
deceived in you. That would be a worse stroke than the
headsman's".

The forlorn girl collected all her strength, and felt the
tumult that was rising in her breast subside, like the

16

uproar of the northern tempest, at the voice of the Reim
kennar. She let his hand go, and stood erect, while he
passed on, followed by several of the party, into another
room. Strange as sorrow had ever been to her bosom,
she could not have anticipated, and was wholly incapable
of supporting the dreadful desolation of spirit which came
upon her after she was left alone. She remained for some
time motionless, in the attitude of one who listens intently,
until she heard the door of a small inner apartment, into
which he had been conducted, close upon her lover; and
then gathering her hands across her bosom, and walking
slowly to the vacant chair, she sank down in a violent and
hysterical excess of grief.

It is strange that the effusion of a few drops of a briny
liquid at the eyes, should enable the soul to give more
tranquil entertainment to a painful thought or feeling;
but it is a fact, however, which Minny experienced in
common with all who have known what painful feelings
are. She pictured to herself the probable nature of the
fate which awaited her betrothed; and from the horror
which she felt in the contemplation, proceeded to devise
expedients for its prevention. This, however, appeared
now to be a hopeless undertaking. The warrant of the
Lord President must needs be executed within the time;
and it was improbable that the White Knight could return before the expiration of the six hours. Would it be
possible to contrive a scheme for his liberation? His
guards were vigilant and numerous, and there was but
one way by which he could return from the room, and
that was occupied by sentinels. If Mun, or the Kerry
thief, his master, were on the spot, of what a load might
they relieve her heart! She would have given worlds to
be mistress, for one night, of the roguery of the adept in
aunt Norry's tale.

We shall leave her for the present, involved, like a
bungling dramatist, in a labyrinth of ravelled plots and

contrivances, while we shift the scene to the unfortunate
hero of the night, who lay in his room, expecting the catastrophe with no very enviable sensations.

The soldiers had left him to make the necessary preparations for his approaching fate in darkness and solitude.
He was now on the point of achieving a character, not
without precedent in the history of his country—namely,
that of a martyr to his own heroic fidelity—and he was
determined to bear his part like a warrior to the last.
Still, however, to a lover, conscious of being loved again—
to a young man, with prospects so fair and present happiness so nearly perfect—to a bridegroom, snatched from
the altar to the scaffold, at the very moment when he was
about to become doubly bound to life by a tie so holy and
so dear—to such an one, though brave as a fiery heart and
youthful blood could make him, it was impossible that
death should not wear a grim and most unwelcome aspect.
Neither is the man to be envied, whose nature could
undergo so direful a change without emotion.   True
bravery consists, not in ignorance of, or insensibility to
danger, but in the resolution which can meet and defy it,
when duty renders such collision necessary.   Fear, in
common with all the other passions of our nature, has
been given us for the purpose of exercising our reason,
and acquiring a virtue by its subjugation; and the man (if
any such ever lived) who is ignorant of the feeling, is a
monster, and not a hero.   The truly courageous man is
he who has a heart to feel what danger is, and a soul to
triumph over that feeling, when it would tempt him to the
neglect of any moral or religious obligation.   Such was
the temper of Cormac.   He believed that he was per
forming his duty, and did not even entertain a thought of
any other line of conduct than that which he was pursuing; but this did not prevent his being deeply and
bitterly conscious of the hardness of his fortunes, in this
unlooked-for and untimely separation.

Exhausted by the intensity of his sensations, he had dropped for some time into a troubled and uneasy slumber, when the pressure of a soft hand upon his brow made him lift up his eyes, and raise himself upon his elbow.   He beheld Minny stooping over him, with a dim rushlight burning in one hand, while with the other she motioned him to express no surprise, and to preserve silence.

"Hush, hush!" she said, in a low whisper, "Cormac, are you willing to make an effort for liberty?"

He stared strangely upon her, and stood on his feet.

"What is the meaning of this, Minny; how came you here?"

"The soldiers have been merrier than they intended, and I drugged their drink for them.   Slip off your brogs, and steal out in your *truis* only.   They are now sleeping in the next room, and I have left them in the dark.   Fear not their muskets; I have drenched the matchlocks for them.   There are only two waking, who are on guard outside the door; and for these, we must even place our hopes in Heaven, and take the chance of their bad marksmanship. Ah, Cormac!—but there is no time to lose; come with me".

"My glorious heroine!" cried the astonished soldier, "I could not have thought this possible".

"Hush! your raptures will betray us".

"But whither do you intend to fly?"

"To the cavern on the western side of the hill, where Fitzgerald lay on the night of the great massacre at Adare Castle.   Keep close to me, and I think it likely we shall pass the sleepers".

She extinguished the light; and both crept, with noiseless footsteps, into the adjoining room, which was the chamber of the heroic maiden herself.   As they endeavoured to steal between the soldiers, who lay locked in slumber on the ground, Minny set her foot on some brittle substance, which cracked beneath her weight with a noise sufficient to awaken one of the soldiers.

"It is the mirror!" said Minny to herself; "my aunt Norry's prophecy was but too correct, and my vanity has ruined everything".

Still, however, her presence of mind did not forsake her. The soldier, turning suddenly round, laid hold of Cormac's *estaigh* or mantle, and arrested his progress.

"Ho! ho!" he exclaimed, "who have we here?"

"Prithee, let go my dress, master soldier", returned the young girl; "this freedom tallies not well with your sermon on grace to the White Knight. I doubt you for a solemn hypocrite".

"I knew you not, wench", replied the sergeant, letting Cormac's mantle fall, "or I would as soon have thought of clapping palms with Beelzebub, as of fingering any part of your Irish trumpery. Whither do ye travel at this time of the night?"

"Even to kindle my rushlight at our hearth-stone in the next room. Turn on your pallet, sergeant, and let me go, else you may be troubled with unholy dreams".

They passed on, and reached the outer room in safety.

"Now, Minny", said Cormac, "it is my turn to make a suggestion. Do you pass out, and await me at the stream that runs by the edge of the wood. The sentinels will suffer you to proceed, and the risk of detection will be lessened. Nay, never stop to dispute the point: its advantages are unquestionable".

Minny would not even trust herself with a farewell before she obeyed the wishes of her lover. A few passing jests were all she had to encounter from the sentinels, and Cormac had the satisfaction to see her hurry on, unmolested, in the direction of the stream. When he supposed a sufficient time had elapsed to enable her to reach the place of rendezvous, he threw aside his mantle, and prepared to take the sentinels by surprise. The door stood open, and he could plainly see the two guards pacing to and fro in the moonlight. Pausing for a moment, he up-

lifted his clasped hands to Heaven, and breathed a short
and agitated prayer of mingled hope and resignation.
Then summoning the resolution which never failed him in
his need, he darted through the doorway into the open
air.

Astonishment and perplexity kept the sentinels motionless for some moments, and Cormac had fled a considerable
distance before they became sensible of the nature of the
occurrence which had taken place. Both instantly discharged their pieces in the direction of the fugitive, and
with loud shouts summoned their comrades to assist in
the pursuit. The bullets tore up the earth on either side
of Cormac, who could hear, as he hurried on, the execra-
tions and uproar of the awakened troop at finding their
arms rendered incapable of service. He dashed onward
toward the wood, and had the happiness, while the sounds
of pursuit yet lingered far behind, to discern the white
dress of his betrothed fluttering in distinct relief against
the dark and shadowy foliage of the elm wood. Snatching her up in his arms with as little difficulty as a mother
feels in supporting her infant, he hurried across the stream,
and was quickly buried in the recesses of the wood.

The morning broke before they had reached the appointed place of concealment. It was one of those
ancient receptacles for the noble dead, which were hol-
lowed out of the earth in various parts of the country,
and were frequently used during the persecutions of
foreign invaders, as places of refuge and concealment for
the persons and properties of the people. When they
found themselves safely sheltered within the bosom of this
close retreat, the customary effect of long restrained
anxiety and sudden joy was produced upon the lovers.
They flung themselves, with broken exclamations of delight and affection, into each other's arms, and remained
for a considerable time incapable of acting or speaking
with any degree of self-possession. The necessity, how-

ever, of providing for their safety during the ensuing day, recalled them to a more distinct perception of the difficulties of their situation, and suggested expedients for their alleviation or removal.

They ventured not beyond the precincts of their Druidical sojourn until the approach of evening, and even then it was but to look upon the sunlight, and hurry back again to their lurking-place in greater anxiety than before. The English had discovered, and were fast approaching the mouth of their retreat.

Cormac, signifying to his bride that she should remain silent in the interior of the cave, drew his sword and stood near the entrance, just as the light became obscured by the persons of the party who were to enter. They paused for some time on hearing the voice of Cormac, who threatened to sacrifice the first person that should venture to place his foot inside the mouth of the recess. In a few moments after, the devoted pair were perplexed to hear the sound of stones and earth thrown together, as if to erect some building near the cave. Unable to form any conjecture as to the nature and object of this proceeding, they clung together, in silence and increased anxiety, awaiting the issue.

On a sudden, a strong whitish light streamed into the cavern, casting the dark and lengthened shadows of the party who stood without, in sharp distinctness of outline upon the broken rocks on the opposite.

" Look there, Minny !" exclaimed the youth, " it is the moon-rise, and we may shortly look for the return of our chief".

" It cannot be, Cormac. The shadows would fall, in that case, to the westwards, and not to the south. It is a more fatal signal, it is the death light of the Rock !"

Cormac paused for some moments. " Fatal it may be ", he replied,—" but do you observe, Minny, that no part of its ghastly lustre has fallen upon us? It is shining bright upon our enemies. There is a promise in that, if there be in reality any supernatural meaning in the appearance".

Minny sighed anxiously, while she hung upon his arm —but made no answer to this cheering suggestion. The party outside continued their labour, and in a little time the light was only discernible, as if penetrating through small crevices at the entrance.

" What can they intend?" said Minny, after a pause of some minutes, during which the party outside maintained profound silence. " All merciful Heaven !" she continued, starting to her feet in renewed alarm,—" we are about to suffer the fate of Desmond's Kernes—they are going to suffocate us with fire !"

A dense volume of smoke, which rolled into the cavern through the crevices before-mentioned, confirmed this terrific conjecture. The practice, all barbarous as it was, had been frequently resorted to by the conquering party in the subjugation of the inland districts of the island. Feeble as he had been rendered by fatigue, anxiety, and want of food, Cormac resolved to make a desperate effort to escape the horrible death which menaced them, and rushed, sword in hand, to the mouth of the cave. But he was met by a mass of heated vapour, which deprived him of the power of proceeding, or even calling aloud to their destroyers. He tottered back to where he had left his bride, and sinking down on the earth beside her, felt a horrid sense of despair weigh down his energies like cowardice. Again he arose, and attempted to force his way through the entrance, and again he was compelled to relinquish the effort. He cried aloud to them—offered to surrender—and entreated that they would at least have mercy on his companion. But no answer was returned, and the dreadful conclusion remained to be deduced, that, contented with having made the work of death secure, they had retired to a distance from the place.

With a sickening heart, eyes swollen and painful, and a reeling brain, Cormac once more resumed his place by the side of his betrothed. She had fallen into a kind of delirium, and extended her arms towards him with an expression of suffering, which made his heart ache more keenly than his own agonies.

"I want air, Cormac!—oh, Cormac, my love! take me home with you—take me into the green fields—for I am dying here.—Air, Cormac! air, for the love of Heaven!"

"My own love, you shall have it—look up, and bear a good heart for two minutes, and we shall all be happy again".

"This place is horrible—it is like Hell! It is Hell! Are we living yet? I have been a sinner; and yet, I hoped, too, Cormac—I always hoped"—

"Hope yet, Minny, and you shall not hope in vain—keep your face near the earth, where the air is freest. Ha! listen to that. The White Knight is returned, and we are safe!"

A rolling of musketry, succeeded by yells, shouts, and cries of triumph and of anguish, was heard outside the cavern. Cormac and his bride stood erect once more; but poor Minny's strength failed her in the effort, and she sank lifeless into the arms of her lover. In a few moments the mouth of the cavern was cleared; and a flood of the cool sweet air rushed like a welcome to life and happiness, into the bosoms of the sufferers. Recovering new vigour with his draught, Cormac staggered toward the entrance, and passed out into the open air, with his fainting bride on his shoulder and a drawn sword in his right hand—presenting to the troop of liberators, who were gathered outside, a picture not unlike that of Theseus bearing the beautiful queen of Dis from the descent of Avernus. His pale cheeks looking paler in the moonlight, his wild staring eyes, scattered hair, and military attire, contributed to render the resemblance still more striking.

The White Knight received him with open arms; but Cormac would hold no more lengthened communication until his bride was restored to health and consciousness.

In this no great difficulty was encountered; and tradition says, that the White Knight was one of the merriest dancers at the bridal feast, which was given at the cottage in a few days after these occurrences.

I learned from a person curious in old legends, an account of the manner in which the "Candle on the Rock" was exorcised,—for it has not been seen for a long lapse of time. About two years after the marriage of Cormac and Minny, they were both seated, on a calm winter evening, in the room which had been the scene of so much tumult and disaster on the occasion above-mentioned. Minny was occupied in instructing a little rosy child (whose property it was, my fair readers may perhaps conjecture) in the rudiments of locomotion; while Cormac— (young husbands *will* play the fool sometimes)—held out his arms to receive the daring adventurer, after his hazardous journey of no less than two yards, on foot, across the floor. The tyro-pedestrian had executed about half his undertaking without meeting with any accident worthy of commemoration, and lo! aunt Norry was bending over him, with a smile and a " *Ma gra hu !*" of overflowing affection, when an aged man presented himself at the open door, and solicited charity for the love of Heaven!

Minny placed a small cake of griddle bread in the arms of the infant, and bade him take it to the stranger. The child tottered across the floor with his burden, and deposited it in the hat of the poor pilgrim, who laid his withered hand on the glossy ringlets of the little innocent, and blessed him with much fervency. At that moment, the fatal Light of the Rock streamed through the doorway, and bathed in its lustre the persons of the wayfarer and his guileless entertainer. The poor mother shrieked aloud, and was about to rush towards the child, when the pilgrim, assuming on a sudden a lofty and majestic attitude, bade her remain where she stood, and suffer him to protect the child.

"I know," said he, "the cause of your fear, and I hope to end it. The evil spirit who possesses that fatal signal, is as much under the control of the Almighty as the feeblest mortal amongst us; and if there be on Earth a being who is exempt from the pernicious influence which the demon is permitted to exercise, surely the fiend may, with utmost security, be defied by innocence and charity".

Having thus said, he knelt down, with the child between him and the Rock, and commenced a silent prayer, while his clasped hands rested on the head of the infant, his long gray hair hung down upon his shoulders, and his clear blue eye was fixed upon the fatal Candle. As he prayed, the anxious parents observed the light grow fainter and fainter, and the shadows of the old man and child become less and less distinct, until at length the sallow hue of the pilgrim's countenance could scarcely be distinguished from the bloom that glowed upon the fresh cheeks of the infant. Before his prayer was ended, the light had disappeared altogether, and the child came running into the arms of its enraptured mother. When the first burst of joy had been indulged in, she looked up to thank the stranger; but he was nowhere to be seen!

The death-light has never since reappeared upon the Rock, although it preserves the name which it received from that phantom. Cormac and Minny long continued to exercise the virtue of hospitality to which they owed so much in this instance; and I am told that the child became a bishop in the course of time. This, surely, is good fortune enough to enable one to wind up a long story with credit; and I have only to conclude, after aunt Norry's favourite form, by wishing : IF THEY DIDN'T LIVE HAPPY, THAT YOU AND I MAY.

CONCLUSION.

By the time this last tale had drawn to its catastrophe, the narrator (the toothless hag before alluded to) found that she had been for a considerable time the sole admirer of her own romance. Alarmed by the increasing strength and harmony of the chorus with which the sleepers bore burden to her tale, she raised her palsied head from beneath the covering she had drawn over it, and gazed upon the circle. The host and hostess sat upright in their lofty chairs, snoring as if it had been for a wager, at the same time that they maintained their attitudes with an unbending dignity that would have struck Cineas mute; while their friends lay scattered about the room in all directions, and some in very queer, comical postures indeed. As it was the tale, beyond all question, which had set them to sleep, so the sessation of the drowsy hum of the old woman's voice produced the contrary effect. The moment that perfect silence reigned around them, all rubbed their eyes, and awoke. The first gray shimmer of a winter dawn stole in upon the revellers—the fowls began to ruffle their feathers upon the roost over the door—and the swinish citizens of a neighbouring piggery gave grunting salutation to the morn.

With hurried and wondering gestures, the guests entered upon the bustle of separation, and the coast was presently left clear of all but the good folks of the house, and their guest, the chronicler of the evening.

CONCLUSION.

Of late years, scenes like this have become rare Ireland. Before the period of the year arrives when ancient and revered custom reminds the peasant of the domestic jollities of his fathers and of his own childhood, the horn of the Whiteboy, or the yell of the more ferocious Rockite, has startled the keepers of the land, and warned the inhabitants to prepare for "other than dancing measures." Without presuming for an instant to venture an opinion on the causes of the change, we may, at least, calculate on the reader's sympathy in expressing a hope that it may be of brief continuance, and that the time may not be very distant, when the Irish agriculturist may enjoy the domestic comforts which at many periods were known to his progenitors, and which are not denied to other nations in our own day—when

> " every man shall eat in safety,
> Under his own *hedge*, what he plants, and sing
> The merry songs of peace to all his neighbours ;"

when he can have his pit of potatoes, his reek of turf, his Sunday coat and brogues, his " three tinpennies" for the priest at Christmas and Easter ; and his family fireside, and his collection of " popular tales" at " Holland-tide."

THE END

SKETCHES

ILLUSTRATIVE

OF

LIFE AND MANNERS

IN THE

SOUTH OF IRELAND.

IRISH SATIRE.

AMONG the many translated specimens with which we
have been furnished from the remains of Old Irish Lite-
rature in all its other branches, I do not recollect having seen any that told us of the existence of a satirical
power. That this was rather the result of imperfect
inquiry on the part of the curious in these matters,
than of its actual non-existence, I always suspected—
for satire is ever keenest when it is *naïve*—and this last
is the characteristic of unreclaimed genius, in all countries. I have been enabled to procure some instances
which are current amongst the peasantry of the South
of Ireland, in their vernacular tongue ; and I shall
venture to subjoin a few, almost literally rendered into
English. They are presented under the form of fables,
and like all early attempts of this nature, have the
fault of being personal. The first is directed against
one of those half gentry who supply the place of the
absentee landlords, (this, it appears, was rather an
ancient grievance,) and let out portions of land, in
acres, half acres, and quarter acres, to the labourer
who wishes to secure himself a store of potatoes
against the idle season ensuing—and who take especial

.are that they do not leave the premises until all
demands have been cleared off by the miserable lessee.
I remember having heard the fable introduced with
great effect, into a harangue, by an orator of this
class.

"John Finnane walked through his grounds—John
was weary, and he sat down upon a ridge of potatoes.
It was Jerry Graham's quarter. How astonished was
John Finnane to hear Jerry's *white-eyes* talking to one
another in the ground under him : He stooped, and
began to listen. 'Will you grow any more?' says a
little potatoe to a big potatoe. 'No,' says the other,
'I am big enough.' 'Well, then,' says the little potatoe, 'move out of the way, and let us grow for poor
Jerry Graham and the creatures.' 'You know very
well,' says the big potatoe, 'that I cant't stir out of this
until John Finnane gets his rent.' 'That's true,' says the
other."

The next was intended to ridicule an extravagant
fellow, who, having no family, neglected his household
concerns, and was ruining himself by indolence, and a
fondness for the chase. The fairies of the Hibernian
bards are a very different race of beings from those of
Shakespeare. They do not hold their meetings

"On the beached margent of the sea,
To dance their ringlets to the whistling wind,'

but are generally represented as a race of chubby boys
in red jackets, with caps on their heads, and invariably
engaged in the diversion of *goal playing*, a game somewhat resembling our cricket.

"So good a rider David Foy was, and so notable a
creature was his horse, that he left hounds, hunt, hare,
and all behind him. On he went, and he was going,
going, going, until he came to a great valley. And
there he saw a number of boys, with red jackets, and

caps on their heads, and *hurlies* in their hands, playing goal. David Foy began to be afraid, for he knew where he was. Presently, an old hag came and offered him something to drink ; he refused it, for he knew it was *not good* to take drink from the like.* 'Take it,' said the old hag, 'and don't spare, it is David Foy's cider, and long may he live, we don't want for the best he has.' David went in, and made merry with them. By and by, in comes an *ounshah* with a fine pail of sweet milk. 'Where did you get that?' said the hag. 'Long life to David Foy, where should I get it but out of his dairy ? He is out hunting, and Betsy was in the *huggart* with Tim Foulou, and I took my share with the cat and the dog.' 'Umph !' says David to himself. Then comes in an *ounshah* with a firkin of butter, and another with a gammon of bacon, and all in the same story. ''Tis no admiration for ye to be so fat,' says David, making as if he knew nothing. In a year after, he came to the same place ; the boys were nothing but skin and bone, and the old hag was scraping a raw potatoe to make a cake for their supper. 'Oh ! the curse of Cromwell on you, David Foy, for a *near* nager as you are ; we haven't made a good meal on you, this twelve-month.' 'The more my luck,' says David."

The last I shall at present give you, is one of more general application, though, as usual, an individual has been made the vehicle of the satirist's spleen, and no less an individual than a saint, and no less a saint than the great patron himself. While its chief point is aimed at those who do much, but stop short of *all*, there is likewise a sly hit at the Western folks.

"How was it that St. Patrick did not reform all Ireland ? When he came over first, he walked along,

* The lower orders of the Irish have a superstition that fairies have power to detain only those who accept refreshments from their hands.

preaching, and converting, and baptizing, wherever he
came. When he came into Ossory, he baptized without preaching. When he came down to Limerick, he
made priests, and told *them* to baptize and to preach;
but when he arrived in Shanagolden, he lifted up his
hands, and said, 'Good people, God bless ye all to the
West!' and returned to Dublin."

SONNET—REPENTANCE.

I looked upon a dark and sullen sea,
   Over whose slumbering waves the night mists hung,
   'Till from the morn's grey breast a fresh wind sprung,
And swept its brightening bosom joyously!—
Then rolled the shades its quickening breath before;
   The glad sea rose to meet it—and each wave,
   Retiring from the wild caress it gave,
Made summer music to the listening shore!

So slept my soul unmindful of THY reign;
   But the kind breath of thy celestial grace
   Hath risen!—Oh! let its sweetening spirit chase
From that dark seat each mist and mortal stain,
Till—as in yon clear water, mirrored fair—
Heaven once more sees itself reflected there!

THE DISPENSARY, VILLAGE LITERATURE.

Host, Page, &c —Bless thee, doctor.—Save you, master doctor.—
Give you good morrow, good master doctor!
Doctor Caius.—Vat be all you, one, two, tree, four, come for ?—Be
gar, de herring is no dead, so as I vill kill!
Merry Wives of Windsor

"Am I not punctual? (said a medical friend, physician to a Wexford Dispensary, on entering my apartment at an earlier hour than was precisely agreeable,)
I am come, according to promise, to accompany you
to our Dispensary. If Hans Holbein, (he continued,
throwing himself into a *sedia d'apoggio*,) had laid the
scene of his *Triomphe de la Mort* in Ireland, I could
supply him with some sketches which, I think, would
form no disadvantageous substitutes for the many flat
common-places with which he has favoured us. Now,
in the first instance, I would take him to a potatoe field,
through which I passed yesterday on this very estate,
(the Earl of * * *'s,) and where I was witness to a
scene which its absentee proprietor, I hope, does not
dream of. I would give him the outline of that scene,
with his own whimsical distortions, and this should be
my etching :—In the centre I should place one of those
portly gentlemen, to whose predecessors it was said,
'Go forth, and take ye your scrip and your staff,' &c. ;
and I would be careful that he had more of the scrip
than of the staff, in the formation of the outward man ;
otherwise, I should not be a faithful historian. He
should point with his cane to an open potatoe-*pit* in the

half distance, on the left : perched upon this goodly *eminence*, I would give you a tithe-proctor with a mallet in his hard, serving in the capacity of auctioneer, and roaring out the biddings of some decently dressed fel- lows, whom, by the use they make of their left hands in examining the devoted *cups*, you may judge to be *Palentines*.* On the left, in the foreground, I should make a group of the miserable, starving family of the lessee. In the distance, on the extreme left, you should see a skeleton horse, and cart, preparing to remove their all—their little winter store ; and on the extreme right, a miserable hovel, or *cabin*. To complete the allegori- cal part of the satire, I would have Death, under the usual figure of a *squelette*, with a spade lifted over the churchman's head, *pour lui casser la tête*. He should have the white shirt of a Rockite thrown over his grisly bones, and his *os frontis* should be smeared with bog- dust."

" I should recommend to you, (said I,) to make a rough draft of the thing, and show it to your friend F——, at the Glebe."

"Then my next sketch should be taken from a Country Dispensary. Death should be here placed be- hind the counter, employed after his own heart, under all the authority of a wig and diploma ; and I would have a junior skeleton at his side, with a mortar in one hand, and a pestle in the other, fiercely engaged in compounding for the miserable looking applicants."

"And would you make this one before us sit for the picture ?" said I.

" Ho ! sir ; no, no, (he exclaimed,) the W—— Dis- pensary is acknowledged to be an exception :—Come

---

* I should suppose there is no necessity for explaining this word. There exists a very sincere hatred of these folks in the southern coun- ties of Ireland, and indeed, I believe there is no love wasted on their side

in, come in."—The door was opened, and a rush commenced, some idea of which may be formed by those
who have waited half-an-hour at the pit door of Drury
Lane, in the first run of "The Cataract."

"Good morrow, doctor. Ah ! then, long life to your
honour ; how does the young mistress, and Master
Tom, and the old man of all, Sir ?   May be you havn't
any time to look at this bit of ticket, plase your honour ; 'tis from old Hartigan*, Sir," (the treasurer to
the concern.)   "Very well, very well, my good man ,
sit down, sit down.—I don't know, (said the Doctor
to me, while he made his arrangements in the surgery,
which was about half again as munificently furnished as
that of Romeo's apothecary,) what these good people
did ten years back, when there was no such thing as a
dispensary in the country ; but since they have been
established, they seem to regard it as a most unreason-
able thing to expect that their little finger should ache
while a doctor was in the neighbourhood, and to think
that it would be a kind of suicidal act if they failed to
make the case known.   An unwise fellow would quarrel
with them on occasions of this kind, but I humour them
—set their minds to rest, save myself trouble, and
make my reputation.   You shall see one of those very
extraordinary cases before we have done.   Well, Mrs.
O'Hierlohee, and what's the matter with you, pray ?"—
"Why, then, Sir, I can hardly tell what ails me, but
I'm very bad entirely."—"Do you sleep well, Mrs.
O'H ?"—"Oh ! very well, Doctor "—"And do you eat
well ?"—"Oh ! then, it is'nt so bad with me, but I can
eat a little, Doctor."—"And drink well ?"—"I can't
say but I do, indeed, your honour."—"Well, then,
what *is* the matter with you, Mrs. O'H.?"—"Why,
then, I don't know, Doctor ; *only* I'm very bad entirely

* This familiar way of naming their betters, *behind their backs*, is
very usual among the peasantry.

—entirely."—"Oh! is that it? Well, we'll get you
over that ; sit down a moment" He let me see the
prescription, which was quite as novel and as nugatory
as the case itself ; it was given in this form :—

Aquæ fontanis -   -   -   iv oz.
⎰ Aquæ puræ
⎱ Aquæ distillæ -   -   -   ā ā ij oz
Tinct Tolut.   -   -   -   gtt ij
Fiat mist. hora somni sumend.

And we had the satisfaction to learn that it was successful *à la merveille.*
"Well, Mr. M'Coy, what has happened to your
hand, that you have bound up there—what ails it ?"—
"Why, then, Doctor, (said the man, advancing his
head obliquely, with a knowing, confidential look,) I
believe 'tis some of my sins that's going to be forgiven
me ! I never had such punishment in my life, since I
was born."—"How did it happen?"—"How did it
happen ! Why, then, I'll tell your honour that same.
To be engaged to cut rape for—there he is—Switzer,
the Palentine, and it to be Michaelmas-day—a retrenched *holiday*, and I, never to know it, till I *run* the
raping-hook right across my fingers !—And, upon the
vestment I could swear, it was unknownst to me I did
it ; for, though it be retrenched, I know 'tisn't good to
break it for all."
The Irish are a nation of intuitive *humbugs;* and
they succeed better in their essays on their superiors,
because they cover their shrewdness with a simplicity
really natural My friend was boasting to me how perfectly he was *au fait* with respect to their qualifications
in this respect, when a woman, who had asked without
avail the four and fiftieth time for a little grain of
ornate, (*ernato,*) turned to one of her companions, who
was being congratulated by another on her perfect
recovery, and said, as if apart, "Ah ! then, Mary, you

may thank the Doctor for that."—"Sure, I know I may, Koth," said Mary.—"'The Lord be good to them that sent us a clever and a civil gentleman, that knows his business."—The *finesse* was irresistible ; and she went off immediately in triumph with her prize.

In the afternoon, I accompanied "the Doctor" to see a patient (on a visiting ticket,) who was ill of a brain fever. The messenger told us he was the great Mr. Davy Dooley, the poet of the village ; and added, as a kind of hint to my friend, if he was at all ambitious of immortality, that David wrote a song in praise of Dr. ——, the last physician who attended him, and that the neighbours said there was a *dale* of very fine English in it. "But I don't know, please your honour, what is it makes poets so unlucky. Davy never did well in his life : I think myself 'tis the curses of the people that they make the songs upon, that falls upon them.* Davy never had any luck since he wrote one upon Father Phelim, where he says,

> "Go, kneel and pray—or fight and play,
>   Or drink, or what ye will ;
> But bring your grist on Christmas-day,
>   To Father Phelim's mill !"

When we arrived at the clay-walled dwelling of this village Juvenal, we found it crowded almost to suffocation with the gossips and the *literati* of the whole neighbourhood. Never was mortal so pestered with queries of "Well, Doctor, what do you think of him? Will he do, Sir?" as my poor friend was on his *sortèe* from the inner chamber, which was separated by a *hurdle* from the outer, where, in the midst of the hushed assembly, stood the redoubted Father Phelim, himself,

---

* This is so curiously characteristic an observation, that perhaps it is worth while to say it is not an invention "With mine own ear heard it."

much to his credit, haranguing them on the absurdity
of the idea that the poet's brain was visited for its own
wicked creations, at the same time that he condemned
these last. Let me here offer a plea for that much
injured, much misrepresented, homely, honest class, the
Catholic priesthood of the country parishes. Nothing
can be more unfair, more untrue, than the allusions
sometimes made to their comfortable mode of living,
and their love for it. A poor farmer will fix on one of
his sons to be made a priest of ; a classical education
can be procured in Ireland for a few pounds ; and this
lad, after having achieved a parish, which may bring
him in about thirty pounds a year—sometimes scarcely
so much—is saddled with the care of a few sisters, a
sister's child, sometimes a young brother, or an old
aunt, or a widowed mother ; and these he must provide
for, until taken off his hands in one way or other.

Of the character of one of this class, Father Phelim's harangue (with the conclusion of which I shall
conclude,) furnished an example. There is nothing
profane or disrespectful in my quoting it, as it was
given in a social, not a ministerial capacity :—

" 'Tisn't any fine, classical poetry we see ye about
writing ; sweet, neat lines, such as—there he is—
Palemon and Daphnis used to make in Horace long
ago. No ; these times are gone by. We have nothing
now but *nugæ canoræ*, as Homer says. Oh ! if Tytyrus
or Virgil were to rise out of their graves, and see such
verses coming after them, I wonder what would they
say to it ? Sorrow a bit, if they wouldn't be ashamed
they ever printed a line, or handled a pen and paper.
Avenis cera junctis tu indocte cum in triviis, &c., as Meli-
bœus says ; as much as to say, " You illiterate fellow,
you go for to sing on the *bortens*, when you should be
closing brogues with wax."

THE IRISH FUNERAL CRY

- - - - - No.—
Porque lo
No quiero que me mejore
Quien cante, sino quien llore!
Calderon's El major monstruo los Zelos.

In all other imitations of human feeling and manner with which poetry furnishes us, (if we allow John Dryden's position—that all poetry is but imitation,) we have only one plain and almost undeviating path by which the imitator tends towards his object ; but the avenues to that deep and single one, the pathos of Nature, are various and innumerable as the different *grades* by which in the hearts of men it ascends to its climax. All men have at least the capability of this feeling, if of no other ; and therefore it is, that in the early life of poetry, when it has *only* nature to imitate, it excels in the naked delineation of the true pathos of the heart. Every poet of nature has pathos, and each a pathos of his own. Read the death scene of Webster's " White Devil ;" read Burns' Epistle to his friend Andrew ; read the " La vida es sueno" of the wild and irregular, but powerful writer from whom I have taken my motto ; read the two last acts of Lear, (not Tate's, but Shakspeare's ;) and read the " But was't a miserable day ?" of the weak and heroic, and mean and noble Belvidera :—you will weep over all, but you will compare none ; it is a different feeling that agitates you in each.

This has been regarded as the prominent and distinguishing merit, both of the ancient poetry and music of Ireland ; but it was not my intention now to speak of these elder worthies ; I merely sat down to tell you a little circumstance of which I was myself a witness, some months since, in a little village in the south-west of Ireland,—a district which has lately excited a melancholy interest. The custom of crying aloud at funerals in that country is well known, and has certainly a very powerful, though not a very pleasing effect on those who have been accustomed to the silent and cold decorum with which we follow the remains of our acquaintances to their long home in this. But those who close their ears at the first intrusion of this strange simultaneous wailing of many voices and few hearts, are very widely mistaken if they imagine that it is the easy acquisition of all, or that it is so unmusical in solo, as it is in the aggregate. It is held just in the same esteem among the peasantry, as a very perfect intimacy with Mozart, Handel, or Rossini, is in circles more polite. An Irish swain, in describing his mistress to you, will place her affections in this ratio : " Ah ! but she is a very *clever* girl, with a white skin ; and (shaking his head) she has a *fine cry with her.*" I have actually known of many conquests made by well-graced maidens ; and what appears still more extraordinary, conquests *planned* by them, in the train of a funeral, and in the wailing of a friend's death ! I have heard the performers in those singular choruses taken to pieces in a cottage *coterie* on the subsequent evening, with as much malice, and as great an affectation of critical acumen, and as little of human mercy, as is here exhibited in the dissection of the young performers in a Lent Concert or Oratorio. " Why, Mary, *you* didn't cry today, at all, at all." " Indeed, then, but it wasn't that there was no room for worse than Mary,' said a third

" Well, to be sure, it isn't good to judge ; but if ever
e'er a girl did make a *muthane* of herself, Kitty Kilmartin was that girl this day. She made the whole church-
yard laugh. There she was, with her *yollow* jock and
her white *handkitcher*, and her *pay* colour *ribbin*, and she
crying for the bare life, and sorrow a note she had, no
more nor the *gorsoon* that *drov* the *truckle.*" " I wonder
what would Thady say if he *seen* her." " Who is
Thady ?" " A *boy* of the Galahoos, that was looking
after her ; but Kitty went in service to a *blue heart*,
(*Anglice*, Protestant,) and—there's a month there since
—she went to mass with one of the mistress's books,
with a fine red cover ; but what should Thady be doing
but sitting behind her, *unknownst*, and she having the
wrong side of the book *to-wards* her. Thady *seen* how
'twas, and he never *come* nigh her after ; and, ('tisn't
good to judge,) but, Kitty Kilmartin ! set up for to cry
over the *dead corpse !—Gondoutha !*"

You see, therefore, that sincerity is not even thought
of. But I have been fortunate enough to hear this
melancholy and wild piece of monotony in its perfection,
for I heard it when it *was* sincere—when it sprung from
and gave expression to the real feeling of the heart.
Perhaps—indeed, I am sure—that I shall be looked on
as a heretic in the musical creed of the day, if I find
the hardiness to affirm, that the compass and modula-
tion and volume of a Catalina would not have produced
such an effect on me ; but I save myself yet, by
acknowledging that this was in a great measure the
result of the attending circumstances. At the east side
of the romantic little village of Adare is an old church,
which has been for some time a prohibited spot to the
sexton's spade ; and a number of mouldering and grass-
covered tombs are seen around its walls, in what was
once a church-yard, but it is now almost a field. I
remember, a few years since, walking from Limerick to

to this village in an evening. It was a Christmas Eve.
Every cottage and cabin on the road-side presented a
picture of at least a temporary cheerfulness. The elder
folks were employed in festive preparations, such as
they were, for the following day ; and the little urchins
gazing with wonder on the great mould candle which,
for one night only, throughout the year, usurped the
place of the little slender rush-light, or still feebler slip
of *bog-deal*,—a simple and frugal substitute, which contents them well for their own convenience, but is not
deemed worthy to honour this season of universal joy-
ance. It was a fine winter night—calm, clear, and
cold. I had fully entered into the pleasant spirit which
breathed all around, when a sudden turn in the road
brought me almost close to the church I speak of.
I stopped to look at the ruin, and a peasant who
accompanied me, pointed out, under an elder tree, a
woman sitting on one of the tombs, her gown turned
over her head, which was bent forward on her knees.
I was surprised and affected by the singular contrast
which the scene presented. Her story may be said in
ten words : She was a widow, who depended for all
upon the exertions of an only son. He loved and honoured her ; but he was misled—he was a *Rockite*. The
policy in those cases recommends the execution of the
culprit who falls into the hands of justice, as near as
possible to his home ; so that this unfortunate youth
had suffered almost opposite his mother's door. It was
from her I heard the *cailach* in its perfection. Every
Christmas Eve since his death, while other parents
laughed at their fire-sides, she had spent at her boy's
tomb, and sung it to his bones. It was a loud and
thrilling cry, followed by a modulated descent, and
ending in broken sobs and half-muttered sentences.
These last, my companion, in his own rude way, rendered into English for me ; but the matter of each, I

thought strongly expressive of the utter solitude of soul, the mournful and desolate feeling, which is occasioned by the reflection that we stand alone in a crowd, —things of the world, yet having no tie of interest or affection with it. The circumstance altogether struck me as being peculiarly characteristic of the almost romantic depth of feeling which stamps the mind of a country, where the ties of relationship are drawn more closely than, perhaps, in any other in the civilized world ; where, to use a phrase current among themselves, "a man's child is always his child ;" for the interests of a family are seldom divided. I speak now, only of the peasantry.

The following are the ideas of the Lament ; but I will not say that the poetical dress has improved them, though I have endeavoured to retain their simplicity :

O, what shall be my Christmas joy
   When the pleasant day is come ?
To think upon my murdered Boy,
   And weep upon his tomb !—
Mothers of children !—should you plain ?
   Oh ! you are stricken light by fate—
A home and love to you remain,
   But I am desolate !—
      Eleu ! Eleu !
And is he dead ! and is he gone ?—
My life ! my child ! my only one !

I saw my father's eyes grow dim,
   And I clasped my mother's knee ;
. saw my mother follow him,
   And my husband wept with me !
My husband did not long remain,
   But his child was left me yet ;
Oh ! my child—my heart's last love is slain,
   And I am desolate !—
      Eleu ! Eleu !
And is he dead ? and is he gone ?
My all in all !—my only one !

ST. SINON'S ISLE.

WOULD not the traditional name of this Saint, Sinon, nave been much better suited to the light and graceful versification of the Irish bard, than the chilling, classical one he has chosen—Senanus? It does not, however, matter much ; for the little song he has founded on this old legend, is one of the feeblest and least popular of all his melodies. Walking some time since, near the village of Kildimo, in the county of Limerick, my attention was directed, by a countryman who accompanied me, to an old dismantled castle between us and the Shannon's side. In the south wall of the ancient pile, I could perceive a round orifice, which he told me was the handi-work of one of Cromwell's cannon balls. The castle, he informed me, belonged in early times to a chief of the Butler family, who had "*come by* his end after a very *quare* manner." I chuckled at the prospect of a traditional story, and begged him to proceed. "Why, sir," he continued, "he was a very savage man ; when a serving man forgot his commands, or a thing of the kind, he made no more ado, but ordered him to be hung up on that old elder tree your honour sees before the gate. It was in these same times that St. Sinon took to the Island of Scattery, near Kilrush, and made his protest that no woman should ever set foot on its ground. When old Butler *heard* *tell* of this, he sent off word to St. Sinon, that he should expect tribute from him. St. Sinon sent him back for an answer, that what he had was God's gift, and he'd pay no' man a tithe on it. To be sure old Butler was very mad at this; and to be sure 'tis he that did raise the great faction to exterminate him from the face of the earth. But Sinon took it easy, and said to them that wanted him to fly, "No," says he, "tisn't me—'tis the blessed Heaven that he's threat'ning; and wee'll see what will come of it—and the sooner the better," says he. And to be sure, true enough the Saint's words *come.* Butler stood on the Shannon's side, with his men around him, and his ships upon the water. When they had embarked, he was about to step into the skiff, when his foot slipped; he shot like an arrow under the boat, and was never heard of after !"

The tale of the peasant excited in me a wonderful desire to visit this far-famed little islet. On returning to the cottage where I made my sojourn, at Ringmoylan, (the estate of Lord Charleville,) I proposed the excursion to Miss O'Shaughnessy of Pallus Kenry, a blooming personification of the *belle ideale* of Irish grace and beauty, and to her sister's husband's cousin, Mr. Thady O'Histin, of Killimicat, a young gentleman who had been once to London, and since his return, affected to despise every thing Hibernian : he cast away his vulgar family name, or rather qualified it, by writing Mr. Thaddeus Hastings on his cards, to the great vexation of his guardian and uncle, an old Histin, who was proud of the name. The blue eyes of Miss O'S. sparkled with rapture when I asked her to accompany us, and Mr. Thaddeus wondered what was to be seen there. "Why," said Miss O'Shaughnessy, "*sure* you have heard of the ruins, Thady ? the eleven churches, and the round tower ?" Mr. T. began to talk of Westminster Abbey and Stonehenge ; and his cousin's wife's sister repeated the word's of Moore's melody, dwelling with peculiar emphasis on the last lines :—

> But legends hint, that had the maid
> 'Till morning's light delayed,
> And given the saint one rosy smile,
> She ne'er had left his lonely isle!

The trip was at length agreed on. We were supplied with all the local information necessary by the Physician of the neighbouring dispensary, a very clever young fellow, (who, I hope, if he sees this, will remember his old companion,) and the next morning we set off for Limerick, in the jingle. On arriving at Swinbourne's Hotel, we found that the Lady of the Shannon, steam packet, was to sail for Kilrush on the following day.

Behold us, then, on the deck—a beautiful and breathless morning—admiring the splendid scenery of the Shannon side. Miss O'Shaughnessy, as she called herself ; or Miss Shannissy, as her sister's husband's cousin called her ; or Miss O'Shochnassy, according to the delicate *euphuisme* of the steward of the vessel—peering through the captain's telescope at the receding summit of Keeper's Hill, and the turrets of St. Mary's steeple ; her brother lying on a bench in affected *ennui ;* and Master Oscar * * taking his notes at the binnacle with a most furious eagerness. We arrived at Kilrush, hired a cot, and proceeded to the isle of St. Sinon. It contains eleven churches and a round tower, which, considering that it is not half-a-mile round, is no trifling allowance. In some of these are many curious pieces of sculpture, and the obelisk itself is one of the most perfect I have seen. It may be discerned on the horizon long before the island is visible. There is a flag in one of the churches, which, say the dwellers of the shore, has been often sought as a curiosity by antiquariai.s ; but, though four men may with ease lift and carry it to the water's edge, no human power can move it into a boat for the purpose of removal ! The island is at present uninhabited.

During a *déjeuné*, which we took on the grass, Miss O'Shaughnessy lamented that we should have no genius to panegyrize such a fine stream as the Shannon, and such noble scenery as we had that day witnessed. Sir, this was touching me in the tender side ; I have been always dabbling in "the crambo jingle," as Burns calls it, and I remembered the words of that poet :—

> The Illisus, Tiber, Thames, and Seine,
> Glide sweet in mony a tuneful line—
> But, Willie, set your fist to mine,
>   An' cock your crest ;
> We'll gar *our* streams and birnies shine
>   Up wi' the best !

I plucked up a sudden courage, and I resolved to surprise Miss O'S. and her sister's husband's cousin. She declared that the lines were " very, very handsome, indeed ;" but I had the mortification to over-hear Mr. Thaddeus whispering to her, "that he would *lee* any *wager* she *pleesed*," that if I sent them to the *Literary Gazette*, they would be rejected ! However, this did not much move me, for I always held his judgment in contempt. To prove this, I shall subjoin them :

A RIVER SONG.

I.

> Merrily whistles the wind of the shore
>   Through the lithe willow,
> But wearily drops the boatman's oar,
>   On the calm billow :—
> 'Tis silent there—although it sing
>   So freshly on the land ;
> The feather shook from the wild duck's wing
>   Scarce finds the strand !—

Then do not fear—up, maiden, and hear
         The gushing billow—
In the deep* silent of the night
         Lie on your pillow;
But wake with the waking of the day-light—
As fresh and as fair, and as blushing and bright.

II.

Is it not pleasanter thus to steal
    O'er the water—than on a dull bed
To toss in the wasting sun, and to feel
    The heavy air over your head—
For this keen, elastic wind ?——Look back!
         Ha! how fleetly
St. Mary's turrets fade from our track—
         And how sweetly
The chime of its bells comes o'er the ear,
With the rush of the Shannon's waters here !—

III.

Oh! it is pleasant to mark the lark,
    When the dark brow of night is clearing,
Give greeting to the dawn—and—hark!
Waked by the dashing of our bark,
    Through the green waves careering ;
The plover and the shrill curlew
         Round us screaming—
Startle thy silent shore, Tiervoe !
         Where the beaming
Of the unshrouded, morning sun,
Finds pleasant scenes to smile upon !—

IV.

'Tis noon! the Race† is past!—'Tis even—
    Ha! see St. Sinon's Isle—
With its high round tower, and churches eleven,
    Bathed in the evening's smile—
And deeper—and fainter—and fainter still
         That smile is growing—
And now the last flush is on the hill,
         Wasting and glowing—
And now in the west there's a flickering bright,
'Tis the triumph of darkness! the death of light !—

* "Dead night—dun night—the silent of the night."
                                  Shakspeare.
† The Race : A part of the Shannon, near Tarbert and Clonderlaw Bay—
here it dilates itself so as to resemble a large lake.

V.

Now steal we under the drowsy shore—
Our toil is done! our sailing o'er!—
How lovely thou lookest, young maiden, now
Thy cheek is flushed— and on thy brow,
　　　　　　White—soft—and sleek—
One purple vein is faintly seen
　　　　　　Like a thin streak
Of the blue sky shown through a silver cloud,
When the dim sun lies in his morning shroud!

THE BELLS OF ST. MARY'S.

" Those evening bells—those evening bells !"
Moore's National Melodies.

THERE is a delight which those only can appreciate who
have felt it, in recalling to one's mind, when cast by
fortune upon a strange soil and among strangers, the
sights and sounds which were familiar to one's infant
days. It is pleasant too, though perhaps, like the
praise of one's own friend, rather obtrusive, to snatch
those memories from their rest and give them to other
ears,--to tinge them with an interest, and bid them
live again. When we perceive, likewise, that places and
circumstances of real beauty and curiosity remain neglected and unknown for want of "some tongue to give
their worthiness a voice," their is a gratification to our
human pride in the effort to procure them, even for
a space :

A forted residence 'gainst the tooth of time
And razure of oblivion.

I shall not in this letter, as in my last, give any thing
characteristic—any thing Irish. I will be dull, rather
than descend from the elevation I intend to keep ; but,
in compensation, I will tell you a fine old Story, and if
you have but the slightest mingling of poetical feeling
in your composition, (and who is there now-a-days that
will not pretend to some ?)—I promise myself that you
shall not be disappointed.

The city of Limerick, though surrounded by some very tolerable demesnes, is sadly deficient in one respect, not an unimportant one in any large town. There is no public walk of any consequence immediately adjoining it. The canal which leads to Dublin is bleak, from its want of trees; and unhealthy, from the low marshy champagne which lies on either side its banks   This however, for want of something better, was for a considerable time the fashionable *promenade*, until the formation of the Military Walk on the western side; to which the beauties of Limerick—(a commodity quite as celebrated, and some malicious wags say, almost as marketable, in an honourable way, as Limerick gloves) —have given, *among themselves*, the witty appellation of the *path to promotion.*

But at the head of this canal, where it divides itself into two branches, which, gradually widening and throwing off their artificial appearance, form a glittering circlet around a small island which is covered with water shrubs—on this spot, I have delightedly reposed in many a sweet sunset—when I loved to seek a glimpse of inspiration in such scenes—to imitate Moore's poetry—and throw rhymes together, about the rills and hills, and streams and beams, and even and heaven, and fancy I was a genius!—"'Tis gone—'tis gone—'tis gone!" as old Capulet says.

But let us recall it for a moment. Have the complaisance to indulge me in a day-dream, and fancy, if you can, that you sit beside me on the bank. We are beyond the hearing of the turmoil and bustle of the town —"the city's voice itself is soft—like solitude's"—and there is a hush around us that is delightful—the beautiful repose of evening. The sun, that but a few minutes since rushed down the west with the speed of a wandering star, pauses ere he shall set upon the very verge of the horizon, and smiles upon its own handi-

work—the creation of his fostering fervour. Hark !
one sound alone reaches us here ; and how grand and
solemn and harmonious in its monotony ! These are the
great bells of St. Mary's. Their deep toned vibrations
undulate so as to produce a sensible effect on the air
around us. The peculiar fineness of the sound has been
often remarked ; but there is an old story connected
with their history, which, whenever I hear them ring
out over the silent city, gives a something more than
harmony to the peal. I shall merely say, that what I
am about to relate is told as a real occurrence, and I
consider it so touchingly poetical in itself,—that I shall
not dare to apply a fictitious name and fictitious circumstances where I have been unable to procure the
actual ones.

They were originally brought from Italy ; they had
been manufactured by a young native (whose name the
tradition has not preserved,) and finished after the toil
of many years, and he prided himself upon his work.
They were subsequently purchased by the prior of a
neighbouring convent ; and with the profits of this sale,
the young Italian procured a little villa, where he had
the pleasure of hearing the tolling of his bells from the
convent cliff, and of growing old in the bosom of domestic happiness. This, however, was not to continue. In
some of those broils, whether civil or foreign, which are
the undying worm in the peace of a fallen land, the
good Italian was a sufferer amongst many. He lost his
all ; and, after the passing of the storm, found himself
preserved alone amid the wreck of fortune, friends,
family, and home. The convent in which the bells, the
chefs-d'œuvre of his skill, were hung, was razed to the
earth, and these last carried away into another land.
The unfortunate owner, haunted by his memories, and
deserted by his hopes, became a wanderer over Europe.
His hair grew grey, and his heart withered, before he

again found a home or a friend. In this desolation of spirit, he formed the resolution of seeking the place to which those treasures of his memory had been finally borne. He sailed for Ireland—proceeded up the Shannon;—the vessel anchored in the Pool, near Limerick, and he hired a small boat for the purpose of landing. The city was now before him; and he beheld St. Mary's steeple, lifting its turretted head above the smoke and mist of the Old Town. He sat in the stern, and looked fondly toward it. It was an evening so calm and beautiful, as to remind him of his own native heaven in the sweetest time of the year—the death of the spring. The broad stream appeared like one smooth mirror and the little vessel glided through it with almost a noiseless expedition. On a sudden, amid the general stillness, the bells tolled from the Cathedral—the rowers rested on their oars, and the vessel went forward with the impulse it had received. The old Italian looked toward the city, crossed his arms on his breast, and lay back in his seat; home, happiness, early recollections, friends, family—all were in the sound, and went with it to his heart. When the rowers looked round, they beheld him with his face still turned toward the Cathedral, but his eyes were closed, and when they landed—they found him cold!

Such are the associations which the ringing of St. Mary's bells bring to my recollection. I do not know how I can better conclude this letter than with the little Melody, of which I have given the line above. It is a good specimen of the peculiar tingling melody of the author's poetry—a quality in which he never has been equalled in his own language, nor exceeded in any other; although, like a great many more of his productions, it has very little merit besides—Why!— you can almost fancy you can hear them ringing!—

Those evening bells—those evening bells—
How many a tale their music tells
Of youth and home—and that sweet time
When last I heard their soothing chime!

Those pleasant hours have passed away,
And many a heart that then was gay—
Within the tomb now darkly dwells,
And hears no more those evening bells.

And so 't will be when I am gone,
That tuneful peal will still ring on—
When other bards shall walk those dells,
And sing your praise—sweet evening bells.

LOCAL SUPERSTITIONS.

Oh monstrous—oh strange—we are haunted!
Pray, masters, fly—masters, help!
Midsummer Night's Dream

THERE is something good humoured in Irish superstition—something *qui donne de la joie aans tu peur.* We
have no witches—none of those ugly, ill-favoured, earthly realities, which brutalize and stupify the minds of a
portion of our own boors ; but there is scarce a hill, a
lough, a dingle, a *fort*, or an old ruin, which does not
call up within the peasant's mind some wild and poeti-
cally fearful association.
Let me see :—Here I have them—all that I was enabled to collect from the country people, who are quite
as communicative as they are inquisitive—I have them
in petto before me in a stoutly bound note book, which
was the constant companion of my pedestrian excursions. A. B. C.—F. K. L.—Limerick—aye, this it the
page. Here I begin my faëry tour—Limerick,—yes :
I have got a great many good things under this head.
Heavens ! what a gorgeous display they make as I let
the pages slip one after another from beneath my
fingers : Traditions—Superstitions—Anecdotes—Points
of Scenery—Character—Rockites—Hush ! What have
I said ?—All in good time : These gentlemen must take
their turn in time, but at present I have quite another

matter in head. I will run through these little memoranda in the order in which I find them set down.

Knuck Fierna.

The hills of the fairies. This is the loftiest mountain in the county above named, and lifts its double peak on the Southern side, pretty accurately, I believe, dividing it from Cork. Numberless are the tales related of this hill by the *carmen* who have been benighted near it on their return from the latter city, which is the favourite market for the produce of their dairies. That there is a *Siobrug* or fairy castle in the Mount, no one in his senses presumes to entertain a doubt. On the summit of the highest peak is an unfathomable well, which is held in very great veneration by the peasantry. It is by some supposed to be the entrance to the court of their tiny mightinesses. A curious fellow at one time had the hardihood to cast a stone down the orifice; and then casting himself on his face and hands, and leaning over the brink, waited to ascertain the falsity of this supposition by the reverberation, which he doubted not would soon be occasioned by the missile reaching the bottom. But he met with a fate scarce less tragical than that of poor Pug, who set fire to the match of a cannon, and then must needs run to the mouth to see the shot go off. Our speculator had his messenger returned to him with a force that broke the bridge of his nose, locked up both his eyes, and sent him down the hill at the rate of four furlongs per second, at the foot of which he was found senseless next morning.

King Finvar's* Cattle.

Between this mountain and the river Shannon, there is a small lake, concerning which a very extraordinary

* A famous fairy monarch

report was circulated a few years back. Some people indeed may imagine it a little too improbable to lend a very ready credence to it, but I can assure them that its veracity was not even questioned at the time it took place. The lake or lough to which I allude is a very pretty one, although it is disfigured on one side by a piece of ugly bog. On the East, it is overlooked by a hill which makes a very sudden descent on its bank ; but the slope is delightfully covered with mountain ash, birch, and hazel trees, so as to form a very pleasant contrast to the dreary flat opposite. At the northern end of the water, among patches of rude crag, and occasional spots of green, a few thatched hovels or cabins are huddled together, so as to form a something indescribably miserable in appearance, which is dignified with the appellation of a village : it is nalled *Killimicat.* Not very far from this, and on the borders of the lake—But what are these stories worth if taken out of the mouth of the original narrator? I shall give this to you as I had it myself :--You see that little meadow there over-right us, Sir,—that was the little spot that Morty Shannon took from the master. Morty was a snug *sculog* then, and very well to do there, as I hear ; but a stronger man than he was could not stand any thing of a loss in such times as they were. Morty wondered what was it that used to spoil the growth of his little meadow. There was no sign of trespass from the neighbours, for the bounds were good, and their cattle were all *spancelled.* But so it was : sorrow a bit of grass did he ever cut on the field for two years. At last, knowing it to be a good bit of ground, he resolved to sit up of a night to see what was it used to be there : and so he did, himself and his two sons. About twelve o'clock, as they were standing, as it might be this way, what should they see rising out of the lake only a fine big cow and seven heifers, and they making towards his

little field. ' *Tha guthine* '' says Morty to himself, ' is
this the way of it ?' So he beckoned to his sons to come
betune them and the lake, and turn them into the pound.
The old cow seen what they were about, and, without
ever speaking a word, made a dart right between the two
sons and into the water with her. But the heifers they
drove home, and inclosed them in a paddock, where
they staid for a year ; until one evening the *gorsoon* forgot to lock the gate, when they all made off into the
lake, and were never heard of more.''

It is said there is a magnificent palace under this
water, one of whose turrets is visible above the surface
in a dry summer. This report is quite as well attested
as the other.

Old Raths.

These very ancient places are a favourite haunt of
the elves ; and woe to the hardy man who dares to apply the axe or the spade to tree, shrub, or soil, in these
hallowed spots. They are very numerously scattered
over the face of the country, and form great eye-sores
to the improving class of landholders, who have acquired wit enough to contemn the superstition, but lack
courage to adventure first in the cause of common
sense. I knew one stout man who lost an eye in the
attempt to root out an old thorn on one of these places ;
another who had a fine meadow *turned up* and destroyed
for his pains ; and a third, who declared that the very
night after he had superintended an exploit of a similar
kind, he saw three *siteogs*, in the shape of strapping
bucaughs, take each a *cleave* of turf from the *reek* in
front of his house. The reality of this latter appearance I was not at all inclined to question.

THE HOAX

NOTWITHSTANDING the title under which I have mar-
shalled this series of lucubrations, and which professes
to confine the sense of the little events described to
"sweet Monomia" itself, I should be very sorry to pay
so much deference to consistency, as to restrain myself
from the pleasure of taking in a flying good thing which
I have caught at in sports to which my attention was
less particularly directed. I shall therefore in this and
my next letters, give you some of my first gleanings on
my arrival in the country, and which in point of fact
were then set down.

Let your philosophical contributors fix the cause, I
content myself with asserting this fact, that in every
considerable town except Dublin, where I have yet
sojourned, practical hoax seems to be the esteemed
relaxation of gentlemen at large of the middle rank,
and men of business and profession, whose facile methods
of despatch, or whose waste time, allows them the
primary means for its indulgence. Passing by countless instances of this scientific waggery, which, if you
had been as long as I have been in Ireland, would
amuse you, allow me to submit one grand *tour* illustrative of the almost desperate extent to which it can
reach. I am about to mention important facts and
dates, and am aware of the authenticity upon which I

ought to base my narrative ; but if my own eyes and
ears may serve, they are your warrant in attaching im-
plicit credence to the sequel. In one word, I shall not
state a circumstance which I do not know of my own
knowledge.

Thus, then, you will easily call to mind, that at the
death of the ever-to-be-lamented Princess, now some
years ago, the day of interment was previously understood throughout the United Kingdom, and every town
and village proposed to mourn the melancholy event
on a Wednesday, I believe, with closed shops, suspen-
sion of business, prayers and homilies. I need not
remind you that I was then in Ireland, partly on your
own mission, and residing in a certain city of Ireland.
The appointed morn rose on that certain city, as on all
the others, and the people duteously attended, or rather
began to attend, to the orders judicially issued for its sad
observance. No shopkeeper unmasked the broad and
shining face of his shop window ; no petty marketing or
cries ushered in the day ; death-bells were knelling ; the
loyal and pious, including the garrison, proposed to go
to divine service ; and all the preachers in the town had
been up two hours before their usual rising time, to
re-con and polish the long-balanced funeral oration.
These were the symptoms down to half-past seven
o'clock ; but lo ! at or about that hour, forth rushes
the town crier, without a hat, his face pale, his looks
wild, his gesticulation vehement, and his voice choked
with precipitancy ; and he rings me his bell at every
corner, and endeavours to pronounce the following :—
"By special orders of Mr. Mayor, the funeral is not
to take place till Friday morning. God save the king !"
The shops were opened, the bells ceased to toll, and
business and bustle proceeded as usual. I went to the
public reading-room to satisfy myself on this extraordinary occurrence   The Dublin mail had not arrived ;

but the Mayor had received the news by despatch from
the Castle the night before, and all was right. It was
eight—half-past eight o'clock, and we heard, at last,
the "twanging horn" of the mail-coach as it drew up
at its allotted resting-place. Many a wistful eye now
peered out of the windows adown the street to recon-
noitre the boy, who had been for an hour before placed
with his shoulder to the little black wooden pane in the
shop window of "the post-office." He came at last,
pale and breathless, and with an ominous pendency in
his jaw—for oh ! he had held whispering converse with
that important inland personage, the guard of the mail,
and his ear still rung with fearful sounds. We tore
open the papers—the Dublin papers of the preceding
evening, despatched at eight o'clock, six hours sooner
than a Mercury could have left town to be in —— at
one o'clock in the morning, which was the case stated.
We tore them open, I say ; our eyes glanced like elec-
tricity to the *readings* of the different journals, then to
the tail of the column, where "second edition," in good
capitals, ought to have been. We did this and more.
We—who ? The magistrates of the city among the rest,
with the Mayor at their head !—the wise caterers for
public order and decorum !—the men of coun*sel* and
coun*cil* !—the "Daniels—I say the Daniels !" Muse
of Hogarth or of Rabelais ! coquet with me only for
one felicitous instant, while I try to paint the vacuity
of horror, yet redolence of the ridiculous, which bespoke
the first full suspicion of a hoax, that was—no doubt—
villainously—good, but also of a blunder that was exe-
crably palpable ! But I dare only leave this scene to
the imagination. Let it suffice that the Mayor ap-
pealed to his despatch from the Secretary—produced it
—and, to mend the matter, "lo, 'twas read !" What
could be done ? The town itself might be managed
after a manner--the crier might make another *sortie* to

cause the shops to be shut, and the customers turned
out—the bells might easily be set again in motion ; but
the country districts, the villages six, eight, ten, fifteen
miles off !   At seven o'clock in the morning the two
troops of horse in garrison had been despatched to
these several places with orders to suspend the homilies
till Friday : there was not a trooper left to pursue them
with countermanding orders !—and again, I inquire,
what could be done ? Nothing but what was done. That
day, while all the rest of the British empire mourned,
the city of —— and her dependencies waxed merry and
busy ; and when the cloud had passed from the world
beside, they had at last their time of exclusive sorrow.
Any comment upon the moral propriety of this hoax
might be out of season,—certainly would be superflu-
ous.   If contemplated to the excess it ran, there can be
no second opinion as to the delinquency ; and in any
view it was most indecorous, and no doubt you and your
readers will call it shocking.   But I am strongly led to
question the first case ; and with the second can have
little to do.   I only state, as in duty bound, facts, that
even in their excesses present to you, I think, a trait
of national character, whose demerits at least contain
some, and a peculiar mental activity—in idleness.

And since we have stumbled on national portrai-
ture, suffer me to present you with another feature
which may interest.   I have met more than one
profound Munchausen in Ireland ; that is, a regular
story-teller, who glories in his talent, who has built up
to himself much fame and admiration from its repeated
exercise, and whose effort is to preserve his character
by a succession of ridiculous fictions.   The king of this
race of queer mortals is now dead ; he abode in the
very metropolis ; was the idol of merry meetings in
taverns, and at respectable private houses too : and,
by all I can learn, never had compeer.   His name was

Sweetman—"Jack Sweetman" Oh! how the bare
mention of his name will set poor Scetch's eyes twink-
ling, and slightly curve the right line of even Mr. O'Regan's mouth!—As master Slender would observe,
however, "He is dead—Jack Sweetman is dead ;" and
those of his unconscious emulators whom I have seen
were not your city wags : Pure rustic geniuses they ;
teeming with their own original conceptions, and flinging them out and about in their own quaint idiom and
slippery tongue. The picture of the cleverest of them
I have encountered, is before me : A comfortable country gentleman, about fifty years of age, tall, a little fat,
a round red shining face, not at all strongly marked, and
no index to his talent, if you should except the sparkle
of two small blue eyes, rebelling against the affectation
of gravity imposed on his well closed lips. At his own
table, or at any other table, he was and is the father
of tempestuous laughter. He knows what is expected
from him—and that is every thing—and without apparent effort he yields full and eternal satisfaction. I have
heard him always with amazement, and, I must own,
often with real excitation of spirits. We have no idea
of such a man in England. He has told in my presence
upon four or five occasions that I have sat with him,
half a hundred stories at least, no one resembling the
other, and, I have been informed by those who knew
him long, unlike any that he had ever told before.· In
fact, during some thirty years of professional practice,
it would appear he scarcely ever finds it necessary to
repeat himself. This you will say is imaginative fecun-
dity with a vengeance. If you proceed to interrogate
me on the merit or style of these extemporaneous
effusions, I fear I can answer nothing satisfactory.
As to matter, they are the most monstrous and
matchless combinations of narrative, out-Munchausening
Munchausen—always new, always jangling against

each other ; and, all I can add is fit to be laughed
at for their very unfitness to any thing else. But
you should hear this man tell them. There is the
whole charm. You shall listen to him as he sits at his
ease with his whiskey-punch before him, and his friends
around him, and his face in its unclouded meridian,
without a muscle wincing, as the fluent words quietly
pour out for ever, and choke every one else with convulsions of mirth. Let your fancy so far assist me as to get
him thus present, and I proceed, as the best mode of il-
lustration, to relate one—though by no means one of the
best of his stories. I select it for its brevity. It would
begin thus : " Arrah, come now—(turning to a grave
guest)—this will never do, father Corkoran—maister,
sir, maister—or maybe you'd be for an oyster ? We'll
get them there ; an' I pray God there mayn't be such
a story to tell o' them as the night last week that the
gauger was here. I was in town that day, an' bought
just as fine a hundred as ever was seen ; Dick put them
down on the dairy floor to keep them cool ; and here
we sat as we are now, God bless us all, after dinner,
when we heard such a screeching an' hubbub as rang
thro' the house, an' brought us out to see what was
the matter. Into the dairy we went—an' I'll tell you
how it happened. The rats came in, you see, in the
dark, an' were for being curious about the oysters ; an'
one of the oysters that was as curious an' just as cute
as any of the rats, opened himself a little to take a
peep about the dairy ; an' when a rat put in his fore
foot to have a crook at the oyster, faith it held him as
fast as it could ; which not being to the rat's mind,
nathing could come up to the passion he got into, an'
the noise he made. We staid some time looking on,
an' then went out for a dog to worry the rat ; an' as
we had to go thro' the yard to the dog, we were for
stepping down stairs quietly, when—what would you

think? By the life of O'Pharoh, Sir, we were forced
to stand aside, and give way to a hundred rats at least,
that were come from borrowing a crow-bar from the
forge, an' they had it between them, walking up stairs
in a body to break open the oyster an' deliver their
namesake from his hands." I shall add no comment
upon this *fanciful* narrative, further than to say, that it
strikes me to be quite as good as the three hundred
rats of which Mr. Hogg has made memorable use in
his last Novel.

THE KILKENNY RANGERS.

THE morning after my arrival in Dublin, I called on my friend Pat Seeteh. He was not at home ; but I understood he might be found at the Dublin Society House, Kildare Street. There indeed I did find him, surrounded by good casts of the Elgin Marbles, and alternately recurring from their god, the Theseus, to a good cast, also, of the Farnese Hercules ; and this, as I afterwards understood, for the purpose of assisting the birth of some strange creation with which his brain was then its full time gone. He sprang to shake my hand, overturning a drawing-desk, chalks, and port-crayons, that now only stood in his way. I requested his aid 'to develope the then immediate place, as the puzzlers call it, of his friend Mr. O'Regan ; and, after appearing to think a second, he touched his forehead and hurried me off. We came, as he informed me, to the Dublin Library, in D'Oliers Street, pushed into the news-room, and, as if by instinct, Seetch picked out from a group of loungers about the fire-place, a grave seeming man ; who, with his back turned to the grate, his hands behind his back, and a deliberate sec-saw motion of body, appeared, with great composure in his own face, to be playing at will the risible muscles of those around him. We were introduced : O'Regan bowed like a Mandarin, and we issued out together to

look at the town. One month exactly I remained in
Dublin under the pupilage of my worthy friends ; one
month we strayed through the county Wicklow ; and
then commenced our true internal campaign. From
the metropolis again, a canal-boat pleasantly beguiled
us of an uninteresting tract of country, depositing us at
Athy, a smart town in the County Kildare, which is
occasionally honoured by a sitting Judge of Assize.
Hence we took a south-west course towards the heart
of the County Kilkenny, on the backs of three sprawling horses, our seats being similar to those we might
enjoy in an inverted rain-bow. They contrived however to transport us to Canticomir, a considerable village, overlooked and governed by the stately mansion
of the Countess Dowager of Ormond ; and there we
divorced ourselves from them and our guide, and joining
hands at the serious proposition of O'Regan, vowed,
like classic pilgrims, to walk the whole extent of our
picturesque tour. So, behold us, with portfolio and
knapsacks hanging at our backs, and note-books and
shilelaghs in hand, attracting an universal stare of
astonishment at every mile of our way. O'Regan carried, though we did not guess it 'till evening, three bottles of Potteen Whiskey, more compactly adjusted than
Gilpin's "bottle at each side ;" and I know not why
I should have omitted to inform you that a servant of
his, as great an original as his master, brought up our
rear with a hand-basket of choice and tangible things,
under which he limped along, a short pipe in his mouth,
and an alternate curse at our bye-roads or hedges
and ditches, or a growling good thing shot off in proper
volumes of smoke, as oftening issuing through his
clenched teeth. I must say a word of this Man-Friday
of ours, Peery, as his master calls him, which appellation is, I take it, a local corruption of Pierce. Peery,
then, is a middle-sized fellow, between fifty and sixty,

inclining to the latter perhaps, straight as a ram-rod, with a pair of squeamish good legs, of which he is not a little proud, a measured pace when he has the city flags or even a smooth road under him, and a round, lumpish, featureless face, which good humour and peevishness, endurance and impatience, sway by turns. He has been an old volunteer ; a corporal of artillery to the " Kilkenny Rangers," and this accounts for his stiff peculiarities of person and manner. Other marks of the old soldier are about him, for I can understand that these volunteer gentlemen may really be called soldiers. He wears a tight knee small-clothes, and short black spatter-dashes, that come a little above the ancle, but toning close to do common justice to the small of the leg. Then he has turned the old oil-silk covering of his helmet into a bag for his hat, and from this union results an uncouth bundle of head-gear, which he has borne about on rainy days in the city, and on country excursions in all weathers, for nearly the last forty years. It looks not unlike a bronze vase turned upside down, and just rescued from the ashes of Herculaneum. One of Peery's privileges is to announce the hour of the day ; and when he is roused towards this office by his master's command, the ensuing operation is rather amusing. He stops short with a " Ha !" then slowly "pulls a dial from his poke," desiring it, by the quaint name of " tell truth," to come forth and declare. First appears a leathern purse suspended by a steel chain, and carefully tied with a running string : after due precaution he takes this off, and then you see a large round machine of I know not what metal, as it is mounted with some kind of green compost ; and at last, looking at it as it reposes on the palm of his hand, with compressed lips and brows and " lack-lustre eye," Peery

" Says, very wisely, it is ten o'clock."

After which the bag is again tied on, and the whole apparatus cautiously returned to its dwelling place. He has
thus carried this ante-diluvian watch since his sixteenth
year, at which time it was bequeathed to him, bag and
all, by a grand uncle in the north, and Peery walked to
the north to claim it. O'Regan never laughs at his
invaluable man, and I can divine that he would not sell
him for worlds. Before dinner Peery is dry and hard
as a sea-biscuit, and you only git bits of him now and
then, which chip off like particles of that same biscuit:
but, still to keep up the comparison, soak him well in
whiskey-punch, and he softens and expands, and be-
comes palatable.

Since I have so far wandered away with this strange
fellow by the hand, I may continue my ramble in his
company, particularly as you will find him versed in
some matters I could not get so well from any other
source. One of our first skirmishing walks about
Dublin was to the Phœnix Park. My friends pointed
out the site of a memorable review of nearly the whole
body of Irish volunteers ; and Peery, after listening
gravely to our observations, came in with his own explanation and anecdotes at last. What he had to
say involved the character and prowess of his native
corps ; and we were treated with a prefatory account
of them, which, linked to the after scenes in which he
put them into particular action, forms, I may say, an
interesting picture of that remarkable time, and of the
national spirit that stamped it. Let me try if I can
collect Peery's own words.

"I ought to know the ground well. The day the
Kilkenny Rangers took the right o' the field, an' I
was corporal an' bombadier of the Artillery, an' auld
Bob Holmes was our captain. The Cork Blues thought
to have id, an' wheeled past us. But they knew little
about id, or the boys they had to deal with either.

There was proud blood an' desperate hearts in the Rangers. They were well known at home in their own town an' county. Before they riz (rose) up, there used to be such things as theevin' an' stalin' in the country parts, but I'll be bound little was hard (heard) in id a month or so afther. The best ir id all was, that whin we had no thieves to hunt, we went out fur the sport o' the business; fur the Rangers liked sport; an' give 'em a crisp frosty road, an' plenty in 'em, good fellows together, with their muskets on their shoulders an' free quarters afore 'em—the Lord knows where, only somewhere at last, you may be sure,—an' the devil a better avvartion they'd ax. To tell God's truth, they might as well lave the robbers alone; fur, from the Lord's cellar down to the ould woman's henroost, sorrow a much was spared afther all the good they done. An' so these were the lads, with ould Lord Ormond an' all the Butlers at their head, an' their ranks made up in estated gintlemen, an' the young an' the stout in the whole neighbourhood,—an' to spake honestly between ourselves, some o' the most finished scape-graces you'd maybe wish to see; these were the lads that the Cork Blues thought to put a wan side that day. Bad look to the finer set o' fellows ever marched into a field. Every man had the gettin' in his own clothin', an' all did their best; an' every cap, coat, an' feather, that mornin' was bran new. Besides, as it was dry summer weather, and we had only to turn out in Dublin into this Park, every man wore his white cassimir small-clothes, white silk-stackins, an' dancin' pumps. Into that gate we came, our drums beatin' an' our colours flyin', an', as I said afore, or somethin' like id, our Cornal an' Officers the hansomest men you'd pick out in three counties. We were in first, an', as we said we'd do id, we took up the right hand place iu the field, an' then, as I tould you, the Blues came in, and were

marchin' a-head on us. "Halt there !" cries our Cornal
as they passed, an' he rode out with his Officers, and
comin' up to the Cornal o' the Blues, the Blues halted,
an' the Officers discoursed together. While they were
talkin', we were doin'. On went our bayonets, an' every
man put in a ball cartridge, out in his private pouch
that we always carried about us. Myself was at the
head o' the line with my two long pounders, an', without sayin' much, I took out my flint an' steel, an' let a
spark fall on the match-rope. My Officer came to me,
an' ' Never better done, Peery (says he,) where's the
key of the ammunition-box ?' ' I think I have id', says
I, showin' a thing like id at the same time. ' Right
(says Captain Bob,) open id, Peery ; an' the first leg
they put afore another, send 'em your compliments.' ' I
will, Captain, as civilly as I can,' says I. By this time
we were all faced about, right fornent the Munster
men, who didn't seem to like how we behaved ourselves,
an', I believe, thought at last we might just as well
have our own frolic. At all events they fell back, an' we
led the day.

"I'll tell you a matter about the Rangers. Afther
the review was over—that is, in a few days afther—we
were for marchin' home, an' passin' through Dublin,
there was a halt in Thomas-street, somehow or other.
As we stood on our arms, a poor fool of a bailiff stept
up to the ranks, and tippin' Tom Kavanah, tould him
he was the King's prisoner. ' No, (says Billy Come-
ford,) he's the King's volunteer soldier an' a gintleman,
and that I'll make you know ;' so he stretched him with
the but-end ir his musket. The poor devil tumbled among
the ranks, an' one axed him what he wanted there, an' another, an' another ; an' there was a bayonet sent through
his body each time. We got the word to march, an'
every man stamped his foot on the bailiff as we passed,
givin' him something else along with it. I saw his

corpse afore we left the street, an' I don't think his mother 'ud know him if she met him. An' these were the men it was so asy to take the lead from in the Park : an' they were some of exactly the same men that the Parliament called saviours of their country to-day, and armed traitors to-morrow ; God for ever bless that Parliament, wherever it is, for sayin' so."

Behold a specimen of my friend Peery's traditional lore. The last anecdote with which he has furnished me is sufficiently shocking : but it serves to show the determined and daring spirit of these famous Volunteers ; the desperate identity of cause and feeling between them ; and, above all, their uncontrolled mastery at that period in Ireland ;—for, as I can authentically learn, if a dog, and not the poor fool-hardy bailiff, had been bayoneted, less notice could not have been taken of the matter.

THE ROCKITES.

I HAVE promised, in a former Letter, that those gentry should form the subject of one of my " hours ;" and as fortune (however singular, always fortunate to a literary gossip) has placed it in my power to lay before your readers a scene—quorum pars *parva* fui— which, I flatter myself, they may not consider uninteresting, I hasten to redeem my pledge.

I was sitting quietly in the house of an acquaintance (a county of Limerick gentleman,) about twelve o'clock at noon, on a fine, still, sun-shiny day : the good lady of the mansion was busily engaged in preparing luncheon ; the master, a quiet, inoffensive, timid kind of man, who by his neutrality during the disturbances had secured himself against injury on all sides, was poring with eyes aghast, and a countenance surcharged with expression which he vainly endeavoured to suppress, over the columns of the last *Limerick Evening Post,* where in all the authenticity of neat long primer, the *doings* of the last week were recorded, not in the most soothing strain of the self-alarmist,—when Pat Cahil, a gentleman who did my friend the honour of officiating as groom of his stables, burst into the chamber, hatless, coatless, and shoeless—his whole frame evidently agitated by the extremity of consternation. It was some time before he could articulate—" Mr. Wardow ! Mr. Wardow ! there they are all !—gone up to the cross by the forge !"

" Who ?" exclaimed my friend, endeavouring to preserve an appearance of dignified calmness.
" The *boys*, Sir—the *boys!* and 'tis thought they're
going to do something that's bad, Sir, by the Peppards,*
Sir, now the army arn't to the fore." " Where are the
military stationed ?" I asked. " Och, your honour, there
isn't a sodger nearer to us than Adare ; and it's but a
poor account you'd have o' the business *be* the time
you'd get there, let alone the road back." The distant
report of a shot instantly convinced us that this was
but too true. I rushed towards the door, however,
rather rudely flinging back my friend, who opposed himself to my exit with the most haggard and woe-begone
look of entreaty I ever beheld. In a few minutes I
reached the hill of Lisnamuck, a place which cut rather
a conspicuous figure as a place of rendezvous on the
nocturnal occasions of those people, and in some part
of which knowing folks will tell you with a wink and a
nod, an old cavern serves as an armory to the worthy
General's forces ; but at all events I reached the summit of the hill, and in an instant the scene of battle lay
before me. Cappa House, the residence of Mr. Peppard
and his two sons, was an elderly-looking edifice, and
apparently well-calculated to sustain a seige in which
musketry were the heaviest modes of assault to be ap-
prehended. It was situated rather on a low ground, with
a slope on one side leaning to a plain still lower, and
surrounded by a lofty wall, the only entrance through
which was a small narrow gateway. In fact it had the
appearance of a regular little fortress. I afterwards
found by the public papers, that the elder Mr. P. was,
at the time the Rockite party suddenly came upon the
house, outside this gate, and unarmed. On seeing them
approach he ran toward it, and closing it after him,

* It may be necessary to remark, that this attack on those gentlemen, and their manly resistance, is pure history.

made what haste he could along a narrow straight passage which led directly from it to the back-door of the
house. This was open. Before he reached it he heard
behind him the grating of the blunderbusses against the
iron railings as the ruffians poked them through to take
a deliberate aim, and he sprung towards the door. It
was shut in his face! The alarm had been given in the
house. Unconscious of Mr. P's absence, and imagining that the assailants had made good their entrance
into this inner passage, they slapped to the door, and
left him to the mercy of the men without, or rather of
their blunderbusses, for these had more than their owners, and contrived to throw their contents harmlessly all
around him. Indeed his escape was almost miraculous.
The door, the panels and jams of which were perfora-
ted by slugs, so as scarcely to leave a hair's-breadth
more than the space necessary for his preservation, was
for a considerable time afterwards an object of intense
curiosity to numerous visitors. Before the discharge
could be renewed, however, he was placed beyond its
reach. The aggressors now (and it was just at this
juncture the scene presented itself to my sight) retired
from the gate, and commenced firing upon the windows.
Only conceive the impression which such a spectacle
must have produced on the mind of a stranger, in the
deep stillness of a summer noontide, and in a populous
country where there was something like civilization
and civil government talked about! Every man went
as cooly and openly to work as if the grey frieze on their
backs had been regular, protected, loyal scarlet, and
the resisting housekeepers the proscribed men of the
law. Very soon after, and while the clouds of smoke
were rolling towards a clump of trees on the south, two
of the windows were suddenly thrown up, and as suddenly a reciprocal discharge commenced from within.
The battle now began to wax earnest; the Rockites

sent forth a yell with every discharge, which came over
the still champagne around with almost a redoubled
loudness ; and the advantage of the housed warriors
became quickly apparent. With all the credit for discipline which the Rockites have achieved, their mode of
battle on this occasion was not very imposing : they
regularly, after discharging a volley *irregularly*, ran
down the slope *a briglia sciolta*, and squatted themselves
behind a hedge, re-loaded, and re-advanced to the charge
in any thing but marching order. Then, again unbur-
thening their fire-arms with all the serious silence in the
world, they again sent forth a shout, and scampered off
to prepare for a new volley. Only one among them
seemed to despise this pusillanimous procedure : he appeared to command the band, and, in fact, did so, as
was afterwards found ; but he was only distinguished
from the rest by a white handkerchief tied round his
hat. He remained during the whole affray in the same
spot, but he did not continue to expose himself with
impunity : as his party advanced to the charge for the
last time, he was in the act of raising his musket, when
a ball from one of the windows struck him on the arm,
and the piece fell to the ground ; he instantly tore the
handkerchief from his hat with his left hand and bound
it round the other, accompanying every twist with what
Hotspur lusciously calls " a good mouth-filling oath,"
alternately directed, in a tremendous roar, to his pol-
troons, as he called them (for they now evidently showed symptoms of tergiversation, and no very equivocal
ones,) and to the bandage, which he hid did not find
ready enough to assist the awkward efforts of the left
hand. He was the last who left the scene of fight,
and he walked off sulkily down the slope, and across
an adjacent bog, trailing his dishonoured musket after
him.

    In a few minutes they all united at the Cross of

Lisnamuck, within rather a scanty distance of the spot where I now lay. There were loud voices for a moment, and words of reproach exchanged in their vernacular tongue. Then ensued the silence and sullenness of defeat—disgraceful discomfiture ; and they walked down the road in a body towards Curra Grove, the estate of Sir Aubrey De Vere Hunt, which, during the occasional absences of the amiable proprietor, was made a frequent place of meeting by those miserably misguided creatures. They entered the wood, and I lost them

A DEATH OF PEACE AND A DEATH OF WAR

.A Dramatic Sketch—Scene, the Empyrean.)

First Spirit

How fare you, brother ?

Second Spirit.

My sweet sister!—Why—
A something weary and a something sad :—
I've stooped into the region of the wind,
A lower flight than those immortal plumes
Have strength to cleave the heavy air : I peered
Through a rifted cloud upon our ancient world—
The pleasant home of our mortality.
I sighed when I looked on the little spot
Of earth. where we last parted, never more
To meet on earth again—and then I laughed
To see how narrow now appeared the distance—
We wept to think should lie between our graves !

First Spirit.

I found mine soon—Come—rest upon this cloud,
And I will tell thee :—What a glorious sight
Is this around us ! The mist-mountains heave
Their sullen fronts into the empyrean light,
And smile, in their despite, against its brightness !
And from their ever-moving sides fling off
Fragments of vapour, spreading, like thin veils,
On the clear ether. These the fair sun-light
Strikes through, and forms the wonder of the earth—
The many-coloured covenant of peace
'Tween man and heaven, whose winged children love
To close their weary wings, and take their rest
In mid air, on those floating splendours—Ha !—
How yieldingly *this* sinks beneath us now !—

It falls—and falls!—and now the clouds of earth
Are o'er us, and the wide dark world beneath!—
Brother, oh! knowest thou not this soil?—The vale
That blooms beneath Potosi's Silver Mount—
A goodly scene is this that lies before us.
The even fall is pleasant—not a breath
Of softest wind creeps on the silent leaves—
Nature seems hushed in rapturous contemplation
Of her own countless charms.—And now—hark!—list!—
The distant murmur of the town, and sound
Of convent bells, mingling their faint heard chime
With the rush of the near rolling Pilcomayo,
Break on the stillr .f the lonely scene
So gently, that '_ .ar of solitude
Scarce notes t_e .trusion!—
So fell the ev' of my death! I pined
And pined, and burned, and wasted with the fire
That fed upon my health—until that came,
And thus it came at length :

A DEATH OF PEACE.

The sun of even
Had looked on me for the last time, (I felt it,)
Aud hid his mighty front behind the Mount ;
And the moonlight was round me, and the air
Sprinkled its viewless tears upon my cheek
Till that was chilled ; aud my heart's pulse grew colder
And slower, and I felt as I could sleep.
Our sister was beside me : on her bosom
I laid my head in weakness—not in fear—
And looked upon the heaven ; and my lips moved,
And words came forth of praise and prayer.—The plain
Of ether glowed with myriads of those gems
Of light that darkling mortals love. I gazed,
With face upturned, until the immensity
Of space did seem beneath me—not above—
And prayed to be released : my pain was great—
I was a weary of my life.—Then felt I
A sudden hope stir in my breast, my blood
Throbbed and flowed slowlier and slowlier yet,
And a cold hand did seem to grasp my heart—
I knew my prayer was heard, and I sprung forth
Upon the bosom of the air.—I rose !
The light wind bore me up—and onward still—
Till the wild music of the seraphim
Was in mine ear, and told me I had found
Impassible being !—
                    I can now remember,
When that strange melody had left my hearing,

A voice of wailing came from the cold earth !
I looked unto the grave which I had left—
The moonlight shone upon a maiden's form
I had known well once.—O'er her sunken brow
Her hair hung, and upon her lap and bosom
A corpse lay, pale and cold—I saw its cheek
Wet with the tears the living mourner gave

Second Spirit.

A waking from a dream of pain and darkness
To the fair mornlight and the voice of music,
Such was *thy* death !—It was not so with me.

A DEATH OF WAR.

Thy life was one of evil : the nepenthe
Of all its sufferings lurked in that dark draught
The happy shrink to look on—death !—But mine
Was full of hope, and joy, and health, and light !
Thy spirit left its earth within the arms
Of a loved friend—Mine on the battle field !—
Thy bones were shrouded—laid with tears in the earth
The mountain winds are shrieking over mine !—
A warning of long years made death to *thee*
Unwelcome nor unsought—A summer morn
Beheld *me* rise to greet its dawn, in health
And hope ————
Its even smile reddened on my bloodless limbs !—
It is before me now !—The flood of time
Hath torn the scene away in its swift course,
But left its bed deep ohannelled in my memory !
I hear the clangour of the opposing trumps—
I hear the tramping of the war steeds' hoofs—
I see the close array of serried hosts—
I see the banner waving on the cleft
Of a rent crag, that crossed the steep ascent
'Twixt us and freedom's victory.—They meet—
And shout !—A thunderpeal had passed unheard
Above them in the shock. Amid the roar
Of that wild sea of war,
I marked the standard where it waved alone,
Rushed on the cleft—seized *that* : and, with a cry
Of triumph, spread its blazonry abroad
Unto the winds above me !—It was echoed,
Till the blue vault rang with the sound again,
And cloud spoke unto cloud of freedom's victory—
A something struck me then—here—on my front—
And all was still !—That pause was nothingness—
And for a space I was not !—When I raised

Mine eyes again, and thought and life awoke—
I stood before the judgment-seat!—
That scene!—
How wonderful it was! The hush that came
After that field of fear!—
The tinkling of the harps of seraphim,
The almost noiseless waving of the wings
Of heaven's bright couriers in their sweeping flight,
And the calm glory of the Almighty presence—
For mortal hate and strife!—I had my guerdon

First Spirit.

Let us now seek it—singing to our joy,
Till its rich light is on us once again!
'Tis twilight on the earth—and darkens slowly

I.

The vales are wrapt in silence now,
    All but the soft wind's melody,
And one small stream that, gurgling low,
    Steals under the grey willow tree,
            Lingeringly—lingeringly
            With its timid minstrelsy.

II.

How sweetly, as we spread our wings
    O'er rocks, and hills, and heather lea,
The even-wind of the mountain sings,
And the red West a lustre flings,
            Tremblingly—tremblingly
            Over his own stirless sea

Second Spirit.

Come away— away—and on,
    Till our own fair heaven we see—
Soon the spirit's flight is done,
    Hand in hand locked, let us flee,
            Lovingly—lovingly—
            As in our earthly infancy!—

THE GRAVE OF MARION.

The wind comes whistling o'er the waste,
  The sand-cloud rises high ;
Our peril is not wholly past,
  Our foes are pressing nigh.
A little farther on, my love,
  A little farther on !
She does not speak—she does not move—
  My love at last is gone !

I press thee to my burning breast,
  No blush is on thy brow ;
These gentle arms that once caress'd,
  Fall round me deadly now ;
Thy lips have still their hue—but chill
  The spirit of their kiss—
I lay mine hand upon thine heart,
  'Tis cold at last to this !

We were young, and closely twined
  Like twin flowers of Love's spring ;
But one the poison blast has pined,
  And one lives sorrowing !
Heart of my heart ! I would I were
  Unloved of thee again—
I'd leave thee as I met thee, fair,
  And waste in silent pain.

Were we beneath a Christian heaven,
  Within a Christian land,
A fairer shrine to thee were given
  Than this bleak bed of sand ;
Yet thou wert single in thy faith,
  And single in thy worth,
And thou shouldst die a lonely death,
  And lie in lonely earth !

And now I've laid thee to thy rest,
  My last look now is given—
The sand is smooth above *thy* breast,
  And mine is still unriven :
No winding-sheet—no matins meet
  Thy perished love can have—
But a lover's sighs embalm thy corse,
  A lover's tears thy grave !

Publications of P. J. Kenedy, 5 Barclay St. N. Y.

Canon Schmid's Exquisite Tales, 6 vols, Illustrated...	$.00
Cannon's Practical Spelling Book	.25
Captain of the Club, a Story for Boys..................	.75
Carroll O'Donoghue. By Christine Faber..............	1.25
Carpenter's Speller and Definer......................	.25
Catechism Third Plenary Council, large, No. 2, paper..	
per 100 net	2.50
The same, abridged No. 1, paper per 100 net.....	1.50
The same, No. 2, cloth flexible, per 100 net.......	5.00
The same, No 1, " " ". " "........	3.50
Catechism, General, National Council, paper per 100 net.	2.00
The same, abridged paper cover, per 100 net.......	1.50
Catechism, Butler's large, paper per 100 net.....	2.50
The same, abridged, paper per 100 net......	1.50
The same, cloth. Illustrated Mass Prayors.........	.30
Catechism, The, or Short abridgment, New York, per	
100 net..............	2.00
Catechism, Boston. Prayers at Mass, etc., paper per	
100 net..............	2.00
Catechism, Koenan's Doctrinal, cloth.............	.50
Catechism, Poor Man's, large and thick.	.40
Catechism, Spanish, Ripalda, paper cover.............	.12
Catechism, Spanish, Astete, paper cover..	.15
Catechism, Spanish, Nuevo Caton, paper cover........	.15
Catholic Christian Instructed, paper .20, cloth...........	.30
Catholic Excelsior Library, 6 vols, per set.....	4.50
Catholic Faith and Morals, By L'Homond.............	1.00
Catholic Fireside Library, 10 vols, per set...	7.50
Catholic Flowers from Protestant Gardens, gilt..	1.25
Catholic Home Library, 8 vols, per set.....	4.00
Catholic Juvenile Library, 6 vols, per set......	2.40
Catholic Keepsake Library, 6 vols, per set...........	4.50
Catholic Missions and Missionaries. By Shea...	2.50
Catholic Offering or Gift Book. By Abp. Walsh	1.00
Catholic Piety, (Prayer Book). Prices range upwards	
from...	.60
Catholic School Book.....	.25
Chambers' English Literature, 2 vols. Octavo..........	5.00

Catholic Prayer-Books, 25c., 50c., up to **12 00**
☞ Any of above books sent free by mail on receipt of price. Agents wanted everywhere to sell above books, to whom liberal terms will be given. Address
P. J. KENEDY, Excelsior Catholic Publishing *House, 5 Barclay Street, New York.*

Publications of P. J. Kenedy, 5 Barclay St. N. Y.

Publications cf P. J. Kenedy, 5 Barclay St. N. Y.